HISTORY and the HOMERIC ILIAD

HISTORY
AND THE
HOMERIC ILIAD

BY DENYS L. PAGE

UNIVERSITY OF CALIFORNIA PRESS
BERKELEY AND LOS ANGELES • 1963

University of California Press
Berkeley and Los Angeles
California

Cambridge University Press
London, England

© 1959 by
The Regents of the University of California

Originally published as Volume Thirty-one
of the Sather Classical Lectures
Second printing, 1963
(First Paper-bound Edition)

Library of Congress Catalogue Card No. 59-5243

Manufactured in the United States of America

PREFACE

THE SIX chapters of this book, all but one in a much abbreviated form, were delivered at Berkeley in October and November, 1957, as the Sather Lectures for 1957–58, at the invitation of the University of California. It is a pleasure to acknowledge at once my appreciation of the honour and my gratitude to sympathetic and generous friends at Berkeley who did so much to make my visit memorable.

I make no apology, and expect no mercy, for intruding upon the reserves of several different classes of specialist. My own interest in these matters goes back to 1930, when one of the most famous of the Sather volumes was published, *Who Were the Greeks?* I still do not know who they were; but over the years I have learnt something of what they were doing in the thirteenth century B.C. I look back now to certain milestones on the path: Milman Parry's proofs of the oral technique of Greek Epic poetry; Sommer's edition of the *Ahhijawā* documents; Blegen's excavations at Troy; Ventris' decipherment of the Linear B tablets; and a clue provided by Miss Dorothea Gray leading through the labyrinth of Homeric formulas to a Mycenaean centre. Here I attempt a synthesis: but even though I focus on a small area, no critic will ever know so well as I do how much I have to leave out of the picture.

Profound knowledge of the Hittite language would appear to be a prerequisite for chapters i and iii: my own knowledge being hardly sufficient to enable me to follow where others lead, I have relied especially upon the works of Sommer, Goetze, Friedrich, and Güterbock; then, wherever it was still difficult to determine precisely the meaning of an important word or passage, I have turned to Professor Crossland, to find exactly the help I needed. Finally, Dr Gurney read both

v

chapters in typescript and made a number of suggestions which I adopted thankfully without question.

This is not nearly the end of my obligations. The chapter on Troy was read and corrected by Dr F. H. Stubbings; that on the Linear B tablets by Mr John Chadwick; and that on the Mycenaean relics in Homeric formulas by Miss Dorothea Gray. I need not say how much happier I felt after my work had been corrected in the light of advice from such authorities: but it would be a serious injustice to these distinguished scholars if I did not avow with more than usual emphasis that they must not be presumed to share all my opinions, and that such errors as may remain must be charged not to their oversight but to my obstinacy.

The two Appendices are not so irrelevant as may appear at first sight. They were planned and partly written while I was still under the impression (in 1954) that the number of Sather Lectures might be eight instead of six; and my purpose was to illustrate two later stages in the making of the Iliad, with one example from the golden age of the Ionian Epic and one from the period of Athenian predominance. They will be grievous to some. "It was vain to hope," wrote Gilbert Murray in 1911, "that even the most pacific and wary walking would take one far into Homeric territory without rousing the old lions that lie wakeful behind most of the larger stones": and I know that my walking, though not unwary, makes the impression of being not always pacific. So I must not complain if there is some growling of old lions. I do no more than restate a case as it has appeared to most of the leading Homeric scholars of the past,—a case never yet refuted, fatal to certain fashionable theories of the present about the making of the Iliad.

In conclusion I must say how grateful I am to the officers and staff of the University of California Press, and in particular to Mr Harold A. Small, for the infinite courtesy and care with which they have treated me and my book.

DENYS PAGE

CONTENTS

MAPS AND PLANS

I

Achaeans in Hittite Documents

GREEK EPIC poetry told of the siege and sack of
Troy: and the ruins at Hissarlik in the Troad prove that a
strong fortress was violently destroyed at a date not far removed from the one assigned by tradition. It would seem that
the Troy of legend preserves the memory of a real Troy,—that
the subject of the Homeric Iliad is at least to this extent historical:—a Greek army destroyed the fortress of Troy about or
soon after the middle of the 13th century B.C.

But if this was a fact, it was for long a lonely one. Archaeologists might tell us much about Greeks in other places: they
might prove the intrusion of Achaeans into the remotest corners
of the eastern Mediterranean during the centuries preceding the
alleged fall of Troy; dubious or incredible conjecture might
bring Achaeans and Danaans into Palestine and Egypt.[1] But
Anatolia, especially northwestern Anatolia, remained for long a
blank space on the map: Troy had no background, apart from
its commercial relations with Mycenaean Greece; the Achaean
siege had no context or confirmation.

From 1907 onwards the excavations at Boghaz-Köy in central Anatolia brought to light not only a great city but also a
great Empire,—the lost empire of the Hittites. Ten thousand
clay tablets re-created Hittite laws, religion, literature, and history. They spread the Hittites over the greater part of Asia
Minor; thrust them southward through Syria into contact with
Egypt; and brought Hittite power and culture to its peak in the
14th and 13th centuries B.C.,—a period when the Greeks were preeminent in the west of the Aegean and adventurous in the east,

[1] For notes to chapter i see pages 19–40.

I

trading in ports subject to Hittite rule, supplying friends and enemies of the Hittites, making new homes on the fringes of Hittite dominion. Surely there was good hope that the Greeks might be found in ten thousand Hittite documents: and in 1924 Emil Forrer triumphantly announced that he had found them.

They were a glittering parade; no wonder many eyes were dazzled. Here, for a start, was a familiar potentate from Greece, friend to the Hittite Emperor,—no less a person than Andreus the founder of Orchomenos. A namesake, at least, of the father of Agamemnon—one could hardly ask for more,—Atreus himself stepped into the pages of history. Or would it not be still more wonderful if we could find an Alexander of Ilios? Seek in the Hittite documents and you shall find not only an Alexander of Ilios but also a city of Troy and an island of Lesbos. Moreover, who should lurk among the pothooks but a priest from Trozen? Who rules in Millawanda—a Mycenaean settlement, whether it be Miletus or Milyas—but Eteocles the Aeolian?

These were wonderful discoveries. And lest you should think that so much Greek history in the Hittite documents is illusion, mark the most important fact of all: over and over again you read in these tablets the name *Achaia*; land of Achaia, King of Achaia; Eteocles the Aeolian is a subject of the King of Achaia, Atreus is a native of the land Achaia. If these things were true, we had found better documentary sources for Greek history in the 14th and 13th centuries B.C. than we shall have again for about seven hundred years. It was therefore well to inquire whether these things are true: but that would be impossible for those who are not masters of the Hittite language, had not Ferdinand Sommer presented us in 1932 with a text so exact, a translation so trustworthy, and a commentary so full of guidance that even the layman can distinguish what is known from what is hypothetical or false or simply unknown.

Even as Satan in Milton's poem surveyed the newly created Paradise from the top of the tree of knowledge, and

> saw undelighted all delight, all kind
> Of living creatures, new to sight and strange,

so Ferdinand Sommer, from the peak of his profession, observed with displeasure the brave new world below. To Sommer, Greek history in the Hittite documents was not a structure of substance, however thin and brittle, of which part might remain after part had been demolished: it was a balloon, a gasbag, to be exploded with sudden and total ruin. He took the field in arms; and one by one they folded their tents, these Bedouin-ghosts of Forrer's fancy, and silently stole away.[2] The priest of Trozen vanished as if he had never been: which was indeed the fact. When the mask was stripped from Andreus of Orchomenos men saw, however sadly, a hook-nosed Hittite. Atreus dissolved, the Aeolian Eteocles resumed his native name Tawagalawas, to the great comfort of his brother and friends, whose uncouth names had resisted such facile turning into Greek.[3] And what of Achaia, the land and its king? The Hittite name is *Akhkhijawā*. The last syllable, the final long *ā*, would imply a country or kingdom, whether Achaiwia or Achaiwa: but was there ever any kingdom so named? And, above all, how is the middle syllable to be explained?—how could Greek $\overline{ai}$ be represented by Hittite *ijă*? Every conceivable philological device has been applied to explain why the Hittites—familiar with Achaeans, on this hypothesis, for many generations—should so persistently misrepresent their name, turning a simple $\overline{ai}$ into *ijă;* this disability being a national defect, common to all officials and all scribes for a couple of centuries.

Now look further and you will see how completely you have been deceived. If there were, in the Hittite documents, much talk of persons and places indisputably or even probably Achaean, connected with this name Ahhijawā, you might think yourself obliged to accept what you cannot explain, the Hittite distortion of the Achaean name. But what if there is *nothing* in the documents to connect Ahhijawā with the Greeks? What if all that is said about Ahhijawā and its people might as well be said about a native state on the mainland of Asia Minor? There would then be nothing left but a general resemblance of names, —and that, on examination, has proved to be only skin-deep.

Ferdinand Sommer went so far as to maintain that this is the true state of the evidence: suppose that the country in question had had some quite different name, such as Zippaslā; nobody would then have looked for connections with the Greeks; we should have thought that it was a 'barbarian' state in Asia Minor, and we should not have found in the documents a single fact inconsistent with that opinion.[4]

In a case where one witness declares that there is much evidence and another replies that there is none at all, it is often possible for the arbitrator to find that there is something—less than the one claimed, but more than the other admitted. The whole of the evidence was reviewed by Fritz Schachermeyr in his book *Hethiter und Achäer*, published in 1935. He invites us to conclude (in brief) that Hittite Ahhijawā is, after all, Greek Achaia; indeed it is the Kingdom of Mycenae on the mainland. Almost all the personal identifications are abandoned: but the documents suffice to prove this one fact, the most important of all, that Ahhijawā is a Greek Empire overseas.

From the arguments employed by Schachermeyr to this end the reader is likely to select for special consideration the following two. First, it is claimed that the Hittite Emperor recognizes the King of Ahhijawā as a *Great King*, equal in dignity to himself and to the Kings of Egypt, Babylonia, and Assyria. The title of Great King is a technical term of Hittite diplomacy: if it is true that the King of Ahhijawā is so called, there is an end of the question;[5] for there was certainly not at that time in the world any power connected with the coast of Asia Minor, except the Achaeans, who could assert or vindicate such a claim. Secondly, the seat of the power of Ahhijawā lay *overseas*: it was not, after all, a native coastal state of Asia Minor; if so, no territory except that occupied by Achaean Greeks will satisfy the conditions imposed by the detail of the documents.

A process of elimination led Schachermeyr to the conclusion that Ahhijawā is to be found on the mainland of Hellas: it is the great realm of the Achaeans, of which Mycenae and Tiryns are the centre. But we must not follow him so far, until we have satisfied ourselves that the facts are truly as stated. Do the Hittite documents tell us of an overseas Ahhijawā; and do they give to its ruler the title of Great King? We hope so, and for a time believe so, for Schachermeyr's is a sober and persuasive book. But we have reckoned without Ferdinand Sommer. He surveys this imposing temple erected to our faith; observes that the overthrow of these two pillars will bring it down; and easily he overthrows them.[6]

For, first, where in all the Hittite documents is it stated or implied that Ahhijawā lay *overseas?* There is indeed proof that it controlled territory on the coast of Asia Minor, and that it possessed ships which might sail to Syria and Cyprus.[7] So far it might well be a maritime state of Asia Minor: what if anything compels us to look further? The first article of Schachermeyr's evidence is a fragmentary text of which the apparent meaning is that the Hittite King Mursilis II, being at the time himself on the coast of Asia Minor, banishes a prisoner to Ahhijawā *by ship;*[8] therefore, said Schachermeyr, Ahhijawā must lie overseas; if you send a prisoner from the coast of Asia Minor by ship, you are sending him out of Asia Minor into territory overseas. It was easy enough for Sommer to refute this once for all: for a ship is often the quickest and safest means of transport from one point of the Anatolian coast to another; here is no evidence at all, *nec vola nec vestigium*, of an Ahhijawā overseas. Let us hear the second witness.

She is a Hittite queen, who in the course of a letter to an unnamed king makes use of the following expressions: "How can you say that you are impoverished?—if the son of the Sun-god, or the son of the Weather-god, *or the ocean*, is impoverished, then so would you be";[9] that is to say, you are no more impoverished than those other three, clearly celebrated for their wealth. Now let it be admitted that the son of the Sun-god denotes the King of Egypt, and that the son of the Weather-god denotes the King of the powerful state of Mitanni: Schachermeyr follows Forrer in declaring that the third member of the trio, the ocean, must therefore likewise denote a great empire—

an ocean empire, comparable with Egypt and Mitanni, a by-
word for wealth. And, if so, there can be no such great sea power
at this time except the Achaeans. I think we must agree with
Sommer that this interpretation of the words is frail and fanciful. We must not build a sea empire on a single word in the
bombastic circumlocutions of an excitable woman.[10] She probably meant no more than this: "When the richest lands are
poor, when the seas are barren . . . ,"—had she meant the
ocean to stand for a third empire, she would probably have continued "And the son of the Sea-god," or whatever else rhetoric
might suggest to her feverish mind as a symbol for an ocean
empire.

So much for one pillar; it is down, if it was ever up. Let us
lay hands upon the second. Is it true that the Hittite King admits the King of Ahhijawā to be a *Great King*, equal to himself and to the Kings of Egypt, Assyria, and Babylon?

There is a single[11] witness, eloquent but ambiguous. Turn to
the treaty of the Hittite King Tuthalijas IV with a prince of
Amurru, and you will read this: "The Kings who are my equals:
the King of Egypt, the King of Babylonia, the King of Assyria,
and the King of Ahhijawā."[12] There is our question answered
once for all: only no sooner was it written than the last words
were struck out,—just these words, "and the King of Ahhijawā," were erased before the clay was dry. Why they were
ever written, we cannot guess: all we know for certain is that
they were struck out, and therefore that they were judged to be
erroneous. We have no right to use this testimony *in favour* of
the Great Kingship of Ahhijawā, since what it actually declares is that Ahhijawā was judged *out of place* in a list of
Great Kingdoms.

The structure erected by Schachermeyr has tumbled.[13] We do
not yet know that any Hittite King ever recognized Ahhijawā
by the title of Great Kingdom; we do not yet know that it lay
overseas from Asia Minor; there is nothing yet to connect it
with the Achaean Greeks. What do we know about Ahhijawā;
and what if any answer have we to Sommer's challenge, that

nothing can be found which is not applicable to a non-Greek princedom on the coast of Asia Minor?

Excluding prejudice and postponing hope, let us sternly require of the documents that they tell their tale unadorned. Whatever and wherever the Kingdom of Ahhijawā may be, what facts are known about it?

Now, first, throughout the period covered by the documents (the 14th and 13th centuries B.C.) there is no indication that it was ever included in the Hittite Empire; indeed there are several plain indications that it was not.[14] And when the two countries come to blows, as once (at least) they do, the quarrel ends in a treaty as between independent states.[15] The greater part of Asia Minor was conquered by the Hittites: but Ahhijawā continued, from one generation to another, free. Was it perhaps not important enough, or not close enough to the Hittite sphere of influence? The documents bear witness to the contrary. The brother of the King of Ahhijawā is entertained by Hittite royalty;[16] there is polite exchange of valuable gifts;[17] and when the Hittite Emperor is sick, in response to "moanfulest broken howl" the friendly gods of Ahhijawā leave their homes and hasten, loud-quacking, to the bedside.[18] Moreover, the bonds of mutual respect and trust are surely strong, if one state deems another a safe prison for its dangerous and distinguished enemies: Ahhijawā is the place to which a Hittite Emperor banishes not only the son of his most troublesome neighbour[19] but also (if the text is not misunderstood) his own refractory wife.[20] Such confidence in friendship is the more surprising since the interests of the two states might at any time come into conflict,—first, because their dominions had a common boundary, at least for part of the period under review; the district of Millawanda, alternatively called Milawatas, subject for a time to the sovereignty of Ahhijawā, extended from the coast of Asia Minor to the boundary of peoples wholly or partly subject to the Hittites. Secondly—a fact of great importance,— *because merchant vessels of Ahhijawā traded with the Syrian coast;* and there were times when her commercial relations with

eastern countries were obnoxious to the Hittites. Thus, when
the Hittites are at war with Assyria, the Great King issues an
order "that no ship from Ahhijawā is to sail to the enemy";[21]
that is to say, ports which might serve the Assyrian enemy are
to be closed to the merchantmen of Ahhijawā. This valuable
document is one of several which prove beyond question *that
Ahhijawā was a seafaring state*,[22] whether coastal or island; and
we proceed to ask whether we can now identify its position at
all precisely.

The name Ahhijawā occurs in some twenty Hittite documents:[23] but so meagre is the evidence for its location that the
most expert judges used to place it so far east as the plain of
Cilicia and so far north as Troy. Others have mapped it overseas, in Crete or on the mainland of Hellas. But there are two
documents which argue strongly, perhaps you may think
decisively, in favour of a site either on the mainland or near the
mainland of Asia Minor. One[24] is a catalogue of frontier lands
(or cities), listed line by line; and the name Ahhijawā appears
on a line following two places which are known to be on the
mainland of Asia Minor. The other[25] refers to a King of Ahhijawā *in person* defending himself against attack on the mainland of Asia Minor: it is obvious that the Hittites regard
Ahhijawā as being, or including, territory on the mainland exposed to attacks by Anatolian states; it would be hard, perhaps
impossible, to reconcile this document with a theory that
Ahhijawā is to be sought in Hellas, and its king identified with
the lord of Mycenae or Tiryns. But while the documents make
it certain enough that Ahhijawā was on or near the coast of
Asia Minor, they still give very little indication of its whereabouts.

The problem might be solved if we knew the location of another country, certain extensive provinces united under the
name *Arzawa*. Early in the 14th century B.C. Arzawa had been
an independent and powerful state, corresponding on friendly
terms with the King of Egypt, and expanding its territory east-
wards at the expense of the Hittite Empire. Conquered by

Suppiluliumas, it alternated thereafter, till the end of the story, between subjection to the Hittites[26] and revolt from them. Now at least one of the territories included in Greater Arzawa—the "Land of the river Seha"[27]—was, if not a neighbour of Ahhijawā, at least very close to it; and certain other lands—especially Luqqā and Karkisa[28]—were more or less contiguous to both Arzawa and Ahhijawā. If we knew where Arzawa was, we could limit the possibilities for Ahhijawā, and in favourable circumstances we could even define its position quite narrowly.

I believe that we do know where Arzawa was, and that its location does indeed solve the first part of our problem. A careful study[29] of the geographical indications provided by the Hittite documents has established beyond reasonable doubt that Arzawa lay in the southwestern sector of Asia Minor, and that it included a stretch of the southern or southwestern coast.[30] These are conclusions of the highest importance: for if Greater Arzawa includes the territories later known as Lycia and Pisidia, there is no room for a powerful seafaring independent kingdom of Ahhijawā except on the *western* coast,—or westwards beyond the coast. We should of course welcome objective confirmation; and for a time it looked as though we had found it. In 1954 the British Institute of Archaeology at Ankara began to excavate a site at Beycesultan on the upper Maeander River. This was an uncommonly extensive settlement, dominated by a great building "almost as large as the palaces of Minoan Crete";[31] and it seemed probable that we had actually found the capital city of Arzawa itself. But later excavations give us pause. The great palace at Beycesultan belongs to the Middle Bronze Age, a later palace to the 13th century B.C.: in the critically important interval—a large part of the 15th and 14th centuries—the site was degraded, thinly occupied by humble folk; evidently Beycesultan was *not* the political centre of Arzawa at the time of its fame and independence in the 14th century. Further work will clarify the history of this exceptionally interesting site; meantime we must not use it in evidence of the location of Arzawa,—we must be content with what we already possess, the indirect testimony of numerous Hittite documents that Arzawa lies in the southwestern sector of Asia Minor, and therefore that Ahhijawā lies on the west coast or westwards beyond it.

Let us now try to define its position more exactly, approaching it through its subject city Millawanda (or Milawatas),[32] which is known to lie on the coast.

Arrived in Millawanda, we ask how it lies with regard to its sovereign Ahhijawā; and we learn two important facts. First, that a man who travels from Millawanda to Ahhijawā does so *by sea*. This is not enough to prove that Ahhijawā is to be located overseas,—we must never forget that the sea is often the quickest and most comfortable route from one point of this coast to another; the fact in itself does no more than suggest that Ahhijawā may have been overseas. But that suggestion is, in my view, confirmed beyond reasonable doubt by our second point, the remarkable conduct of a Hittite Emperor who brought his army into Millawanda and stayed there some considerable time, writing to his temporary landlord one of the most interesting of ancient letters. The document in question deserves our scrutiny; for you may think that it answers once for all the question whether Ahhijawā lay overseas, and (if so) where. Moreover, if this document does not answer our question, it is certain that no other document will.

The text is a letter[33] addressed to a King of Ahhijawā by a Hittite Emperor, whether Mursilis II or Muwattallis, in the latter part of the 14th or the earlier part of the 13th century B.C. There is still no direct clue to the location of Ahhijawā; but the Hittite Emperor's actions and words compel us to take the first important step to an exacter identification. We must remember throughout that the writer of the letter is one of the greatest of the Hittite conquerors, and that the period is the zenith of Hittite power and prestige. With his army at his back he enters Millawanda, a city on the west or southwest coast subject to Ahhijawā; and here is a brief summary of his long tale of woe:

"I have to complain [he writes] of the insolent and treacherous conduct of one Tawagalawas. We came into contact in the land of Luqqā; and he offered to become a vassal of the Hittite Empire. I agreed, and sent an officer of most exalted rank to conduct him to my presence: he had the audacity to complain that the officer's rank was not exalted enough; he insulted my ambassador in public, and demanded that he be declared vassal-king there and then without the formality of interview. Very well: I order him, if he desires to become a vassal of mine, to make sure that no troops of his are to be found in Ijalanda when I arrive there. And what do I find when I arrive at Ijalanda?—the troops of Tawagalawas, fighting on the side of my enemies. I defeat them, take many prisoners, devastate the district,—scrupulously leaving the fortress of Atrija intact out of respect for my treaty with you.[34] Now comes a Hittite subject, Pijamaradus by name, steals my 7,000 prisoners,[35] and makes off to your city Millawanda. I command him to return to me: he disobeys. I write to you: you send a surly message, unaccompanied by gift or greeting, to say that you have ordered your representative in Millawanda, a certain Atpās, to deliver Pijamaradus up. Nothing happens, so I go to fetch him. I enter your city Millawanda, for I have something to say to Pijamaradus, and it would be well that your subjects there should hear me say it. But my visit is not a success. I ask for Tawagalawas: he is not at home. I should like to see Pijamaradus: he has gone to sea.[36] You refer me to your representative Atpās: I find that both he and his brother are married to daughters of Pijamaradus; they are not likely either to give me satisfaction or to give you an unbiassed account of these transactions, though they have had the pleasure of listening to the speech which I had prepared for their father-in-law, and they have promised under oath to make a true report to you. Meantime I receive from you a most insolent message, adopting a tone tolerated only between equals,[37] forbidding me to remove Pijamaradus from Millawanda. Now I have a proposal to make: give me Pijamaradus, and I promise that he shall come to no

harm. I will send a high dignitary of the Hittite court, a kins-
man by marriage of my own queen, as a hostage for him.[38] If I
can make a satisfactory settlement with Pijamaradus, well and
good; if not, he shall return to your territory unharmed, and
you shall keep my royal hostage until then.[39] Are you aware,
and is it with your blessing, that Pijamaradus is going round
saying that he intends to leave his wife and family, and inci-
dentally my 7,000 prisoners, under your protection while he
makes continual[40] inroads on my dominions? Kindly tell him
either to settle down peacefully in your country, or to return to
my country. Do not let him use Ahhijawā as a base for operations against me. You and I are friends.[41] There has been no
quarrel between us since we came to terms in the matter of
Wilusa: the trouble there was all my fault, and I promise it
shall not happen again. As for my military occupation of your
city Millawanda, please regard it as a friendly visit. I am sorry
that in the past you have had occasion to accuse me of being
aggressive and of sending impolite messages: I was young then,
and carried away in the heat of action. I may add that I also
have had harsh words from you: and I suggest that the fault
may lie not with ourselves but with our messengers; let us bring
them to trial, cut off their heads, mutilate their bodies, and live
henceforward in perfect friendship."

Here is a most soft-spoken, down-looking emperor; or perhaps rather "a chafing, stamping king, struggling much to be
composed"? At any rate an abject, questionable letter, surely
our most important evidence—I believe, our *only* decisive evidence—for the exacter location of Ahhijawā. Its subject city[42]
Millawanda lies on the west or southwest coast of Asia Minor,
adjacent to Hittite territory and defenceless against Hittite invasion. There is nothing to stop the Hittite Emperor walking
in and staying in; and that is what he does. Now shall the
citizens of Millawanda tremble; for surely there shall be
slaughter and burning and outrage. Has not its military leader
Tawagalawas proved an enemy, and a treacherous one? Did not
the city give refuge to a dangerous rebel from Hittite dominion,

together with thousands of prisoners stolen from the Hittite King? Is not its governor Atpās tainted and suspect, married to the daughter of the Great King's enemy? Are not insolent messages arriving from Ahhijawā? And here, in our midst, at the head of his army, is the man whom we have insulted and betrayed, the Great Emperor in person, whether Mursilis, who has conquered a quarter of the world, or Muwattallis,[43] whose name is dreaded from the Black Sea to the Nile. What will he do? He will sit down and dictate a letter, apologizing for his intrusion, taking all possible blame upon himself, making large concessions to shifty and impudent rascals; he will do what he can to justify himself in the sight of a king whom he considers his inferior, from whom he has suffered injury. *Egregie cordatus homo*, he shall stand out in history—on this occasion only—as the most soft-spoken, down-looking, of Hittite Emperors. He has been careful to commit no formal breach of treaty; he hopes that his occupation of Millawanda will not be thought unfriendly; he sees some justification for the discourtesy of messages sent from Ahhijawā; he waives his right to the surrender of his own rebel subject; he will send a member of his royal family as a hostage; he takes all blame for past misunderstandings.

And where, all this time, is his correspondent, the King of Ahhijawā? Nothing is more certain than that, if he is anywhere within reach, his days are numbered. There is no room, on the west or southwest coast of Asia Minor, for a kingdom powerful enough to take this tone with the Hittites. A word from the Emperor, and as much of Anatolia as he needs is on the march. The large and powerful kingdom of Arzawa has been crushed;[44] Syria has learnt the folly of rebellion; the unruly tribes of north and east are counting their dead;[45] Kizwatna is at last a vassal state;[46] the assembled might of Egypt is outwitted and checked at Qades on the Orontes.[47] We are bound to answer this question: why is Ahhijawā, herself and her defenceless satellite Millawanda, alone immune from harm; and not only immune from harm, but free to insult and injure the Great Emperor with absolute impunity, confident that he will do no more than

protest apologetically through the proper channels? If the
Hittite Emperor wants Pijamaradus, what is to stop him going
and fetching him? How can the King of Ahhijawā be so sure as
he evidently is that there is no prospect of an embarrassing
personal interview with the much greater King whom he has offended? At the very least, would not the spectacle of Millawanda demolished and depopulated teach him a timely lesson?
Why is it that, in a dispute of this gravity with Ahhijawā, the
normal principles of Hittite action are altogether suspended?[48]
Common sense dictates to us that there can only be one answer
to these questions: if the Hittite King refrains from laying
rough hands on Ahhijawā, *the reason must be that it lies beyond
his reach; and that means that it lies divided from him by the sea.*
When Pijamaradus fled to Ahhijawā from Millawanda by ship,
he was crossing the sea, not cruising up the coast.[49] The conduct
of the Hittite King on this occasion is, in my submission,
absolutely unintelligible unless Ahhijawā is out of reach of the
Hittites. It may, and does from time to time, possess territory
on the mainland coast; but the seat of its power is overseas.

An overseas kingdom, controlling at least one district on the
mainland coast; trading as far as Syria; independent of the
Hittites, their mutual interests regulated more or less by treaty;
presuming to talk to the Great Emperor as to an equal; a power
so much respected by the greatest of the Hittites that he will
swallow insult and injury rather than offend her by exacting
overdue retribution from an impudent satellite on the coast:
where can it be? I think the most important clue to an answer is
given by a passage in this same letter from Millawanda. When
Pijamaradus fled by sea to Ahhijawā, he took with him his
wives and children and domestics *and the prisoners stolen from
the Hittite King;* and he intended to use his new home as a base
for operations against Hittite territory near the coast of Asia
Minor.[50] It is surely common sense to infer that his base must
have been near the coast,—certainly not so far away as the
Greek mainland, probably not so far away as Crete: are we
seriously asked to contemplate the arrival in Hellas of many

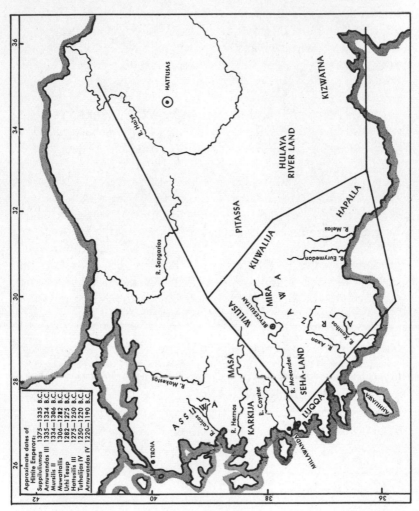

Hittite Anatolia, the subject kingdom of Arzawa with its frontier districts, and neighbours in approximate relative positions. Adapted from Garstang, *American Journal of Archaeology* (1945).

Approximate dates of
Hittite Emperors:

Suppiluliumas	1375—1335 B.C.
Arnuwandas III	1335—1334 B.C.
Mursilis II	1334—1306 B.C.
Muwattallis	1306—1282 B.C.
Urhi Tesup	1282—1275 B.C.
Hattusilis III	1275—1250 B.C.
Tuhalijas IV	1250—1220 B.C.
Arnuwandas IV	1220—1190 B.C.

hundreds, perhaps thousands, of Anatolian subjects of the Hittite King, living under the protection of the Greeks while *pater familias* crosses the Aegean from time to time in order to make raids on Hittite territory, and the Hittite Emperor sends complaints to Hellas, bleating in cuneiform across the wine-dark sea? The letter expressly says that Ahhijawā is a base from which Pijamaradus will raid the mainland, and to which he will withdraw when defeated: surely the place to which the rebel transports his family and his prisoners, and from which he contemplates raids upon the coast, lies very close to the mainland? Remember too that document in which the King of Ahhijawā appears *in person* on the mainland, defending his territory against attack: does he come all the way from Cnossos or Mycenae, when his trading-post in Asia Minor is threatened? Is not this again a clear indication that Ahhijawā itself lies close to the mainland?

My general conclusion has become so obvious that it may as well now be stated bluntly. Is there at this time any island state, close to the west or southwest coast of Asia Minor, a seafaring commercial state powerful enough to be so greatly respected by the unconquerable Hittites? The hard facts of archaeology assure us that there is such an island state—*one only*, as it happens; and that is *Rhodes*.

This is (I need hardly say) not the first time that Rhodes has been mentioned in this connexion. There is, I think, no possible place which could now be named for the first time. Hellas, Lesbos, northwest Asia Minor, Caria, Pamphylia, Cilicia, Crete, and Cyprus have all been proposed:[51] not one of them, in my opinion, can be upheld against the evidence of the Hittite documents—not even Cyprus, despite the advocacy of Schaeffer in his great work on Enkomi-Alasia five years ago,[52] and despite the support of Kretschmer recently. Rhodes was first suggested as the site of Ahhijawā by Hrozný in 1929:[53] but the greater part of his argument was easily refuted, and the identification remained one of the least popular. Within the last few years, however, it has been revived by Karl Völkl of Innsbruck, whose

sober and well-documented article[54] presents the evidence in
favour of Rhodes, and that against all other places, in a very
clear light. He does not make use of the matters on which I
chiefly rely: but I rejoice—and so, I hope, will he—that our
different approaches have brought us together at the same
destination.

It needs no special pleading nowadays to show that Rhodes
fulfils all the necessary conditions. From at least the beginning
of the 14th century B.C. onwards the Achaean Greeks were
established on this island in considerable force. It was not here
a question of traders' outposts or of local settlements amid a
dominant native population: in the time of Hittite Mursilis and
Muwattallis, Rhodes was a Greek island, strong, populous, and
wealthy. She must certainly have been the most formidable sea
power in that neighbourhood; she must have played a part—
probably a leading part—in the expansion of Mycenaean commerce into all corners of the eastern Mediterranean during this
period.[55] The markets of Greek trade included numerous districts directly or indirectly under Hittite control: nobody will
suppose that the Hittites were unaware of, or indifferent to, the
power that ruled the sea for hundreds of miles of Hittite coast;
whose merchants and markets were to be seen for many generations in the ports of countries so interesting to the Hittites as
Cilicia, Cyprus, and Syria. If the Hittites identified the seat of
this formidable power with Rhodes, that was natural enough,
indeed it was presumably the truth; certainly there was no
greater island power eastward of the Greek mainland.

We shall no longer wonder why the Hittites thought it so
important to preserve the peace; why Ahhijawā remained independent and inviolate; why it was prudent to overlook the mis-
demeanours of such easy prey as Millawanda. So long as the
peace is preserved, the Hittites have nothing to fear from these
islanders, and their subjects and allies have much to gain from
their commerce. If the peace is broken, there will be hundreds
of miles of coast exposed to raiders and ruffians; support for
maritime rebels; ruin for friendly markets. Ahhijawā may con-

trol a small area, probably little more than a trading-post, on the west coast of Asia Minor,[56] just beyond the limits of the Hittite Empire: that is no menace to the Hittites, provided that the two states agree (as they do) to respect each other's boundaries. There is no clash of interest, for the Hittites have no ships[57] and the Rhodians have no continental ambitions. The letter from Millawanda illustrates just what we might expect of Hittite diplomacy toward a powerful island state of traders: peace at any price on the coastal fringe; on either side of it, let each recognize the plain facts, that the sea belongs to the islanders, the land to the Hittites, and that the one is out of reach of the other.

We have answered our question finally: Rhodes is Achaean Greek, and Rhodes is Ahhijawā;[58] there really are Achaeans in the Hittite documents. Is it not vain to resist any longer the temptation to identify the names?[59]

Earlier in this lecture I left that question where it stood twenty-three years ago: and indeed there has been little if any progress to report until just recently. Völkl in 1952, Crossland in 1953, Kretschmer in 1954, and P. B. S. Andrews in 1955 have all returned to the problem of the Hittite name for the land of the Achaeans. The waters are deep, and nobody but Völkl has deemed them crystal-clear. I am not myself satisfied that anyone has yet solved the problem of the second syllable, the Hittite equivalent of Greek $\overline{ai}$; but I suggest that that problem has now become one of philological interest only and is no longer a matter of historical importance. The identification of Ahhijawā with an Achaean land is to be proved, if at all, by documentary and archaeological evidence, apart from all speculation about place names. We have followed the evidence, and found that it guides us to Rhodes, whatever the Hittite name for Rhodes may have been; and the proof has not made use of any coincidence of names. We are now at last free to mention the fact that one of the Achaean fortresses in Rhodes, at Ialysus, was later said to have been called by the name Ἀχαία πόλις,[60] and we may conjecture (since nothing much depends upon it) that this was the Mycenaean Greek name of the place, and that the Hittites called Rhodes Akhkhijawā because *Akhaiwā City* was in fact the name of its sovereign centre.

I should be the readier to believe that the similarity of names is fortuitous if the coincidence were not double. First, the greatest Achaean power in the eastern Aegean was called by the Hittites Ahhijawā. Secondly, the only considerable Achaean settlement on the west coast of Asia Minor at this time was *Milatos*, and the only settlement on that coast assigned by the Hittite documents to the realm of the Achaeans was *Milawatas*. That is to say, the only two place names ascribed by the Hittite documents to Greek dominion both bear a strong superficial resemblance to their Greek equivalents.[61] I am very anxious to avoid using jingles of names as historical evidence: but we might perhaps go so far as to remain on speaking terms with those who hold that the double coincidence, or at least half of it, may be more than fortuitous.

The men of Ahhijawā in the Hittite documents are Greeks of the two centuries preceding the sack of Troy. Predominant in the eastern Aegean is the island of Rhodes: for the Hittites, Greek means Rhodian; and for two hundred years the island state enjoys a privileged position in Hittite diplomacy. It owes allegiance, at home, to one King, who sends valuable gifts to the Hittite Emperor, and whose brother is an honoured guest at the Hittite court; it is allowed to control a small district on the mainland, with frontiers regulated by a treaty which the greatest of Hittite Emperors is sedulous to observe; mutual interest preserves the peace, even under provocation, with the Hittites, who think Rhodes a safe and suitable place of exile for distinguished persons from the imperial or vassal courts; Rhodian gods will leave their island temples and journey to the Hittite capital when a dying Emperor calls for their magic or medicine; Rhodian King treats Hittite King as an equal, and is nearly—perhaps quite—treated so by him.[62]

I was looking for the historical background to the Iliad, and soon discovered that the Hittite documents afford one,—provided that the Ahhijawans really are the Achaean Greeks. Nothing further could be done until that question was answered. Most scholars nowadays take the equation for granted: but a study of the Hittite documents in the light of Sommer's commentary undermines and overthrows all easy confidence. If the argument which I have founded on the Tawagalawas letter be not acceptable, I do not know where to turn for anything worthy of the name of evidence in favour of the equation of Ahhijawā with an Achaean state.[63]

We are now confident that Achaeans and Hittites were in contact for a hundred and fifty years (more or less) preceding the sack of Troy VII[a]. We must proceed to ask whether there is any evidence in the Hittite documents of contact between Hittites and Trojans, and between Achaeans and Trojans, towards the end of our period: but first let us turn our attention to Troy itself. Troy remains something enigmatic, while the searchlight of the Hittite documents passes fitfully across Achaeans and Asiatics from Lycia to the frontier of the Troad. Who were the Trojans, and what sort of place was Troy?

NOTES

PRINCIPAL ABBREVIATIONS USED

AS.................*Aḫḫijavāfrage und Sprachwissenschaft:* F. Sommer, *Abhandlungen der Bayerischen Akademie der Wissenschaften*, phil.-hist. Abt., N.F. 9 (1934) 1–101

AU...............*Die Aḫḫijavā-Urkunden:* F. Sommer, ibid. 6 (1932) 1–469, with 9 plates

AUKE............"Aḫḫijavā und kein Ende?": F. Sommer, *Indogermanische Forschungen* 55 (1937) 169 ff.

Bittel, *Grundzüge*   K. Bittel, *Grundzüge der Vor- und Frühgeschichte Kleinasiens*, 2nd ed., 1950

Breasted, *Records*   J. H. Breasted, *Ancient Records of Egypt: Historical Documents* (Chicago, 1906–07)

Güterbock.........H. G. Güterbock, "Neue Aḫḫijavā-Texte": *Zeitschrift für Assyriologie* N.F. 9 (43) (1936) 321 ff.

Kup.............."Der Vertrag Muršiliš' II. mit Kupanta-ᵈKAL von Mirā und Kuwalija": *Mitteilungen der Vorderasiatisch-Aegyptischen Gesellschaft* [*MVAEG*] 31 (1926) 95 ff.

Madd.............*Madduwattaš:* A. Goetze, Hethitische Texte III, *MVAEG* 32 (1927) 1–178, with 6 plates

M-D.............."Die Reste des Vertrages Muršiliš' II. mit Manapa-Dattaš": J. Friedrich, Staatsverträge des Ḫatti-Reiches in hethitischer Sprache, 2. Teil, *MVAEG* 34 (1930) 1 ff.

Mercer............S. A. B. Mercer, *The Tell el-Amarna Tablets* (Toronto, 1939)

Murs.............*Die Annalen des Muršiliš:* A. Goetze, Hethitische Texte VI, *MVAEG* 38 (1933)

Schachermeyr, *HA* ..F. Schachermeyr, *Hethiter und Achäer: Mitteilungen der Altorientalischen Gesellschaft* 9 (1935)

Targ.............."Der Vertrag Muršiliš' II. mit Targašnalliš von Ḫapalla": J. Friedrich, Staatsverträge des Ḫatti-Reiches in hethitischer Sprache, 1. Teil, *MVAEG* 31 (1926) 49 ff.

Taw.............."Der Tavagalava-Brief": F. Sommer, *Die Aḫḫijavā-Urkunden*, Kap. I, *Abh. d. Bayer. Akad. d. Wiss.*, phil.-hist. Abt., N.F. 6 (1932) 2–194

Wil.............. "Der Vertrag des Muwattalliš mit Alakšanduš von Wiluša": J. Friedrich, Staatsverträge . . . 2. Teil, *MVAEG* 34 (1930) 42 ff.

The bibliography of the 'Aḫḫijawā Question' is best given by Völkl, *Nouvelle Clio* 4 (1952) 329 ff.; L. A. Stella, *Il poema di Ulisse* (Firenze, 1955) 72; and at the end of O. R. Gurney's masterly survey, *The Hittites* (Pelican Books, 1952; reprinted 1954).

[In the Notes to this and later chapters, certain abbreviations are explained where they first appear. Other abbreviations, used throughout, are:

AJA .... *American Journal of Archaeology*
BCH .... *Bulletin de Correspondance Hellénique*
BSA .... *Annual of the British School at Athens*
CAH .... *Cambridge Ancient History*
CQ .... *Classical Quarterly*
CR .... *Classical Review*
JHS .... *Journal of Hellenic Studies*
JNES .... *Journal of Near Eastern Studies*
RE .... Pauly-Wissowa, *Real-Encyclopädie der klassischen Altertumswissenschaft*
RHA .... *Revue Hittite et Asianique*]

[1] *a*) The *Aqiyawasa* (for this spelling of *iqjws* see Albright, *The Vocalization of the Egyptian Syllabic Orthography*, New Haven, 1934, p. 34, admitting the alternative *Aqiwasa*):

The equation of *Aqiyawasa* to Ἀχαιοί, difficult enough linguistically (*AS* 84 f.), is put beyond the bounds of probability by the fact, if it is a fact, *that the Aqiyawasa practised circumcision*. For the evidence see Breasted, *Records* III § 574 ff. (the Karnak Inscription) and § 601 (the so-called Athribis Stela; reëdited by G. Lefèbvre, *Annales du Service des Antiquités de l'Égypte* 27, 1927, 19).—In the fifth year of the reign of Merneptah (c. 1220–1205) Egypt was invaded by the Libyan king Meryui assisted by Aqiyawasa, Turusa, Ruku, Sak(a)rusa, and Sardina, described as "northerners coming from all lands" and "of the countries of the sea." The point at issue is briefly as follows. In the Karnak Inscription the phalli of the Libyans are said to be "with *qrnt*, "and the phalli of the Aqiyawasa "without *qrnt*." "*Qrnt*" is believed to signify "foreskin"; indeed the only conceivable alternative seems to be the suggestion so powerfully advocated by Schachermeyr (*HA* 144 ff.) that *qrnt* means *Phallustaschen*. But this alternative cannot be upheld in the face of the Medinet-Habu Relief, in which the Meswes and the Libyans are identically represented, *except that the Meswes do wear Phallustaschen whereas the Libyans do not*; therefore "with *qrnt*," of the Libyans, cannot mean "with *Phallustaschen*," but only "with foreskins"; and the Aqiyawasa, who are "without *qrnt*," are a circumcised people. So Hölscher, *Aegyptologische Forschungen* 4 (1937), quoted by Schraff in his contribution to Sommer, *AUKE* 288 ff.

Moreover, two of the Medinet-Habu pictures have "*qrnt*" with the determinative "flesh" or "part of the body." In these circumstances it is perverse, even if it is possible, to deny that the Aqiyawasa are explicitly said to be "without foreskins"; and the equation with the Achaeans can only be maintained by those who are willing to accept the consequence,—that these Achaeans practised circumcision.

It has long been generally accepted (on the basis of the superficial similarity of names) that the Achaeans took part in the raids on Egypt, and scholars are showing the utmost reluctance to abandon this article of faith. Prentice (*AJA* 33, 1929, 216 ff.) found support here for his opinion that the Achaeans were not of Mycenaean (Greek) race. Völkl (*Nouvelle Clio* 4, 1952, 358 f.) suggests that the Achaeans in the eastern Mediterranean adopted the custom from native peoples; M. I. Finley, *The World of Odysseus* (1954) 7, suggests that the Achaeans who raided Egypt c. 1220 "were evidently in the formative stage of becoming Greeks, still non-Greek as well as Greek"; but the date is much too late for a formative stage of becoming Greeks. Kretschmer, *Glotta* 33 (1954) 14, and Matz, *Kreta, Mykene, Troja* [*KMT*] (1956) 144, believe in circumcised Achaeans. C. F. A. Schaeffer, *Enkomi-Alasia* I (1952) 352 n. 3, suggests that "à Chypre, où les Achéens s'étaient installés dans un milieu oriental, on comprendrait qu'ils aient pu pratiquer la circoncision,"—but it is an exaggeration, to call Cyprus a "milieu oriental"; and the time allowed is short; and the fact remains that there is no reason in the world to suppose that any Greeks ever practised circumcision, except the force of the traditional faith in the identification of the names Aqiyawasa and Ἀχαιοί. Bury-Meiggs, *History of Greece* (3rd ed., 1955) 44: "the Achaïwasha are almost certainly Achaeans"; but the obstacle to the identification is not mentioned.

b) The *"Danaans"* in Egyptian records:

About 1172 B.C. occurred the second and greater of the two invasions recorded by Ramses III at Medinet-Habu (Breasted, *History of Egypt*, 2nd ed., 1952, 474 ff., and *Records* IV § 64 ff.; H. H. Nelson, *Medinet Habu* I [1930], II [1932]: Univ. of Chicago, Oriental Inst. Publ. VIII, IX, and *JNES* 2, 1943, 40 ff.): "The northern countries, which are in their isles, are restless in their limbs; they infest the ways of the harbour-mouths. . . . Their main support was Peleset, Thekel, Shekelesh, Denyen, and Weshesh" = Philistines, Tjikar(a) or Tjikal(a), Shak(a)rusha, Danuna, Washasha; Albright, l.c. Since all except the third are new to the Egyptian documents, it is imprudent to attach any significance to the superficial likeness of Danuna to Δαναοί. It is much likelier that these Danuna are a

Syrian or Palestinian tribe: *Tell el-Amarna Tablets* I p. 395 no.
117.92 (Mercer), D(a-n)una is a person named in a letter from Rib-
Addi to the Pharaoh; II p. 496 no. 151.52, Abimilki of Tyre reports
to the Pharaoh on affairs in Canaan, "*The king of Danuna* is dead,
and his brother has become king in his stead, and his land is quiet.
And fire has consumed Ugarit . . ."; clearly Danuna is a kingdom
on the mainland.—Burton-Brown, *The Coming of Iron to Greece*
(1955) 97, thinks that these mainland Danuna may nevertheless be
identified with the Danaoi: if so, we should have to agree with Hall
(*BSA* 8, 1901-02, 183) that "the mention of the Danuna in the Tell
el-Amarna letters merely shows that in the 15th century B.C. they
[the Danaoi] already possessed a settlement on the coast of Palestine"; but what we need is *a kingdom with a hereditary succession*,
and there was no such Greek place on the coast of Palestine or Syria
at that time.—There remains the further possibility that these
Danuna are the Danuna of Karatepe: if so, it is very unlikely that
they were of Achaean race (cf. Seton Lloyd, *Early Anatolia*, 1956,
179 ff.).

Albright calls the Medinet-Habu record "clear-cut" evidence of
the participation of Danaan Greeks in the sea raid: to me it seems
nothing but the basis for an exceptionally adventurous guess.

[2] For the "priest from Trozen" see *AU* 222; for "Andreus," *AU* 291 ff.
They have all been long dead and buried, and there is no need to
say another word about them. "Atreus," for which Attarssijas
could not possibly be a Hittite equivalent, was abandoned by Forrer
himself (it is a "Ding der Unmöglichkeit," *AU* 330). Nor is there
anything plausible or attractive in the speculation that Attarssijas
might be "a Hittite rendering, or misrendering, of Ἀτρείδης,"
as Barnett suggests (*The Aegean and the Near East: Studies Presented to H. Goldman*, 1956, 215; the same suggestion was made by
Brandenstein, *RE* VII A 2, 1948, col. 2504); when he adds that
"Tawagalawas, though not necessarily Eteocles, turns up as a
name in the Pylos tablets," we must change the names round—
Eteocles, though not necessarily Tawagalawas, turns up in the
tablets.

The equation Tawagalawas = Ἐτεϝοκλέϝης is an improbable guess:
in the only document in which he appears, Tawagalawas looks much
more like a "barbarian" than a Greek; and nobody will succeed in
making a Greek out of his brother Lahurzi (*AU* 373 f., *AS* 58).
Matz, *KMT* 137, by no means rejects the identification of Atreus
with Attarssijas and of "Tavogalassia" (sic) with Eteocles. Ventris
and Chadwick, *Documents in Mycenaean Greek* [*DMG*] 138, say

that "the two occurrences of the patronymic *Etewokleweïos* at Pylos confirm the Mycenaean connexions of the name Eteocles, and make it more probable that Forrer was right in identifying it with the name of *Tawakalawas*." But the existence of this name "Eteocles" in Greece is all that is proved by the Pylos Tablets: they afford no new information whatsoever on the question whether that name is to be identified with the Asiatic Tawagalawas.

The place name Lazpas could be Lesbos; but the identification is a blind guess, incapable of verification. The only other mention of Lazpas is in *Keilschrifturkunden aus Boghazköi* [*KUB*] XIX 5 Vs. 8, where it is apparently attacked by Pijamaradus: Forrer, *Forschungen* I i (1926) 90, "Wie aber hat mich (Pija)maradus ins Unglück gestürzt! Denn er hat mir den Adbas vorauf (? über mich) hingesetzt. Dann schlug er das Land Lazbas." Cf. Gurney, *Hittites* 49 f.

For Troy and Ilios see pp. 106 ff. below.

As for Alaksandus: see *AU* 365 ff., *AS* 30 ff., *AUKE* 187 ff. There is no difficulty in the equation Alaksandus = 'Aλέξανδρος, provided that we derive the latter from the former, not vice versa. 'Aλέξανδρος is a Greek representation of an Asiatic name: the native termination *-andus* is sufficiently attested (*AU* 366); and it is to be noted that *-ανδρος* is a rare element in specifically Greek names (at least before the 5th century); observe too that *-ανδρος* in the Homeric Epic is almost entirely confined to the names of Trojans and their allies; but all these interesting matters are discussed at length and with consummate skill by Sommer, ll.cc.

Kretschmer's speculations, l.c. 20 ff., seem to me to have no contact with reality.

The identification of Luqqā with Greek Λυκία is generally accepted: even Sommer agrees (*AUKE* 272), with the warning that the location may not have been the same in Hittite as in later historical times; and indeed it is highly probable that the territory in question is what was later called *Caria* (see Garstang, *AJA* 47, 1943, 42 f.). It is certain that Luqqā included coastal territory: *Tell el-Amarna Tablets* I p. 203 no. 39 (Mercer), from the king of Alasija to the king of Egypt, "People of the land of Lukki year by year take a small city in my land"; and they are among the sea raiders who attacked Egypt (see the note on Danuna above).

³ His brother's name was Lahurzi; his associates in Millawanda are named Atpas and Avajanas.

Kretschmer, *Glotta* 33 (1954) 10 f., attempts to revive ἐτεϝοκλέϝης and adds the identification of Dapalazunaulis (son of Uhha-LÚ-is, an Arzawan) with Greek δαπανάω+ναῦλον!

[4] Sommer says this explicitly, *AUKE* 286 f.

[5] In the context of the relevant document (*AU* XVII, see n. 12 below) this is true; apart from a confirmatory context it might not be true; Sommer *AU* 101 n. 2.

[6] In "Ahhijavā und kein Ende?"

[7] If Cyprus and Alasija are the same. Syria: *AU* XVII. Alasija: *AU* XIX fin. (= *Madd.* 36).

[8] *AU* XV, quoted n. 19 below. For the detail see *Annalen des Mursilis* pp. 221 ff. Schachermeyr calls this a "most important piece" and stresses "its significance for an overseas Ahhijawā"; but, as Sommer says (*AUKE* 282 f.), however it may be supplemented, all that is stated is that Mursilis sent a person from the Arzawan coast to Ahhijawā by ship; and that he might very well do, if Ahhijawā itself lay on the same coast.

[9] *AU* VI, a letter from Queen Puduhepa to a king in whose realm Urhi-Tesup was exile. The critical passage is Vs. 15 ff.: "Mein Bruder hätte ganz und gar nichts? Wenn der Sohn der Sonnengottheit oder der Sohn des Wettergottes nichts hat oder das Meer nicht(s) hat, so hättest auch du nichts. Du aber, mein Bruder, willst dich von mir aus noch in etwas bereichern?—Das ist kein feiner Ruhm," etc.

[10] Sommer observes that she has already given an example of her tendency toward "etwas affektisch geladenes Pathos" in Vs. 12: "welche Tochter *des Himmels und der Erde* soll denn ich aber [mein]em Brud[er] geben, mit welcher soll ich ihn vermählen?"

Kretschmer, *Glotta* 33 (1954) 8 f., returns to Forrer's view, showing that *aruna* elsewhere may mean rather "sea-land" than "sea"; but he does not (and could not) show that *an island* is meant.

[11] For *Taw.* II 13 ff. see n. 37 below.

[12] *AU* XVII iv 1 ff.: "Und die Könige, die mir gleichgestel[lt] (sind), der König von Ägypten, der König von Babylonien, der König von Assyrien, (*erased:* und der König von Ahhijawā)."

The idea that the erasure was made appreciably later than the writing is not technically untenable, but (as Sommer shows, *AU* 323 ff.) is rendered specially improbable by the sequel. See further *AUKE* 283 ff., a refutation of Schachermeyr on this point. Völkl rightly follows Sommer, "Irgendwelche historisch bedeutsamen Schlussfolgerungen dürfen wir daraus nicht ziehen wollen"; contrast Dussaud, *Prélydiens, Hittites, et Achéens* (1953) 74 ff.

This text is discussed also by R. Ranoszek in *Archiv Orientální* 18.3 (1950) 236 ff. He argues that the erasure is good evidence that the king of Ahhijawā was *not* recognized by Tuthalijas as a "Great

King"; and observes further that Muwattallis had not included him in his list (*Wil.* p. 68 § 14).

13 The review of Schachermeyr's book by Sommer in *AUKE* 265–287 is very damaging. There is no doubt that Schachermeyr makes altogether too much of the Ahhijawan ships, of their trade, and of the "Grosskönigtum"; that he does not solve the linguistic problem of the Ahhijawā-Achaia equation; that his exclusion of the claims of Pamphylia was unjustified; and that his treatment of *AU* XVI in particular is a confession of weakness. Sommer's one really weak point is his constant playing down of the extent of Achaean strength and influence in the eastern Mediterranean and on the coasts of Asia Minor in the 14th and 13th centuries.

14 Sufficient evidence is assembled in *AU* 377.

15 *Taw.* IV 7 ff.

16 *Taw.* II 59 ff.: from the Hittite Emperor to the king of Ahhijawā, "Dabala-DU ist aber nicht ir[gend ein] Mensch von unterstem Rang: Als Hofstallmeister (?) seit Jugendzeit pflegt er mit mir auf den Wagen zu steigen, auch mit deinem Bruder u[nd] mit Tavakalava ist er oft [(auf den Wagen ?)] gestiegen." See Barnett, *The Aegean and the Near East* 216.

17 *AU* IV: the Hittite Emperor (perhaps Hattusilis) declines a request from an unnamed king to pass on to him a gift made by Ahhijawā to the Hittite court. Cf. Güterbock p. 321: inventory of clothes, draperies, etc., ends with reference to a copper object described as "from Ahhijawā" or "in the Ahhijawan style."—I say "exchange" of gifts, since Ahhijawā was independent of the Hittites; such courtesies must have been reciprocal. Even a Hittite "protectorate," such as Arzawa, paid no tribute (Pirenne, *Archiv Orientální* 18.1, 1950, 378 ff.).

18 *AU* X: the sick Emperor is Mursilis; he appeases the offended gods of his own land, and seeks help from the gods of foreign countries (cf. the sending of the cult figure of Ishtar from Nineveh to Egypt to heal the Pharaoh; *AU* 290; *Tell el-Amarna Tablets* I p. 95 no. 23.13 ff.). The Emperor sends for "die Gottheit von Ahhijawā und die Gottheit von Lazpa," but he does not know what their proper ritual may be. (This is the notorious Antaravas text; *AU* 291 ff.)

19 *AU* XV, also edited by Goetze, *Annalen des Mursilis* p. 67, as follows: "der S]ohn des Uhha-LÚ-is [ ] und er [ging] aus dem Meere [hinweg, und er kam . . .] zum König des Landes Ahhijawā [weg. Da] entsandte ich, [die Sonne, den . . .] zu Schiffe [und der König von Ahhijawā liefer]te [ihn ihm aus] und sie führten ihn weg."

20 *AU* XIII: Suppiluliumas' wife (mother of Mursilis) was accused of

diverse crimes and banished from the palace; the question arose
whether the treatment of the Queen had not offended the gods and
caused great misfortune in Hatti,—justification of the action taken
against her is the subject of numerous fragmentary prayers. The
critical part of the text runs:

Rs. 3 Auch solange mein Vater am Lebe[n war, . . .
4 nun er (or sie) mit meiner Mutter (et)was (?) [. . .
5 [nu]n sie (or ihn) in das Land Ahhijawā [. . .
6 [a]bseits beförderte er [

As Sommer says, it is conceivable that the text said not that
Suppiluliumas banished his Queen but that he protected her and
banished someone else. He admits, however, that the likelier interpretation is: "So long as the Queen did nothing wrong, she suffered
nothing in the time of my father; but when she and my father
quarrelled, he banished her to Ahhijawā"; cf. also Schachermeyr 37.
Sommer absolutely rejects Forrer's attempt to bring an *overseas
journey* to Ahhijawā into this context: the document says no more
than "abseits," i.e. "ausser Landes"; Forrer supplied "jenseits über
(das Meer) verbannte."

Schachermeyr's arguments for an overseas Ahhijawā are easily
refuted by Sommer in *AUKE* 280 ff.

[21] *AU* XVII iv 23: "vom Lande Ahhijawā darf kein Schiff zu ihm
[sc. the Assyrian] fahren."

[22] Cf. *AU* XV: the son of Uhha-LU was banished *by ship* to Ahhijawā.
Also *Taw.* (quoted below), Pijamaradus escaped from Millawanda
to Ahhijawā *by ship*. If Alasija is Cyprus, *Madd.* 37 ff. shows that
Attarssijas the Ahhijawan travelled overseas.

[00] Ahhijawā is named certainly or probably in sixteen of Sommer's
Ahhijavā-Urkunden; add two more texts from Güterbock, *Zeitschrift für Assyriologie* N.F. 9 (1936) 321 ff., and two from Schachermeyr 41 ff.

[24] *AU* XVIII. See Sommer's reply in *AUKE* 279 f. to Schachermeyr
40. The latter's objectivity fails him altogether here. The ideogram
ZAG, he says, *"can mean, among other things,* 'frontier,' "—as if
there were any doubt about what it means in this context. The first
three lines contain no more than ZAG-ma, ZAG-ma kuis, LUGAL
ZAG kuis, then follow (v. 4) *Dattassa,* (v. 5) *Mirā,* (v. 6) *Ahhijawā,*
(v. 7) another place name. Schachermeyr argues that if vv. 5–7 are
still concerned with frontiers (ZAG), the reference can only be to a
country which had a common frontier with both Mirā and Ahhijawā, and for which Dattassa was a frontier town; and he objects (i)

that it is improbable that the frontier in relation to Mirā can have
been disposed of in a single line; and especially (ii) that geographical
considerations exclude the possibility that Dattassa and Mirā
bordered one and the same land. Sommer has no difficulty in refuting this: there is no reason whatever to suppose that vv. 5–7 give a
list of common frontiers of any one land (indeed it is likelier that
they give simply a list of lands; hence the division of one line from
another by underlining throughout); and Schachermeyr's geographical problem is illusory (see Garstang, *JNES* 3, 1944, 17 ff.).

No certain inference can be drawn from this severely mutilated
document; but there is an obvious probability that Ahhijawā is
being included in a list of Asiatic lands. At least it is apparent that
this document is a thorn in the flesh of those who would like to believe that Ahhijawā is to be sought *on the mainland of Hellas*.

[25] *AU* XVI Vs. 3 ff., and Ranoszek, in *Rocznik Orjentalistyczny* 9
(1933) 52: from the Annals of Tuthalijas IV. When the Land of the
river Seha rebelled against the Hittites, "der König von Ahhijawā
zog sich zurück." Sommer says all that is necessary (*AUKE* 278)
in reply to Schachermeyr on this point. The appearance of the king
of Ahhijawā *in person* on the Asiatic mainland (especially in such a
context as this) is extremely unwelcome to those who would locate
Ahhijawā on the mainland of Hellas, or indeed anywhere else except
on the Asiatic coast or very close to it. Schachermeyr (39) will not
look the fact in the face: "Perhaps the reference is to *a passing
appearance* (vorübergehendes Auftreten) of the king of Ahhijawā in
the Land of the river Seha"; later (86 n. 1) he goes so far as to suggest that the king was "*not present in person*," though the document
says that he was present. Such evasive action leaves the obstacle
unmoved: when the rebels rose, the king of Ahhijawā withdrew;
the suggestion that the king was not there at all, or only happened
to be passing through at the critical moment during a visit from
Mycenae (or Cnossos), is not even remotely indicated by anything
in the text, and may securely be ignored. Völkl (351) sees the importance of this matter, and (as we must all do) agrees with Sommer.

There is some doubt about the meaning of the phrase which,
following Sommer (and Gurney, *Hittites* 51), I have translated
"withdrew": *AU* XVI 5 f., *LUGAL KUR Ahhijawā EGIR-pa e-ip-
ta* [. . . *E]GIR-pa e-ip-ta LUGAL GAL-ma* etc. I have discussed this
passage with Mr Crossland: *EGIR-pa e-ip-ta* means "took back,"
and the question is whether the usage is transitive or intransitive;
Sommer gives parallels for the intransitive usage, and decides
definitely for "took (himself) back"; Mr Crossland agrees that the

context favours this, but stresses the fact that a transitive usage, "withdrew (his troops)," possibly implying *withdrew support,* cannot be ruled out; it remains possible, therefore, that the Ahhijawans were withdrawing not from the rebels but from the advancing Hittite army.

I agree that this is possible in itself, but I believe that the context almost if not quite rules it out. V. 5–6 tells us that "(the king of the Seha-land) made war, and the king of Ahhijawā withdrew, but [when the king of Ahhijawā] had withdrawn, I advanced . . ."; it is strongly suggested that the Ahhijawans' withdrawal is a withdrawal from attack, and is contrasted with the successful advance of the Hittites. Sommer adds that the expression in v. 1, "the king of the Seha-land again *offended doubly,*" is most easily understood to mean "attacked both the Ahhijawans and the Hittites (or their lieges)." See further Cavaignac, *RHA* 3 (1934–36) 149 ff.: he supplements differently, but agrees that the document proves the interest of Ahhijawā in the affairs of the Seha-land at this period.

Mellaart, *Anatolian Studies* 5 (1955) 83, says that "the king of Ahhijawā . . . retreats at the approach of Tuthalijas": what the document seems to say is that he retreated at the approach of the king of the Seha-land. Bittel, *Grundzüge* 69, says, "Der König von Ahhijava griff in das Scheha-Flussland ein": on the contrary, he withdrew when the Seha-land rebelled.

[26] For the political status of Arzawa in relation to the Hittites (a "protectorate," not a vassal kingdom) see Pirenne, *Archiv Orientální* 18 (1950) 378 ff.

[27] Cf. *AU* XVI. Like Mellaart (*Anatolian Studies* 5, 1955, 83), I follow Goetze in identifying the Seha with the Maeander. Dr Gurney tells me that he too formerly agreed, and thinks there is still much to be said for it, though he himself has now decided in favour of one of the more northerly rivers. The identification with the Eurymedon (Hrozný, *Archiv Orientální* 1, 1929, 328, accepted by Völkl, *Nouvelle Clio* 4, 1952, 341 n. 6) seems to me impossible. Other Arzawan districts, especially Mirā (*AU* XVIII, cf. *AU* V pp. 250 ff.), are also obviously close to Ahhijawā.

[28] For Luqqā see esp. *Taw.* I 3 ff.; cf. *Wil.* 67, with Commentary 95. For Karkisa see *Taw.* III 53 ff. (Pijamaradus will cross to Masa or Karkisa leaving his family in Ahhijawā); *AU* XII (Karkisa probably in the same context with Ahhijawā); *Murs.* 69, *M-D* 5 ff. (a king of Seha takes refuge in Karkisa); *Kup.* 113 (a king of Mirā takes refuge in Karkisa).

[29] See esp. Garstang, *AJA* 47 (1943) 35 ff. and *JNES* 3 (1944) 14 ff.

The political geography of Hittite Asia Minor is a most complex subject, not to be elucidated by the amateur. But before I ever saw Garstang's map or read his articles, I had made a map of my own based on a cross-reference index of all the facts I could find relative to the positions of Arzawa, Ahhijawā, and all places apparently connected with them: the resulting map was, for the area of interest to me, almost identical with Garstang's. There was one serious discrepancy: I had reversed his locations of Mirā and Hapalla. I am still not perfectly convinced that I am in the wrong on this point (and I find some support in Goetze, *Madd.* 152); but we must wait for the publication of the authoritative book on Hittite geography by Garstang and Gurney.

[30] This is absolutely proved by *Murs.* 51 Vs. II 31 f.; 61 Vs. II 50 ff.; 55 Rs. III 39 ff. See further Garstang, *AJA* l.c. 39 f. Mursilis chased the Arzawans "nach dem Gebirge Arinnanda. Besagtes Gebirge Arinnanda aber (ist) sehr steil, ins Meer geht es hinaus, ferner (ist es) sehr hoch und unzugänglich," etc. (*Murs.* 55 Rs. III 39 ff.). Garstang shows cause for placing the Arzawan coastline in Lycia rather than (what I had thought likelier) Pamphylia.

[31] Seton Lloyd, *Early Anatolia* 210. See esp. *Anatolian Studies* 5 (1955) 39 ff., 6 (1956) 101 ff.; the London *Times*, September 24, 1954, June 17 and 28 and August 1, 1955, August 31 and December 10, 1956. For the area around Beycesultan see the map at the end of A. Philippson's *Reisen und Forschungen im westlichen Kleinasien* IV (=Ergänzungsheft Nr. 180 zu *Petermanns Mitteilungen*, Gotha, 1914), Geologische Karte, Blatt 4.

[32] See nn. 42, 61, below.

[33] *Taw.* (=*AU* I); cf. Gurney, *Hittites* 47 ff.; Cavaignac, *RHA* 2 (1932–34) 100 ff.

[34] *Taw.* I 36 f.: ". . . liess ich, da ich das ganze Land vernich[tete, dort doch] die Stadt Atrija als einzige Festung übrig, in Vertragstreue zu [   ]."

[35] For the number of prisoners see *Taw.* III 9 ff.: "Gefangene sind in grosser Zahl über die Grenzen meines La[ndes] gelangt, und 7000 Gefangene von mir hat mein Bruder (=the king of Ahhijawā) geno[mme]n (?)." These are the prisoners stolen from the Hittite Emperor by Pijamaradus, ibid. III 12, "Weil er [eini]ge (viz. of the prisoners) mit Gewalt über die Grenze geführt hat"; III 52, "(Pijamaradus) pf[le]gt das zu sagen: 'ins Land Māsa (oder) Karkija werde ich hinübergehen, die Gefangenen aber . . . werde ich hier (viz. in Ahhijawā) zurücklassen!' "

Mr Crossland warns me that the meaning of the word (NAM.-

RA.MEŠ) here translated "Gefangene," "prisoners," is uncertain; perhaps "serfs," or "persons deported."

[36] *Taw.* I 59 ff.: " 'Die Worte, [die] ich dem Pijamaradu sagen will, die sollen auch Untertanen meines Bruders (sc. the king of Ahhijawā) zu hören bekommen!'—Nun war Pijamaradu zu Schiffe [auf und dav]on! Die Vorwürfe nun, die ich ihm zu machen hatte, [di]e haben auch Atpā und Avajana [ange]hört."

[37] *Taw.* II 13 ff. I play for safety and follow Sommer: but I incline to think that this passage is good evidence at least for the Ahhijawan's *pretension* to the title of Great King. Thus Sommer:

> v. 11 da sagte ich das: "Wenn irgend einer meiner Thron-
> herren (??)
> 12 gesprochen hätte oder (meinetwegen) einer meiner
> 'Brüder,' so würde ich auch dessen
> 13 Wort . . . gehört haben! Jetzt aber hat mein Bruder mir
> als ein Grosskönig, ein mir
> 14 Gleichgestellter, geschrieben! Das Wort eines mir
> Gleichgestellten
> 15 höre ich nicht!"

I have discussed this critical passage with Mr. Crossland: the Hittite text says, "If some great lord of mine (?), or my brother [*or*, one of my brothers], had spoken, I would have listened to him. *But now my brother a Great King my equal has written, and I do not listen to the word of an equal.*" The italicized words make no sense, as Sommer observes: but they will make very good sense if they be taken to be (what is very common in these documents) *a rhetorical question:* "I would have listened to lesser kings: now a Great King, my equal, has written, and do I not listen to an equal? (Of course I do!)." This is surely, both in itself and in its context, a much more natural interpretation than Sommer's, in which the expression "my brother a Great King my equal has written" is taken to mean "my brother has written *as if he were* a Great King my equal"; and the relation of this to what precedes is much obscurer. (Sommer paraphrases the words "If some lord . . . listened to him" as follows: "If the tone of your speech had been, as it ought to have been, that of one of my subordinate kings or some allied sovereign, then I would not have refused to listen"—surely a forced interpretation.) Though I believe that my rendering* is very much likelier than

---

* I find at the last moment that it is not mine: it was proposed by R. Ranoszek in his review of *AU* in *Indogermanische Forschungen* 56 (1938) 38 f.

Sommer's, yet it is not *certain*, and at most it would only prove that the king of Ahhijawā *claimed* the title of Great King (as the king of Assuwa probably did; Seton Lloyd, *Early Anatolia*, 1956, 144 f.) or simply adopted the tone of one, and the Hittite Emperor thought it politic on this occasion to let it pass.

There is a good modern example of the matter at issue here in Kinglake's history of the Crimean War, II 62 f.: the Czar Nicholas (in 1852) absolutely refused to treat Prince Louis Bonaparte as an *Emperor*; "he would call him his 'good friend,' but no earthly power should make him add the word 'brother.'"

[38] *Taw.* II 73 f. (about the hostage): "Was aber diesen Hofstall-meister (?) betrifft, (so ist) er, da er (eine Frau) aus der Familie der Königin hat—im Lande Hatti ist die Familie der Königin hoch-angesehen—(nur) nicht ganz ein Schw⟨ag⟩er (?) von mir."

[39] *Taw.* II 76: "Der (sc. the hostage) soll sich für ihn (sc. Pijamaradus) so lange an seine Stelle setzen, bis er (sc. Pijamaradus) kommt (und) bis er wieder zurückkehrt."

[40] *Taw.* III 59: Sommer translates, "Er aber wird mein Land *immer wieder* überfallen"; and the context suggests repeated attacks, which surely presuppose a base close at hand. I have discussed this passage with Mr Crossland, who tells me that the Hittite *ụalḫ-ḫeškizzi* (iterative, *AU* 429; cf. *Taw.* I 51) does not absolutely require the "*immer wieder*"; it may be interpreted either "keeps attacking" or simply "is attacking."

[41] *Taw.* IV 10.

[42] *AU* III (the Milawatas letter) shows that Milawatas had a common frontier with lands under Hittite control, and strongly suggests that it was (at the time when the letter was written) itself subject to the Hittites; see Sommer *AU* 207 ff. *Taw.*, on the other hand, proves that Millawanda (which is identical with Milawatas; *AU* 206 n. 1) was at that time subject to the king of Ahhijawā; though his control cannot have been very firm, since Tawagalawas offers himself as a vassal of the Hittites, and since the Hittites can (and indeed do) walk in and occupy the place. I suppose that this district (like others in the neighbourhood) may have varied its allegiance from time to time. If the Ahhijawans are Achaeans, their standing in Milawatas may well have been limited to a trading-settlement more or less dominating the native population. For proof that Milawatas lay on the coast see *Taw.* I 61: Pijamaradus escapes from Millawanda to Ahhijawā by sea.

[43] But see Güterbock, *Zeitschr. f. Assyr.* l.c. 326: there is a possibility (envisaged by Sommer also, *AU* 36 n. 1) that *Taw.* is the work of

Hattusilis III. Mursilis or Muwattallis is, however, likelier, since Pijamaradus recurs in a letter of Manapa-Dattas, who died in the reign of Muwattallis (Forrer, *Forschungen* I i 90, transcription and translation of VAT [Vorderasiatische Schriftdenkmäler, Berlin Museum] 7454 + Bo. [Boghazköi-Texte] 2561; the force of this argument weighed especially with Sommer, *AU* 35 f.).

44 For the conquests of Arzawa by Mursilis and Muwattallis see esp. Friedrich, *Wil.*, and Goetze, *Murs.*

45 Especially the Gasgas in the north and the Azzi in the northeast; for these and others see *Murs.* passim.

46 For the history of Kizwatna see esp. Goetze, *Kizzuwatna and the Problem of Hittite Geography* (Yale Oriental Series, Researches, XXII, New Haven, 1940) 26 f., 75 ff. It seems to have been a vassal state of the Hittites in the reigns of Mursilis and Muwattallis (indeed from the time of Suppiluliumas to the end of the Empire; Bittel, *Grundzüge* 71).

47 The great battle at Qades between Ramses II and Muwattallis is dated early in the 13th century (usually 1286/5; c. 1296 according to Yeivin, *JNES* 9, 1950, 101, cf. Cavaignac, *RHA* 2, 1932–34, 180 ff.).

48 Mr Crossland warns me not to underestimate the Hittites' predilection for diplomacy rather than force (cf. Gurney, *Hittites* 113 ff.): but the Annals of Mursilis afford sufficient examples of Hittite methods of retaliation against inferior peoples within their reach. Insult and injury were, as a rule, severely or even savagely avenged *unless there was some special reason for a milder course;* cf. also Mursilis' account of the Deeds of Suppiluliumas, now published by Güterbock in the *Journal of Cuneiform Studies* 10 (1956) 41 ff., 75 ff., 107 ff. *Kup.* 113 provides a striking contrast to the present case: "If you do not seize him and give him up, *I shall come and destroy you and the whole of your territory*,"—that is what we should expect the Emperor to say to the king of Ahhijawā concerning the surrender of Pijamaradus. Contrast also the fate of Arzawa, a much more powerful place than any *mainland* Ahhijawā could have been; and of the Seha-land in *AU* XVI (next door to the Achaeans' Millawanda preserve; the Hittite Emperor crushed his rebellious subjects and took their chieftain "together with his wives" away to Arinna).

49 Laurenzi (l.c. at n. 53 below) notes that in Bo. 2825 (Forrer, *Forschungen* I ii 206 f.) Pijamaradus is again in the same context with *ships*.

50 *Taw.* III 52 ff.: "er (Pijamaradus) pf[le]gt das zu sagen: 'Ins Land Māsa (oder) Karkija werde ich hinübergehen, die Gefangenen

aber, meine (?) Frau(en ?), Kinder (und) Hauswesen werde ich hier (= in Ahhijawā) zurücklassen!' "

[51] Against identification with Crete (supported by Cavaignac, *BCH* 70, 1946, 58 ff.) or Hellas: Völkl 349 ff. Against Cilicia and the "Hypachaioi": ibid. 341 ff., with Schachermeyr 84 ff. Against Pamphylia: ibid. 338 ff., with Schachermeyr 117 f., 124 f.

[52] Cyprus: see Schaeffer, *Enkomi-Alasia* I (1952) 1 ff., 350 ff.; Kretschmer, *Glotta* 33 (1954) 1 ff.

R. Dussaud (ap. Schaeffer, op. cit. 2 ff.) would like to believe that "Alasija" was a name limited to the eastern part of Cyprus and often signified only the one place, Enkomi. The extreme weakness of his position is revealed by his own "principal arguments," of which "les plus typiques sont d'abord qu'Enkomi s'est révélée comme le siège d'une importante industrie du cuivre, et aussi que le vocable d'Alasia est resté longtemps attaché au territoire d'Enkomi dans le vocable de sa divinité Apollon Alasiotas." The fact that Enkomi was an important centre of the copper industry is no reason whatever for confining *the name Alasia* to this one place alone; and there is not an atom of evidence to connect Apollo Alasiotas more closely with Enkomi than with other places (e.g. Tamassos, the source of two of his statues; Enkomi supplies one).

The idea that Ahhijawā is to be identified with Cyprus, or with any part of it, is not supported by anything in our evidence; indeed one would suppose Alasia to be sharply distinguished from Ahhijawā in *Madd.*, where a man from Ahhijā joins a mainland prince in an attack on Alasia, which the Hittite Emperor claims for his own realm. Schaeffer, 356 n. 2, says that Madduwattas was right in protesting that nobody ever told him that Alasia belonged to the Hittites: "le roi hittite semble avoir considéré les possessions achéennes de Chypre comme dépendant d'une puissance alliée avec laquelle il tenait à rester en bonnes relations." A glance at the Madduwattas text shows that no such interpretation can be entertained for a moment; the Hittite Emperor says that Alasia belongs to him, and complains that his vassal Madduwattas has made a raid upon it together with the Ahhijawan Attarssijas; the text itself rules out the suggestion that the Hittite Emperor is intervening to protect the territory of an allied power (Madduwattas himself admits that he must restore to the Hittite Emperor the prisoners taken from Alasia).

I must add that I do not share Schaeffer's confidence that the chiefs who lived in his "bâtiment 18" in the 14th/13th cent. were Achaeans; the cranial deformation practised by their women points

to a non-Greek race; and the evidences of Mycenaean culture
(whether imported or local) prove nothing about the nationality of
the ruling house; traders and artisans had long been settled on the
island. It comes as a surprise, to be told (342 ff.) that "bâtiment
18" is a Mycenaean type of building, especially that the plan of the
central part reproduces that of the typical Mycenaean house of
Late Helladic III; the Plan seems not to confirm it.

(Kretschmer, l.c., identifies Alasia with Cyprus, Ahhijawā with
Enkomi, but brings no new evidence in support; his conclusions
from the Puduhepa and Uhha-LU documents are invalidated by
the simple fact that neither of them makes any reference to Cyprus.)

[53] Hrozný, *Archiv Orientální* 1 (1929) 323 ff. See Schachermeyr, *HA*
129 ff.: after rightly dismissing certain weak arguments adduced
by Hrozný, he proceeds (131) to admit that Rhodes does fulfil most
of the conditions required (distance from the Hittites; suitability as
a home for Hittite exiles; position relative to Cyprus, Syria, and the
coast of Asia Minor; power to intervene on the mainland; density
of Mycenaean settlement), but rejects the identification because:

i) It is said to be doubtful whether Rhodes, occupied by Mycenaeans c. 1400 B.C., had time to attain so high a peak of power
already in the time of Suppiluliumas (1375–1335).—As if some fifty
years were not sufficient for the building of a prosperous commercial state.

ii) The "most serious objection" is this: if Rhodes is Ahhijawā,
it follows that the Rhodians called their island Ἀχαίϝα, and that
is said to be improbable.—If this really is "the most serious objection" that can be brought against the case for Rhodes, that case
must be very strong indeed. Schachermeyr seems to have overlooked the likelihood that what the Rhodians called themselves was
"Achaiwoi," and that the Hittites simply called the country by the
name of its people; and we must not forget that the fortress on
Ialysus was actually called Ἀχαία πόλις (see n. 60 below).

iii) It is said to be doubtful whether Rhodes was important
enough to bear the burden of all the activity attributed to Ahhijawā
and Aqiyawasha in Asia Minor and the eastern Mediterranean.—
But (a) we must not bring the Aqiyawasha into the picture of
Rhodes (n. 1 above); (b) the amount of activity attributed to
Ahhijawā in the Hittite documents is not at all great; it is far less
than we might easily reconcile with the prosperity of Rhodes in the
14th and 13th centuries. This section of Schachermeyr's book makes
on the reader the strongest impression of special pleading, all the

more noticeable since much of the book is exceptionally sober and judicious.

Völkl, 353 n. 4, gives a list of those (relatively few)* who have expressed themselves in favour of the identification with Rhodes; add Crossland, *Compte rendu de la IIIe rencontre assyriologique*, 161 n. 13; Mellaart, *Anatolian Studies* 5 (1955) 83 (Ahhijawā must include especially the Mycenaeans in the islands off the southwest coast), cf. Taylour, *Myc. Pottery in Italy* (1958) 187 f. Bittel, *Grundzüge* 69 ff., makes the good point that the importance of Ahhijawā presupposes some greater territory than a few coastal stations in Asia Minor; he thinks that Rhodes (and perhaps Samos) must be included in the realm of Ahhijawā.

[54] Völkl's admirable essay (*Nouvelle Clio* 4, 1952, 329 ff.; my own work was done before I saw it) shows in detail, with excellent documentation, that Rhodes, unlike all other potential sites, suits the evidence from all sources to perfection. It still cannot be said that he offers *positive proof;* that need is not supplied by the identification of Piggaia with Φαγαιεῖς (356: a very long shot), or by stressing the value of the evidence of ᾽Αχαία πόλις (355: it is mere assumption that the colonists of Rhodes were "Angehörige der verschiedensten Stämme, ... die sich gegenüber der einheimischen Bevölkerung einen Gesamtnamen beigelegt haben müssen").

[55] See esp. F. H. Stubbings, *Mycenaean Pottery from the Levant* (1951): the evidence "amply proves that a Mycenaean settlement flourished at Ialysos from the beginning of Myc. III (i.e. 1425–1400), and was in all probability established even a little earlier" (p. 11); a good case is made for Rhodes as the principal source of Mycenaean exports to Syria, Palestine, and Egypt in the 14th century (68 ff., 106); the density of the Mycenaean population in Rhodes is well shown in fig. 1, p. 6. For detail of excavations in Rhodes see G. Monaco, *Clara Rhodos* 10 (1941) 43 ff.: "Scavi nella zona micenea di Jaliso (1935–36)"; G. Jacopi, *Annuario della Regia Scuola Archeologica di Atene* XIII/XIV (1930–31): "Nuovi scavi nella necropoli micenea di Jalisso"; A. Maiuri, ibid. VI/VII (1923–24) 83 ff.: "Jalisos. Scavi della missione archeologica italiana a Rodi"; and *Clara Rhodos* 1 (1928) 60 ff.: "La necropoli micenea di Jalisso"; Hiller von Gaertringen, *RE* Suppl. V (1931) 731 ff. The warlike disposition of the colonists is well shown by the fact that some

---

* Pride of place should perhaps go to Laurenzi, "Rodi e l'Asia degli Ittiti," *Nuova Antologia*, genn.-febb. 1940, 372 ff.: brief, lucid, complete, and cogent in its presentation of the *general* case for Rhodes: there is still no *specific* argument, such as (I believe) the Tawagalawas letter provides.

seventy tombs excavated by Maiuri and Jacopi yielded 5 swords, 10 lances, 16 other blades, 4 arrowheads, and 1 battle-axe. Cf. also Laurenzi, l.c. (see fn. to note 53 above), and Schaeffer, *Enkomi-Alasia* I 325 n. 1, 343 ff., 419, al.

[56] For Mycenaean activity on the west and southwest coast of Asia Minor see esp. Hanfmann, *AJA* 52 (1948) 135 ff.; Karo, *RE* Suppl. VI (1935) 612 f.; Völkl 336 f.; on the west coast south of the Troad, the only demonstrable Mycenaean settlements are at Miletus and (Goldman, *AJA* 27, 1923, 67 f.) Colophon; scanty finds at Pitane, Phocaea, Larisa, Assarlik, Mylasa, Telmessos afford no proof of settlement. The overlap of Hittite and Achaean spheres of interest is well illustrated in Schachermeyr's map, *HA* 119; cf. Bittel, *Grundzüge* 71 and map 5.

[57] There are numerous later historical parallels to the immunity of the East Aegean islanders from attack by mainland powers; cf. Herodotus I 143, 151. Apart from lack of naval power, it is likely that the Hittites treated certain great coastal cities (centres of commerce) with special favour: compare the degree of immunity enjoyed by Ugarit in the 13th century (Schaeffer, *Ugaritica* I, 1939, 38 ff.),—perhaps because Mycenaeans were in that period "la classe possédante" (ibid. 103 f.).

[58] It may be asked whether this might not be true only from the Hittite point of view,—if Pijamaradus goes to an adjacent island under Ahhijawan control, it would be natural for the Hittites to say "he has gone to Ahhijawā" even though that island were merely an outpost of an Ahhijawan empire based on the Greek mainland. This possibility seems practically ruled out by *Taw.* and other documents: the Hittite's correspondent in *Taw.* is clearly a king *close at hand*, indeed in the same territory as Pijamaradus. And the suggestion that he might be merely a local ruler subordinate to a sovereign in Mycenae (or elsewhere) is hardly to be reconciled with the fact that it is *this* king, the one close at hand, who claims equality of status with the Hittite Emperor.

[59] Ahhijawā, spelt ahhijawā, ahhiuw(ā), and ahhijā; never ahhijāw-: see esp. *AU* 350 ff., *AS* 73 ff., *AUKE* 254 ff. Later discussions include Schachermeyr 69 f.; Völkl 344 ff.; Crossland, *Bibliotheca Orientalis* 10 (1953) 120 f.; Kretschmer, *Glotta* 33 (1954) 2 ff.; Andrews, *RHA* 13 (1955) 18 f.

The termination is reasonably explained by the hypothesis that the Hittites turned a race name into a place name, Ahhijaw-ā like Mir-ā, Pal-ā, al. I suppose, on the evidence of the Greek Epic, that the Achaeans used no general place name Achaea. We must not say that the reason why 'Αχαιϝία does not occur in the Epic is because it will not fit into the verse (so, most recently, Ventris and Chadwick, *DMG* 141): there was nothing to prevent the formation of a dozen such formulas as τοὺς ἔθρεψεν Ἀχαιίη ὑλήεσσα, ἐν Ἀχαιίηι (cf. Xenophanes fr. 2.3 D.-K. ἐν Ὀλυμπίηι), and normal practice would have created such expressions as Ἀχαιίης ἐρατεινῆς (cf. ἀτιμίη, ὑπεροπλίηισι, and the like). In Tablet C 914 from Cnossos *A-ka-wi-ja* may, as Ventris and Chadwick say (*DMG* 138), "conceivably represent" Ἀχαιϝία; but there is no certainty that it is the correct interpretation, and if it were we should still not know what place (? a town in Crete) it signified.

The greatest difficulty is presented by the alleged equation of Hittite *-ĭjă-* to Greek *-aĭ-*. I am not convinced that anybody has found a reasonable explanation for this; for me, the last word is said by Sommer (*AUKE* 269): "Those who wish to stand by the equation of Ahhijawā with the land of the Achaeans will serve their purpose best by keeping entirely clear of linguistics, renouncing a spurious wishful thinking, and relying on the power of faith"; and again (*AS* 89, 91), the equation is one which we must tolerate if the other facts demand it; it cannot be rationally explained.

Völkl, 346, passes rapidly over the point: the equation is acceptable, "denn aus einem unbetonten griechischen -ai- wird, soweit wir heute schon von Lautgesetzen sprechen können, im Hethitischen einfaches -i-, und der Schwund von intervokalischem -w- ist im Hethitischen gleichfalls belegbar. So scheint mir der Weg einfach von Ἀχαιϝία über Achchiwia zu Achchija zu gehen." I can see that Ahhijā may be thus explicable; but that is a form which occurs only in one document. What we have to explain is Ahhijawā, particularly the *-ija-*; and to that problem Völkl makes, so far as I can see, no contribution. Kretschmer suggests a progress from Ahhaï- to Ahhäï- to Ahhaji- to Ahhija-; it is a relief to the layman to find that his impression that this is mere hariolation is shared by Sommer, *AS* 90.

Schachermeyr's attempt to explain the phenomenon includes two fatal errors, exposed by Sommer, *AUKE* 267 f.

Andrews' solution I doubt whether I have fully understood; so far as I follow, I find it speculative and unconvincing.

Ventris and Chadwick, *DMG* 209, refer to "the form Ἀχαιϝία postulated as the Greek original of the Hittite *Ahhijawā*": what ought to be so postulated is not Ἀχαιϝία but Ἀχιάϝα.

⁶⁰ *Inscr. Graec.* XII 1.677 = Schwyzer *Dialect. Graec.* nr. 284, "(saec.) III utique non recentior"; inscribed stelae to be set up, μίαμ μὲν ἐπὶ

τᾶς ἐσόδου τᾶς ἐκ πόλιος ποτιπορευομένοις, μίαν δὲ ὑπὲρ τὸ ἱστιατόριον, ἄλλαν δὲ ἐπὶ τᾶς καταβάσιος τᾶς ἐξ 'Αχαίας πόλιος. Ergias' Rhodius ap. Athen. VIII 360ᵉ φησὶν ὡς οἱ περὶ Φάλανθον ἐν τῆι 'Ιαλυσῶι πόλιν ἔχοντες ἰσχυροτάτην τὴν 'Αχαίαν καλουμένην κτλ. Schol. Pind. Ol. 7.34ᵃ, i p. 206 Dr., Δίδυμος δέ φησι καὶ τετάρτην εἶναι πόλιν τὴν νῦν 'Αχαίαν καλουμένην ('Αχαιῶν codd.: -αίαν Wilamowitz, Hermes 14, 1879, 457 n. 3).

Schachermeyr (130) supposes that the name 'Αχαία πόλις may have been given first by the Dorian settlers: Völkl (354 ff.) makes the appropriate reply, "So gut die Bezeichnung von den späteren Doriern gesetzt sein kann, ebenso gut kann sie auch schon von den mykenischen Ansiedlern herrühren"; we simply do not know.

[61] The identification of Milawatas with Milatos has been rejected by some (e.g. by Sommer, AU 361 f., AUKE 272) on the ground that, if it were true, the Ionic form would have been Milātos, whereas in fact it is Milētos; for αϝα contracts to ā, not η, in Ionic (cf. O. Hoffmann, Gr. Dialekte 3.326 ff.). This objection is not so cogent as it may appear at first sight. It would not be valid, if the contraction to Milātos had already occurred before the change from ā to η began in Ionic: and indeed we have reason to believe that the name was Milāt- already in the Mycenaean era (Pylos Tablet Aa 17; whether the Cretan or the Asiatic town), and that the change from ā to η began later than this (Risch, Mus. Helv. 12, 1955, 65). Moreover, the name was presumably non-Greek: foreign place names may sound differently to different peoples, and Greek Milāt- may have been as good an approximation to the truth as Hittite Milawat-. Finally, though the Ionians later as a rule preserved ā in foreign names (e g Dāreioo), they might substitute η for ā in any such name if it became so familiar as to be considered virtually a native word (Hoffmann, l.c.); it is likely enough that in the course of time the name of their own metropolis would be pronounced in the native manner, Milētos not Milātos, whatever the ultimate origin of the ā might be.

The identification is quite strongly supported by an independent argument well stated by Garstang, AJA 47 (1943) 41: "Mursil's line of approach to this place (Milawatas) was marked by two other site names in the sequence Waliwanda—Ialanda—Milawatas, and the sites suggested by the classical equivalents of these other names, namely Alabanda and Alinda, mark an actual route toward Miletus parallel with the Maeander. We cannot reject the significance of these pointers."

[62] I mention in passing the alleged discovery at Boghaz-Köy of a

Hittite cuneiform text with Linear B writing at the foot: see
Friedrich, *Minos* 3 (1954) 5 ff.; Peruzzi, ibid. 4 (1955) 118 ff.; and
esp. Dow in *AJA* 58 (1954) 101 ff., "a discussion which may suffice
so far as Linear B is concerned." If more is needed, it will be found
in Friedrich, *Minos* 5 (1956) 117 ff.

In *Minos* 3 (1954) 8 f., Laroche discusses a seal and sherd inscribed with alleged Linear A signs: this too is a false trail.

[53] "Nearly all scholars are now agreed that we have here [viz. in the
Hittite documents] the first documentary evidence for the Achaeans," Bury-Meiggs, *History of Greece* (1955) 43: so indeed they are,
but they have no right to be, for not one of them has refuted Sommer's attack upon the identification. Forsdyke was entirely justified
in saying (as recently as 1956: *Greece before Homer* 83) that "there
is not yet any reason beyond the resemblance in the place name to
connect the people of Ahhijawā with the Achaians of Greece."

The question is the more important since we have learnt that there
are points of close contact between Hittite and Greek mythology
and theogony: I owe my introduction to this interesting subject to
three papers by Albin Lesky: "Hethitische Texte und griechischer
Mythos," *Anz. Oesterr. Akad. d. Wiss.*, phil.-hist. Kl., Nr. 9, 1950,
137 ff.; "Zum hethitischen und griechischen Mythos," *Eranos* 52
(1954) 8 ff.; "Griechischer Mythos und Vorderer Orient," *Saeculum*
6 (1955) 35 ff.; cf. also Güterbock, *AJA* 52 (1948) 123 ff.; Gordon,
ibid. 56 (1952) 93 and *Minos* 3 (1955) 126 ff.; Webster, *Minos* 4
(1956) 104 ff.; Walcot, *CQ* n.s. 6 (1956) 198 ff.; Barnett, *The
Aegean and the Near East* 218 ff. We have now to reckon seriously
with the opinion expressed by Dunbabin, *The Greeks and Their
Eastern Neighbours* (1957) 56, that "the closeness with which
Hesiod's version follows the Hittite epic in places, and the undi-
gested nature of much of the matter, by no means hellenised and
humanised as are Homeric stories about the gods, argues strongly
against this view [viz. the theory of continuous transmission from
the Mycenaean era]. The more probable hypothesis is that the
Greeks learnt these stories in the Levant in the eighth or seventh
century."

II
The History of Troy

HEINRICH SCHLIEMANN began to excavate the hill of Hissarlik in 1870, and led seven major campaigns before his death in 1890. The work was continued by his architect and assistant, Wilhelm Dörpfeld, who conducted elaborate excavations in 1893 and 1894 and published his findings in one of the great books of its time, *Troja und Ilion* (1902). Some years ago I wrote down a short list of questions to which the excavations had not, so far as I could see, provided answers:

i) Who were the Trojans?

ii) Was the "Sixth City"—that is, the fortress to some extent contemporary with Mycenaean Greece—continuously occupied by the same people from beginning to end?

iii) What was the end, and how did it occur?

iv) What was the relation of Troy to the great empire of the Hittites, who dominated the greater part of Asia Minor for hundreds of years, and especially from about 1400 to 1200 B.C.?

v) What were the sources of Troy's prosperity for so long a period of time?

From 1932 to 1938 seven campaigns of excavation were organized by the University of Cincinnati and carried out under the command of Carl Blegen. The results of his work are now published in a series of wonderful books entitled *Troy*. I have examined the work of Blegen and his colleagues from start to finish in the hope of finding answers to my questions. I doubt whether there is any other source of factual information which will ever answer them; and in this section I shall confine myself wholly to the results of excavation at Troy.

The occupation of the site of Troy begins toward the close of the fourth millennium B.C.;[1] and the American excavators have proved that it was from the first a fortified stronghold, designed for the accommodation of a chieftain, presumably together with his family and retinue. The first settlement passed through ten successive phases of building,[2] perhaps a period of some five hundred years. The type and scale of the building may be illustrated by the example of a great house of the second phase,[3] a megaron in plan, measuring some 56 by 21 feet,[4] with built-in beds, fireplace, kitchen with kitchen table, and latrine.[5] It is improbable that the circuit at that time would leave room for more than a dozen such houses,[6] if so many; it is therefore certain that the subject population lived on the slopes and in the plain outside the royal precinct. For a subject population there must have been: the scanty material remains[7] attest the activity of farmer, fisherman,[8] potter,[9] metalsmith[10] in copper and lead, and especially stonemason and builder.[11] The great houses and still more the great wall testify at once to the power of a supreme ruler, and to the skill of numerous labouring hands. The fortification wall is by far the most impressive of the remains of the first settlement of Troy; some five thousand years after its erection it was found standing about 10 feet high; its course was traced for 100 yards, which may be not much less than half its original circuit; and in its south face was a gateway, flanked on each side by sturdy towers.[12] The most unexpected discovery was a limestone slab with a human (or divine) head carved in a manner which shows that already, at this very early date, sculpture in relief had passed the stage of primitive scratching on stone and had developed a formal style.[13] The decorative arts and the practical crafts flourished in this ancient kingdom; their religion survives only in a few small amulets and idols[14] of stone or terracotta and two stone tablets pitted with saucer-like concavities, discoloured with blood of sacrifice.[15]

It was by no means secluded from the wider world: there are idols fashioned of a marble which is not native to the Troad; there is pottery which was almost certainly imported from the

[1] For notes to chapter ii see pages 74–96.

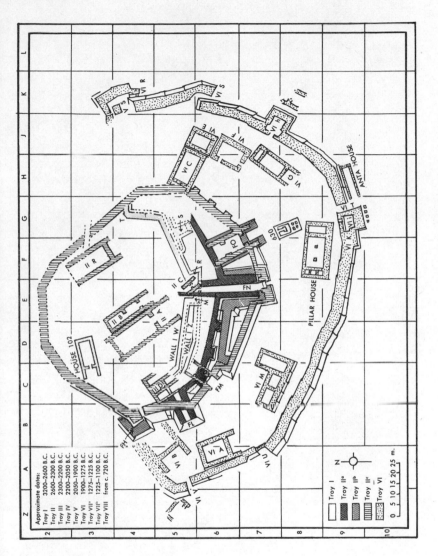

Approximate dates:		
Troy I	3200–2600 B.C.	
Troy II	2600–2300 B.C.	
Troy III	2300–2200 B.C.	
Troy IV	2200–2050 B.C.	
Troy V	2050–1900 B.C.	
Troy VI	1900–1275 B.C.	
Troy VIIa	1275–1225 B.C.	
Troy VIIb	1225–1100 B.C.	
Troy VIII	from c. 720 B.C.	

☐ Troy I
■ Troy IIa
▨ Troy IIb
▥ Troy IIc
░ Troy VI

N

0 5 10 15 20 25 m.

Troy I, II, VI. After Blegen's adaptation (*Troy* III 2, fig. 446) of Dörpfeld's plan (*Troja und Ilion*, Taf. III)

Greek mainland or the Cyclades; there is a flake of obsidian which may have come from so far away as Melos or Mersin.[16] Trade and fishery alike suggest that the earliest Trojans were no strangers to seafaring.[17]

Such in brief is the picture of the earliest settlement on the site of Troy: it is the castle of a royal house which fosters art, religion, commerce, and many crafts among its numerous subjects. It lives impregnable within its walls for five or six hundred years; and when at last the fortress is consumed by a great fire,[18] the same people[19] level the ruins and ashes, build a far bigger and stronger fortress, and live there until the total of their years on that hill has reached at least seven or eight hundred. There was no break in culture, and therefore presumably no change of people, between the first and second fortresses of Troy:[20] the differences are of scale, not of kind. The second fortress passed through eight building-phases,[21] of which the most brilliant was the third. In this phase the circuit wall, already much greater and grander than that of the first fortress, was enlarged and rebuilt in magnificent style with monumental gateways;[22] and in the centre of the enclosed citadel arose the largest building so far discovered on the prehistoric site. It is a megaron in plan, more probably an official than a domestic building; it is hard to guess what it might have been, except a palace or a temple.[23] From a vestibule 10 feet square you might enter a main room 30 feet wide and perhaps as much as 60 feet long. This great building[24] stood in a courtyard which must have occupied nearly half the area of the citadel; the entrance to the courtyard lay through an imposing portal, of propylon style; and the inner walls were adorned with roofed and pillared porticoes.[25]

As in the first settlement, so in the second, there cannot have been room for more than a dozen dwelling-houses of moderate size within the fortress walls. It is still therefore the castle of a king; the massive walls and stately houses are the work of a subject population residing on the slopes and plain outside the fortress. There is evidence that the craftsmen have made progress, not only in architecture but also in domestic arts: in the second phase of the settlement we find the first wheel-made pottery.[26] In most walks of life, however, comparison between Troy II and Troy I shows rather development than difference. They still spin and hunt and fish and farm; with stone and bone and terracotta they make tools and weapons, rings and necklaces, beads and pendants; they work in lead and copper, but not yet in bronze; they develop their own styles of pottery, and practise especially the modelling of lids or necks of vases into the likeness of human (or divine) faces;[27] at the same time they import freely from peoples overseas in the west.[28] In general, and for the most part in detail, Troy II is simply Troy I "writ large"; there is a fire which burns steadily and strongly, bursting into sudden and continued splendour at rare intervals,—particularly in the Early and Middle Phases of the Second Settlement.

And then, in the latest phase of this second fortress of Troy, a cloud gathers over the scene, and in the growing darkness we discern, first, an invasion of the palace area by humbler buildings, and, thereafter, the greatest of catastrophes,—the devastation of Troy by fire, a fire so violent that the citadel was reduced to a vast heap of cinders, concealing all but the split and discoloured stonework of the great walls.[29] We observe the events, and can only guess at their meaning. Towards the end of the second settlement of Troy the great courtyard itself was partly demolished: down goes the whole of the southwestern angle of this venerable place, pillars and porticoes tumble, and over the site creeps a network of unworthy lodgings.[30] All the stranger, since the encroachment follows quite soon after a substantial *enlargement* of the courtyard.[31] Whether temple or royal palace, this precinct must have been holy of holies: what cause could there possibly have been to invade its privacy, to destroy the courtyard walls and allow the spread of humbler houses to the very doors of the great mansion? And what connexion may there be between this and a deeper mystery,—the enigma of the golden treasures of Troy II?[32]

Beneath a deep stratum of débris from the burning of Troy, in or about a fairly large house adjacent to the fortress wall,[33] a great treasure of gold, silver, and bronze lay hidden, abandoned by its owner on the day of wrath. Its discovery by Schliemann in 1873 was the first of a series: sixteen other treasures, comparable in kind but not in quantity, are listed in *Troja und Ilion;*[34] and the American excavators added to the sum of precious metals 1,472 beads of gold, and 9 other gold and

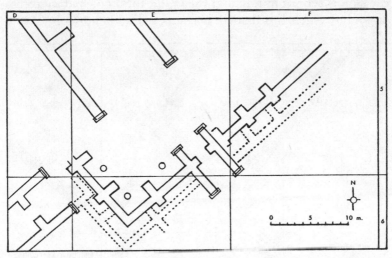

Troy II, extension of courtyard: from Blegen's *Troy* I 2, fig. 451. Extension from II^c (solid lines) to II^d (broken lines).

3 silver objects.[35] These wonderful treasures are fully described elsewhere, and I need do no more than stress the variety and delicacy of the goldsmith's art by referring briefly to one or two items in the catalogue. No. 5873 is a silver vase, containing 2 golden diadems, 1 headband, 4 ear pendants, 6 gold bracelets, 56 gold earrings, and 8,750 gold beads. No. 5875 is a diadem of gold, "20.4 inches long across the top . . . it consists of a gold chain, composed of 295 rings of double gold wire, from which are suspended on each side 8 chains, 15.8 inches long. Each of these consists of 360 rings made of double gold wire,

and between every three of such rings is fastened a lancet-shaped leaf. At the end of each of these chains is suspended a figure 1.3 inches long. . . . Between these ornaments for the temples there are likewise 74 small chains, 4 inches long, each of which consists of 84 rings of double gold wire, and is adorned with 28 lancet-shaped leaves. At the end of each chain is suspended a large leaf of a similar form. Let us compute the number of double rings and leaves of this wonderful headdress"[36]— the sum is set out in full, and the grand total of separate pieces of gold of which this diadem is composed adds up to 16,353.

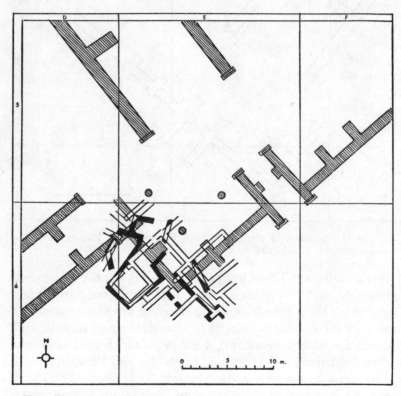

Troy II, encroachment on courtyard: from Blegen's *Troy* I 2, fig. 458 superimposed on fig. 457. Encroachment on SW angle of Great Court: in II[d], shaded; in II[f], solid; in II[g], open.

I dwell for a moment on this matter, for it is one of the greatest mysteries of Troy. You may ask, were there not gold mines within reach of Troy?[37] And why may not the Trojan goldsmith excel in one art, as the Trojan architect in another? True, but perpend the facts:

These treasures are unique in Troy. They have neither past nor future. It is very nearly true[38] to say that no object in gold has ever been found in any phase of any of the first six settlements—a period of nearly 2,000 years—except in this, the last phase of the second settlement. Yet the quality of the goldsmith's art is such that we are compelled to postulate a period of development. That golden diadem was not created in the first generation of the craft. It must have had a history: but it had no history at Troy itself; and there must be a reason why the goldsmith's work should be thus excellent at a time when the craftsmen in other materials were plodding, without much progress, at a far lower level of artistry.[39] In brief, the facts indicate that these golden treasures were not created at Troy; and this immediate inference is confirmed by the observation that the treasures include objects of bronze,—for bronze is not found elsewhere in the relics of the second settlement[40] from first to last.

Now, if these treasures came to Troy from outside, how did they come? Consider first that they may be the spoils of war or of a raid; and remember the treasures from the shaft graves at Mycenae. Those also (many of them) are isolated in the history of their place and period;[41] and we believe that the craftsmen (if not the artefacts) came—or rather were dragged—from Minoan Crete.[42] Just as the Mycenaean treasures were isolated and enigmatic before the resurrection of Minoan art, so the Trojan gold was inexplicable[43] until a later excavation provided some contemporary background;—I mean the wonderful discoveries made in 1935 at Alaça Höyük,[44] a few miles to the north of Boghaz-Köy in central Anatolia. It is a matter of opinion, whether the best of the Alaça goldware is equal to the best of the Trojan:[45] but it is certain that the two treasures are more or less contemporary,[46] comparable artistically, not without family resemblances.[47] The goldsmith's craft was flourishing in central Anatolia in the time of Troy II: we do not yet know how widespread it may have been,[48] but we may now safely assume that there were places within reach of an expedition or even a raid from Troy,[49] whence the Trojans might return with treasures of the type and quality discovered under the ashes of the second settlement.

Still there is no cértainty: the Trojan treasures may have been imported by traders. And we have now to reckon with the discovery of similar golden treasures at Poliochni in Lemnos, nearly forty miles westwards over the sea: here are pins and earrings and torques and beads (in thousands) of gold; very like the Trojan in workmanship, more or less contemporary in date.[50] Troy II and Poliochni were closely related in culture:[51] whether also politically, we shall never know, and so the other question must go unanswered; for spoils of a raid may be shared with allies as well as with vassals, and traders may deal with both. Only we are now still surer that these treasures were not made by native craftsmen for native purchasers: the large number of unpaired earrings, or broken or twisted pins and torques, has an obvious tale to tell,[52]—this is miscellaneous bric-à-brac, not a select and systematic jewelcase. Certainly it all came to Troy and Lemnos from the same source, by whatever path; you may think the warpath likelier to bring home such odds and ends.

The treasures of Troy were abandoned on the day of wrath, some previously hidden, some simply left lying.[53] And the owners never returned to dig out their splendid possessions. The great fire which incinerated Troy II was surely the work of man, a deliberate destruction;[54] and we must suppose that the owners of the treasures—presumably the great men of the day —perished together with their fortress. They knew where their gold was lying, in cellar or niche or cupboard; they could not fail to recover it if they tried. But they did not find it: and the modern excavations prove, wherever traces of ancient digging would have been left,[55] that they did not even look for it,—

neither did their destroyers; that is more surprising, and we must ask, what exactly happened at the end of Troy II?

The story is more complicated than at first it appears. We can only state the sequence of events, and guess at their causes. Let it be remembered especially that the abandoning of the treasures occurred long after the demolition of the great courtyard, and the building of disrespectful houses on hitherto holy ground. But before setting out the events in sequence, let us look for a moment at the men who founded the third settlement at Troy: who were the men who made their homes on the rubble and ashes of the burnt fortress?

The material remains of the third settlers are enough to prove continuity of culture:[56] they were Trojans; but there is good evidence that they were not the same family or group of Trojans as their predecessors on the citadel. First, there were fundamental differences in their building and town planning. They seem not to know, or not to care, what lies beneath the débris on the surface: their houses and streets are laid out independently of what must have been an immemorially old traditional plan.[57] Moreover, in place of stately buildings, standing in spacious courts or areas, the third settlers build a crowded little town of narrow streets and passages running between blocks of houses.[58] It would be strange if a people who for so long had treated their citadel as a royal castle suddenly brought the suburbs inside it, especially strange if they did so despite the recent memory of what the fire had done to a much less crowded enclosure. And whereas the houses of the first and second settlements of Troy had been for hundreds of years built of clay-brick walls on stone foundations, the third settlers build the exterior walls of houses as a rule wholly of stone.[59] It is worth noticing, besides these differences of plan and technique, a difference of domestic usage: the third settlers, unlike their predecessors, were untidy people; indeed they were among the most slovenly housekeepers in recorded history. Their streets, and the floors of their houses, were a shameful sight; they moved, so far as they could move, amid heaps of oystershells, bones, pins and needles, broken pottery and millstones, and a mass of other litter. When the refuse raised the floor so high that you could no longer stand upright in the room, what you did was not to remove the refuse but to build the walls higher, and raise the roof.[60] About the housekeeping of one Trojan lady the excavators have this to report: the floor of her house was "filled with débris to a depth of 1.60 m. to 2 m. Most of it seemed clearly to be the product of gradual accumulation: when a floor became offensively encumbered with rubbish of animal bones, shells, potsherds, and other litter, it was covered by a new floor of fresh earth or clay which in its turn suffered the same fate. A great many such floors could be distinguished."[61] It is further reported that the street outside her house "served regularly as a repository of rubbish of all kinds thrown out from the neighboring houses," and that this rubbish raised the level of the passage no less than six feet.[62] Secondly, there is a sudden great increase in the numbers of bones of stag and deer, and of objects fashioned out of such bones and horns, on the citadel in this period.[63] It is perfectly apparent that the deer is, for this people, an important article of diet, and its horns and bone important material for manufactures. This great increase "suggests," according to the American excavators, "that new or more efficient weapons or methods of the chase had been invented."[64] It is possible: but is it really probable that the natives of the burnt city suddenly became great hunters, about the time when they were occupied in building the third settlement above the cinders? Does not the fact more promptly suggest that the rebuilders of Troy are huntsmen ready-made, and therefore a different family from the earlier occupants?

Let us now return to consider the sequence of events. In the *fourth* phase of Troy II the great courtyard was enlarged and embellished. In the *sixth* phase its southwestern angle was demolished, and relatively small buildings began to creep over the site. In the *seventh* phase this encroachment continued, up to within a few yards of the front of the great palace itself; in the same period the treasures were placed where they were to remain for the next four thousand years. In the *last* phase the citadel of Troy was reduced to a heap of ashes. Thereafter it was occupied by newcomers, of Trojan culture, a cruder sort of countryfolk, who did not know that untold wealth lay not many inches under their feet.

What happened? We can say for certain that the great kings of Troy II[e] and II[d] have been eliminated; we are confident that the burners of Troy II were not the folk who built Troy III, a humble people evidently unfamiliar with the ground. The rest is guesswork. It is easy to imagine that Troy II was destroyed by a local rival, or by a wandering horde such as the Cimmerians in later history. But neither the one nor the other would explain the desecration of the royal precinct which began so long before the great fire, and which continued to make headway for many years. Mere increase of population,[65] or even the exigency of a protracted siege, will not account for this mutilation of a sacrosanct area. There was room to build, if building must be, without demolishing the royal courtyard and squatting on the royal doorstep. The facts suggest—they do no more; but can they do less?—that Troy at this time underwent a social and political upheaval;[66] that this is the time when the great kings of Troy II[e] and II[d] fell from power; and their treasures presumably passed into their supplanters' hands.[67] There was no break whatever in material culture: if there was such a catastrophe, it was local or internal, a civil war. And the day of the regicides was brief enough: certainly they did not survive the destruction of the citadel; and perhaps they were easier victims than the great kings would have been, when the enemy[68] came with sword and fire, and Troy burned as seldom a fortress had burned before, and one of the strongest places in Anatolia was left a desolation of cinders and rubble.

The third settlement passed through four building-phases, covering perhaps a period of 100 years. Above it was built a fourth settlement; no miserable hamlet, as it was formerly called, but a solid community enclosed in a circuit wall[69] which spread well beyond the limits of the great fortifications of Troy

II. It passed through five building-phases,[70] covering perhaps a period of 150 years. It preserves more or less unbroken the chain of Trojan culture[71] which now links a thousand years together in this little place. The fourth settlers build small houses with party walls, facing on narrow streets,[72] ignoring both the layout and the methods[73] of their predecessors. The standards of housekeeping are slightly improved; and a large number of domed ovens attest proficiency in the art of cooking. So far as one can read what is written in the ruins, Troy IV is a second and revised edition of Troy III.[74]

The fourth settlement was followed by a fifth, which passed through four building-phases, covering perhaps a period of 150 years. The continuity of cultural tradition remains unbroken; but the people have now begun to make steady progress towards a more civilized and comfortable life. Their houses are larger and more orderly, including such comforts as built-in corner seats and benches, and an improved style of hearth and oven;[75] the floors are swept clean with frequent broom.[76] The remnants of bone suggest that deer has gone out of favour; beef and pork are preferred to venison.[77] The art of the potter, now more than a thousand years old at Troy, flowers with a final grace and freshness in this period; and at long last the secret of making bronze is mastered.[78] Commerce continues in the west and extends into the eastern Mediterranean.[79] There is some but not sufficient evidence that the citadel was surrounded at this time by a new fortification wall.[80]

So far we have traced the history of Troy from the bedrock to the end of the fifth settlement at a date not far removed from 1900 B.C. It is not very much that we know; but it is a great deal more than we expected to learn; and at least we have the assurance that almost the whole of it is founded on hard fact. It is certain that throughout this long period of time the citadel of Troy was occupied, without interruption, by one and the same race of men, however often one tribe or family may have replaced another within that race. For two thirds of the time, from the beginning up to the end of Troy II, the story is one of continuous development at a fairly high level of civilization, within which a few periods of specially rapid progress can be discerned. The last third of the time begins at a lower level but steadily advances until, at the end of the fifth settlement, we seem to be in an age of change, of progress, and of good hope for the future; hope that will never be fulfilled, not at least by these Trojans.

Hitherto, as we passed upward from one settlement to another, we found a continuous chain of culture. Materials and manufactures remain essentially constant. The Trojan craftsmen develop and adapt and imitate; they are never interrupted, make no spectacular innovations. But now suddenly, without trace of battle or burning, comes an end: the thread that runs through a thousand years is abruptly broken. The tokens of change are already manifest at the beginning[81] of Troy VI, and a continuous development is visible throughout six building-phases covering a period of some five or perhaps six hundred years. Architecture and pottery are our most substantial and safest guides: they are joined by one other most important and unexpected witness to the truth; and a number of smaller sign-posts point in the same direction.[82]

In architecture the break with the past is very obvious. A much greater space was now enclosed by walls of monumental scale and superb masonry, distinguished in particular by a most unusual and at present inexplicable feature,—the addition of shallow "offsets"[83] in the wall face. Internally the citadel took a form which is said to have no parallel, east or west.[84] Within the oval orbit of the fortification walls the ground now arose in a series of terraces concentric to the hilltop, with radial roads or alleys leading upward from the walls and converging on the summit. On the terraces stood the interior buildings, domestic as well as public, spacious, freestanding, some of elaborate design. If we suppose that the crown of the hill was occupied by royal palace or chief temple,[85] we shall hardly find room for more than three concentric terraces: the first, that nearest the walls, might hold about 20 or possibly 25 buildings; the second,

about 12 or possibly 15;[86] the third (if there was a third), about
6. In short, it is possible, but not likely, that the fortress of
Troy VI enclosed so many as 50 buildings,[87] of which not all
were domestic residences. The number of people who slept under
a roof inside the walls might be estimated at a few hundred.

The citadel is thus revealed as the castle of a king, as it had
been during the first two settlements. It was now much larger
than before; but still the circuit of its walls was not much
more than 550 yards.[88] You could still saunter from side to side
in less than two minutes; and a moderate sprinter could cover
the ground in twenty-five seconds.[89] The castle will accommodate the king's family and servants and attendants; there is
room for a priest or two, and no doubt a few men-at-arms. The
entire community, except the royal family and its retinue, must
have lived outside the walls; and so numerous must they have
been (as we shall see)—nobles and craftsmen and farmers and
labourers of all kinds—that the fortress could not have been
designed to serve, and certainly would not have served, as a
place of refuge for more than a small proportion of the whole.
Moreover, Troy had no subsidiary enclosure of the type to be
seen at Tiryns, no fortified annex designed to preserve not only
the people but also the herds and flocks which stand between
them and starvation in time of siege.[90]

Consider secondly the sudden change in shape and style of
pottery. Of 97 shapes of vases from Troy VI, only 8 reveal the
influence of the Trojan past.[91] That fact alone would be good
evidence of the change from one culture to another: but there
is something much more significant,—the presence in Troy VI,
from the start, of that unique type of pottery called "Gray
Minyan Ware."

It is most important to appreciate the fact that the term
"Gray Minyan Ware" stands not only for a pottery type but
also for a potter's technique. In the words of the American
excavators,[92] "Gray Minyan Ware both in fabric and shapes is
a distinctive product, different from other gray wares, and of
limited geographical distribution. It is a product not of any one

specific kind of clay, but of some particular technique in handling the clay, in finishing the surface, and in firing the pot under reducing-conditions in a well-controlled kiln. It was the knowledge of this technique the invaders [of Troy] brought with them, and not the actual pottery itself." The technical details have often been described,[93] and there is no need to repeat them here. Even the layman observes at once that Gray Minyan is different from any other pottery he has seen; and the expert fully confirms the truth of this immediate impression.

Now the presence of Gray Minyan Ware in Troy VI from its beginning is a matter of surpassing interest. For this extraordinary technique is characteristic of one other people only,—the people who invaded Hellas at a date not very far removed[94] from that of the foundation of Troy VI: that people whom, after some centuries of settlement in Hellas,[95] we shall call the Greeks. It is certain that Hellas was overrun and permanently occupied by invaders at the beginning of the Middle Bronze Age, say about 1950 or 1900 B.C.;[96] it is generally agreed that these invaders were the bringers of the Greek language to Hellas;[97] and it is certain that the characteristic pottery of these Greek-speaking invaders was, from the beginning,[98] this same Gray Minyan Ware. This peculiar ceramic technique is not known to have been practised anywhere except (a) at Troy and some western Anatolian settlements exposed to the influence of Trojan culture,[99] and (b) in Hellas and some of the Greek islands; or at any time earlier than the occupation of Hellas by the invaders of c. 1950 B.C.

Here is a solid and remarkable fact, with an obvious implication. Hellas in the west and Troy in the east of the Aegean are occupied by invaders in the same era. Common to the two bodies of invaders is a distinctive, indeed a unique,[100] process of making pottery, a refined and complicated technique shared with no other people in the world. The implication is thus carefully stated by the American excavators: that the founders of Troy VI "may have constituted one branch in the folk-movement that overran the mainland of Greece. . . . The abundant use in both areas of Gray Minyan Ware in the same distinctive forms can hardly be otherwise explained. The original connexion thus postulated seems not to have been closely maintained, once the two branches had established themselves in their new homes; and the divergent development in the two areas may perhaps reflect the different influence exercised in each region by the surviving elements of the earlier population that was gradually absorbed. Contacts across the Aegean there may have been from the first; but it is clear that they became close only in the late stages of Troy VI when the western off-shoot, through its relations with Minoan civilization, had been metamorphosed into Mycenaean."[101]

That is halfway towards saying, in paradoxical form, *that the Trojans were Greeks;* more accurately, the founders of Troy VI were people of similar cultural background to the Greek-speaking invaders and occupiers of Hellas, and were involved in the same migration.

Is there any escape from this implication? Theoretically there might be one or two loop-holes. First, is there any objection to the theory that Gray Minyan Ware might have been introduced to Troy by way of commerce? If the Trojans of the sixth settlement were not, after all, invaders,[102] such a theory would be unattractive but not quite untenable. It is possible, however contrary to normal conduct, that Troy might suddenly import a number of potters, possessed of a peculiar technique, from the newly established occupants of Hellas. It is very unlikely, since Troy at this time reveals only slight contact with Hellas in all other respects; but perhaps it is not impossible. I say no more of it, since I believe that the facts compel us to conclude that Troy VI is the foundation of alien invaders. Granted the invasion, the theory is surely ruled out.[103] *Gray Minyan Ware was being made at Troy VI in its earliest phase:* the invaders brought the technique with them, and applied it at once. There was no interval in which the invaders might look about them, establish relations with peoples overseas, organize commerce, import potters. The invaders of Troy VI brought no merchant fleet

with them: seaborne trade was conducted by the peoples of the
Aegean and Hellas, not by the new Trojans themselves. What
the theory requires us to envisage is the *immediate* export, from
Hellas to the new foundation of Troy, of a number of these
specialist potters, and apparently of nobody and of nothing else.
Nothing compels us, and we shall surely decline, to do any such
envisaging.

A second loop-hole concerns only the alien invaders. It is
theoretically possible that the Troy-invaders might have
adopted the Gray Minyan Ware technique from the Hellas-
invaders in circumstances which include no implication about
community of culture. The two parties, though involved in the
same great migration, might be racially different, and the Troy-
invaders might have moved later than the Hellas-invaders. The
former might have settled for a time *en route* somewhere near
the fringes of the latter—in the region of Macedonia and
Chalcidice, perhaps,—remaining in contact long enough to
learn the technique of this ceramic art (and apparently nothing
else).[104] I do not see how this suggestion could be positively
refuted. It enjoys a status well known in academic circles and
doubtless elsewhere,—that of the Remotely Conceivable
Alternative, contrary to the obvious implication of the facts,
incapable of proof or disproof. The Aegean shores were invaded
in the same era by two peoples sharing a specialized and otherwise unknown technique in pottery: common sense will always
insist that the two peoples were kindred in culture,—that their
association was not brief, peripheral, and more or less fortuitous,
but protracted and intimate.[105]

I mentioned just now another most important and unexpected witness to the truth,—the truth of the conclusion that
the founders of Troy VI were a people of alien culture who sup-
planted the native rulers on the citadel. The relics of the sixth
settlement include, from the beginning, something wholly unknown on the site or in the neighbourhood of Troy: *the bones,
in considerable quantities, of the horse.*[106] Let us bear in mind the
likelihood that this forms another link between Greeks and

Trojans; for it is highly probable that the horse was introduced to Hellas in this same era by the invading Greeks.[107]

The introduction of the horse may well explain the fact that the settlement immediately previous to Troy VI shows no sign of having ended by violence.[108] No wonder there is no trace of burning or destruction: for the greater part of the native population must have lived on the slopes and plain outside the citadel, easily to be overridden by the invaders, even if panic had not possessed them, as it possessed the Aztecs of Montezuma when they first saw "the strange animals which fear had clothed in such supernatural terrors."[109]

The invaders of Troy came with horses; and we must consider what bearing this fact may have on the route by which they came. In the lack of special appliances both ashore and afloat, the embarking of horses from shore to ship, their transport over the sea and disembarking, are very difficult operations.[110] It is questionable whether they are even possible operations, given the sort of boat which may fairly be postulated at the beginning of the Middle Bronze Age; particularly since the waters of the narrows—or even of the wider reaches—in the areas of Dardanelles, Nagara, and Bosporus are exceptionally unfavourable to such operations, and since it is to be presumed that the Troy-invaders had little or no previous experience of the sea. There is room for doubt: but it seems likelier that these horsemen came by a land route. It is a long way to Troy from the regions beyond the Caucasus: but others had come, or were soon to come, as far if not farther along the same track; and the path of the Cimmerians in the 7th century was not very different.

Let us now look more closely at the walls and buildings, not only for their own sakes but also because they will convince us that the sixth fortress of Troy was the centre of a large and prosperous community, whose political and economic system remained stable for a very long time,—not so long as that of the first and second settlements, but still for a half-millennium.

I. The Walls

The walls[111] of Troy VI have been traced, and to a considerable extent exposed, over about two-thirds of their original circuit. They are pierced by four [112] gates facing more or less the quarters of the compass; and they are strengthened by projecting towers[113] which enable the defence to act against the flank of a force attacking the wall itself. The construction is twofold: a wall of solid stone, with vertical inner face but sloping outer face, is crowned with a vertical superstructure originally made of brick, later of stone. The height of the sloping wall varies with the contour of the ground: the long reach in the southeast rises to 5.25 metres above the contemporary ground level, and sinks another metre or more below the earth to bedrock or nearly to bedrock. The superstructure consists of a breastwork on the outer edge, about 2 metres thick, behind which a platform runs, about 3 metres wide. The original height of this breastwork cannot be determined; it was not less than 2 metres. Thus wall and superstructure together, in this section of the wall, rose to a height of 24 feet at least above the outer ground level.

The wall is not all cast in one mould: it consists of several sections unequal in style and technique, evidently built in different periods; and a continuous development can be traced, over a period of some two or three hundred years, from the cruder style of a short section in the southwest, through the greatly improved technique of the east and southeast, to the superb artistry of the south range. Here, for a reach of 121 metres, the wall was built of a hard limestone cut into squared blocks laid in ashlar style, avoiding superimposed joints, for the most part in alternate headers and stretchers, with few chinks and fissures. Both inner and outer faces were dressed smooth after the structure was completed. It is a masterpiece of masonry, both elegant and monumental;[114] it is "a striking demonstration of the power and wealth of the later Sixth Settlement," as the American excavators say; it is also a testimony to the uninterrupted progress of the architectural art over a very long period of time. And it is obvious that such a wall was not thrown up to defend the citadel against any particular enemy, present or potential; it was built carefully, at leisure, under no shadow; it is the work not of panic but of pride.

The walls of Troy VI introduce one or two novelties in technique which are not at all easy to explain. First, the line of outer and inner faces is broken by "offsets."[115] The wall describes its orbit not in a continuous curve or series of curves, but in a series of straight lines each about 9 metres long, and each starting afresh with a slight projection from the face of the wall.[116] These offsets are wholly independent of the jointing of the stones, and are cut in each sector after the laying of the stones. Now it is obvious that they serve no structural or other practical purpose: why, then, did the mason add so much to his labour? Evidently he is acting under the compulsion of a traditional technique; and we may guess that he or his masters appreciated, as we do, the aesthetic value of this breaking of the line at intervals. But what was the original function of this device, which is now merely decorative? The least unconvincing explanation is this, that it was invented to counteract the difficulty of building sloping walls along irregular contours, where differences in the ground level would involve "differences in the degree of slope in contiguous sections of the wall. A vertical offset might then be cut so as to coincide neatly with the change in inclination, and an unseemly bulge in the face of the wall could thus be avoided."[117] Whatever the true reason may have been, we are obliged to infer that these builders did not learn their craft from the native inhabitants of Troy: they brought with them a technique of their own, already highly developed; this is a people who lived in stone-walled fortresses long before they came to Troy.[118]

Secondly, at some points the foundations of the wall are laid not on the bedrock but on a pad or cushion of earth above the bedrock.[119] It is very improbable that this was done without a purpose; and it is hard to see what the purpose could have been except to create a shock-absorber against earthquakes. Rock, in the words of the American excavators, "is a more active conductor of vibrations than loose or even hard-packed earth"; a fact which the builders of Troy "had no doubt often had occasion to observe."[120] The effect may be seen in the southeastern sector of the fortifications: a tower which rests on bedrock projects in front of a wall which rests on a cushion of earth; the tower has been distorted by earthquakes, the wall has not.[121] Surely these masons were far in advance of their times.

Of the great towers and portals the most interesting is the complex facing (more or less) south.[122] Here was the main entrance to the fortress, a narrow passage overlooked on the west by a tower. From this area comes almost all the little that is known about the religious or superstitious practices of the inhabitants of Troy VI. Inside a flanking tower, on the ground floor, is an area paved with stone; near its eastern edge is a massive squared block of limestone, on the surface of which the outline of two circles can be discerned, presumably the feet of the legs of a table. If this was, as it appears, an altar standing on a raised dais,[123] it is a most unusual thing to find on the ground floor of a tower protecting the main entrance to a castle; and it may well have some necessary connexion with the next object to be considered. Outside this tower, along the front wall and very close to it, a row of rectangular stone pillars was set up. These pillars (at present four, perhaps originally six) were firmly embedded in slots cut into massive blocks of foundation stone;[124] they rose, to whatever height,[125] sloping backwards to parallel the wall of the tower; there is no means of determining whether they carried any superstructure, or were carved in their upper portions.

What was their purpose? They discharge no structural function; they are useless for defence; they cannot have been merely decorative. Clearly they were designed to resist the attempt of an enemy to overturn them; what can they be, but idols representing king or god, invested with power to protect the fortress at its most vulnerable point, the main entrance?[126] And, if so, it is probable that there was some connexion between these monolithic idols just in front of the tower wall and the altar erected just behind it: surely the gods would repel the onslaught of the enemy at the gates, just so long as their priest, secure within the tower walls, refreshed their altar with flame or blood. Now, further: adjoining this same gate, outside the walls, stood the queerest of Trojan buildings: a long, lean, barnlike structure,[127] with open face[128] looking toward the idols and the

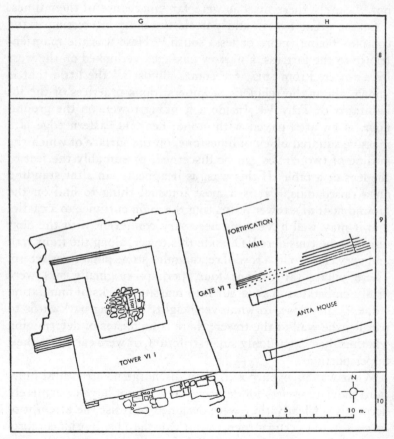

Troy VI, south gate and tower, with altar, monoliths, and Anta House: adapted from Blegen's *Troy* III 2, fig. 452.

altar only a few yards away. Its secret is revealed by what lies under it: for hundreds of years, from the beginning to the end of the sixth settlement, extensive fires were kindled in this place, and burnt offerings left their débris on the floor, until ten or a dozen strata of bone and ashes had accumulated. This was a place of burnt sacrifice, which may have been offered in the open air until the latest phase of Troy VI, when the long, lean barn was built.[129] Its position suggests that its priests were charged with the duty of appeasing the idols which protected the entrance to the citadel: an office which might be transferred to the altar inside the tower if an enemy attacked the gate.[130]

II. The Buildings within the Walls

Substantial remains of eight buildings, and traces of half a dozen more, have been unearthed within the circuit of the walls. The two most impressive are:

1) The Pillar House.[131] This is one of the largest of all the mansions at Troy,[132] measuring (externally) about 80 by 37 feet. Thick walls, strong pillars, and a staircase built into the main room, argue in favour of at least one upper story. The evidence of the débris indicates that this was a public building, later converted to domestic use.

2) The house labelled VI F.[133] This is the most elaborate in construction. In its floor are twelve stone bases, "designed to hold wooden columns. They are arranged in two rows of five each, along either side of the hall, with a further pair in the central axis."[134] The number and close spacing of the lateral columns prove the intention of supporting a heavy super-structure,—at least one upper story, perhaps more than one.

These were two solid and splendid mansions, ambitious in design and elegant in execution; they are creations worthy of the men who built the most beautiful fortress walls in the pre-historic Aegean.

The people who built so well and so much over so long a period of time must have been, to use a vague word, prosper-

ous. What was the source, and what the nature, of the prosperity of the sixth settlement at Troy? It is impossible to estimate,
except in the broadest terms, how many people—nobles and
fighting-men, craftsmen and farmers and fishermen and labourers—lived on the slopes and in the plain outside the walls.[135] It
is likely that at least a few hundred men were employed at once

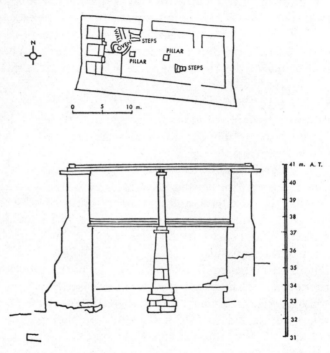

Troy VI, the Pillar House: plan (adapted) and conjectured reconstruction:
from Blegen's *Troy* III 2, figs. 451, 466ᵃ.

in the stonemason's craft alone, cutting and carrying stone,
digging foundations, shaping and laying blocks, designing and
overseeing and labouring. And then there were farmers and
millers and spinners and potters and armourers and workers in
bronze and lead, bone and ivory, stone and paste and clay.[136]
It cannot have been a very small population, a mere thousand

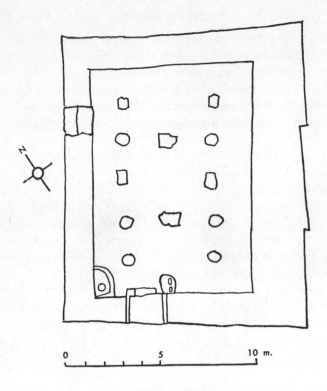

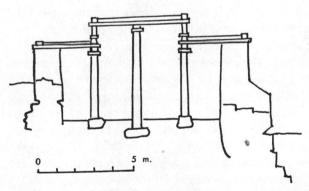

Troy VI, House VI F: plan and possible scheme of reconstruction: from Blegen's *Troy* III 2, figs. 487, 484.

or two; it is safe to say at least several thousand; but how many thousands, we have no means of telling.

There is no sign of a break in the political system: the fortress remained a royal castle throughout. We can see positive signs, in walls and mansions especially, that throughout the life of Troy VI craftsmen became more skilled, labour not less abundant, from one phase to the next. What was the source of this prolonged prosperity and apparently uninterrupted progress?

First, were the Trojans traders, and if so, what did they buy and sell? The life of this fortress coincides in time with the growth and expansion of the mighty Hittite Empire.[137] Before the end of Troy VI, Hittite control or influence extended into almost the whole of Asia Minor,—excepting the northwest sector; it would be natural, if there were some going and coming between the Trojans and the Hittites. The Iliad, though the events which it narrates are assigned to the last days of the Hittite Empire, reveals no awareness that any such people ever existed:[138] excavation might have told a different story, but in effect tells the same one. The relics of Troy VI include very few objects which did or might have come, directly or indirectly, from Hittite territory or from territory subject to Hittite influence,—"nor in all the enormous mass of pottery that has been recovered is there even a sherd that has been identified as Hittite."[139] The meagre evidence could not possibly have led us to presuppose a centre of commerce in central Anatolia, let alone a vast empire. For all that Troy can tell us, the very existence of the Hittites would have remained unguessed.

The Trojans and the Mycenaean Greeks once shared a common culture: it is natural that a Trojan should look west (as Troy had always done); and indeed the evidence for trade with Mycenaean Greece is abundant. From mainland or islands in the west come arrowheads, bronze daggers, sword pommels of marble and alabaster, beads of carnelian, steatite, vitreous paste, objects of ivory, and (from however far afield) the shells of ostrich eggs. The last period of this fortress, say 1400–1300 B.C., is the zenith of Mycenaean influence on the arts and crafts

of Troy. Over and above earlier discoveries, the American excavators unearthed the relics of seven or eight hundred imported
Mycenaean vases; and it is worth noticing that the majority
of these are what might be called table vessels,—drinking-cups
and the like; that is to say, they were bought for their own sake,
because they were admired for their beauty; they are not (for
the most part) containers, bought for the sake of their contents.[140]

What did the Trojans offer in return? What were the indus-
tries, of which the surplus was bartered for Mycenaean wares?
Let us begin by mentioning certain things which, so far as our
evidence reaches, they did *not* offer in return. First, there is
nothing whatever in the relics of Troy VI to suggest that the
Trojans at this period practised the fine arts, let alone that they
could compete with the products of the Mycenaeans. The western invaders, on the mainland and in the islands, came under
the spell of Minoan Crete; and the blend of cultures, native and
newcomer, created a new spirit of art, the art of Mycenaean
Greece. No such destiny awaited their former companions on
the march in the lonely fortress at Troy: these went their own
way in isolation, developing their own culture continuously. In
architecture alone they rivalled or surpassed the Mycenaeans;
as for the manifold creations of art and craft, it simply is not
possible to speak of east and west in the same terms—for on the
one side there was nothing but steady progress along traditional
lines, on the other there was one of the great revolutions in
ancient art. Secondly: there is no evidence whatever that the
Trojans at this time mined or manufactured in gold and silver.
This surprising lack of precious metals has been explained in
various ways: the fortress was thoroughly plundered; or the inhabitants took away all their gold and silver when they left.[141]
But it is incredible that *nothing* should have been overlooked,
that *nothing* should ever have been lost and buried in hundreds
of years. The most likely reason why no gold or silver is found
is that no gold or silver was ever there. This is not a mere argument from silence: buried gold is practically indestructible;[142]

and, if gold there was, it is simply not to be believed that the extensive and infinitely careful excavations of the Americans would have brought to light nothing more than "one infinitesimal bead" of gold, and one pin of silver.[143] Thirdly, there is nothing to indicate that the Trojans possessed what might be called a merchant navy: they were not traders in that sense, and their prosperity was not maintained by the profits of exchange. Fourthly, we must decline to entertain a notion which used to be fashionable,[144]—that Troy controlled the passage of the Dardanelles, and derived its wealth from taxes on the trade of others; that it was a tollhouse, the douanier of the Dardanelles. Much might be said in refutation of this theory. The Dardanelles have never been, and never could be, a link between European and Asiatic land routes; and although Troy might interfere with seaborne commerce entering the straits, there was certainly not in the time of Troy VI any considerable volume of seaborne trade between the Aegean and Propontis (let alone the Euxine). Nor can it be maintained that Troy was the terminus of an Anatolian trade route serving as a market for the lands and islands to the west: such western traders would have to approach Troy by sea, and on all the west coast of Asia Minor there is no more unlikely site for such a market,—no point more difficult of access for sailing-boats or rowboats than this northern corner, where the Hellespont rushes through the straits; nor in fact has Troy ever served any such purpose in the centuries of recorded history. But it is not worth while to discuss further a theory which is contradicted by the fact that there is no trace of any such market or commerce at any time in the material relics of Troy,—and traces there must have been, if Troy controlled a trade route from Propontis to Aegean, from Asia Minor to the Balkans, or indeed from anywhere to anywhere.[145]

There is no hope of progress in this direction. We know nothing about fine arts or precious metals or merchant navies or tollhouses at Troy; we cannot attribute her prosperity to any of these sources. Perhaps we have been altogether on the wrong track. It may be mistaken in principle, to search for special causes. If we ask again, why was the site of Troy so favourable for so long to its inhabitants, and what did it produce and sell to the Mycenaean traders, the relics of Troy itself return a simple and perhaps sufficient answer. There is no great mystery about the continuous occupation of a site, and the steady progress of its people, given three conditions: security from external attack; food in plenty; and the discipline imposed by an absolute power at the centre. And that is the picture painted by the relics of Troy; it may be misleading, but at least it is not obscure. Here in the remotest corner of Anatolia, half surrounded by the sea, the Trojans are isolated from the greater world; not even the Hittite Empire reaches quite so far as this. They are firmly controlled by the power of a royal family. What further proof of that power do we need, when we look at the massive and monumental walls of Troy, built by thousands of labouring hands over so long a period of time, rather to gratify the pride than to insure the safety of a few dozen families at most, perhaps of one single family? And, then, why should a people not be content and prosperous, where food was so plentiful? Incalculable quantities of shells and bones attest not only the variety and abundance of supply, but also the industry of farmers and fishermen, of hunters and herdsmen. But we must not simply call the Trojans an agricultural community: they are much more than that. There are royalty and its retainers; there are fighting-men; there are wall-builders and workers in manifold arts and crafts. And they live in a land of plenty, where the herds increase and grain grows and the seas are inexhaustible, and the destroyer comes but twice in two thousand years.

Still, what did they sell to the Mycenaeans? We can make a guess or two. There is one object found at Troy in quantities unparalleled on any other site,—*the spindle whorl*.[146] Schliemann's collection includes 7,737 specimens, the Americans found another 400. This is proof, not subject to confirmation or rebuttal, that the spinning of yarn must be counted among the commonest and most productive occupations at Troy. "The abundant bones of sheep and goats found in all layers (of the sixth settlement) indicate that there can have been no shortage of wool";[147] and the craft of the spinner is manifest for six hundred years. What an obvious and likely commodity of exchange, whether spun yarn or textile; here is an object of which the Trojans might have a surplus, and a craft which they practised so long and so assiduously that they might not have a rival in the Aegean world.

That is one possibility; and here is another,—*that the Trojans specialized in the breeding and export of the horse.*[148] The Homeric poems call Ilios alone of all cities εὔπωλος, "of good horses," and the Trojans alone of all peoples ἱππόδαμοι, "horse-tamers"; thus in the old formular poetry Troy was associated especially with the breeding and management of horses; and there is reason to believe that they would find many an eager market in the East and in the West.[149]

Let us now look back to the questions from which we started. We have learnt that the inhabitants of Troy VI were newcomers to the site; that they were kindred in culture, perhaps also in race, to the Mycenaean Greeks; and that there was no break in their occupation of Troy up to the last phase of the Mycenaean era. We know that they lived just beyond the furthest reach of the Hittite Empire, with which they had little if any commercial contact throughout its existence; their faces were turned westward, towards a familiar people on the mainland and in the islands of Greece. We have seen what sort of community they formed, what work they did, and why they and the natives before them might live and prosper at Troy for so vast a span of time. This is much to learn, to be sure of; most of it was unknown or unverifiable before the latest excavations on the hill of Hissarlik.

This is the Troy which we shall look for, and may possibly discover, in the Hittite documents. Its history is illuminating. The Trojans, alone of all peoples in the East, have shared the earlier fortunes of the Achaeans; the ancient bond had been renewed by exchange of commerce, and the Achaeans knew well that the Trojans were in possession of the strongest fortress and perhaps the most prosperous territory on the western coast of Asia Minor. Therefore we shall not wonder if the Achaeans, when they begin to invade that coast, must sooner or later come to terms or to blows with this powerful and prosperous community. Troy was the strongest and most spectacular place in all Asia Minor of which the Achaeans had personal knowledge; and it was held by dimly remembered companions of the march. It is not surprising that the battle for Troy was so long remembered in Greek tradition.

The sixth settlement of Troy collapsed in an earthquake;[150] the great buildings, and in part even the great walls, lay in ruins. The date was a year not far distant from 1275 B.C.: and we turn with curious attention to its successor, the early period of Troy VII (to be called "Troy VII[a]"), for this is the fortress which is likely to come down to a time within reach of the traditional siege of Troy by the Greeks. Since the last volume of Blegen's *Troy* is not yet published,* I cannot take the story in detail to its natural end. I can only give broadest outlines; and it is good fortune, that the preliminary excavation-reports give answers to our most important questions,—answers which the final publication will certainly not upset. The questions and answers are as follows:

First, was Troy VII[a] simply a continuation of Troy VI? Was it inhabited by the same people; did they rebuild their fortress as soon as possible after the earthquake; was their culture continuous with the immediate past? The answers are, Yes. There is no break.[151] Troy VII[a] was "constructed directly over the fallen ruins, with no intervening layer of habitation";[152] there is complete continuity of culture.[153]

What is left of the buildings indicates that Troy VII[a] was a pinched and meagre offspring, unworthy of its robust and

---

* *Troy* IV reached me after my book was in proof. It confirms and enlarges the conclusions which I had drawn from the preliminary reports, leaving me with little to subtract but much detail to add; I have attempted to draw the larger picture in *Antiquity* (1959).

monumental parent.[154] A series of sheepish cubicles huddles in
the gangway between the great walls and the first of the interior
terraces; for the most part, they are built directly onto the
great wall, which serves for a back. These little houses, many
of which share a party wall, are penned in a circle round the

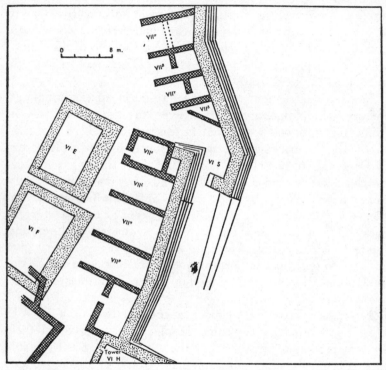

Troy VII[a], new houses (1): after Dörpfeld, *Troja und Ilion*, figs. 71,
72. Troy VI, stippled; Troy VII[a], cross-hatched.

citadel; in places a second ring of them stands opposite, and
presumably the interior terraces and summit were similarly occupied. If this was the Troy which the Achaeans besieged and
sacked, part of their work was done for them by the earthquake before they came, and their opponents were less capable
of resistance than Troy VI would have been.

Let us ask at once the second question: how long did Troy VII[a] endure, and what happened to it in the end? Chronology is relative, determined mainly by sequence of pottery types. Translated into years, within the commonly accepted pattern, the date of the fall of Troy VII[a] is now assigned by Blegen to a year near, at least not long after, the middle of the 13th century B.C.;[155] perhaps half a century earlier than the most popular of

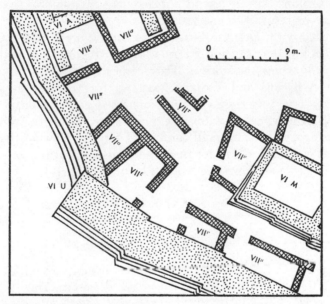

Troy VII[a], new houses (II): after Dörpfeld, *Troja und Ilion*, fig. 72. Troy VI, stippled; Troy VII[a], cross-hatched.

the traditional dates. The cause of its termination is established beyond doubt: Troy VII[a] was devastated by a fire of exceptional violence.[156] Blegen tells of a "desolation stamping the ruins of Troy VII[a], when all the houses on the citadel were apparently gutted by a devastating fire."[157] There are very strong indications that the conflagration was caused "by human agency."[158] If we ask for confirmation of the Greek legend that the city of Priam was destroyed by the Achaeans in this era, the excavations do confirm it up to this point: at a date quite close to that of tradition,[159] Troy was most thoroughly burnt; and the burning was evidently the work of man,—that is to say, of an enemy who captured Troy.

The survivors of the sack of Troy lingered on the site for another generation; then they came under the domination of a people of cruder and alien culture,[160] certainly neither Greeks nor Trojans. Greek legend consistently maintained that the Achaeans returned home after the sack of Troy, that they did not occupy the site: the excavations cannot prove that the tale is true, but they can and do prove that it is consistent with the truth. For now the story of Troy comes to its gloomy end; at least Achaeans and Trojans have no further interest in it. Nearly two thousand years have passed since civilized men made their homes on Hissarlik. Only once, about six hundred years ago, was the chain of continuity broken. Now for the first time the citadel will lie for many generations obscure, and send no echo ringing down the halls of history.

NOTES

In this lecture I have relied most on *Troy* (= *Troy: Excavations Conducted by the University of Cincinnati, 1932–1938*, edited by Carl W. Blegen with the collaboration of John L. Caskey and Marion Rawson, Vols. I–III, the fourth imminent); *Troja und Ilion* (= *Troja und Ilion: Ergebnisse der Ausgrabungen in den vorhistorischen und historischen Schichten von Ilion, 1870–1894*, by Wilhelm Dörpfeld, Athens, 1902); and *Trojanische Altertümer* (= *Heinrich Schliemann's Sammlung Trojanischer Altertümer*, by Hubert Schmidt, Berlin, 1902). Schliemann's *Ilios: The City and Country of the Trojans*, I have used in the New York edition of 1881; his *Troja: Results of the Latest Researches and Discoveries on the Site of Homer's Troy*, in the New York edition of 1884. The other works most often used and abbreviated in the notes are *AKG* (= F. Schachermeyr, *Die ältesten Kulturen Griechenlands*, 1955), *RE* XXII (= F. Schachermeyr, *Prä-*

historische Kulturen Griechenlands, in Pauly-Wissowa, 1954), and *Grundzüge* (= K. Bittel's *Grundzüge der Vor- und Frühgeschichte Kleinasiens*, 2d ed., 1950). The background, both in time and in space, has now been delineated in a masterly survey, Seton Lloyd's *Early Anatolia* (1956).

1 See *Troy* I 1.40 f.; dates and periods are rough approximations. A much later date for Troy I is finding favour in some quarters (see now Schachermeyr, *AKG* 32:2650–2400 B.C.).

2 *Troy* I 1.36 ff.; I 2 fig. 418 shows the superimposed foundations of at least seven houses.

3 House 102, a megaron, "one of the most ancient examples of that type yet known in the Eastern Mediterranean region" (*Troy* I 1.37). It is built partly over an earlier house from the first phase (House 103), which "seems to have had an apse, the earliest known appearance of that form along the west Anatolian coast" (ibid.). See Bittel, *Kleinasiatische Studien* (1942) 138 ff.; Tahsin Özgüç, *Türk Tarih Kurumu, Belleten* 10 (1946) 13 ff.

4 Exterior length 18.75 m., breadth 7 m. House 115 (*Troy* I 1.134 f.) seems to have been slightly larger.

5 *Troy* I 1.89 ff., I 2 fig. 426; the "beds" are low stone platforms adjoining the walls.

6 Especially because all the houses traced are freestanding, i.e., surrounded by their own courts or precincts, not semi-detached or wall-to-wall.

7 The surviving materials are mostly stone, bone, and terracotta; 16 objects in copper (no bronze), 2 pieces of lead.

8 Shellfish were common diet; also tunny.

9 Pottery from Troy I is all handmade, not turned on the wheel.

10 Including armourer: actual or potential weapons are dagger blades, hammer-axes, arrowheads.

11 As Dr Stubbings points out to me, we must not assume that all trades were specialized at this time, though some of them probably were. I say nothing, therefore, of the evidence for spinning, milling, hunting (bones include stag, pig, hare, sheep, goat, ox, dog, tortoise).

12 See *Troy* I 1.145 ff., with I 2 figs. 183 ff., 417, 436. The wall is built of flattish unworked stones; its inner face was not found, so its thickness is conjectural. In places the wall is a stone-faced clay embankment, elsewhere it has a stone-filled backing. Interstices between stones are filled with clay mortar. Its outer face is for the most part (except near the foot) but not everywhere markedly sloping. At one point six courses of brickwork superstructure were

preserved (I 1.148). In the late phase of Troy I, extensive altera-tions were made.

[13] *Troy* I 1.155 ff.: the sculptured slab is one of three which were set up in line on edge outside the easterly flanking tower of the great South Gate. It was transferred to this use from elsewhere. The pur-pose of the "barrier" of three slabs outside the tower, and the func-tion of the sculptured slab before its transference thither, can only be conjectured; perhaps, as the excavators suggest, it came from a tombstone or a secular or religious monument. Schachermeyr, *RE* XXII 1403 f., observes that the sculpture has no parallel anywhere at this period ("weicht . . . von allem Orientalischen völlig ab, steht auch Sesklo und der Ägäis nicht näher").

[14] See esp. *Troja und Ilion* i 362 ff. with Beilage 44.v.

[15] *Troy* I 1.157 f. with I 2 figs. 193–194; behind the "saucers" in the "table" depicted in fig. 193 was the dark discoloured patch which suggests the stains of blood sacrifice.

[16] *Troy* I 1.45 f., 53 ff.; but see also II 1.227, "the incompleteness of modern knowledge of obsidian deposits along the Anatolian littoral leaves us just short of certitude." Imports of pottery from the Middle phase onwards, not earlier; the obsidian belongs to the Late phase.—Obsidian is found at Polatli (*Anatolian Studies* 1, 1951, 21 ff.) in the early Copper Age, contemporary with Troy II; and in the Neolithic flint industry at Mersin,—there is said to be "a likely source just north of the Taurus mountains" (Seton Lloyd, *Early Anatolia*, 1956, 76).

[17] No clear picture has yet emerged of the detail of the external rela-tions of Troy I and II. (*a*) It is reasonable to suppose that this powerful fortress dominated small places in its immediate neigh-bourhood (e.g. the contemporary settlement at Kum Tepe). (*b*) Presumably Troy stood in some relation, politically as well as cul-turally, to contemporary settlements of similar type a little further afield, such as those at Yortan (cf. Bittel, *Grundzüge* 20), at Thermi in Lesbos and Poliochni in Lemnos (*RE* XXII 1402 ff., with literature). (*c*) It is certain that the culture of Troy I and II had much in common with that of the northern shores of the Aegean, through Thrace to Macedonia; and that there was commerce with the western Aegean lands (islands and mainland). (*d*) It is never-theless maintained that Troy I–II was essentially an *Anatolian* foundation, with family connexions on the central plateau (Alaça and especially Alishar: Bittel, *Grundzüge* 26) and in the south beyond the mountains (Mersin). See Bittel, *Kleinas. Studien* (1942) 130 ff.; *Grundzüge* 20 f., 32 ff., 58 f.; *Gnomon* 26 (1954) 441 f.; Schachermeyr, *AKG* 161 f., 169 ff., and *RE* XXII 1403 f.;

Troy I Index s.v. "external relations"; Seton Lloyd, *Early Anatolia* 86 ff., 108 ff. Important new contributions to this subject will be found (*a*) in *Istanbuler Mitteilungen* 6 (1955) 53 ff., by Mellaart, establishing relations between Troy I–II and the Inegöl–Yenisehir–Iznik region, south of the gulf of Izmit at the eastern end of the Sea of Marmora; (*b*) in the *Illustrated London News*, August 3, 1957, 197 ff., by Luigi Brea, on the settlement at Poliochni in Lemnos in the time of Troy II (see n. 51 below).

The further question, whence came the founders of Troy I, is discussed by Schuchhardt, *Abh. d. Preuss. Akad. d. Wiss., Berlin,* phil.-hist. Kl., 10 (1940) 1 ff. (criticized by Bittel, *Kleinas. Studien* l.c.; cf. Özgüç, *Belleten* l.c. n. 3 above).

[18] *Troy* I 1.39, 169: "Stratum I^k . . . seems to represent an ambitious project of regrading and of readjustment of levels preparatory to rebuilding, rather than a real habitation layer"; "merely an interval between Phase I^j and the initial phase of the Second Settlement which follows immediately."

[19] *Troy* I 1.15, 82, 204, al.

[20] Ibid.—Schachermeyr (*AKG* 199, 202; cf. *RE* XXII 1446, and Lorimer, *Homer and the Monuments* [*HM*], 1950, 6 f.) is tempted to infer from the *Schnurkeramik* and battle-axes of Troy II a "Zuwanderung von Streitaxt-Leuten": the evidence seems inadequate, cf. Bittel, *Grundzüge* 56 f.; and Schachermeyr himself recognizes that there was no break in the culture of Troy.

[21] *Troy* I 2 fig. 432 illustrates superimposed houses of the first five phases.

[22] For the detail see *Troja und Ilion* i 52 ff., with additions and corrections passim in the second half of *Troy* I 1. The wall consisted of a sloping lower part, of unworked limestone cemented with clay mortar, and a (presumably vertical) superstructure of clay brick. The height of the lower part varied from 1 to 8.50 m. according to the contour of the hill; the height of the clay superstructure (which was probably topped with timberwork) was appreciably more than 3 m. The thickness of the wall is a filling of small stones, in some parts cemented but in others not.

[23] Or both, if Troy II was ruled by a priest-king. *Troy* I 1.263: "striking evidence that the buildings in this area were public or state edifices rather than private dwellings is furnished by the almost complete absence of animal bones, which are normally found in great abundance on house floors and in the adjacent open yards and streets." Apart from a copper and a bone pin, the list of objects found includes nothing but a small quantity of pottery.

[24] It rested on a stone foundation 1.70 m. wide and 1.30 m. deep. A

socle of stone supported clay-brick walls (1.44 m. thick) ribbed with timber; the roof was composed of clay and reed laid on cross-timbers (which must have been 30 feet long, for there was apparently no internal pillaring). Some evidence for the nature of the roof survives in House II S, where the fallen roof clay retains impressions of reeds or twigs, and blackened remains of wooden beams were found in the débris (*Troy* I 1.374 and I 2 fig. 351).

[25] See *Troja und Ilion* i fig. 23 p. 81, and *Troy* I 1.261 f. with I 2 figs. 287, 455.

[26] *Troy* I 1.205. Schachermeyr, *RE* XXII 1405 f., notes that the potter's wheel is not in evidence in inner Anatolia until a much later period; he thinks it must have come to Troy "from remote Mesopotamia"; we now know that wheel-made pottery existed at the same period at Polatli (*Anatolian Studies* 1, 1951, 45 f.).

[27] See esp. W. Lamb, *BSA* 46 (1951) 75 ff.; Frankfort, *JNES* 8 (1949) 194 ff.

[28] Frankfort, l.c. 210 f.

[29] *Troja und Ilion* i 99.

[30] The encroachment is well illustrated by the diagrammatic plan in *Troy* I 2 fig. 458 as compared with fig. 457.

[31] *Troy* I 1.278 f., with I 2 fig. 451. The enlargement occurred in Phase II^d, the encroachment began in Phase II^f. Phase IIe is scantily represented, and it seems likely that not more than one generation is needed for the interval between II^d and II^f.

[32] See esp. Schliemann, *Ilios* 40 ff., 453 ff.; *Troja und Ilion* i 325 ff.; *Trojanische Altertümer* 225 ff.; *Troy* I 1 Index s.v. "treasures," and esp. 350 ff., 366; Becatti, *Oreficerie antiche* (1955) 147 and Tav. I; Bittel, *Grundzüge* 32; Seton Lloyd, *Early Anatolia* 106 ff.; Schaeffer, *Stratigraphie comparée* (1948) 223 ff. (his theory, that the "Treasure of Priam," with others, is to be assigned to Troy III, seems to have won few adherents). I concentrate on the artefacts of gold: the silver and bronze are theoretically easier to account for.

[33] The so-called "House of the City-King"; see *Troy* I 1.372. The site of the find is near the northeast corner of Square C 5 on the Plan.

[34] *Troja und Ilion* i 325 ff.

[35] *Troy* I 1.214.

[36] *Ilios* 456 f.; photograph in *Troj. Altertümer* opposite p. 232; in *Ilios* no. 687 (p. 457); and in Becatti, op. cit. Tav. I.

[37] See Schliemann, *Ilios* 253; Leaf, *Strabo on the Troad* 134; Blümner, *RE* VII 2 (1912) 1562; Rüge, ibid. VII A (1939) 533.

[38] Cf. Wace, *JHS* 72 (1952) 150 col. ii. The only certain exception appears to be "an infinitesimal bead of gold" (*AJA* 39, 1935, 30 =

Troy III 1.373, a "speck of gold" in burial urn no. 14) from the
late VI cemetery. Also from Troy VI is a pin which may be of
electrum (*Troy* III 1.21 with fig. 297); *Troy* III 1.318 n. 34 refers
to a "small tubular gold bead," but of uncertain date. *AJA* 39
(1935) 571 refers to a gold ornament in the form of a coiled ser-
pent: presumably from Troy VII? And is the rosette disc in gold
(*Troj. Altertümer* 6030, illustrated, = *Troja und Ilion*, Beilage
46.x) also to be assigned to Troy VII?

It is difficult to tell how far the gold artefacts were in use in Troy
II apart from the Treasures: only three "Einzelfunde" of gold are
listed in the Schliemann Collection (of silver, only two dozen small
objects), from unrecorded strata.

[39] The contrast was noticed first by Schliemann himself; he thought it
likely that the golden treasures came into Troy from outside (*Ilios*
467). It is to be recognized that a similar contrast appears at
Alaça Höyük: Miss M. Mellink, in *The Aegean and the Near East:
Studies Presented to H. Goldman* (1956) 45, notes that the technical
proficiency of the Alaçan metalwork is "in clear contrast to the
primitive aspect of the ceramic inventory of the royal tombs."

[40] *Troy* I 1.210: the argument is *ex silentio,* but is strong in confirmation of a point established by other means.

[41] Karo, *Schachtgräber von Mykenai* 350 ff.; what he says of the Mycenaean treasures is true of the Trojan: they are a "geschlossenes
Bild selbständiger Eigenart"; they "stand out in splendid isolation" (Bury-Meiggs, *History of Greece*, 1955, 23).

Bittel, *Grundzüge* 32, says that the Trojan treasures "deshalb
nichts so Aussergewöhnliches mehr darstellen, weil der Besitz von
Geräten und Schmuckgegenständen aus kostbaren Steinen und
Metallen, wie die noch reicheren Funde von Hüyük zeigen, bei den
Fürsten der anatolischen Stadtkultur des 3. Jahrtausends offenbar
zur normalen Hofhaltung gehörte": but the evidence of Troy insists that its treasures of gold were isolated, not "normal"; Alaça
throws no great light on that aspect of the problem, however much
else it may illuminate.

[42] Lorimer, *HM* 19, on the shaft-grave treasures: "For so spectacular
an accession of riches a natural and obvious cause is the capture
and spoliation of some wealthy city" (suggesting Cnossos; the artefacts include many that are "unmistakably Cretan in style though
not as a rule in subject"). Matz, *Kreta, Mykene, Troja* [*KMT*]
(1956) 133, agrees that the treasures are the spoils of raids, whether
on Cretan or other territory: but Dr Stubbings warns me to tread
carefully here,—not all the shaft-grave treasures are Minoan in

character; and where style and workmanship seem Minoan, actual Minoan parallels may be wanting; it is perhaps more likely that the "capture and spoliation" was rather of artificers than of artefacts.—For the historical background of the alleged Mycenaean invasion of Crete see esp. Schachermeyr, *Archiv Orientální* 17.2 (1949) 331 ff.

⁴³ The only fit objects for comparison in respect of material, place, and time were the treasures discovered by Richard Seager at Mochlos off the coast of northeastern Crete in 1908 (R. B. Seager, *Explorations in the Island of Mochlos*, 1911, with illustrations of the best gold objects). Their date is Early Minoan II, close enough to Troy II. But it is not easy to find any necessary connexion between the two: the goldwork at Mochlos is, as Seager says, "for the most part, of the simplest character"; differences from the Trojan treasures are much more striking than resemblances; and there is a fundamental disparity in context,—"in view of the high development shown by the stone vases of this settlement, the profusion of gold ornaments [nearly 150, not counting beads] in the Mochlos graves is not so surprising": whereas in Troy II the goldwork far surpasses all other comparable arts, in Mochlos it is only one—and very far from the best—example of artistic talent. (The influence of Ur upon Troy seems to me, for reasons of place and time, to be most unlikely; but see *RE* XXII 1407.)

The question remains, how far the alien origin of the Trojan gold treasures is confirmed by differences, other than that of the material, from local types of artefact. To the layman, the number and quality of the differences appear great; and the resemblances need no further explanation than the reference to generically Anatolian, rather than local Trojan, types.

⁴⁴ R. O. Arik, *Les Fouilles d'Alaça Höyük* (1937), with illustrations clxvii ff.; Bossert, *Altanatolien*, pls. 297–314; H. Z. Koşay, *Ausgrabungen von Alaça Höyük* (1944), *Les Fouilles d'Alaça Höyük* (1951), and *The Aegean and the Near East* 36 ff.; Schachermeyr, *RE* XXII 1400 ff., *AKG* 167; Seton Lloyd, *Early Anatolia* 35 ff., 96 ff.; and now esp. Mellink, *The Aegean and the Near East* 39 ff.

⁴⁵ Bossert, *Altanatolien* 35: "Innerhalb der anatolischen Kunst des 3. Jahrtausends ragt die Kunst von Alaça Höyük dermassen hervor, dass alles bis jetzt Bekannte, einschliesslich Troja, dahinter zurückstehen muss"; Seton Lloyd, *Early Anatolia* 107: "on the whole primitive and the workmanship very rude," of the Trojan treasures. I am surprised, if there is anything in the Alaçan goldwork surpassing the quality of *Troj. Altertümer* 5863, 5876, 5878, 6133, among others. Schachermeyr (*AKG* 167) rates the Trojan high

above the Alaçan goldwares, and in some respects above those of Ur; I would add, above those of Mycenae the greater part of a millennium later; Vaphio and Dendra put everything else in the shade. Some of the Trojan gold artefacts are now very well illustrated in Matz, *KMT* Taf. 5 f.

46 The graves (from which the gold comes) of Alaça are assigned to c. 2350–2100 B.C. (Bittel, *Grundzüge* 27 ff.), overlapping Troy II (latest phases) and III.

47 Resemblances between Alaçan and Trojan artefacts are noted or suggested by Arik, op. cit., throughout his catalogue; cf. Schachermeyr, *RE* XXII 1407 f., and Mellink l.c. 47 ff. So far as the goldwares are concerned, it must be admitted that here again the differences are more numerous and striking than the resemblances.

48 "A chance find in 1950, in a somewhat equivocal setting in a site near Amasya, has produced a fluted jug and chalices of gold, together with a quantity of silver and copper objects, identical with those in the Alaça tombs," Seton Lloyd, *Early Anatolia* 100 f.; see also Mellink, *The Aegean and the Near East* 46 n. 18.

49 Cf. Mellink, op. cit. 57, "recent discoveries suggest that a series of small kingdoms can be reconstructed along the route from Troy to Alaça, and that the rise of metallurgy was one of the main factors which made these sites locally powerful."

50 See L. Brea, *Illustrated London News*, August 3, 1957, 197 ff.

51 The site at Poliochni is described as "an urban settlement surrounded by a solid curtain of walls." In culture, generally, it was closely related to Troy II, but more complex and much larger,—"its extent during the period of Troy I and Troy II is more than double that of Troy." Its destruction, "due certainly to an earthquake," is more or less contemporary with the Burnt Layer of Troy II. Thereafter it played no noticeable part in history, though tenuous traces indicate occupation of some sort up to the middle of the second millennium.

52 This point is stressed by Brea (199); he suggests that "this treasure, as is probably the case with some of the Trojan finds also, represented some family's gold reserve, for use as a medium of exchange."

53 It is generally very difficult to discover in just what conditions the Schliemann Treasures were found; Goetze in *Troja und Ilion* i 325 ff. reports as much as is known.

54 Among other reasons: if the fire had been accidental, most people would easily have escaped; they would then certainly have dug out their treasures.

We must resist the temptation to associate the collapse of Troy

II with that of Poliochni, "due certainly to an earthquake": decades may have divided the two catastrophes; and in fact the destruction of Troy II was not apparently caused by an earth-quake.

[55] See *Troy* I 1.321, 366 f.

[56] *Troy* II 1.6: "In general, the pottery of Troy III is almost indistinguishable from that of the later phases of Troy II, demonstrating unimpeachably the continuity of ceramic tradition"; 10 ff., in materials (copper, stone, bone, terracotta) and in manufactures (articles listed pp. 11–16) the link with Troy II is unbroken; 8 f., commercial relations with the West continue as before.

[57] *Troy* II 1.4 f.: compare esp. II 2 fig. 263 with I 2 fig. 459 (Phases e, f), and still more significantly with I 2 fig. 451 (showing the same area in Square E 6 up to Phase IIe).

[58] See *Troy* II 2 figs. 263 ff. It is not certain that Troy III was not a walled fortress: the evidence in general suggests that it was not, but it is safer to say with the American excavators that the matter is simply "undetermined."

[59] *Troy* II 1.5.

[60] Ibid.

[61] Ibid. 65 f.; cf. Schliemann, *Ilios* 518.

[62] *Troy* II 1.38. For a similar floor in the fourth settlement see the photograph in *AJA* 39 (1935) 10.

[63] *Troy* II 1.38.

[64] Another explanation is offered by Bittel in his review of *Troy* I and II (*Gnomon* 26, 1954, 440).

[65] *Troy* I 1.321: this suggestion is there made tentatively together with others.

[66] When the visitor to Buckingham Palace finds a large angle of the forecourt demolished to make room for small houses extending almost up to the front portal, he may safely conclude that Royalty is no longer at home there.

[67] We have no right to assume either (*a*) that the Trojan treasures were not introduced into Troy until the phase (II^g) in which they were found embedded; or (*b*) that they did not change hands in the course of time.

[68] Bittel, *Grundzüge* 57, suggests that the burners of Troy II may have been passing raiders, "etwa von der See her, nach dessen Gelingen die Invasoren wieder abzogen, oder aber sie strebten weiter ins innere Kleinasien"; on p. 58 he allows the possibility that they were outrunners of the Hittite invasion. Seton Lloyd, *Early Anatolia* 63 ff., 93 f., stresses the parallel between Troy II

and (a) Alaça Höyük: in both, the wonderful treasures "date from a period which terminated in a great cataclysm, and was followed in both cases by notable changes in the habits and tastes of the local inhabitants"; (b) Polatli: there are striking cultural resemblances to Troy II at a level immediately preceding a destructive fire. These events and circumstances play an important part in the general theory of Schaeffer, *Stratigraphie comparée;* they are discussed in a wider context also by Mellink in *The Aegean and the Near East* 41 ff.

[69] *Troy* II 1.102, 105, 139 f.: but perhaps the evidence indicates no more than a particularly massive retaining wall for a terrace.

[70] See esp. *Troy* II 2 fig. 297.

[71] *Troy* II 1.108. Materials and manufactures remain as before; the ceramic tradition is uninterrupted (though wheel-turned pottery now becomes commoner); commercial relations with the West are continued, and there are some points of contact with central Anatolia and the Near East (II 1.107).

[72] See esp. *Troy* II 2 fig. 271.

[73] Troy IV reverts to clay brick instead of stone for walls of houses.

[74] Bones of *cervus* are still common in Troy IV; there is an apparently absolute continuity of culture in general, with some differences (mostly for the better) in details.

[75] See esp. *Troy* II 2 fig. 304, representing House 501, with main room about 4 m. wide and at least 10 m. long; its remarkable cooking-stove is excellently photographed in fig. 192. The sugarloaf cubes on the edge of the stove are presumably intended as stands for pots and pans. Another interesting house is no. 504, ibid. fig. 308 with text II 1.283.

[76] *Troy* II 1.223.

[77] Ibid.: "bones of deer show a sharp decrease, while bones of *bos* and *sus* rise almost to their maximum proportional incidence."

[78] Ibid.

[79] Probably to Tarsus, perhaps to Cyprus, possibly to central Anatolia; *Troy* II 1.227 ff.

[80] See esp. *Troy* II 1.221 f., 297, with II 2 figs. 230 ff.; Dörpfeld's V[ede] probably belong to the earliest phase of Troy VI (see n. 88 below). There is a mass of thin slabs of stone, with crude brick super-structure, which "looked as if it might have been part of a fortification wall of the Fifth Settlement."

[81] Bittel in his review of *Troy* III (*Gnomon* 28, 1956, 243 ff.; cf. *Kleinas. Studien*, 130 f.) denies that the evidence suffices to prove a change of culture at the end of the fifth settlement, and suggests

that "Early VI" may have been a period of transition from Troy V
to Troy VI ("ob nicht faktisch das ganze frühe VI den Charakter
des Überganges von V zu VI hat?"); such changes as the facts force
us to admit are at no period sufficient, he believes, to prove a break
in the continuity of culture at Troy.

He deals *seriatim* with the principal arguments:

I. *The architecture.*—(*a*) Only one house from Early VI, "House
630," is well preserved. About this Blegen says (III 1.122) that,
"though a certain neatness in the style of construction recalls the
houses of Troy V, the general character of the building, its regular-
ity of plan, and its free-standing position look forward to the great
houses of the later phases of the Sixth Settlement of which it is
surely a forerunner. Its importance therefore lies in the evidence it
gives that the introduction of the new architecture . . . goes back
to the initial phases of Troy VI." Bittel replies (i) that it is hazardous to make a single house the foundation of inference about the
general character of the building in Early VI, and (ii) that House
630 is not in fact so different from the houses of Troy V as to exclude the possibility of direct evolution. He does not consider the
important point that this Early VI house, which certainly represents a marked improvement on anything that Troy V can show,
contains relics both of Gray Minyan Ware and of the horse: the
improvement in architecture was contemporary with these astonishing innovations, and its evidential weight should be assessed
in conjunction with them, not in isolation.

b) Blegen believes that Walls V^e, V^d (III 2 fig. 503), assigned by
Dörpfeld to Troy V, must now be assigned to Early VI: Bittel
thinks that the claim of Troy V remains open. The point is of considerable importance, for this wall has the "offsets" which are so
distinctive a feature of the architecture of Troy VI: if the "offsets"
were already present in Troy V, Bittel's case would acquire some
substance. There is a conflict here which the layman must not presume to discuss. Blegen states categorically (III 1.212): "This
latter [=Wall V^b] cannot be assigned to the Fifth Settlement, but
must have been constructed later, though how much later could
not be determined"; Bittel replies that "so viel ich sehe, haben sich
neue stratigraphische Anhaltspunkte, die für die Zuweisung dieser
Fortifikation zwingend wären, nicht gefunden." He does not discuss Blegen's further statement (112), that "a short section called
V^e, lying underneath House VI G in Square H 7, which Dörpfeld
plausibly suggested might be part of the same fortification, . . .
is certainly a work of the early Sixth Settlement"; it is possible,

however, that V^e is not part of the same fortification (142: "whether a retaining wall or the foundation of a building or a defensive wall"). In summary, Bittel has not succeeded in showing cause why we should disbelieve the explicit statement of the excavators that V^b "cannot be assigned to the Fifth Settlement, but must have been constructed later."

II. *The pottery.*—Bittel stresses the fact that in Early VI the new shapes occur together with old shapes; it is not until Middle VI that the break with the past is almost complete. As for the Gray Minyan Ware, Bittel suggests that, since it was highly fashionable in the Aegean world about the period in question, its presence in Early VI may be due simply to "import and inspiration from the Aegean area or from the West Anatolian neighbourhood" (for the latter area, see n. 17 above). He suggests further that Gray Minyan Ware, which first appears in Hellas, must have been invented there (this seems to me a most improbable assumption); therefore, if the founders of Troy VI were invaders who brought the technique with them, either they must have come from Hellas itself (which nobody will believe), or they must have acquired it *en route*, perhaps on the periphery of the Greek world; but this (he argues) is an unnecessary complication, for if Trojan G.M.W. was adopted from Greek the adoption could just as well have occurred in Troy itself.

III. *The horse.*—Bittel suggests that local influences in Asia Minor might at this time have caused the introduction of the horse to Troy. A conquest of Troy is not to be inferred "unless there is real proof of the beginning of a new epoch at Troy simultaneously with the appearance of the horse"; and he simply denies that the architecture and the pottery constitute such proof.

His general conclusion (p. 246) is that, so far as the archaeological material allows a judgement, the advances in Troy VI "developed organically" out of the recent past; there is no need to infer even a change of dynasty at Troy, let alone a conquest and a change of population.

Although his argument is overstated in places (the Gray Minyan Ware is not "*the only thread*" that runs all through Troy VI, and among the things which did *not* "develop organically" out of the Trojan past are the Gray Minyan Ware and the horse), and although he seems to make insufficient allowance for the cumulative value of the evidence, yet it must be admitted that he has argued the case with great skill and force. He has not succeeded, as he claims, in setting up "one possibility against another": he has set up a theoretically conceivable proposition against a common-sense inference. It is theoretically conceivable that a people might suddenly subvert their own culture, importing the potters of newly arrived strangers in a land overseas to teach them a new fashion in ceramics, at the same time as they were remodelling their citadel with a new architectural art and introducing the already domesti-cated horse,—though nobody knows where either the new archi-tecture or the horse came from. It is, in effect, simply to say that change of culture does not mean change of people: for Bittel's argument that Early VI was a transitional phase seems to me to fail entirely. Of the three most significant changes, two certainly and the third also according to the excavators are definitely manifest in the earliest phase of Troy VI; not to mention numerous lesser changes. In all respects Troy VI is as unlike Troy V as it could well be; it seems probable that the general opinion will be in favour of Blegen's judgement that the change in culture in Troy VI from its beginning is of such a quality that a change of people is the only reasonable inference to be drawn (so also Schachermeyr, *RE* XXII 1449 f.: "Troia VI . . . zeigt einen ebenso plötzlichen wie durch-greifenden Wechsel des kulturellen Bestandes. Mit Recht nehmen die amerikanischen Forscher eine Einwanderung an, welche mit derjenigen der Griechen nach Hellas am Beginn von M. Hell. irgendwie zusammenhing." Wace, *JHS* 76, 1956, 121, agrees that "Troy VI marks a new era in the history of Hissarlik").

[82] I do not use in this connexion the evidence of the cremation ceme-tery discovered in the vicinity of Troy (*Troy* III 1.391 ff.). This is assigned to Late VI, and may be unconnected with the change of people at Troy after Troy V. (*a*) The custom of cremation might have been introduced at any time during the life of Troy VI through Anatolian influence (the Trojan crematory has points in common with the crematory discovered at Boghaz-Köy in 1952; Bittel, *Gnomon* l.c. 251 and *Kleinas. Studien* 69 f.); (*b*) the Trojan crematory was used not by the great families but by more ordinary people; it is possible that cremation was an existing local practice adoped by the commoners after the invasion though not necessari-ly by their leading families. Schachermeyr, *RE* XXII 1493, and Matz, *KMT* 138, think that the Trojan crematory is an indication that the founders of Troy VI were not of the same race as the Greeks; for the two reasons given the inference is unacceptable. The question has recently been discussed in a wider context by Burton-Brown, *The Coming of Iron to Greece* (1955) 140 ff., 153 ff.

[83] For the "offsets" see p. 60.

[84] Bittel, *Gnomon* l.c. 251: "Die Häuser des späteren VI sind auch

im Grundriss, in der—mindestens—im Untergeschoss beschränkten Raumzahl und in ihrer Anordnung auf Terrassen durchaus eigenwillige Schöpfungen und mit der Bauweise keines anderen bekannten Ortes oder Gebietes direkt vergleichbar. Es besteht keine Verbindung zur östlicheren kleinasiatischen Architektur, aber auch keine zur ägäischen."

[85] *Troy* III 1.3: "the high central terraces, on which the principal palace presumably stood, had been cut away and removed, together with all their monuments, in Hellenistic and Roman times when a pretentious temple of Athena was erected."

[86] Houses Q, E, F, G, M, A, P belong to the first terrace; C, D, O, N, to the second.

[87] I have deliberately put the figure as high as possible: this is a maximum, perhaps theoretically attainable. I have no doubt that the true figure was very much lower, probably not more than half as many. Blegen (III 1.10) speaks of "a score or more of large houses in which the members of the ruler's family and his immediate subordinates lived"; that is surely the correct estimate.

[88] See the plan (facing p. 42): the discovery of a fragment of wall in Squares F–G 3 allows a reasonably precise estimate.

[89] From wall to wall along line 5/6 is about 180 m.

[90] It may be wondered what the royal strategy may have been: the castle will not accommodate the subject population together with flocks and herds and fodder for more than a very short period. The problem is by no means peculiar to Troy, and perhaps not very important. It might be expected that the fighting-men would defeat the enemy in the field; and that the walls would hold the greater part of the population (the rest dispersing on the hills) during the transit or assault of a too powerful enemy. It is quite possible that no special provision would be made for that unlikely and in fact extraordinarily uncommon event, a regular and protracted siege. (Blegen, *AJA* 39, 1935, 31, suggests that Balli Dagh may have been "a natural stronghold in which the surrounding rural population could take refuge in times of danger"; also Eski Hissarlik, ibid. p. 33.)

[91] *Troy* III 1.39.

[92] Ibid. 15 f.

[93] Schachermeyr, *RE* XXII 1464, 1468; Forsdyke, *JHS* 34 (1914) 126 ff.; Blegen, *Korakou* 15; Goldman, *Eutresis* 135 ff.; Persson, *Asine* 261 f.; Myres, *Who Were the Greeks?* 263 ff., and *Archiv Orientální* 17.2 (1949) 199; Kraiker, *Antike* 15 (1939) 210 f.

[94] Bittel (*Gnomon* 28, 1956, 247 f.) and Schachermeyr (*RE* XXII

1450) believe that Troy VI begins c. 1800 B.C., whereas the main
Greek invasion of Hellas had occurred c. 1950 B.C. Both agree that
the difference in dates would not in itself be an argument against
the theory that the Hellas-invasion and the Troy-invasion were
historically interconnected (indeed Schachermeyr insists that they
were so connected: "so erweist sich die Begründung von Troia VI
als der jüngste Akt einer umfassenderen Bewegung, der auch die
griechische Einwanderung angehört hat," *RE* XXII 1450). It is
therefore not misleading to speak of the invasion of Hellas and the
founding of Troy VI as being "events of the same era," as I have
sometimes done in suitable contexts. The dates are in any case
highly artificial, and it is an open possibility that the two events
occurred much closer together in time than Bittel and Schachermeyr suggest.

[95] *RE* XXII 1458 f. It would carry me far beyond my present limits
to discuss the complex problem whether there was a change of
dynasty at Mycenae at the end of the Middle Helladic period, and,
if so, whether the new rulers were of the same race as the old. It
seems certain enough that the great fortresses of Hellas were occupied by Greeks throughout the period with which I am primarily
concerned, the Late Helladic era; on the uncertainties relating to
the Middle Helladic period see Burton-Brown, *The Coming of
Iron to Greece* 45 ff.

[96] *RE* XXII 1452 f.; cf. Kraiker, *Antike* 15 (1939) 195 ff.; Haley and
Blegen, *AJA* 32 (1928) 141 ff.

[97] *RE* XXII 1489 ff.; this is now as certain as such things can be.

[98] This is flatly denied by Schachermeyr, *RE* XXII 1463 ff. (and by
Kraiker, l.c. 210 f.): "Völlig irrig war es, sie [sc. Gray Minyan
Ware] mit der Einwanderungskatastrophe zu Anfang der Periode in
Verbindung zu bringen." (He adds: "Keramik wird von Ein-
wanderern ja sehr häufig gar nicht aus ihrer früheren Heimat mitge-
bracht, sondern an Ort und Stelle übernommen": yes, but the
extraordinary technique of Gray Minyan Ware was certainly not
"*taken over on the spot*" by the Greek invaders.)

The origins of Gray Minyan Ware are a much-debated mystery.
It is said to have no prototypes, no previous history at all in Hellas
or anywhere else before its appearance early in the Middle Bronze
Age, when its distribution is confined to Hellas (including Macedonia and Chalcidice, but not Thrace), some of the islands (Cyclades, but also Leucas and Ithaca), and Troy (for finds elsewhere
in Anatolia see next note). It seems to be generally agreed that it
is an imitation in clay of metallic vessels: but nobody knows

where either the metallic originals or the clay imitations came
from. Schachermeyr is confident that the former must have been
Anatolian, but admits (1468) that we know nothing which would
account for the combination of distinctive features comprised in
Gray Minyan Ware.

Schachermeyr denies that the Greek invaders brought this
peculiar technique with them: he believes that it was invented in
the Aegean area after the invasion,—"somewhere in the Aegean
region, whether in Macedonia, Thrace [this seems particularly im-
probable], Chalcidice, or on the Greek mainland, the decisive step
was taken towards the creation of Minyan Ware,—the imitation
in clay of East Anatolian metallic vessels." The essence of his case
lies, as it is presented, in the fact that excavation at certain
places in Hellas shows an interval, a *Zwischenstufe*, between the
first occupation by Greek invaders and the first appearance of Gray
Minyan Ware: "erst im Abklingen dieser Zwischenstufe stellt sich
das Neue zuerst in Gestalt des Minyschen allmählich ein." At
Tiryns, Eutresis, Aegina, Gonia, it is stated (1463), there is "a
kind of transitional stage, which at Asine and Malthi actually ex-
pands into a subperiod, in which Matt-painted Ware is wholly
wanting and true Minyan makes only a hesitant début."

I do not argue about facts which only the field archaeologist is
competent to judge: but I suggest that, given these facts, the inference drawn from them by Schachermeyr is far from cogent. Even
supposing (what is not stated, and so far as I can discover would
not be true) that this transitional stage was a fairly uniform characteristic of all relevant sites excavated, it is surely natural enough
that an appreciable interval should elapse before the characteristic
pottery of the invaders asserts itself. We do not know how long the
invaders took to establish themselves securely; and we may
reasonably postulate a lapse of some considerable time before a
normal economy was reëstablished under the new conditions. At
Troy, where the invasion affected a single small settlement, no
delay need be presumed and none in fact occurred; but in Hellas
the conquest may well have been a protracted and arduous operation, and we have no reason whatever to expect that Gray Minyan
Ware will make an immediate appearance,—the highly skilled
craftsmen of this peculiar technique may not have been very
numerous, and may well not have been represented on all sites
alike at an early stage in the occupation of Hellas. It is intrinsically
much likelier that the technique was brought by the invaders than
that it was invented so soon and so suddenly after the invasion—in

an area where there was nothing whatever at the time which could possibly lead to this particular technical process.

On p. 1493 Schachermeyr himself says that "Anregungen zur minyschen Töpfertechnik könnten gleichfalls vom Balkan ausgegangen sein."

⁹⁹ For Gray Minyan Ware in Asia Minor (apart from Troy) see Bittel, *Gnomon* l.c. 252 (Brussa, Old Smyrna, Eskisehir); *Anatolian Studies* 1 (1951) 31 ff. (Polatli); and esp. Mellaart, *Istanbuler Mitteilungen* 6 (1955) 61 ff. G.M.W. is common in the mounds investigated in the areas of Iznik, Yenisehir, and Balikesir (south of the eastern end of the Sea of Marmora): all these settlements lie on or near the main roads from the Anatolian plateau to the Troad (l.c. 55). It is certain that further investigation will add greatly to our knowledge of these matters, but there is at present nothing surprising in the discovery of this attractive ware in places near Troy or further afield on the main roads to the Troad. (See now Mellaart, *AJA* 62, 1958, 9 ff., esp. 15 ff., on the distribution and origin of Minyan wares. He argues that "Aegean archaeologists have perhaps laid a little too much stress on the colour and the technique of the grey Minyan ware," and maintains that "in seeking the origins of the Minyan wares the real criterion should be not colour or soapy surface, but *shape*." The case is then stated for the West Anatolian origin of the Minyan wares of Middle Helladic Greece, and the conclusion is drawn that the invaders of Greece c. 1900 B.C. came from Anatolia, not via the Balkans from the north. If this was so—and the case so far is persuasive, however hard it may be to accept much of what follows on pp. 19–32,—it becomes even likelier than before that there was some very close association between the invaders of Greece and the founders of Troy VI; and Mellaart of course agrees with Blegen in linking "the arrival of a new culture at Troy with that which brought the Minyan wares to Greece.")

¹⁰⁰ Dr Stubbings points out that the evidence from the plain of 'Amq is relevant here: see R. J. Braidwood, *Mounds in the Plain of Antioch* (Univ. of Chicago, Oriental Inst. Publ. XLVIII, 1937). A ware similar to Minyan is found on tells in the plain of Antioch at a comparable date (Braidwood's Period VIII = 2000–1800 B.C.: "the Minyan wares begin here"). The reference under Period VII (1800–1600) to "Minyan wares and local copies" suggests that the Minyan wares were not of local manufacture, and it is noticeable that these wares are very far from being characteristic of the area in the earlier period. Period VIII is represented on only three certain-

ly and two more probably out of 178 mounds; the period was one of "very light occupation," and its characteristic pottery was "probably imported."

[101] *Troy* III 1.10 f.; cf. Wace, *JHS* 76 (1956) 121 col. ii.

[102] See n. 81 above.

[103] Schachermeyr accepts Blegen's inference that the founders of Troy VI were invaders (from the north), *RE* XXII 1449 f., *AKG* 249; but nevertheless maintains that the presence of Gray Minyan Ware in early Troy VI is due to transplantation from the Aegean world, ibid. 1469 ("mit Völkerwanderungen hat die Verbreitung dieser alsbald so weithin beliebt werdenden minyschen Gattungen ... nur insofern zu tun gehabt, als sie durch die Begründer von Troia VI von Makedonien, Thrakien, der Chalkidike oder von Griechenland her nach Westkleinasien verpflanzt wurden").

[104] Bittel, *Gnomon* l.c. 249: "das ältere Troia VI hat in allem übrigen mit dem mittelhelladischen Griechenland überhaupt nichts gemein"; but I wonder if this is not overstated. The invading Greeks have in common with the founders of Troy VI the practice of building walls round their settlements: such walls were built at Mycenae, Tiryns, Malthi, and doubtless elsewhere; this is a marked contrast with the past in Hellas (where "the only city wall of the Early Helladic era yet discovered" is the one at Aegina, *RE* XXII 1456 f.; add now Lerna and Khalandhriani [Syros]; *JHS* Suppl. 1957 pp. 9 f.). It is likely too that both Greeks and Trojans first introduced the horse to their respective regions (see n. 107 below). See further *Troy* III 1.15 f.: Early Troy VI imported Matt-painted Ware from the West.

[105] The Iliad does not suggest that the Trojans were of a different race, or spoke a different language, from that of the Greeks; but I should not use this fact in evidence of their cultural kinship.

[106] *Troy* III 1.10 f.

[107] Schachermeyr, *RE* XXII 1453; *Poseidon* (1950) 53 ff.

[108] Bittel, *Gnomon* l.c. 247, draws attention to this fact, which is of course in his favour (n. 81 above). He admits that Blegen's explanation (the impact of the cavalry) is possible, but justly comments that the theory of a change of power at Troy would have gained much force if there had been evidence of a violent end to the Fifth Settlement; in fact the evidence makes it clear that the citadel (at least) was not at that time destroyed by violence.

[109] Prescott, *Conquest of Mexico* III 9.

[110] Cf. General Maurice's remarks in *JHS* 52 (1932) 16 f.

[111] For what follows see *Troy* III 1, esp. 81 ff.

[112] In their final phase; not counting the blocked-up Gate VI^u or the small gate of Tower VI^g.

[113] VI^g, the great tower which protected the principal water supply; VI^h, added in the latest phase of Troy VI; VI^i and VI^k, flanking the main (southern) entrance on the left as you enter.

[114] *Troy* III 2 figs. 38 ff.: contrast fig. 19 (middle phase) with fig. 68 (early phase).

[115] See esp. *Troja und Ilion* i 119 ff., *Troy* III 1.87.

[116] *Troy*, l.c.: "usually ranging from 0.10 m. to 0.15 m., sometimes reaching 0.30 m."; see also *Troja und Ilion* l.c.

[117] A similar technique is exemplified the greater part of 2,000 years earlier in the Middle Chalcolithic fortress walls of Mersin: Garstang, *Mersin* (1952) 133, with fig. 80 A, "Turns in the main wall were covered by stout offsets, each sector of the masonry continuing straight." (Matz, *KMT* 137, is entirely mistaken in saying that the great fortress at Gla [p. 165 n. 40] has offsets comparable with the Trojan: the walls of Gla are built in a series of retreating angles; there are no "Vorsprünge.")

[118] Tahsin Özgüç, *Belleten* 10 (1946) 13 ff. (see Caskey, *AJA* 52, 1948, 455 ff.), rightly rejecting the view of Troy VI as a "typical Mycenaean citadel," discusses its architecture (walls, houses, megara) and looks to Anatolia for its ancestors and relations.

[119] *Troy* III 1.85 f.

[120] Ibid.

[121] *Troy* III 2 fig. 31.

[122] Ibid. figs. 448, 451.

[123] Ibid. fig. 55: the paved area is about 2.75 m. in diameter, the "altar block" is 1.22 m. long, 0.60 wide, 0.40 thick, and rises 0.13 above the paving.

[124] Ibid. figs. 47–51. Pillar no. 1 is 0.78 m. wide, 0.51 thick, still 1.05 high above its foundation block, which measures 1.94 m. long, 1.12 wide, nearly 0.60 thick, with a slot 0.25 deep in its long side to receive the foot of the pillar. Four pillars are partly preserved, and there is room for another pair.

[125] The top was cut off in the Hellenistic period: *Troy* III 1.96.

[126] Not only at the main entrance: a similar pillar still stands beside (and outside) Gate VI^v (*Troy* III 2 fig. 74). See further Knight, *JHS* 54 (1934) 210.

[127] The Anta House: *Troy* III 1.249 f., III 2 fig. 471.

[128] It is at least very probable that the building was open at its western end; ibid. 250.

129 There is no indication that any building preceded the Anta House on this site, though fires were burning here for ages before.

130 We really know next to nothing about the religious beliefs of these people. For the significance of the fact that they cremated their dead (*Troy* III 1.370 ff.: a cemetery of cinerary urns about a quarter of a mile south-southwest of the citadel) see Rohde, *Psyche* 19 f. (Eng. transl.). It is among the greatest mysteries of Troy, that no other burial ground has been discovered, and that human skeletons are so rarely found on or near the citadel; see further *Troy* III 1.378 f.

131 *Troy* III 1.219 ff. with III 2 figs. 124 ff., 465, 466[ab] for conjectural reconstruction.

132 II[a] was larger, VI[acm] are comparable, VI[b] may have been larger.

133 *Troy* III 1.285 ff. with III 2 figs. 183 ff., 478, 484 for conjectural reconstruction. The exterior lengths of walls are 15.87 m. (east), 14.70 (west), 12.50 (north), 12.60 (south). The east wall is 2.66 m. thick, the others from 1.46 to 1.68.

134 *Troy* III 1.291.

135 Buildings outside the walls were traced in Square K 8 (close to the face of Tower VI[h], a "modest house with meagre floor deposit"), and in Square Z 5 (just outside Gate VI[v]).

136 See the tables in *Troy* III 1.21 ff.

137 I.e., from 1900 to 1300 B.C.: the Hittite Old Kingdom dates from about the beginning of the second millennium; the age of the Great Empire is from about 1450 to 1200.

138 Bowra (*Homer and His Forerunners*, 1955, 38), followed by Webster (*Minos* 4, 1956, 104) writes of "memories of the Hittite Empire" in connexion with Iliad B 856 f., Γ 184 ff., Z 183 ff., Odyssey λ 519 ff.: it is therefore worth while emphatically to restate that no awareness of the Hittites is shown in these or in any other passages of the Greek Epic; nor is there any awareness of the existence of a great Anatolian empire under any name. The Κήτειοι of Od. λ 519 ff. are no more "Hittites" in their Odyssean context than in Alcaeus fr. 413; see further *RE* XI (1921) 360.

139 *Troy* III 1.17 f. Numerous resemblances between Trojan and Hittite are noted throughout this volume of Troy, but the reader will find nothing to contradict the summary statement on p. 17 that "apart from two cylindrical seals . . . there is hardly a single object that could be regarded with any degree of probability as an actual import from the east." On the remarkable absence of material traces of contact between Hittites and Mycenaeans see Nilsson, *Archiv Orientální* 17.2 (1949) 210 ff.

140 *Troy* III 1.16.

141 *Troja und Ilion* i 402; *Troy* III 1.21 f.

142 Cf. Woolley, *Ur of the Chaldees* 59.

143 See n. 38 above. The Schliemann Collection is in accord. There is nothing specially significant in the absence of silver, "a metal which ill resists the action of the acids in the soil" (Woolley, op. cit. 48).

144 Leaf, in his *Troy: A Study in Homeric Geography*; contested by Allen in *JHS* 30 and *Homeric Catalogue of Ships* 175 ff. Cf. *Troy* III 1.10, "another (additional to agriculture) source of revenue may have been provided by control of the sea passage through the Dardanelles and the land route that led from the western coastal areas of Asia Minor to a crossing of the straits,"—but there never was such a land route. Cf. also Matz, *KMT* 19 (on Troy II), the kings of Troy controlled the "völkerverbindende Strasse" and increased their wealth thereby. He speaks of the site of Troy as "the place where the old *Völkerstrasse* touched the Aegean": he does not see that Troy is a *terminus*, and is geographically so placed as to be exceptionally difficult of access (*a*) by land from Europe (nobody in his senses would make the détour down the harsh Gallipoli peninsula in order to cross to Asia at the actual straits of the Dardanelles), and (*b*) by sea from European waters (if the fact is not too well known to need illustration, I refer to the British Admiralty's *Mediterranean Pilot* IV 338 ff.; cf. Bittel, *Kleinas. Studien* 130 n. 14. In ancient practice, as Leaf showed, traffic from the Aegean took to the land much further south, often at Assos).

Bury, *CAH* II (1924) 490 f., justifiably objected to Leaf's theory that there was no evidence of any kind to support it: at the same time he asserted (what geography refutes) that "a number of converging lines of traffic met" at Troy (*History of Greece*, 1913, 48; these lines have disappeared from the latest edition, 1955, 46 ff., but we are still told that Troy "owed its power and wealth to its strategic position").

145 Bittel, *Grundzüge* 32, makes this point with reference to Troy II: it applies with equal or greater force to Troy VI.

146 *Troja und Ilion* i 424 ff., *Troy* I 1.216 ff., III 1.32: "the occurrence at Troy of terracotta whorls in vast numbers . . . is a phenomenon that seems not to be matched at other contemporary sites, east or west, and that must presumably point to some special and peculiar feature in Trojan culture."

147 *Troy* III 1.33.

148 See p. 252 below.

149 On the inadequacy of most native Greek cavalry forces, and their

need for imported horses, in the classical period, see now Adcock, *The Greek and Macedonian Art of War* (1957) 47 ff.

I owe this suggestion to Dr Stubbings, who further reminds me of Iliad E 640 (Heracles went to Troy ἕνεχ' ἵππων Λαομέδοντος).

[150] *Troy* III 1 Index s.v. "earthquake."

[151] *AJA* 39 (1935) 16 f.: "A study of the ceramic sequence revealed in F 8–F 9 leads logically to the conclusion that there was no break in continuity between Troy VI and VII^a"; *Troy* III 1.15, "the same culture still maintained itself in Settlement VII^a as it was reconstructed after the earthquake."

[152] *AJA* 41 (1937) 40.

[153] Ibid.; *AJA* 39 (1935) 550 f., al.

[154] *Troja und Ilion* i 192, with figs. 70–72.

[155] I have had the advantage of a conversation with Professor Blegen on this topic, and am obliged to Dr Stubbings also for advice. The date of the fall of Troy VII^a is, scientifically speaking, "Mycenaean III B," in terms of pottery sequence; what that may mean in terms of years is a complex question, likely to be widely discussed when the fourth volume of *Troy* becomes available. Relevant is Schaeffer's discovery of a bronze sword with the cartouche of Merneptah in an apparently Myc. III B context at Ras Shamra: *Illustrated London News*, April 10, 1954, 574 fig. 2; *Antiquity* 29 (1955) 226 ff., with plate; Wace, *The Aegean and the Near East* 133 f. Merneptah's date is given as 1234–1224 by Drioton and Vandier, 1224–1204 by Rowton (see Schaeffer, *Antiquity* l.c. 226 n. 5): it seems to be generally agreed that this is somewhere near the end of Myc. III B, but there is room for difference of opinion about how long thereafter it lasted—Dr Stubbings tells me that in his opinion Myc. III B may have lasted till c. 1180 B.C.

[156] See the preliminary reports in *AJA*, passim: e.g., 1934, 236; 1935, 17, 550 f., 569, 571, 574; 1937, 35, 36, 39, 575, 577, 579, 584.

[157] *AJA* 39 (1935) 17.

[158] Ibid., and ibid. 550 f. A little detail is given in the preliminary reports, but we must wait for *Troy* IV.

[159] The "traditional dates" (for which see Robert, *Gr. Heldensage* iii 2.1288 f.; Forsdyke, *Greece before Homer*, 1956, 28 ff.; Bérard, *Recherches sur la chronologie de l'Époque mycénienne*, 1950, 6 ff., and *Studies Presented to D. M. Robinson* I, 1951, 135 ff.) are merely speculative guesses, based at best on shifty and quarrelsome genealogical traditions, especially the Lacedaemonian king-lists. No Greek in historical times ever possessed reliable evidence from which a scientific approximation to the date of the Trojan War

might have been calculated. There is no point in trying to harmonise such guesses with the results of archaeological research: if, as Broneer believes (*Antiquity* 30, 1956, 15), "the destruction of the Mycenaean cites [viz. Mycenae, Tiryns, Prosymna, al.] took place about 1200 B.C.," whereas Eratosthenes dates the Trojan War a little later, there is still no "chronological dilemma." The absolute date suggested by the archaeologist may be a little uncertain, but that given by Eratosthenes is nothing but a guess proceeding from flimsy premises which could not possibly have led to a scientific calculation.

The sequence of events (1) fall of Troy VII[a], (2) decline and fall of the great Mycenaean kingdoms, seems still to be the teaching of the archaeological record. If it were ever upset, we might be forced to fall back on the position prepared by Schachermeyr (*Poseidon* 190 ff.),—that Troy VI was the Homeric city, and Troy VII[a] destroyed by barbarians. Meantime we may derive comfort (*a*) from the most recent pronouncements of the leading experts in the archaeology of Mycenae, Wace (*The Aegean and the Near East* 132 ff.) and Mylonas (*Ancient Mycenae*, 1957, 15), who place the fall of Mycenae a good deal later than 1200 B.C.; (*b*) from Blegen's assurance (*AJA* 61, 1957, 133) that the fall of Troy VII[a] occurred appreciably earlier than the fall of the palace at Pylos, whatever the absolute dates may be.

[160] These are the people who introduce pottery of the type called *Buckelkeramik: Troja und Ilion* 193 ff., 402 ff.; *Troj. Altertümer* 172 ff. For a short time (perhaps one generation) Troy VII[b] "shows a direct continuity of the culture represented in Troy VII[a]," but "in its second phase, VII[b] 2, it seems to come for a time at least under the domination of a crude intrusive culture" (*Troy* IV 1.142). The site seems to have been virtually unoccupied from c. 1100 to c. 700 B.C.

III

The Historical Background of the Trojan War

So FAR I have defined who the men of Ahhijawā
were and where they lived. Now let us consider what they did.
In broad outline the answer has already been given: they built
a powerful state in Rhodes; they exchanged courtesies and
quarrels with Hittite royalty; they maintained an establish-
ment on the coast of Asia Minor; their merchant vessels sailed
as far as Syria. But is there anything in the history of Ahhijawā
which might provide a background for the Greek siege of Troy?
We now turn to a document which guides us halfway along the
path,—the record of an Achaean warrior buccaneering on the
mainland of Asia Minor about the end of the 13th century B.C.
A summary of the tale is in place here, not merely for its own
sake but rather for the light which it throws on conditions in
western Asia Minor during the period which is of primary interest to us. The Achaean buccaneer plays quite a small part: it is
the principal villain, one Madduwattas, who will teach us most.

The document in question[1] is addressed to Madduwattas by
the last of the Hittite Emperors, Arnuwandas IV.[2] Written on
both sides of a single tablet, it runs to about 3,000 words in
translation, ending with the grim synopsis, "First Tablet of
the Crimes of Madduwattas." The story begins with Madduwattas in danger and desolation, only too glad to accept from
the Hittite Emperor the security of a petty princedom on the
edges of his Empire; and it ends with Madduwattas in command of the greater part of the Hittite provinces in southwestern Asia Minor.

[1] For notes to chapter iii see pages 112–117.

97

Attarssijas[3] the Achaean drove Madduwattas out of his land and pursued him into the interior; Madduwattas, together with his wife and children and troops, was rescued by the Hittites,—"Otherwise," says the Hittite monarch, "hungry dogs would have devoured you; if you had escaped alive from Attarssijas, you would have died of starvation."[4] He was given beer and wine and bread and cheese and a land to live in, Zippaslā,[5] on the frontier of the province of Mirā; and he swore a great oath of loyalty to the Hittite Emperor. He vowed that he would remain within his own frontiers; that he would instantly report all rumours of revolt; that he would deliver up all refugees from Hittite territory; and that he would "bathe his hands in the blood"[6] of the Emperor's enemies. In particular he would treat as enemies the ruler of Arzawa, Kupanta-KAL,[7] and the Achaean Attarssijas.

The ambitions of Madduwattas were first revealed in one or two ill-starred enterprises. He led his troops against Kupanta-KAL, and suffered a heavy defeat. The Hittites came to his rescue, destroyed his enemies, and restored him to Zippaslā. But not for long; here comes his old enemy, the Achaean Attarssijas, threatening deeds of most black and odious import. Madduwattas took to instant flight. Once more the Hittites came to the rescue, and their general Kisnapilis had the better of a battle in which the Achaean led one hundred chariots and one thousand infantrymen.[8] After the defeat of Attarssijas, the Hittites restored Madduwattas for the second time to his little land of Zippaslā; and there for a time he rested "snuffing with haggard expectancy the hungry wind."

So far the spirit of Madduwattas seems dim and low: from this time onward he began to smoulder and burn. The towns (or districts) of Dalawa and Hinduwa were guilty of offence against the Hittites: let us profit by their punishment. Here is a plan, gratefully approved by our benefactor, the Hittite general Kisnapilis.—I, Madduwattas, will march to Dalawa and take it by surprise, while you attack Hinduwa. I will attack Dalawa, so that it cannot go to the help of Hinduwa. So Kisnapilis led his forces against Hinduwa: and "thereupon Madduwattas marched to Dalawa, but not to fight; on the contrary, he wrote to the people of Dalawa saying, 'Look! Hittite forces are on the way to fight at Hinduwa: why not ambush them and fall upon them?' And so they brought troops from Dalawa to the road, and they arrived, and ambushed the Hittite forces and destroyed them, killing Kisnapilis and Partahullas. And the man who prompted them to do it was Madduwattas, who thereupon detached Dalawa from the Hittite Empire and persuaded it to render allegiance and tribute to himself."[9]

From this small beginning Madduwattas advanced to greater things. He made a treaty with Kupanta-KAL, ruler of Arzawa, the Hittites' most dangerous enemy in this region. To the Hittite Emperor he explained that his intention was to lure Kupanta-KAL into his own house by promising him a daughter in marriage; "when he comes, I will seize him and kill him." The Hittite Emperor was not deceived: "I have entered very deeply into the soul of Madduwattas," he wrote back; he knew well enough that Madduwattas' true intention was different, but such was his weakness or his folly that he must end his letter with the words, *act as seems best to you*."[10] What seemed best to Madduwattas was to take the land of Arzawa for himself; of Kupanta-KAL and of the decoy daughter no more is heard. To this important territory he added the province of Hapalla, attempting by the way to ambush and destroy a Hittite governor of high dignity, GAL.GESTIN, Gentleman of the Wine Cellar. A most slippery smouldering man, this Madduwattas, looming large in the dusk of Hittite history.

He now turned to the west,[11] and conquered a long list of places all more or less subject to the Hittites,—Zumanti, Wallarimma, Jalanti, Zumarri, Mutamuttassa, Attarimma, Suruta, Hursanassa; their troops and tributes were henceforth diverted from the Hittite Emperor to himself. And whenever I protested, says the Emperor, "you always wrote back about something else." It is clear that at this time Madduwattas is in control of the greater part, perhaps the whole, of the Hittite provinces in southwestern Asia Minor; the Hittite Emperor is at last compelled to retaliate. He sets out with an army, but Madduwattas is too quick for him; at the very outset the Hittites are delayed on their own frontier by a rebellion provoked by Madduwattas: the people of Pittassa rise in arms, cross into Hittite territory, destroy a garrison and burn a town. The Hittite Emperor contents himself with sending an ambassador to complain about the seizure of Hittite provinces and the reception of a Hittite refugee, Niwallas. Madduwattas replies with treasonous irreverent growlings, asserting his right of conquest over all regions except Hapalla; as for the refugee Niwallas, he knows nothing about him,—a position hard to maintain when the Hittite ambassador arrives at Madduwattas' court and finds Niwallas living there. But Madduwattas has an answer for everything: Niwallas is nothing to do with me; he is living with my son, and I cannot be expected to control my son's lodgers.[12]

The last item in the catalogue of Madduwattas' crimes is the most interesting to us, provided that Hittite Alasija is Greek Cyprus.[13] The charge, frankly conceded by Madduwattas, is that Madduwattas, hand in glove with his old enemy the Achaean Attarssijas, and an obscure person called "the man from Piggaia," has invaded Alasija and taken prisoners from it. The Hittite Emperor claims Alasija as his own territory, and demands the return of the prisoners. Madduwattas replies that he is very sorry; why did nobody ever tell him that Alasija belonged to the Hittites? Of course the prisoners shall be returned at once.

Such are the contents of "The First Tablet of the Crimes of Madduwattas," a unique historical document from the last phase of a great Empire. On its last two lines is the inscrutable phrase,[14] "Now will I squeal like a pig, and then die," *nuwa ugga SAH-as iwar wijami, nammawa agallu:* however fortuitously, a true account of the present behaviour and impending doom of the Emperor. Within a few years of these events Hittite dominion will have passed forever from the map of central and western

Asia Minor; here we see the tokens of a decline that went before the fall. The great provinces of the West are snatched away by the unspeakable Madduwattas; hovering dim-seen on the frontier is Attarssijas the Achaean, "rolling large eyes, questionable of the coming time." What happened in the end we can only guess: we know that, when this tablet ends, the Hittite Emperor has lost the greater part of his dominions in the West, and we are left wondering what he will do in the face of this unholy alliance between Madduwattas and Attarssijas the Achaean. The probability is that he will write letters and send ambassadors so long as he has a court to send them from; and that is now not very long The last of the Hittite Emperors fades from sight "with wostruck minatory air, stern-beckoning."

These events are illuminating, when we look for the historical background of the Trojan War. At some time not far from 1200 B.C. the Hittite Empire in central Anatolia collapsed. The "Crimes of Madduwattas" were committed in the years of decline before the fall,[15] and show us what must happen in southwestern Asia Minor when the Hittites have lost control. For more than a hundred years this area had been dominated by the Hittites through their vassal kingdom Arzawa. There was no other power equal, or nearly equal, to Arzawa itself, let alone to an Arzawa supported by the Hittites. Achaean interference on the mainland had met the barrier of Hittite military force at Millawanda. But now the last king of the Hittites lies on the deathbed of his Empire: who shall move into the vacant places along that more or less neutral fringe of coast which had for so long divided the Achaean from the Hittite sphere of influence? Surely the Achaeans will move into it: for several generations the tide of their commerce has been lapping on the shores of Hittite territory; and we must think of Attarssijas as only one of many Achaeans who scampered up and down the coast, south and west, when the decline of Hittite power left the field free for competition. Among the competitors, perhaps Arzawa: it had been crushed by the Hittites in the previous reign; the

palace at Beycesultan was destroyed by fire c. 1225 B.C.;[16] but
the documents make it clear that Achaeans in this area will
have to reckon with the like of Madduwattas.

And now, what of the northwest, the regions from Miletus to
the Troad? Is there any power in that quarter which might intervene? Is there any evidence that there was such a power,
and that it did intervene? That it tried to assert itself in the
days of Hittite decline, or rushed in to fill the vacuum created
by the Hittite withdrawal? Might Achaeans and Asiatics really
meet in conflict on this coast at this time?

Once more we are favoured by uncommonly good fortune.
The Hittite documents include a record from the reign of King
Tuthalijas IV,—a record which takes us back within a very
few years of the new date for the fall of Troy. One fact emerges,
plain and persuasive: that the Hittite Emperor, for the first
time in Hittite history,[17] came into conflict with some sort of
league of places in the central or northwestern region of the
coast of Asia Minor; and one possibility presents itself,—that
in the list of places allied against the Hittites, Troy and Ilios
are named side by side.

The document in question[18] comes from the Annals of Tuthalijas IV, whose sculptured image may still be seen in the famous
sanctuary called Yazilikaya.[19] Emperor of the Hittites from
about 1250 to about 1220 B.C., father of the last Emperor
Arnuwandas, he tells how he suppressed a great rebellion in
Arzawa and returned to his capital city with many prisoners.
And then, he says, the following countries took up arms against
me: and we read a catalogue of no fewer than twenty-two
places, starting with Luqqā,[20] the Lycians, in the south, and
ending with a place which has been identified with Troy in the
far north. These, the Emperor continues, gathered together and
drew up their forces in front of me: but I surrounded them in
the night, and the gods gave them into my power; with the aid
of "the goddess of the city Arinna, the celestial god of the storm,
the tutelary deity of the city Hatti, Zababa, Istar, the divinity
of the moon, Lelwanis, I completely destroyed the city of the

rebels."[21] He now advanced into the rebel country, subjugated the people, and took their cattle, sheep, and wealth away to his own court. And now he tells us the name of the rebel district: it was *Assuwa;* he concludes this part of the record by saying, "When I had laid waste the country of the city Assuwa, I went back thence to Hattusas, and into captivity 10,000 infantry, 600 war chariots and lords of the bridle-men . . . to Hattusas I brought."[22]

But the story did not end there. Two leaders of the rebels were "given to the god of the storm," surely an uncomfortable ending: but Kukkullis, son of the king of Assuwa, was set up as a vassal of the Hittite Emperor. And Kukkullis "stirred up rebellion in the low country (?): 10,000 infantry and 600 war chariots and lords of the bridle-men, having their origin in the country Assuwa, he induced to conspiracy, and stirred up rebellion."[23] And now the conventional phrases recur: "The gods gave them over to me; therefore their affair was revealed; (the Hittites) completely defeated them, and killed Kukkullis." Then the Hittites had to hurry away to deal with a rebellion in the mountains north of their country, and we hear no more of the men of Assuwa.

Here let us ask a question or two. First, in general, what is the district involved in the first rebellion? One or two facts appear clearly enough: (i) the area in general is the western end of Asia Minor: among the rebels are Luqqā and Karkija, which are known to be near the southwestern coast; (ii) it must be a fairly extensive district, if it is bold enough to oppose the Hittite armies even after these had overthrown the formidable power of Arzawa, and if it is strong enough to muster an army from which 10,000 infantry and 600 war chariots might be taken prisoner;[24] (iii) apart from Luqqā and Karkija, the catalogue of rebels consists of places hitherto almost if not quite unknown to us: now, if the territory of Greater Arzawa is correctly located on the map, we can assert with confidence what has hitherto been a guess,—that the "kingdom of Assuwa" must lie north of (say) Miletus. It could not possibly be accom-

modated in Greater Arzawa:[25] the northern half of the west coast
of Asia Minor is the only area which satisfies three conditions:
that it be a large and potentially powerful district; that it be
so placed that Luqqā and Karkija can send contingents to it;
and that it can supply a large number of place names not elsewhere recorded in the Hittite documents.

So much being independently established, we are free to consider the evidence of mere names. I take to heart the words of
Albrecht Goetze, among the greatest of Hittite scholars and
geographers: the correct method of defining locations lies in
"the determination of relationships between various countries.
A system of such relationships must be established, and only
then can an attempt be made to establish their absolute position
on the actual map. Identifications with names of later periods are
only permissible when reasons other than coincidence in name
warrant a position which corresponds to that of the place compared."[26] Now in the present inquiry we have satisfied the preliminary conditions: we know for certain where the district in
general lies, and we have not used coincidence of names to assist us in reaching our conclusions. We are therefore justified in
pointing, at this stage, to a verbal resemblance:

We have securely placed the kingdom of *Assuwa* in a region
which was known to the Greeks as *Asia:* Asia is a name earliest
associated with the district of the River Caÿster and, not far
north of it, the territory of Sardis.[27] The greatest and strictest
of Hittitologists admits that Hittite *Assuwa* and Greek *Asia*
may well be the same word.[28] I think we must conclude that the
resemblance is, in this instance, more than fortuitous; and welcome this striking confirmation of our results.

So far we are guided by the documents; now we must ask a
question which can only be answered by a guess. Granted a
powerful Kingdom of Assuwa on the western coast of Asia
Minor, so influential that its allies include people from the
remote south in Lycia, what are we to say about its relation to
one of the strongest and most prosperous places that ever

existed on this coast,—the fortress of Troy in the extreme northwest?

We can only guess. Though Troy might go to war in alliance with Assuwa, we must not assume that it was subject to that kingdom, or even that the two had much in common. The Troad is geographically isolated from its southern neighbours; and there is plenty of room for a separate Kingdom of Assuwa in the valley of Caicus or Hermus or Caÿster. These are the areas in which Assuwa is to be found; and there is at least one good reason why we should refrain from postulating any close political connexion between them and Troy.—Mycenaean traders were active on the west coast of Asia Minor in two sectors: first, in Miletus and the southwestern islands; secondly, at Troy. But there was little or no such trade with the long reach of coast between these points;[29] and that is a contrast for which there must have been a reason. The most obvious reason would be this, that the intervening area was controlled by a power or powers which differed from Troy in the policy adopted toward Mycenaean traders. The Hittite documents assure us that there was such a power, at least in the second half of the 13th century B.C., somewhere in this very region,—the Kingdom of Assuwa; and it is easy to think of a reason why Troy and Assuwa might go different ways in the field of commerce. The founders of Troy VI had been associated with the Greeks in their migration to the Aegean: their commerce with the Greeks had proceeded more or less continuously since the time when the two had shared a common culture. But we have no reason to suppose that the Kingdom of Assuwa had any such history, any such affinity in culture and perhaps in race to the people on the mainland of Hellas. It may well be that Assuwa, like Arzawa, excluded the Mycenaean traders; and it is evidently possible that it might act independently of Troy in other fields of policy, —that it might form a league and march against the Hittites, while the Trojans complacently pursued what seem to have been their favourite occupations, spinning wool and eating shellfish.

But is there not another piece of documentary evidence? Has it not been common knowledge for a generation that the catalogue of places led by Assuwa actually includes the name of Troy, and perhaps the name of Ilios too?

The list of twenty-two places in the league of Assuwa begins with a district in the south (Luqqā) and later (in the eighth place, Karkisa) names a district north of it. It is generally supposed that the catalogue offers (more or less) a geographical sequence, starting in the south and ending in the north.[30] Now the last two places, which should therefore be the two most northerly places, are (21st) *Wilusija*, and (22nd) a name which is capable of being interpreted *Truisa*.[31] The question is, whether Hittite *Wilusija* and *Truisa* can be identified with Greek *Wilios* and *Troia*.

Here is a boxing-ring in which none but the fully trained philologist is likely to remain standing for more than a round or two. The layman may occupy a ringside seat; but unfortunately there is no knockout, and it is doubtful whether the onlooker is competent to decide who has won. I have devoted much time and trouble to this matter, and give here a summary judgement on the apparent facts.[32]

So far as the requirements of philology are concerned, the equation of Hittite *Truisa* with Greek *Troia* is possible. *Ta-ru-i-ja* would be a natural Hittite equivalent for *Tro-i-ja;* and the termination -*sa*, instead of -*ja*, has an apparent parallel in the fluctuation between *Karkija* and *Karkisa*. To say that the equation is possible is by no means the same as to say that it is correct; it means only that philology cannot disprove it, or even disapprove of it. The case for the equation of *Wilusija* with Greek *Wilios* is less satisfactory: the stem *Wilu-* might well correspond to Greek *Wilo-*; but the termination -*sija* or -*sas* remains inscrutable.[33] We should have to suppose that the Hittites, who were unfamiliar with this region except for a few years in the reign of Tuthalijas, have so distorted the ending of the name of this place that it cannot be explained to our satisfaction.

It may be that we gain more than we lose, if we abandon Ilios and concentrate on Troy: the equation of *Truisa* and *Troia*, taken by itself, is a little more than merely possible. Geography is satisfied, for this is the last place listed, and so may be the most northerly among the allies of Assuwa. Philology admits that the stems are satisfactory, and finds a parallel to the terminations. And the excavations assure us that Troy at this time was a place of importance,—though the period must then be not too late in the reign of Tuthalijas, for the days of Troy are now numbered. Troy and Assuwa were probably independent powers: but that is no reason why the one should not march beside the other to battle; and it looks as though this Hittite document is saying, but inarticulately, that Troy did march with Assuwa against the Hittites. So far, but no farther, we can go without trespassing on the "good land of Fancy, between the arbitrary mountains of Invention and the whimsical river of Device."

Whether Troy is actually named or not, we have learnt one fact of high importance: that in the generation of the fall of Troy there existed on the west coast of Asia Minor a league of warlike and aggressive people, capable of mustering large forces against the Hittites; and among their confederates we note especially the men from Luqqā, whom we last met[34] in the Achaean sphere of interest, south of Miletus. The stage is evidently set for a conflict between the aggressive armies under Assuwa and the long-established power in the southwest, the Achaeans. It is to be expected that the two will come to blows when the Hittites leave the field open; and a long mutual hostility is the likeliest reason for the exclusion of Mycenaean commerce from the regions in which the league of Assuwa is to be located. We should now like to be reassured that the Achaeans were still active in their quarter of the mainland at this time; and we are again so fortunate as to find what we are looking for.

These same Annals of Tuthalijas include the only extant mention of the King of Ahhijawā acting in person on the mainland of Asia Minor. They tell us[35] that when the Land of the river Seha—a province of Arzawa—rose in rebellion against the Hittites, "*the King of Ahhijawā withdrew*," but the Hittites advanced and overcame the rebels and took their chieftain prisoner. The implication is—as we should expect—that the King of Ahhijawā depended on the Hittites to preserve the peace in western Asia Minor, and was attacked by the rebels as being friendly toward the Hittites. What then must have been the Achaeans' reaction a few years later, when the Kingdom of Assuwa rose against the Hittites, and summoned allies from the south, the Achaean sphere of interest? Surely they stood again on the Hittite side, at least in sympathy; and surely they must be alarmed by the influence of Assuwa over regions so far south as Karkija and Luqqā, neighbours to the Achaean coast. It is not by chance that the name of Ahhijawā is not to be found in the league of Assuwa.

This is not quite the end of the story of Assuwa. From the reign of the last Hittite Emperor, Arnuwandas IV (c. 1220–c. 1190 B.C.), comes a fragmentary document of some interest.[36] Though nothing can be made of the detail, we can read a reference to the defeat of Assuwa by Tuthalijas in the previous reign, and the kings of Assuwa and Ahhijawā are named almost in the same breath. It is obvious that the activity of Assuwa is the principal theme, and that the Achaeans are somehow involved.[37] We may regret that the documents are not more numerous and better preserved: but there was a time when it would have seemed a fond foolish hope to expect that we should ever possess documentary evidence of the Achaeans in contact, and perhaps in conflict, with a powerful kingdom on the coast of Asia Minor at this time.

I say, *at this time:* what time? What is the sequence of events? During the first half of the 13th century B.C. the Hittites controlled (directly or indirectly) the greater part of western Asia Minor, excepting the northwestern sector. Soon after the middle of that century the Hittite power was challenged in several quarters: in the reign of Tuthalijas IV, c. 1250–1220 B.C., Arzawa revolted and must be subdued; Achaean Attarssijas provoked battle with Hittites on the mainland; and the Hittite Emperor himself advanced into the northwestern sector to meet a new danger, the challenge of a league of cities led by the Kingdom of Assuwa. The Hittite Empire was already slipping down to destruction; and at this time the Great King addressed to his peoples one of the most moving of Hittite documents,[38] an appeal tense with anxiety, eloquent of the gloomiest forebodings.[39] Imagine what a falling-off is there, when the Emperor himself must plead for loyal service; complain of inefficient engineering in the field; exert his royal authority to stop quarrels about leave and garrison duty. But there is no need to do any imagining: the King tells us that men are actually deserting from his army,—not only common soldiers, but even officers.[40] As for the high command, there is much more anxiety than faith in the Emperor's heart when he utters these words: "Lords who command my troops and charioteers and strongholds, stand by with loyal heart; as you love your own wives and your own children and your own homes, even so love your King's commands and practise them well!"[41] I say, more anxiety than faith: for while all ranks are exhorted to obey their general officer, there is yet a significant proviso,—that if *he* gives way to despair or disloyalty, his men shall arrest him and bring him before the King.[42] And so this passionate gloomy appeal draws to an end with the words, *"The second Tablet of the commands of Tuthalijas to all peoples is finished"*; and not far from finished is the power of the Hittite palace to issue commands to all or any peoples.

In the following reign, c. 1220–1190 B.C., the men of Assuwa are on the move again; Arzawa is finally taken from the Hittites by Madduwattas. Towards the end of the 13th century the tide of Hittite dominion has receded from western Asia Minor, never to return: and the historical background of the war of Greeks and Asiatics, the Trojan War, is to be found precisely here,—in the conflict between rival forces, Achaeans and the League of Assuwa, over the territory at long last vacated by the Hittites. The decline of Hittite control coincided in time with the rise of that turbulent ambitious power, the Kingdom of Assuwa, which challenged the armed forces of the Hittites and exerted influence over allies within the sphere of Achaean interest. When the Hittites withdrew, these two forces were rivals for the vacant sovereignty: the natural consequence is a conflict between the Achaeans and the aggressive confederation on the mainland. Now darkness falls and hides the scene for several hundred years; and when the dawn breaks again, all was forgotten except what the Greek Epic poems preserved,— and that is the story of a war between Achaeans and a league of native places on the northwestern mainland. We can only guess where the fall of Troy VII^a took place within this context. We are not certain that Troy is actually named in the League of Assuwa, and we are not certain whether its fall occurred in the reign of Tuthalijas or rather in that of Arnuwandas. It appears at present likely that the Achaeans attacked Troy soon after the defeat of Assuwa by Tuthalijas, perhaps within a decade (either way) of 1230 B.C. It is a time when the Hittites have departed from this region for ever; when the field is open to the first comer; and when the Kingdom of Assuwa has hardly recovered from a defeat in the field.

So far the documents have guided us: they have taken us not onto the field of battle but to a point commanding a general prospect, whence at least the identity of the opposed forces can be clearly discerned, the League of Asia swelling and grumbling in the northwest, and the Achaeans swarming round the coast, occasionally visible on the mainland. Nor is it difficult to suggest what they might be fighting about: for several generations the Achaeans have been trading prosperously with the coast from Troy to the Egyptian Delta—excepting the central-western coast of Asia Minor. The Hittite withdrawal occurred at a time when the tide of Achaean commerce was running high; now at last the barrier was removed, and the tide spilt over onto the western shore,—most coveted of coasts, as a thousand years of Greek history will later demonstrate. It is the most obvious lesson of archaeology, now confirmed by the Linear B Tablets,

that the Mycenaean Greeks were great men of business: the
attack on the western coast of Asia Minor is the last chapter
in the tale of two hundred years of economic penetration in the
East.

To call them "great men of business" is not to detract from
those heroic qualities on which the Greek Epic exclusively con-
centrated. The Achaean adventurers in the East were not men
with a mission: they were men with a quest. But—in this like
the Spanish *conquistadores*—they were at the same time men of
high courage and enterprise, emissaries of a society in which
the ultimate allegiance was owed to the fighting-man's stern
code of honour. And, apart from the normal channels of peaceful
commerce, we must imagine from time to time some great
Achaean prince, an Attarssijas or a Tlepolemus with his companions, setting forth to find new homes and new wealth abroad,
to be won if necessary—and it *will* be necessary—by the sword.

Thus the Iliad illustrates a chapter of the story recorded in
the Annals of King Tuthalijas; and yet there are large and
obvious differences. The Iliad's league of natives is led by Troy,
not Assuwa; and the Achaeans who attack them are not the
Achaeans familiar to the Hittites—the men of Ahhijawā from
Rhodes,—but an expeditionary force from the mainland of
Hellas. Let us recognize, however, that these are differences,
not disagreements; and that the Hittite documents are few and
fragmentary, touching only the fringes, telling only a fraction
of the whole. It is at once apparent that our two sources—the
Hittite records written at the time, and the Iliad four hundred
years later—fit easily enough together. The Iliad is concen-
trated on one incident, the siege of Troy; that is natural enough,
for Troy had long been one of the strongest and most prosperous
fortresses on the whole coast from the Dardanelles to Syria.
We are not sure that we have actually found its name in the
documents, though we may have done so; but it is now reasonable to assert, in the light of the wider scene, that the event
which the Iliad commemorates is one which blends harmoni-
ously with the historical background. The Iliad does not dis-

agree with the Hittite documents: it supplements them, saying that the contest for power was not confined to the centre and south, but extended to the north also; and that the Achaeans engaged on the coast came not only from Rhodes and its neighbourhood, but also from the mainland of Hellas.

Still it may be asked whether this last assertion, that the siege of Troy was conducted by an expeditionary force from Hellas, may not be a fiction or at least a distortion of the truth. Four hundred years of poetic tradition might easily exaggerate a simpler tale, connected with the conflict between the League of Assuwa and the Achaeans from Rhodes and Miletus, into a grand Epic about the siege of Troy by the great kings from Hellas. Is there any means of deciding this question?

I believe that a definite answer is given by the second half of the Second Book of the Iliad, the Catalogues of Greeks and Trojans; let us now consider what they tell us.

NOTES

[1] Madduwattas [*Madd.*]: *Mitteilungen der Vorderasiatisch-Aegyptischen Gesellschaft* 32 (1927) = Hethitische Texte III; ed. A. Goetze. References are to pages.

[2] Reigned c. 1220–1190 B.C. I call him the last, though there is some evidence that he was followed by one more king for a short period.

[3] This is Forrer's Atreus, Brandenstein's Atreides; "If you are permitted to put in and pull out any letters you please, names are easily made, and any name may be adapted to any object" (Plato, *Cratylus* 414ᵈ).

    For the spelling of the name see Goetze, *Madd.* 41 ff. It occurs nine times in the form AT-TA-RI-IS-SI-IA-AS, seven times in the form AT-TAR-SI-IA-AS; these harmonise in ATTARS(S)IJAS. He is described (twice) as LUᵘʳᵘ *Ahhiiā*, "the man from the land Ahhijā"; this does not exclude the possibility of his being a king or prince (see *Madd.* 53, with Sommer's comments in *AU* 330 f.), but there is no justification whatsoever for calling him "the brother of the king of Ahhiyava" (Bury-Meiggs, *History of Greece*, 3rd ed., 1955, 43).

The identity of Ahhijā with Ahhijawā is admitted even by the generally sceptical Sommer (*AU* 351).

[4] *Madd*. 5.

[5] Zippaslā: *Madd*. 25, the Hittite Emperor gave Madduwattas "das Land vom Flusse Sijanta zum Wohnsitz." The river Sijantas was an eastern boundary of the province of Mirā (*Kup*. 117 f.); the Achaean Attarssijas has penetrated a long way inland.

[6] *Madd*. 7, 31.

[7] This is not the king of Mirā under the Hittite Mursilis, but presumably a descendant of the same house, now in control of a substantial part of Greater Arzawa and in revolt from the Hittites. See Goetze, *Madd*. 157 ff.

[8] *Madd*. 17 with Commentary 127 f.: the number of infantry, which is not preserved, is supplied by inference—based on analogies—from the number of chariots.

[9] *Madd*. 19 (verbatim except the last half-dozen words, which summarize).

[10] *Madd*. 21.

[11] Wallarimma, Jalanti (if the same as Ijalanda), and Attarimma recur in *Taw*. and in *Tuth*. (see n. 18 below) in conjunction with places in the region of the west coast.

[12] *Madd*. 35 (the last clause, "and I cannot . . . ," is supplement).

[13] The identification of Alasija (a place rich in copper, *Tell el-Amarna Tablets* I 195 ff., nos. 35–36) with Cyprus is strongly suggested but not (so far as I can tell) absolutely proved by a number of indications. See Hall, *BSA* 8 (1901–02) 167 ff.

[14] Unless it is explicable in the light of KBo. IV 14 II 35, quoted by Goetze ad loc.: "*wenn ich solches tue, dann will ich sterben.*" (KBo. = Keilschrifttexte aus Boghazköi, in *Wissenschaftliche Veröffentlichung der deutschen Orient-Gesellschaft* XXX and XXXVI.)

[15] But the beginning of the story, especially the defeat of Attarssijas by the Hittites supporting Madduwattas, is dated to the reign of Tuthalijas (c. 1250–1220). Goetze, *Madd*. 158 f.

[16] *Anatolian Studies* 5 (1955) 51, 80.

[17] I do not think that the "Dardanians" in the Hittite army at Qades deserve more than a footnote in the pages of history (cf. Hall, *BSA* 8, 1901–02, 179). Albright (*AJA* 54, 1950, 169) goes so far as to say: "That the Troad was under Hittite control half a century earlier, under Muwattallis, is certain from the list of Hittite vassals in the inscriptions of Ramses II celebrating his alleged triumph about 1286

B.C. Among the names are, in varying succession; Egyptian Pi-da-sa = Hittite Pidassa (Pitassa); Egyptian Da-ar-d(a)-an-ya; Egyptian Ma-sa = Hittite Māsa; Egyptian Qa-r(a)-qi-sa = Hittite Kar(a)-kisa; Egyptian Ru-ku = Hittite Lukka; Egyptian 'rwn = Hittite Arawanna." The coincidences of Māsa, Karkisa, and Luqqā are indeed striking: this is clearly a list of Hittite allies or subjects from southwestern Asia Minor. But there is no justification for assuming that the Dardanya are the Δάρδανοι from the Troad: there is no evidence that the Hittites ever penetrated into northwestern Asia Minor before the reign of Tuthalijas IV; and there are decided indications to the contrary,—the silence of the archaeology of Troy, and of such documents as the Annals of Mursilis. "It is doubtless an accident," says Albright, "that they [the Dardanya] are not explicitly named in the Hittite cuneiform documents": it is an unlikely accident; and the Dardanya are not even among the twenty-two places named in the league of Assuwa in the time of Tuthalijas (see p. 102). If the Dardanya are indeed the Δάρδανοι, we must rather suppose that they, like Māsa and Karkisa and Luqqā, lived in the southwest in the time of Muwattallis, and later migrated to the Troad.

18 The only text with translation of this known to me (and apparently also to M. van der Kolf, *RE* XXII 2, 1954, col. 1904) is given by R. Ranoszek in "Kronika króla hetyckiego Tuthaljasa (IV)," *Rocznik Orjentalistyczny* 9 (1933) 43 ff. I have been so fortunate as to obtain a very careful translation from the Polish into English made by my friend Dr S. Trenkner; and I have had the guidance of Dr Gurney and Mr Crossland in certain difficult places.

19 For another portrait of this king see Woolley, *A Forgotten Kingdom* (1953) pl. 15 (a).

20 L]uqqā: but Sommer (*AU* 362) describes this as a *certain* supplement.

21 Ranoszek 55.

22 Ibid. 56.

23 Ibid. 57: "In the low country" is a very doubtful rendering. Dr Gurney has rescued me from a pitfall here. At first sight it looked as though Kukkullis was sent back to Assuwa as vassal governor, and aroused a new rebellion there (and so it is taken by Van der Kolf, "kehrte in seine Heimat zurück"): but it would then be an incredible coincidence, if the numbers of his infantry and chariots were *exactly the same as those captured by the Hittites in the previous campaign*. Clearly the identical numbers refer to the same persons: Kukkullis aroused the captives to rebellion in some district (*not* Assuwa) of which he was governor subject to the Hittites.

24 I suppose some allowance should be made for exaggeration by the Hittite annalists; but, as Seton Lloyd says (*Early Anatolia* 148), the magnitude of the number "even allowing for a little understandable exaggeration, classes him [the Assuwan King] as a formidable enemy." It is quite possible that the famous rock sculpture in the Karabel Pass (not far east of Smyrna) is a representation of the king of Assuwa; if so, we learn that he was so proud as to style himself "*Great King*" (*Early Anatolia* 144 f., 148; Bossert, *Altanatolien* nos. 557–559).

25 Quite apart from the fact that Greater Arzawa had only just been pacified and subjugated by Tuthalijas.

26 Goetze, *Kizzuwatna and the Problem of Hittite Geography* (1940) 49; cf. Sommer, *AU* 350, "Man kann auf solcher Basis nach meiner Ueberzeugung die Geographie der hethitischen Zeiten nicht rekonstruieren."

27 The Iliad (B 461) favours the connexion of 'Ασι- with the central area: 'Ασίῳ ἐν λειμῶνι, near the river Caÿster (cf. "Ασιος, a brother of Hecuba, Π 717; "Ασιος a Trojan ally from Arisbe, B 837); Mimnermus (fr. 12.2) refers to the area round Colophon; Herodotus (IV 45), to the area round Sardis. In Archilochus fr. 23, Sappho fr. 44.4, the contexts are indecisive.

28 Sommer, *AU* 362 n. 1, 370 n. 1; first suggested (so far as I know) by Forrer, *Reallex. d. Assyr.* i. 227.

29 See I n. 56: the facts are stated, and a similar inference drawn, by Mellaart in *Anatolian Studies* 5 (1955) 83. It remains uncertain, how far the islands of Lesbos, Chios, and Samos may have been under the control of the alleged anti-Mycenaeans; for Mycenaean relics on Chios see *JHS* 75 Suppl. (1955) 20; on Lesbos see Matzouranis, *The First Greek Settlements at Lesbos* (1949).

30 I should not put this assumption higher than Sommer does: *AU* 362, "einigermassen wahrscheinlich."

31 The spellings TA-RU-I-SA, TA-RU-U-I-SA, admit the interpretations *taruïsa, tarwisa* (trisyllabic), *taruïsa* (uï diphthong), *tru-i-sa*, and *truïsa* (disyllabic).

32 On the identification of "Taruisa" with Troy see esp. Sommer, *AU* 362 ff.; Gurney, *Hittites* 56 f.; on that of Wilusija with Wilios, *AU* 370 f., *AS* 54 ff., *AUKE* 170 ff.; Kretschmer in *Glotta* 18, 21, 24, and elsewhere. So far as I can judge, I find in favour of Sommer on all essential points; but the failure of the philological argument is not decisive against the identifications, and Sommer himself seems to allow that if *Truija* instead of *Truisa* and *Wiluuas* instead of *Wilusas* had been offered, no linguistic fault could have been found with the identifications; indeed it would have been an excess of

caution to resist them, in the light of their approximately known location.

33 If Wilusas in *Tuth.* (see n. 18 above) is Ϝίλιος, what are we to make of its relation to that Wilusas which was a province of Greater Arzawa under a vassal king Alaksandus in the time of Muwattallis (1306–1282 B.C.)? "Alexander of Ilios" has naturally been an object of the greatest interest, and much regret has been expressed that he lived so far south and so long before the traditional date of Priam's son. I do not know whether there is much profit in such speculations, but offer one or two observations: (i) there is not, so far as I see, any mention of Wilusa as a province of Greater Arzawa later than the reign of Muwattallis (it is a doubtful reading in *Taw.* IV 8; and, if it does occur there, the context strongly suggests that it is not then a province subject to the Hittites); (ii) the evidence indicates that Wilusa, when it belonged to Greater Arzawa, lay in the northwest sector thereof; it might therefore be inferred that the house of Alaksandus of Wilusa migrated in the first half of the 13th century the relatively short distance northwest to the Troad, and settled in "Ilios."

34 In *Taw.*, init.

35 *AU* XVI = Ranoszek 52; see above, n. 25 to chap. i.

36 *AU* IX.

37 There is a possibility that this letter was actually addressed to the King of Ahhijawā. See *AU* 270 f.: it is quite likely that only one line is missing from the top of the tablet, and the first extant line runs "[He]rr des [La]ndes Ahhijaw[ā]": prima facie one would suppose that this is the name of the person addressed, and that the missing top line contained the name of the writer (Arnuwandas IV). Sommer objects that the MS evidence (which I have discussed in detail with Mr Crossland) excludes the possibility that the person in the first extant line was called "*King* of Ahhijawā," and makes it likely that he was called "*Man* of Ahhijawā"; if so, it was surely not part of a formal address, for he must then have been given the title "King," as he is a dozen lines below. We must therefore reckon with the possibility that this is *not* the first tablet of the letter, in spite of appearances. The matter does not affect the main points at issue, but it would have strengthened our hand if we had known for certain that the Hittite Emperor actually addressed a letter to an Achaean king on the subject of the kingdom of "Asia" at this time.

The text offers no connected sense: the nearest approach to an intelligible context is made in vv. 9–14: "Nun Tuth[alija . . .] /

und unterwarf ihn (= presumably the king of Assuwa, probably named in v. 7 above). Nun [. . .] / (dar)über habe ich geschrieben [. . .] / und (?) des (?) König(s ?) des Landes Ahhij[avā . . .] / einst aber [. . .] / der König des Landes Assuv[a . . .").

[38] Hittite text with English and Turkish translations by Sedat Alp, *Türk Tarih Kurumu, Belleten* 11 S. 43 (1947) 403 ff.

[39] L.c. 404: "an attempt to hold together the political and military forces of the empire and prevent a coming disaster."

[40] Doc. cit. A I.3 ff.: "If a subaltern or a man of the lowest rank flees back from the campaign, let his captain and major not hide him, and let them report him immediately to the palace." Cf. E II. 1–18, earnest and detailed instructions to all persons to apprehend deserters.

[41] Doc. cit. A I.28 ff., verbatim.

[42] Ibid. I.26 f.: "But if that prince or lord brings bad word before the army, and offends my majesty, seize him and bring him before my majesty." It is clear also that the commanders have been abusing their juridical powers: A I.32 ff., the king forbids them to extend a criminal's punishment from his person to his family,—this they have evidently been doing "for gain of bread and beer."

IV

The Homeric Description of Mycenaean Greece

THE BRILLIANT civilization of Mycenaean Greece declined and fell during the 12th century B.C.: before the end of that century its dwindling lights were submerged for ever by a wave of ruder and gloomier Greeks,—the Dorian invaders who occupied most of the southern and much of the northern half of Greece. The history of that invasion is obscure, but of one consequence there is no doubt whatever: the Dorians brought with them a horror of great darkness, and shakings of the world. "The eleventh and tenth centuries were, to judge from their material remains, a time of poverty and disorder, far less civilised than the preceding centuries, with scarcely any of that free communication between the different districts that is a characteristic of the later Bronze Age"; it was "a period of cultural decay," "a disintegrated and materially degenerate society"; these, we are told, were "the Greek Dark Ages, whose darkness far surpasses the Dark Ages which follow the fall of the Western Roman Empire. We know little of them, and that little is at first sight unattractive—poverty, shrunken population, decline of art and skill, loss of the art of writing."[1] There was an end of building great palaces and fortresses; an end of abundant commerce with the rich lands of the eastern Mediterranean. Precious metals and stones were no longer commonly worked; luxuries were no longer in demand; the wonderful arts and crafts of Mycenaean Greece were disused or debased. From these long and illiterate Dark Ages the later world inherited nothing memorable in history or delightful in legend. So wide

[1] For notes to chapter iv see pages 155–177.

and profound is the gulf which divides us from the heroic past when we stand on the verge of History in the 8th century B.C.: the glory that was Mycenaean Greece lies buried under the dismal deposits of the impoverished and parochial Dorians.

Towards the end of this period of eclipse a single voice was uplifted loud and passionate enough to ring through the ages. On the summit of a stony, rugged hill near Mount Helicon, among the untrodden ways, stood the joyless hamlet of Ascra, —a bad place in winter, and disagreeable in summer, according to old farmer Hesiod. The earliest Greek personality known to us since the Mycenaean era, he tells us what he and others thought of the times in which they lived,—not only the immediate present, but all the years since the age of heroes ended. And the emphasis falls not so much on the material as on the spiritual degeneration of Greece. Here are his words, spoken from a full and bitter heart after generations of darkness have passed over the land, and the dawn is not yet in sight:

"Now is a race of iron: would that I had never been born among them, but either had died before or been born after! Never by day shall they have rest from labour and anguish, nor by night from the spoiler. The gods shall fill them with hard cares. . . . The father no more kind to his children, nor the children to their father, nor the guest true to the host that shelters him, nor comrade to comrade: the brother no more dear to brother, as in the old days. Parents shall grow old quickly and be despised, and shall turn on their children with a noise of bitter words. Woe upon them: and they hear no more the voice of their gods. . . . Their righteousness is in their fists; and a man shall sack his brother's walled city. There shall no more joy be taken in the faithful man nor the righteous nor the good: they shall honour rather the doer of evils and violence. . . . There shall be a spirit of striving among miserable men, a spirit ugly-voiced, glad of evil, with hateful eyes."[2]

But one thing survived the long night of catastrophe: when the day breaks again, the Greek Epic emerges already full-fashioned, at the end of a long period of development. And there, near the beginning of the Iliad, is a faded picture of the past—a description, in effect, of the vanished world, kingdoms and kings and lists of places as they existed before the Dorian occupation. Here is a bedrock of fact, fit to serve as our foundation: *the Catalogue of Achaeans in the Second Book of the Iliad wholly ignores the Dorian occupation.* It knows nothing of Dorian Corinth or Argolis or Messenia; its map is blank where Megara should be; its Lacedaemon is very different from the later Dorian state; and, in the north, it knows nothing of Thessalians, who occupied their land during the Dark Ages.[3]

Here at least is something beyond dispute: the political divisions of Greece described in the Homeric Catalogue are fundamentally different from those which existed after the Dorian occupation. What the Catalogue offers is a description of Greece as it was in the Mycenaean period: and the questions must be answered, is it a fictitious description, or is it wholly or partly true? And, if there is truth in it, how did the truth survive through the Dark Ages into the Iliad?

The Catalogue's places are real places, and they are coherently grouped into kingdoms which have their centres in capital fortresses such as Mycenae, Tiryns, Orchomenos, and Pylos. But how can we prove that the portrait painted is true to life, a list of towns and kingdoms as they really existed in the Mycenaean era? The first long stride was taken in 1921 by T. W. Allen,[4] who observed that the majority of the identifiable places—indeed nearly all of those which had been excavated—were in fact occupied by the Mycenaeans.

It is well to be as precise as possible about this. The evidence was fully reviewed and brought up to date by Viktor Burr in 1944:[5] much of the detail is disputable, but the general conclusion is now established beyond reasonable doubt. There is indeed a fairly extensive limbo of conjectural identifications; but the most cautious critic will have to admit that of the 164 places[6] named in the Catalogue some 96 have been more or less certainly identified; and that archaeology has already proved the Mycenaean occupation of at least 48 of these 96. As for the

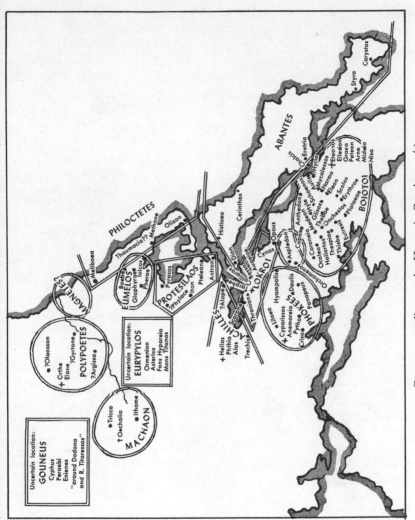

Greece according to the Homeric Catalogue (I)

Uncertain location:
GOUNEUS
Cyphus
Perrabi
Enienes
"around Dodona
and R. Titaressos"

Uncertain location:
EURYPYLOS
Ormenion
Asterios
Fons Hypereia
Mons Titanos

MACHAON
Tricca
†Oechalia
Ithome

POLYPOETES
?Oloosson
?Gyrtone
Orthe
Elone
?Argissa

GONNISSA

MAGNETES
Meliboea

PHILOCTETES
Thaumacia??
Olizon
Methone

EUMELOS
Boebe
Glaphyrae
Iolcos
Pherae

PROTESILAOS
Pyrasos
?Phylace
Iton
Pteleon

ACHILLEUS
†Hellas
Phthia
Alos
Alope
?Trechis

Antron

Histiaea

Cerinthos

Dion

Pelasgia

LOKROI
Cynos
Opous
Calliaros
Tarphe
Augeiai
Scarphe
Thronion
Boagrios
Bessa

ABANTES
Chalcis
Eretria

Styra
Carystos

PHOKESS
Hyampolis
Iliaea
Cyparissos
Anemoreia
Daulis
Pytho
Crisa
Panopeus

Orchomenos

BOIOTOI
Aspledon
Copae
Anthedon
Mycalessos
Heleon
Hyrie
Schoenus
Eteonos
Hyria
Eilesion
Harma
Eleon
Peteon
Graea
Mideia
Arne
Nisa
Coroneia
Medeon
Ocalea
Haliartos
Glisas
Thebe
Thespia
Onchestos
Scolos
Erythrae
Plataeae
Hypothebae
Eutresis
Thisbe

other 48, the evidence of place names or intimate connection with earliest legend assigns about a quarter of them to the Mycenaean era. The same cautious critic will allow that the number of places whose approximate location is known, or whose exact location is probably known, amounts to a further 33; and that at least a quarter of these are known to be Mycenaean sites. There is a remainder of some 35 places whose location is unknown or very doubtful; but several of these have names which support their claim to be pre-Dorian. In brief, not one of the identifiable places is known to have been founded later than the Dorian occupation; at least half the identifiable places, and almost all the excavated places, are known to have been inhabited during the later Mycenaean period.[7] That is to say, so far as we can judge, the portrait of Mycenaean Greece is true to life.

But we must not overlook (as Burr and Allen did) the sceptic's objection to our argument. He might ask, is it not true that Mycenaean Greece was densely populated, and that many Mycenaean sites were still occupied in historical times? Would not any ordinary list of Greek towns necessarily include many that were Mycenaean? A final and decisive proof of the Mycenaean origin of the Catalogue would therefore be welcome:[8] and surely it is to be found in the observation *that many places named in the Catalogue could not be identified by the Greeks themselves in historical times: and that some of them were abandoned before the Dorian occupation and never resettled.* How could a poet of the post-Dorian era have selected such places for his list? How could he even have known that they existed, or what their names were? The importance of the great fortresses, such as Mycenae, might have been conjectured from visible remains: but how could the poet learn about *Dorion*,[9] abandoned at the close of the Mycenaean era and never reoccupied? How could he come to select numerous other places for which the geographers in historical times sought high and low without ever finding a trace of them?—*Nisa*, which "cannot be found anywhere in Boeotia";[10] *Calliaros*,[11] which "is no longer inhabited";

Bessa and *Augeiae*, which "do not exist";[12] *Mideia* and the vineyards of *Arne*, which must have been "swallowed up by the lake";[13] *Eiones*, which has "disappeared";[14] *Aepy*, a name unknown to posterity;[15] *Pteleos*, which was identified with an uninhabited copse;[16] the Arcadian places, *Rhipe*, *Stratie*, and *Enispe*, of which Strabo says, "It is difficult to find these and you would be no better off if you did find them, because nobody lives there";[17] *Parrhasia*, which survived only as the name of a district;[18] *Elone*, which has "changed its name" and "is in ruins";[19] *Neritos* and *Aegilips*, *Ormenion* and *Orthe*, and at least a dozen more?

It soon becomes clear that something like one-quarter of all the places in the Achaean Catalogue were unidentifiable, except by guesswork, in the historical period. Some forty names were known only from one source, the Catalogue. The most diligent geographers of the second and first centuries B.C. were unable to bring this large proportion of the Homeric list into harmony with anything known or recorded about their own country. It is inconceivable that such a list should have been first compiled during or after the Dark Ages; for there was never again a time in the history of Greece when so many places might disappear from the memory of man. It is vain to plead that the places might have fallen into oblivion at some time between the 9th and the 3rd century: the supreme authority of "Homer" was an absolute guarantee that places mentioned in the Catalogue which still preserved their names in (say) the 8th century would never again lose those names,—or at least the memory of them.

There is no escape from this conclusion: the names in the Catalogue afford proof positive and unrefuted that the Catalogue offers a truthful, though selective, description of Mycenaean Greece. The further question, how this lengthy and detailed list of places survived through the Dark Ages, is easily answered: there is no scrap of evidence, and no reason whatever to assume, that the art of writing was practised in Greece between the end of the Mycenaean era and the 8th century B.C.[20] There is only one alternative,—that the Catalogue survived by word of mouth; and that means through the oral tradition of Epic poetry.[21]

These results of our inquiry—that the Catalogue describes Mycenaean Greece, and that it was preserved orally by the Epic poets—are confirmed by a study of the noun + epithet combinations.[22]

Descriptive epithets are attached to some fifty of the place names; and it seems certain that many of these epithets must have been inherited by the Ionian poets together with their place names. The proof of this important fact is simple enough:

Many of the epithets are distinctive, not generally applicable. One place is meadowland, another is rocky; one place is rich in vineyards, another is famous for its sheep; one place is rugged, another has many flowers; one place is on a riverbank, another on the seashore. Let us ask, how could an Ionian poet living in the 10th or 9th or 8th century B.C. know how to describe so many places—some of them very obscure places—all over Greece? How could he know that there were many doves at Messe (if anyone could still find the place); and vineyards at Arne (if it had not yet been swallowed up by the lake); that Aegilips was rugged, Oloosson white, Enispe windy, Pteleos a meadowland, Helos on the coast? Nobody supposes that a Boeotian, or an Ionian from Asia Minor, travelled in the Dark Ages round the mainland, blazing a trail for Pausanias and Baedeker; indeed, it is doubtful whether the most tactful tourist would have got far in the Dorian Peloponnese at that time. But what is the alternative? That he *invented* these epithets, hoping for the best? That he avoided the use of noncommittal epithets, such as were supplied by the Epic tradition in abundance,[23] and scattered doves and vineyards and meadows and rocks and positions on hilltops or by the sea, sowing not with the hand but with the sack? Surely he did nothing so irresponsible and so exposed to ridicule: many of the places continued in occupation, and the poet must reckon with the disgust of the natives if his random distribution of natural beauties planted—as it sometimes must—flowers on a rocky peak and vineyards in a marsh. Distinctive epithets must originally have been applied to their place names for one reason only,—because they were true. But it is certain that nobody living after the Dorian occupation of Greece could have known how to describe so many places as are distinctively described in the Catalogue—unless the descriptions had been handed down from the Mycenaean era, attached to their place names in ready-made formulas.[24] Even if the evidence of the place names alone had not proved that the Catalogue is truthfully descriptive of Mycenaean Greece, the evidence of the epithets would have suggested and indeed insisted on that conclusion.

Let us now consider the relation of the Catalogue to the rest of the Iliad.[25]

Since the Catalogue is substantially a Mycenaean composition, and the Iliad the final development of a poetry which had been in the making for hundreds of years since the Mycenaean era, it is not surprising that we find great differences between the two. It is indeed immediately obvious that the Catalogue was not originally designed to occupy its present place in the Iliad; and it is easy to prove that, while Catalogue and Iliad have certain presuppositions in common, each was composed independently of the other. When at last the Catalogue was incorporated into a continuous Iliad, nothing was done to eliminate the largest and most obvious incompatibles, though minor discords were softened by the addition of a note or two. The most important factors in this calculation are as follows:

First, the Catalogue describes the gathering of the Greek army in Greece at the beginning of the war; and it describes it in imperfect tenses, as being still in progress. This description is inserted into the Iliad, tenses unchanged, at a point where the war is in its tenth year. It suits the poet's purpose very well, to prefix to his first battle in the Iliad a review of the total forces engaged on either side; nobody seems to care if the passage introduced to describe the forces arrayed for battle at the present moment actually describes something wholly different—the assembling of armies at a Greek harbour ten years ago.

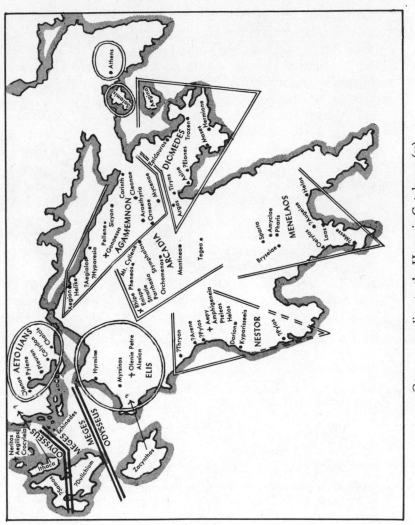

Greece according to the Homeric Catalogue (II)

Secondly, the Catalogue begins with an entry which could not possibly have been suggested by the Iliad, and to which the Iliad makes no attempt whatever to adjust itself: *pride of place is given in the Catalogue to the Boeotians*. About one-fifth of its whole length is reserved for Boeotia and her neighbours, the Phocians, Locrians, and Euboeans. In the Iliad, these are among the most insignificant of peoples;[26] in the Catalogue, they claim more than a third of all the place names, though

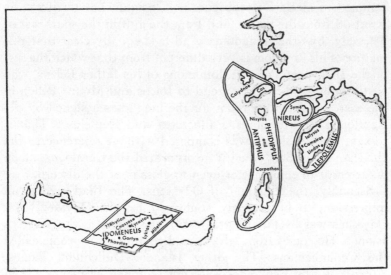

Greece according to the Homeric Catalogue (III)

twenty-four other districts are waiting for admission. Whoever composed the Catalogue knew more and cared more about Boeotia than about Agamemnon or Achilles or the siege of Troy. It is particularly to be noticed that the Iliad makes no attempt to adjust itself to this incompatibility: it neither adds anything within itself nor subtracts anything from the Catalogue at the time of its inclusion in the Iliad.

Thirdly, the Catalogue and the Iliad are in most violent disagreement about the nature and extent of the kingdoms of three of the principal heroes,[27]—Achilles, Odysseus, and Agamemnon.

First, the kingdom of Achilles. According to the Catalogue, the area later known as Thessaly[28] was divided among nine chieftains, and the portion assigned to Achilles was a small one, extending over Hellas and Phthia, and including the towns of Alos, Alope, and Trechis. This does not tell us much, for we cannot be sure what is meant by Hellas and Phthia; and though Trechis and Alope may be known, Alos is not.[29] But one thing is clear enough,—that the greatest hero of the Iliad is being confined to a relatively obscure and insignificant territory; he is cut off from the plains, and from the gulf in the southeast of Thessaly, by other kingdoms. And it is equally clear that this picture of his kingdom is very different from that which the rest of the Iliad portrays: the dominions of his father Peleus, who is still living and ruling, extend to Iolcos and Mount Pelion in the east, and leave no room for the kingdoms assigned by the Catalogue to Protesilaus, Philoctetes, and Eumelus.[30] That is to say, the Catalogue was composed without reference to the Iliad; and the Iliad, when it incorporated the Catalogue, made no attempt to eliminate or even to gloss over the discord.

Secondly, the kingdom of Odysseus. The Iliad creates an impression, to be strongly confirmed by the Odyssey, that Odysseus was by far the greatest of the rulers in the Western Islands. He comes from Ithaca, and commands a people called the Cephallenians. The other islands—Dulichium, Samos, Zacynthus, the Echinades—are not so much as mentioned in the Iliad; and there is no suggestion that any other hero, important or unimportant, was a ruler of any of them. It goes without saying that Odysseus is the only great hero from that area present in Agamemnon's army; and there is the strongest possible implication that he rules an important kingdom without a rival at home. Once more the picture drawn by the Catalogue is entirely different:[31] the greatest kingdom in the Western Islands is that of Meges, who rules over Dulichium and the Echinades, and commands a fleet of forty ships; what is left over—right, left, and centre of Meges' dominion—is bundled together to make a kingdom for Odysseus; and the best fleet he can muster is a mere dozen ships, one of the most insignificant contributions in the whole Catalogue. In the Iliad, Meges moves over to the mainland, where he rules a different people, the Epeians; he is a person of no importance in the story, though not so utterly insignificant as most of the Catalogue's commanders. Here again the Catalogue and the Iliad are in violent conflict.[32]

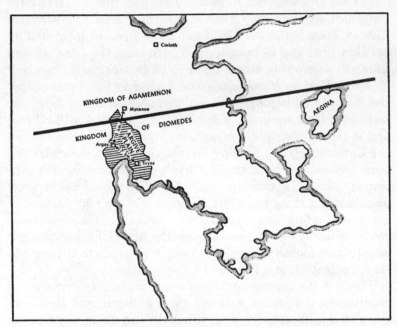

The Kingdoms of Agamemnon and Diomedes

Thirdly, the kingdom of Agamemnon. Earlier in the Second Book we were told how the sceptre of divine right descended from Pelops by way of Atreus and Thyestes to Agamemnon, so that he might be "king of many islands and all Argos." Whether "all Argos"[33] properly signifies a political or a geographical unit, it is obvious that in this context the territory which we call the Argive Plain is included in it; and indeed the Iliad often

tells of "Argos" as the home of Agamemnon. Now look at Agamemnon in the Catalogue: he is not ruler of all Argos, and he is
not ruler of many islands. All Argos is taken away from him
and given to Diomedes; and since Diomedes rules over the
coast of the whole peninsula and the island of Aegina, it is impossible to find "many islands," or indeed any islands, for
Agamemnon to be king of. The Catalogue pushes Agamemnon
out of the area assigned to him in the Iliad, into the area later
controlled by Corinth,[34] Sicyon, and the eastward district of
Achaea. Here is the third example of an irreconcilable conflict
between Iliad and Catalogue; and once more the Iliad refrains
from any attempt to eliminate or to gloss over the difference.[35]

Walter Leaf, in *Homer and History*, observed and fully stated
the facts: but his judgement on them was vitiated from the
start by a misconception. For him, the truth was in the Iliad;
and if the Catalogue disagrees with it, so much the worse for
the Catalogue. The unhappy Catalogue, we are assured, "has
been reduced to the absurd; it has even attained to the gro-
tesque." It is "a curious product," a "work of dismember-
ment"; it is a thing to be left, in order that we may "return to
more interesting and instructive themes"; "the murderous
stroke which it has driven through the heart of Agamemnon's
empire is as foolish as it is criminal. It contradicts at once history, geography, and Homer."

This is a fundamentally mistaken approach. It is proper to
observe the differences between the Catalogue and the Iliad,
and to judge impartially; to say that the two differ, not that the
one contradicts the other, as if we knew which of them spoke
first. As for "history and geography," the Catalogue and Iliad
are themselves by far our most voluminous sources of information on both topics. Archaeologist and geographer can sometimes (all too seldom, as it happens) provide us with external
and objective evidence related to our primary sources: and our
proper task is to inquire whether the Catalogue or the Iliad
contains anything either intrinsically unacceptable or in conflict with such external evidence as we may happen to possess.

If we do this, we shall find many obscurities in the detail of both sources; but we shall not find anything objectionable in the important matters which we are now considering. The kingdom assigned by the Catalogue to Achilles is quite an ordinary district; so is that implied by the Iliad. There is no cause for comment, let alone incredulity. The only problem arises from the *difference* between the two accounts: one of them is misleading us, but there is no objective means of deciding which one it is.

It remains to consider the kingdom of Agamemnon. Here is indeed a notorious problem; but it is a problem which would present itself even if there were no Catalogue in the world. There is nothing intrinsically objectionable in the Catalogue's division of land between Agamemnon and Diomedes:[36] the one controls the Argive peninsula and Aegina, the other controls the territory to the north and northwest. Geography has nothing to say against the recognition of Diomedes' kingdom as a separate political unit; yet something problematic remains. Agamemnon rules in Mycenae, at the northern apex of the Argive plain; about six miles away, in the plain, stands the fortress of Argos itself; four or five miles farther on rise the massive walls of Tiryns. But Argos and Tiryns are in the realm of Diomedes, Mycenae belongs to Agamemnon. The question suggests itself, in what circumstances might two such massive fortresses as Mycenae and Tiryns be erected so close together, and so close to Argos and one or two other great Mycenaean strongholds in the vicinity? If they shared the plain, the territory under the direct control of each fortress must have been very small: the grandeur of Mycenae and Tiryns suggests some greater dominion than their own suburbs; and one would have thought it impossible to build on such a scale without employing the skilled and unskilled labour of a wide area.

This, I insist, is a problem which would arise even if the Iliad and its Catalogue had not survived: what political conditions are presupposed by the building of these colossal fortresses, Mycenae and Tiryns, only about ten miles apart?[37]

At any given time in the Late Bronze Age, Mycenae and

Tiryns must have been ruled (i) by independent kings, or (ii) by the same king, or (iii) by two kings, of whom the one was dependent on the other. Perhaps we can say which of these three possibilities is the least exposed to objection.

i) *They were governed by independent rulers.*—One or two points are suggested by common sense. The building of such a fortress as Mycenae or Tiryns was the labour of years: and it follows that whoever built the one was not, while he was building it, independent of the other; otherwise he would not have been left in peace for a period of years while he built his rival fortress a few miles away. Moreover, it is unlikely that Tiryns and Mycenae were often if ever occupied, after their building, by wholly independent rulers: for both were surrounded by extensive residential areas which were not protected by fortification; it is inconceivable that this form of community should have been adopted, or should have survived, if it was exposed to attack by day and by night at a few minutes' notice.[38] The adjacent and unprotected suburbs offer a strong argument against the supposition that Mycenae and Tiryns were built and governed by independent rulers; let us look further afield.

ii) *They were built and ruled by the same royal house.*—There is one obvious objection: the fact that they are only ten miles apart. Why should a king build two colossal fortresses so close together? We are in the realm of conjecture, or even of dreams: there is no lack of conceivable motives,—mere ostentation; mere love of large building; assertion of supreme power; protection of the Argive plain at both ends.[39] But there is one reason why we may decline to believe in any of these motives or anything like them. Greek legend, which has much to tell about Mycenae and Tiryns, never suggests that they were subject to the same ruler. We must not ignore the guidance of legend; there is no other guide, and we have no reason to suppose that it is misleading. In this example it merely confirms what we were already inclined to believe,—that two such palaces so close together were not built to serve one and the same ruler.

iii) The process of elimination has led us to what you may

think was in itself the likeliest answer: *Mycenae and Tiryns must have been governed by different but not independent rulers.* There must have been some bond uniting them. We think first of a dual kingship,—two brothers, perhaps; but neither the Epic nor legend at large is in favour of this. A single possibility remains,—that one place was subordinate to the other; and that is what the Catalogue asserts, and the Iliad confirms. Tiryns was not directly under the rule of Agamemnon; it was a fortress in the realm of Diomedes, and Diomedes, like the other Greek commanders, acknowledges the divine right of Agamemnon as overlord. If the Catalogue had not survived, the fortresses of Mycenae and Tiryns would still have posed their problem, and this would have seemed the least unlikely answer to it; but the Catalogue did survive, and this is precisely the answer which it gives.

There are still those who find a conflict between the alleged political and the actual geographical conditions: politically Mycenae belongs to Agamemnon; geographically it belongs to the Argive plain, the realm of Diomedes. So Thomas Allen wrote Mycenae off as a mere summer palace; and Leaf took the Argive plain away from Diomedes and gave it back to Agamemnon. The true explanation is surely simple enough: precedent and prestige are sufficient reasons for Agamemnon's occupation of this particular fortress. Mycenae had been the home of great kings for hundreds of years; and I suppose that it was the grandest building in the whole of Achaean Greece.[40] The overlord had ruled in Mycenae from time already immemorial. We do not know why that site was chosen, or what were the personal dominions of the earlier kings: but we do know that in the later 13th century it was still occupied by the overlord of the Achaeans, Agamemnon; and the Catalogue tells us that at that time the great king's personal dominions extended over a large and important area to the north and northwest. If the position of Mycenae enables him on the one hand to supervise the Argive plain and the numerous fortresses in that neighbourhood, and on the other to control the roads leading north, nobody will say that it was ill-chosen. The Catalogue's division of territory between Agamemnon and Diomedes creates no problem: on the contrary, it solves one—it gives a reasonable explanation, which even without its help we should have guessed to be the likeliest explanation, of the problem posed by the two great fortresses in the Argive plain.

We have vindicated the Catalogue: but it is right that we should look, and shudder, at the doom which impended if we had failed. We should have been compelled to believe in the Catalogue of Walter Leaf, composed in the Ionian period by a poet of the utmost eccentricity. That poet must have been familiar, at that time, with the main streams of tradition which flow into the Iliad; but he is possessed with a mania for contradiction. What shall he do with the great Achilles? Confine him to an insignificant parish, incapable of supplying so many ships as the obscure Arcadians. How shall he treat the overlord, Agamemnon? Take away all his Argos, take away his many islands, and give them to Diomedes. How can he humble the celebrated Odysseus? Reduce him to a third-rate power even in his own remote and foggy district, let him bend the knee to a bogus Meges. Who shall have pride of place in the armies arrayed before Troy? The Boeotians, of whom the Iliad knows nothing but their insignificance. To use moderate language: it is very unlikely that the Epic tradition in Ionia could have created, or would have tolerated, such aberrant innovations. The picture drawn by the Catalogue may very well be early and true: as a late fiction, created in contradiction of the Iliad, it would be so absurd as to be inconceivable. And what should we think of the poets who went out of their way to incorporate this ultramodern, iconoclastic, and irresponsible fiction into their Iliad, and to preserve it therein for evermore with all its imperfections on its head?

I touch briefly on one other discrepancy between the Catalogue and the Iliad. The Iliad contains a few little catalogues within itself: and the distinctive feature common to these is their disagreement with the great Catalogue in the Second Book.

I 149 ff.—Agamemnon offers amends to Achilles, including the splendid gift of seven towns in the western Peloponnese. Now look at the seven place names, and try to find them in the great Catalogue: not one of them is there. Agamemnon's offer discloses to us an entirely unfamiliar district, something of which no mention whatever was made in the great Catalogue.[41] And, as if disregard were not enough, contradiction is added: for it is obvious that the Catalogue's division of the Peloponnese deprives Agamemnon of the power to dispose at will of places in the southwest.[42]

N 685 ff.—This is a trifle in comparison with the insolence of the little catalogue in the Thirteenth Book. Here are *Ionians*, trailing their tunics, for the first and last time in the Greek Epic. Here are *Phthians*, of whom nothing has been or will again be heard. Here is a most uncomfortable verse (691) introducing three new Athenian commanders, Pheidas, Bias, and Stichios, all persons of the utmost obscurity. Here is Meges, formerly sole ruler of a powerful island state, now sharing with two nonentities the command of a different people. Here is Medon, whom we left in the great Catalogue succeeding to the command of Philoctetes: now he has moved his command to the Phthians, and his home to the kingdom of Protesilaus. In brief, this poet either knows nothing of the great Catalogue, or has thought fit to treat it with the utmost disdain.[43]

It remains only to add, what we are now well prepared for, the proof that the great Catalogues sit very loosely in the framework of the Iliad. Some poems achieve catalogues, this one has a catalogue thrust upon it.[44]

At the head of the Catalogue stands an invocation to the Muses,[45] preceded by a simile describing how the Greek army first rushes out of the ships and tents onto the plain (464 ff.), and then is marshalled into order by its commanders (476 ff.). This is a very good introduction to the Catalogue: but unfortunately the whole of it has already been anticipated in the immediately preceding passage (444–458). Listen to the sequence of events: the army assembles (444 ἠγείροντο); the commanders marshal it into order (445 f. βασιλῆες θῦνον κρίνοντες); Athene urges it to go to battle (446 f. Ἀθήνη ὀτρύνουσ' ἰέναι); and it actually goes to battle (457 ὡς τῶν ἐρχομένων). And now the whole procedure is repeated: having started out in good order towards the enemy (457), the Greeks again rush from ships and tents into the plain (464 f. νεῶν ἄπο καὶ κλισιάων ἐς πεδίον προχέοντο), are again marshalled into order (476 ἡγεμόνες διεκόσμεον), and again prepare to go to battle (477 ὑσμίνηνδ' ἰέναι). Nothing could be more obvious than that these two lengthy passages are alternatives:[46] they were never intended for continuous recitation. The Catalogue was an independent composition; when it was incorporated into the Iliad, it was necessary to add something at the beginning to connect it with the narrative of the Iliad. At least two[47] such connecting passages stand side by side in our standard text; a clear proof that the present form of our text owes something to *editorial* arrangement.[48]

It is now established that the Catalogue is substantially an inheritance from the Mycenaean era; that it has survived independently of that version of the story which culminates in the Iliad; and that it has been rather carelessly inserted into the Iliad after the composition of the Iliad in something like its present form. It remains to inquire, *What is the Catalogue?* For what purpose was it originally composed?

Let us begin with the observation that the Catalogue is not simply a list of places and persons: *it is a list of participants in a military campaign.* This theme, the assembly for battle, is an integral part of its pattern; in this respect, matter and form are inseparably united. The Catalogue does not say that "in Diomedes' kingdom were certain places, Argos, Tiryns, Asine, and the rest": it says, "Those men who dwelt in Argos and the rest were being commanded by Diomedes; of the Locrians who dwelt in such and such places, Ajax was the leader." Let this be recognized and frankly admitted. Many scholars have spoken as though the Catalogue were a sort of topographical survey, whether Domesday Book or Baedeker's Guide, reconstructed and adapted to the requirements of an Epic about the Trojan War.[49] But they overlook, as a rule, two points:

i) The Catalogue shows not the slightest internal trace of ever having been anything but what it is, an Order of Battle. The expedition to war is integral to the form as well as to the matter; the peoples and their commanders, not the places, are the subjects of the sentences and the movers in the action. The notion that Baedeker or Domesday Book has been converted to suit the requirements of the Trojan War is an idle speculation, destitute of all factual support; it is an arrow shot in the dark.

ii) And the one target which the arrow will certainly miss is the one it was aimed at. For the only old Epic about the Trojan War about which anything was ever known is the one which culminated in the Iliad: and we have already seen proof enough that one of the most distinctive features of the Catalogue is its ignorance of, or indifference to, some of the most elementary requirements of the Iliad. It is proper to ask the holder of the 'adaptation theory' one or two pungent questions. First, is there any internal or other factual evidence or indication that the Catalogue, as a whole, ever existed in any form but that of an Order of Battle? No answer. Secondly, if the Catalogue were an adaptation of something different to suit the requirements of the Trojan War, how has it come to pass that it does not suit the requirements of that story of the Trojan War which culminated in the Iliad? What can you tell us about the version to which it was, on your theory, adapted?—a version in which the Boeotians were very prominent; in which Agamemnon was excluded from Argos and the islands; in which the kingdoms of Achilles and Odysseus were reduced to insignificant parishes; in which many places and persons unknown to the Iliad were specially distinguished? Profound and prolonged silence; which let us not disturb, unless it be to ask, "Since neither the nature of our Catalogue nor its relation to the Iliad is explained by your theory, what is the use of that theory?"

Now although the Catalogue was composed without special reference to the Iliad, yet it has much in common with the Iliad. The principal heroes are the same in both, and have the same formular epithets. And the mutual independence of the two makes it all the more significant that the majority of the obscurer persons mentioned in the Catalogue reappear in the Iliad, though nine of them do not. And not only do they reappear: they retain the same characters as they have in the Catalogue. Consider for example the shadowy Boeotians, Peneleos and Leitos. They are mentioned very seldom in the Iliad,— Peneleos four times, Leitos thrice; but in two of the three places where Leitos reappears, he is in the company of his brother officer, and it is remembered that they are Boeotians. Among the Boeotian commanders are two still dimmer persons, Clonios and Arcesilaos: they reappear once only in the Iliad— and they reappear *together*.[50] Nobody could be much more insignificant than Ialmenos, one of the two leaders of Aspledon and Orchomenos: but when he makes his single reappearance in the Iliad it is not forgotten that he must be coupled with his fellow chieftain Ascalaphos,[51] as he was in the Catalogue. In the Catalogue, the name of Diomedes is coupled with that of Sthenelos: in the Iliad, Sthenelos is never mentioned except in the same combination. These and other examples prove that the Iliad knows, as well as the Catalogue, who goes with whom: it handles its long list of obscure persons—114 are named on the Achaean side—with astonishing consistency and clarity.[52] The only reasonable explanation of the fact that the Catalogue and the Iliad diverge[53] so far as they do and coincide so far as they do is that both have ultimately a common origin in poetry about the Trojan War. The Iliad is the final product of a continuous development over a very long period of time, whereas the Catalogue, being essentially nothing but a list of names, has naturally changed comparatively little throughout that same period. It is reasonable to expect, as we actually find, many harmonies and many discords between the two.

We cannot much longer postpone the question, was the Catalogue originally connected with the Trojan War or not? We have already observed, first, that the Greece which it describes is the Greece which existed within a century, more or less, of the historical destruction of Troy VII[a]; secondly, that it is in structure as well as in contents an Order of Battle, and shows no sign of ever having been anything else. It is a list of contingents assembling for an expedition overseas; and it is so close in time to the historical event with which it is connected that it seems improbable—to me, inconceivable—that that connexion should be fictitious. Now let us hear one more witness— the Catalogue of Trojans.

Is the Catalogue of Trojans also substantially of Mycenaean origin? If it is, then the answer to our question is given with a very high degree of probability. A catalogue of Greek towns and kingdoms might theoretically serve a variety of purposes (though in fact the Homeric catalogue serves only one): but who can conceive the Mycenaean Greeks making a versified list of peoples and places in Asia Minor for any purpose except one connected with an expedition into that area? I do not say that there is no remotely conceivable alternative: there is almost always some loop-hole for escape from the clutches of common sense. But it is obvious that the poets could not have known what they do know unless the Greeks then or earlier had visited Asia Minor; and it is not easy to think why they should make a versified list of Trojans and their allies except in connexion with a war. You may well judge that the making of such a list would have been an improbable conception and an impossible achievement in any other circumstances.[54] So everything depends on the answer to this question: whether the Trojan Catalogue, like the Greek one, is of Mycenaean origin. If it is, we may regard it as proof positive of a war of Greeks against Trojans in the Mycenaean period. Let us inquire of the Trojan Catalogue what its date may be.

We begin with a general observation. The contrast between the Greek and the Trojan Catalogue is very sharp.[55] The one is opulent and plump, the other has a lean and hungry look. The one has 265 lines, and is full of information; the other has only 61, and gives little away. Those who believe that the Catalogues were composed by Ionian poets in Asia Minor after the Dorian occupation of Hellas are deeply embarrassed by this in-

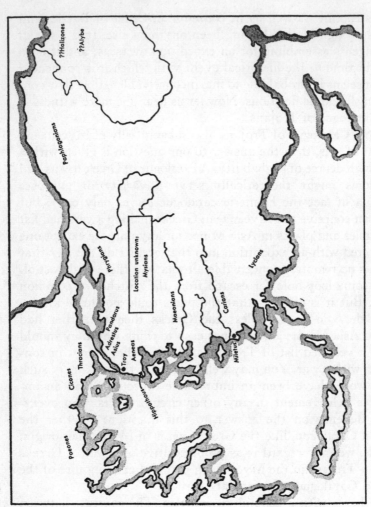

Troy and Its Allies according to the Homeric Catalogue

convenient observation. The Ionians lived on the west coast of Asia Minor, and might be expected to know much about it; they might be pardoned if they knew little about the detail of Thessaly, Boeotia, Phocis, Locris, and Arcadia. But in fact their knowledge of the latter is profound, of the former very slight. We have learnt that their acquaintance with mainland geography was derived from the Mycenaean Epic: but how are we to account for their lamentable ignorance of the area adjacent to their own homes? It is obviously probable that in this matter also they are reporting not what they know from personal experience but what was handed down to them from the past when very much less was known. To an Ionian living in (say) Miletus in the 8th century B.C. the Catalogue of Trojans must have seemed an extraordinarily jejune and reticent composition, already a museum piece. Not a word about Bosporus or Black Sea;[56] not a mention of Smyrna or of any island or coastal place south of the Troad—except that the chief Ionian city, Miletus, is selected for celebration as the home of Carian barbarophones on the enemy side. In the region around the Troad, not a word about Ionian colonies, or such well-known peoples as the Bithynians and Mariandynians, already familiar to the most parochial of Boeotians.[57] Nor was anything ever added by local pride or patriotism: such was the historical sense of the Ionian poets, and such their self-denial, that they made up this list of Asiatic peoples and places without allowing the slightest intrusion of any matter of interest to themselves: "The claims and vanity of no one are served by it. The colonists among whom it was sung first are not allowed the slightest prophecy or indication of their future existence; the *nostos* of no hero affects it."[58] For this reason alone, even if there were no other, it would be hard to reconcile the facts given in the Trojan Catalogue with a theory of its origin in Ionia during or after the Dark Ages.

But this is not all. We observe further that the Trojan Catalogue, like the Greek, was not originally designed to suit the requirements of the story as told in the Iliad. The Iliad needs

many Trojan names, mainly for cannon fodder; indeed, the
number of Trojans named is nearly twice the number of Greeks,
—114 Greeks, but 216 Trojans, of whom no fewer than 180 bite
the dust; and the need for names is so pressing that so many as
twenty names are used twice. But still the Catalogue is not
pressed into service: of its 26 Trojans, 8 make no reappearance,
and only 5 play any noticeable part in the Iliad,—Hector,
Aeneas, Sarpedon, Pandaros, and Asios. There is no mention
of Priam or Paris or Polydamas or Helenos or Deiphobos. Moreover, scanty as the Trojan Catalogue's information is, it is contradicted time and again by the Iliad: B 858, Chromis and
Ennomos command the Mysians; Ξ 511 ff., they are commanded by Gyrtios. B 858, the Mysians are a tribe in Asia
Minor; N 5, they live in Thrace. B 827, the bow of Pandaros was
given to him by Apollo; Δ 105 ff., it was made by a craftsman
from the horns of a goat which Pandaros had killed. B 830 f.,
Amphios is son of Merops; E 612, he is son of Selagos. B 846,
Euphemos is commander of the Cicones; P 73, the Cicones are
commanded by Mentes. B 848, Pyraechmes leads the Paeonians; P 348, the Paeonians are led by Apisaon. B 860, 874 f.,
Ennomos and Amphimachus were killed by Achilles in the
battle at the river; but when we come to that battle in the
Twenty-first Book, there is no mention of Ennomos and Amphimachus. In brief: the greater part of the scanty information
given by the Trojan Catalogue is either flatly ignored or briskly
contradicted by the Iliad.[59] Nobody who had in mind the Iliad,
or the material of which the Iliad is composed, could possibly
have concocted a catalogue so laconic and recalcitrant. Con-
versely, nobody who had this catalogue in mind could have
treated it with such disdain during the composition of the Iliad.

Still we have not positively proved that the Trojan Catalogue
is of Mycenaean origin: is there any means of doing this? Walter
Leaf, who knew more about the Trojan Catalogue than anybody before or since, maintained that "the Trojan Catalogue
. . . seems to represent accurately a state of things which must
have existed at the time of the Trojan War, and could not have

existed after it, nor for long before. . . . It would seem to follow
that there existed from the first some sort of a metrical narrative of the war, of which the Trojan Catalogue at least has survived in something like its original form."[60] He stresses also the
fact that the Iliad gives a great deal of information about the
Troad, and yet makes few if any mistakes—"this negative consideration seems to me of the greatest weight, and to attest not
so much the autopsy of a particular poet as the reality of the
material on which he is working." Thomas Allen agrees: "This
list appears to represent the knowledge of Asia and North
Europe current in Greece before the Ionic migration."[61] Very
well: but what is the proof of it? What should we accept as
proof? In the case of the Greek Catalogue the argument was at
least clear, whatever may be thought of its cogency: the places
named are all, so far as we know or may conjecture, Mycenaean sites; many of them were unoccupied and unidentifiable
in historical times; a few of them are known to have been unoccupied since the end of the Mycenaean era. These are very
strong reasons for believing that such a list of places must have
been made in the Mycenaean era; that nobody during or after
the Dark Ages could have drawn *de novo* a picture of Mycenaean
Greece so true to life. But the Trojan Catalogue is not so helpful: instead of 164 places it offers only a dozen,—the rest are
names of tribes, mountains, rivers. It seems unlikely that the
proof which we need is to be found in a record so slight and
superficial. And yet I believe that the evidence exists, and is
sufficient. What we need is the mention of names which were
not in use after the end of the Mycenaean era, and which could
not have been known to the Ionian poets except by way of a
continuous oral tradition from that era. There are at least
three[62] separate signposts pointing to our destination; I believe
that they are reliable guides.

First, the birthplace of silver, called *Alybe*. It is generally
agreed that the position of Alybe in the Catalogue assigns it to
the remote regions across the river Halys, where silver is indeed
abundant. Now let us concede that the Eastern Greeks may

have become familiar with this region, and may have known
that it was the source of silver, in the 8th century or even a
little earlier: but if we suppose that the entry in the Catalogue
was made at that time, how can we explain the fact that nobody
at any *later* time ever knew what place was meant by Alybe?
From the 8th century onwards geographical knowledge of this
area expanded rapidly and widely: the Ionians ventured farther
and farther afield, founded colonies, opened routes for commerce. It was no longer possible to *forget* places: if Alybe, the
birthplace of silver, was familiar to Ionians in the 8th century
(or even the 9th), it cannot have been forgotten by them in the
7th and 6th centuries;[63] on the contrary, it will have become
very much better known. Yet in the late 6th century Hecataeus
of Miletus, the first great geographer, could find no trace or
record of the whereabouts of Alybe: he is the first of a long line
of inquirers who make guesses about Alybe or alter it into
something else.[64] This was a notorious puzzle in the text of
Homer: nobody ever again knew a place called Alybe. Not even
Demetrius of Scepsis, who lived in the Troad early in the 2nd
century B.C. and spent many years composing a work in thirty
books on the 61 lines of the Trojan Catalogue,—not even
Demetrius could find a trace of Alybe. But that is proof positive of the sort we were looking for: this entry in the Catalogue
is older than the Ionian migration to Asia Minor; the silver
mines of Alybe are merely a name to the Ionians,—a name
handed down from the Mycenaean past.

Alybe is not the only example of the kind. Nastes commanded the Carians, whose home was Miletus, *and the mountain
Phthires*, and the river Maeander, and the heights of Mycale.
Now everybody knew Mycale and the Maeander: but what is
meant by "the mountain Phthires"? Evidently a further landmark; and it seems clear enough what it must be. Hecataeus,
himself a native of Miletus, naturally supposed it must be the
most obvious landmark, the celebrated mountain range of
Latmus. But how could he have to do any *supposing* at all? "He
thought Latmus was the same as Homer's Phthires," Strabo

records; and others thought differently.[65] But how could there be any question about it? If this great range of mountains, the landmark of Miletus, bore the name Phthires in the 8th century, how could that name have been forgotten in the 7th or 6th centuries?—*forgotten by the natives of the place?* Mountain ranges which are local landmarks do not lose their names, at least locally. If this was the proper name of that mountain (or of any other local mountain) after the Ionian occupation of Miletus, it is inconceivable that nobody should have had any idea that it was so called after a few generations had elapsed,—that not even the authority of "Homer" was sufficient to preserve it in use, or even in memory, in the great city above which it towered. This mountain, with its unique epithet, ἀκριτόφυλλον, tells the same tale as Alybe: it tells of a time earlier than the Ionian occupation of the eastern Aegean; it preserves a name which was never known to the Ionians except through the Trojan Catalogue.

The same lesson is to be learnt from a pair of places not in the Catalogue but in the Iliad. The Catalogue, it is very noticeable, has nothing to say about the south coast of the Troad:[66] but the Iliad preserves the memory of two raids by Achilles into that area. First, he captured Thebe, the town of Eetion, father of Andromache, in the land of the Cilices, a people unknown to the Catalogue. At the same time he sacked *Lyrnessus*, and took Briseis captive. Secondly, he chased Aeneas down from Mount Ida and destroyed *Lyrnessus and Pedasus.* Where are these two places?[67] There is not, I think, any dispute about the site of Pedasus. It is described in the Iliad as being "steep" and "on the banks of the river Satnioeis"; it is the place known to the later world as Assos, the most important of all settlements ever made on the banks of this river, and the only one in the whole of its brief course to which the epithet "steep" could be applied.[68] As for Lyrnessus, an obscurity in the text of Strabo hides the truth from us: it is probably the other chief settlement on this coast, Antandros; but the identification cannot be proved. Now let us ask the explanation of this fact: the Iliad knows of two places in this region, Lyrnessus and Pedasus; but it does not know the only two names of any importance in the same region in historical times, Assos and Antandros. An Ionian poet who wished to introduce prominent place names into his work from this narrow strip of coast has no choice but to take Assos and Antandros; no other name is worth mentioning or generally known. But the Greek Epic, his own Epic, chose Pedasus and Lyrnessus, of which nobody ever knew anything at all from the earliest historical period onwards.[69] The answer is the same as before: these names were never known to the Ionians except through the Iliad; if they had existed in the 9th and 8th centuries, they could not have been forgotten again, and they would not have been changed again. Pedasus and Lyrnessus, like Alybe and Mount Phthires, have been inherited from the Mycenaean past, and have survived through the continuous tradition of oral poetry.

It is now established that the Trojan Catalogue includes heirlooms from the Mycenaean past;[70] and I stress the observation that these are in perfect harmony with their surroundings. The Trojan Catalogue as a whole is so uninformative[71] and old-fashioned that we should be very unwilling to ascribe its making to the Ionian settlers in Asia Minor. We should find it impossible to explain why a Trojan Catalogue, composed in connexion with the Ionian Iliad, ignores the Iliad and is ignored by it; and why no part of it takes any notice of the Ionians or of anything which might interest them. Some parts of it are certainly of Mycenaean origin, and all may be: that is as far as we can go; and it is far enough, for it tells us what we wanted to know,— whether the Greek Catalogue was originally connected with the expedition to Troy. The Mycenaeans must have had a special motive for composing a catalogue in verse of places in the far northeast; and it is hard to conceive any motive but one connected with, or even directly inspired by, an expedition to that area. If so, there is no longer any reason to doubt that the Mycenaean catalogue of Greeks was originally connected with the same event; and we must constantly bear in mind that the catalogue of Greeks is in fact an Order of Battle, and so far as we can tell has never been anything else.

Before I turn to the question, how far the Catalogues have been altered in the course of their long lives, I draw attention to one more Mycenaean element common to the Catalogue and the Iliad: the person of the Athenian commander, *Menestheus the son of Peteos*.

Athenians in the Iliad have long been under a cloud. They hardly dare lift their heads but somebody brands them bogus and interpolated. The facts are at once less lurid and more interesting. The city or fortress of Athens,[72] named in the Catalogue, never reappears in the Iliad. Athenians, under that name, are mentioned in only four places, of which two are unfavourable to their reputation as fighters.[73] Individual Athenians, specifically named, play an insignificant part: *Iasos* does nothing whatever except die;[74] *Stichios* is barely mentioned twice, and the third time bites the dust;[75] *Pheidas* and *Bias* share half a line between them.[76] That is the grand total of Athenian activity in the Iliad,—except what is said of the leader, Menestheus; and that is little enough. In Δ 327 ff. he and Odysseus are reproached by Agamemnon for slackness; Odysseus defends himself, Menestheus does not. In M 331 ff. he is frightened and sends for help. In N 195 he carries away the corpse of a comrade-in-arms,—but not until Ajax has driven Hector away from it. In O 331 he loses a comrade, Stichios, killed by Hector. In N 687 ff. he is assisted by Boeotians, Locrians, and Epeians in repelling Hector. A dismal record, which could have been improved by adding his name to more glorious exploits here and there; one can only admire the self-restraint of the Athenian editors of the Iliad.

The plain fact is that the Iliad inherited no knowledge whatsoever about the Athenians except the name of their commander; and that had been preserved from time immemorial in half a line, υἱὸς Πετεῶο Μενεσθεύς. And there are two reasons why Menestheus the son of Peteos cannot possibly have been first introduced to the Iliad by Ionian poets at any date. First (negatively) *because nobody in historical times ever knew anything about him except the name*. He is not mentioned in the Odyssey, or by any lyrical or elegiac or early iambic poet, or by any tragedian or comedian, or by Herodotus or by Thucydides, or by any Alexandrian poet, or—except in one place—by any Attic orator. He and his father are mere names: not one single fact apart from those names survived in history, and it is very doubtful whether one single fact survived even in legend.[77] Second (positively) because, if it had been necessary to invent a leader for the Athenians, the power of legend, both local and international, would have enforced the introduction of the family of *Theseus*. Later poetry was not so conservative as the Iliad: in the *Iliou Persis* the sons of Theseus are present at Troy; that example is followed by Greek Tragedy in general, and Euripides puts a son of Theseus in command of the Athenian army. Only the Iliad holds aloof: the name of Theseus, greatest of all persons in Athenian legend, was not so much as mentioned.[78]

The historical Athenians and others had the utmost difficulty in fitting Menestheus into the pattern of Greek legend. The king of Athens at the Trojan War ought to be one of the most famous of all heroes: unfortunately he was one of the obscurest, a nonentity and something of a ninny. His subsequent fate in Athenian hands is a tale of torture: he is stretched on the rack of hypothesis, elongated until he touches Theseus in a much earlier generation than his own; and a synthetic potion of theory is brewed to a thin consistency, palatable to the omnivorous.

Menestheus the son of Peteos repeats the lesson of Alybe and Phthires and Pedasus: he is preserved in the Iliad because he is part of the inheritance; the Ionian poets know nothing whatever about him, and there is no means by which they could have known his name and his father's name except by way of the continuous tradition from the Mycenaean period. He cannot have gladdened their hearts, but they could not expel him; what they received they must pass on, whether it be an unintelligible phrase like πτολέμοιο γεφυραί or a forgotten landmark like Mount Phthires, or the name of an inscrutable nonentity like Menestheus the son of Peteos.[79]

Let us now consider the question, how far the Catalogues have been preserved intact from the Mycenaean era into the Iliad. Are they, in their present form, substantially or even wholly Mycenaean compositions? There is a general probability that many or even most of the place names, especially those combined with descriptive epithets, have remained unaltered[80] through the Dark Ages. But there is also a general probability that whatever else was susceptible of change has suffered change in the course of centuries of oral transmission; and it soon becomes apparent, from evidence both external and internal, that additions were made to both Catalogues in the Ionian period and even later.

In the Trojan Catalogue the list of places on or near the Black Sea coast (853–855) was not in the text of the Iliad recognized by the great Alexandrian scholar Eratosthenes, or in the text used by Apollodorus, who wrote a large book *On the Catalogue of Ships*; evidently the lines were added in the 2nd or 1st century B.C. Already in the late 4th century two additional lines had been added at the same point by Callisthenes; and these were accepted by Apollodorus as part of the tradition.[81] In the Greek Catalogue the entry for the great Ajax is presumably not of Mycenaean origin: Ajax belongs to a generation much earlier than that of Agamemnon; he cannot have been included in a Mycenaean list of commanders in the Trojan War; and it is significant that he alone[82] of the Iliad's great heroes has no place of his own in the Catalogue,—somebody at some time inserted him apologetically with a single lonely line to his credit, and much later a second line was added by somebody else. Another apparent anachronism is the entry which, as it stands,[83] describes Tlepolemos as the first Achaean colonist in Rhodes, and the founder of the Achaean settlements at Lindos, Cameiros, and Ialysos. It must have been common knowledge in Greece in the 12th century B.C. that Rhodes had already been a powerful Achaean community for several generations; and nobody at that time would have included the first colonist of Rhodes in Agamemnon's army. This entry presumably bears more than a casual relation to the only episode in the Iliad (E 627–698) in which Tlepolemos reappears: there he is killed by Sarpedon, king of the Lycians on the mainland opposite Rhodes. In Gilbert Murray's words, "one can guess what may have happened. A local legend of battle between the Rhodian and the Lycian has been torn up from its natural context and inserted into the midst of the fighting about Troy";[84] and, in the words of Martin Nilsson, "There is no apparent reason for supposing that Tlepolemos represents the Dorian Colonists of Rhodes who made attacks on Lycia. He may as well belong to Mycenaean times in which the Greeks made repeated attacks on the southern coast of Asia Minor."[85] It is possible that the entry in the Catalogue was not made until after the Catalogue had been incorporated into the Iliad: but, if so, it nevertheless represents a very old tradition. Many scholars, misled by the appellation "son of Heracles" and by the threefold division of the Rhodians, διὰ τρίχα κοσμηθέντες, have jumped to the conclusion that the Dorian state of Rhodes, and the Dorian division into three tribes, are here described. Nothing of the sort is true. The descendants of Heracles who "returned" with the Dorians belong to a much later generation; Tlepolemos is son of that Heracles, well known to the Iliad, who lived a long time before the Trojan War. And the threefold division refers, in its context, to nothing but the three great cities founded on the island by the Mycenaeans,—Lindos, Cameiros, and Ialysos.[86] We are therefore at once deprived of the right, and relieved of the burden, of maintaining that an addition made to the Catalogue in the Dorian interest could muster no more than a mere 9 ships— against 60 from Arcadia and 40 from the unspeakable Argissans in the heart of Thessaly; and that the one passage introduced into the Iliad in the Dorian interest described not the glory of the Dorian hero but his defeat and death at the hand of his bitterest foe. As Thomas Allen said, "The story in the Iliad is not what the powerful state of Rhodes would have invented as a heroic past. The few ships and the death of the oecist appear to represent fact."[87] It is indeed probable—one can put it no higher—that the story of Tlepolemos in the Iliad had its origin in the fighting between Ahhijawā and the fringes of Hittite Asia Minor in the 13th century B.C.

There is nothing intrinsically improbable in the Catalogue's account of the coming of Tlepolemos to Rhodes: the family quarrel, ending in bloodshed, the flight of the killer to a far land, accompanied by his adherents; the founding of a prosperous community overseas,—nothing is here for incredulity. It may be just a yarn; or it may be true. The one thing certain is that the Catalogue's account abbreviates a fairly long and well-known story which survived independently[88] of the Iliad; and I do not know why anyone should suppose—or how anyone could make it seem probable—that the story was first invented during or after the Dark Ages.

The two persons who gave the Ionians most trouble were Philoctetes[89] and Protesilaus. They had been in command at the time of the gathering of the clans described in the Catalogue: but the one had been dead for ten years when the Iliad begins, and the other had never come to Troy at all. It was necessary to add in each context a brief explanation, and to incorporate the names of their successors in command: 699–709, 719–728. Another passage designed to adapt a first-year Order of Battle to a tenth-year Iliad was added to the entry concerning Achilles. The Catalogue says that he was the commander: but in the Iliad he and his men are withdrawn from the war; they have no place whatever in a list of troops arrayed for fighting today. Therefore the story of his wrath and withdrawal from the fighting is briefly inserted in verses which the first of the great Alexandrian editors of the Iliad knew to be uncanonical.[90]

Other additions were made here and there, all designed to give a little more information about persons and places named in the Catalogue. The ancient Homeric scholars assure us that a number of these insertions had no right to a place in the true text: 528–530, the lines added to distinguish the smaller Ajax from the greater; 553–555, something to provide Menestheus the son of Peteos with what he sorely needs, a personality; 558, the notorious Athenian interpolation;[91] 579–580, for the greater glory of Agamemnon; 612–614, a particularly interesting insertion: the Arcadia known to the Ionians was an inland district, having no access to the sea, yet the Catalogue says that it provided 60 ships; let us add three lines to point out that Arcadians are not seafaring folk, and that their ships must have been borrowed from Agamemnon; 641–642, a note to explain why the commanders from Aetolia are not of the dynasty of Oeneus; 673–675, welcome information about Nireus, whom we shall never meet again. Modern scholarship has detected two or three further examples: 547–551, probably an expansion of the entry about Athens;[92] 658–667, the exceptionally interesting history of the Achaean settlement in Rhodes; 594–600, the story about Thamyris; and perhaps a few other passages (513–515; 831–834; 871–873). It appears that the text of the Catalogue recognized by the Alexandrian editors of the Iliad as being canonical included nearly all of the persons and places, but excluded much of the explanatory comment. The Ionians inherited a Mycenaean Catalogue, to which they made a considerable number of additions designed either to adapt a first-year Catalogue to a tenth-year Iliad or simply to give information about places and persons named in the Catalogue.

I say that the Catalogue included *nearly all the persons*, because names of commanders are indispensable in an Order of Battle constructed in the manner of the Catalogue. If this Order of Battle is, as we have seen reason to believe, of Mycenaean origin, so presumably are the names of the commanders. Even if the Catalogue was not originally an Order of Battle, it is unlikely that there was ever a Catalogue which described the kingdoms without naming the kings; or that the kings named in it were other than those upon whose names the Iliad and the Catalogue agree.

The point is of great importance, for names and epithets are inseparably combined in the traditional formular vocabulary; and if the names were in the Mycenaean Catalogue, so must their epithets have been. This will afford a proof of what we had already learnt to expect,—that the traditional formular phrases for the great heroes were already stereotyped in the Mycenaean Epic. For the significant fact is that the Iliad and the Catalogue, in other respects so discordant, agree absolutely in their noun + epithet formulas. In both sources Agamemnon is κρείων Ἀγαμέμνων, Menelaus is βοὴν ἀγαθὸς Μενέλαος, the smaller Ajax is Ὀιλήιος ταχὺς Αἴας, Diomedes is βοὴν ἀγαθὸς Διομήδης, Nestor is γερήνιος ἱππότα Νέστωρ, Idomeneus is Ἰδομενεὺς δουρίκλυτος, Meriones is ἀτάλαντος Ἐνυαλίωι ἀνδρειφόντηι, Menestheus is υἱὸς Πετεῶο Μενεσθεύς, Eurypylus is Εὐρύπυλος Εὐαίμονος ἀγλαὸς υἱός, Hector is μέγας κορυθαίολος Ἕκτωρ; and there are numerous other old formular phrases common to both, for example Ϝισόθεος φώς, Διὶ μῆτιν ἀτάλαντος, δῖα γυναικῶν, τόξων ἐὺ Ϝειδώς, ὄζος Ἄρηος, ἐγχεσιμώρων. The fact is, I repeat, significant: but it is the reverse of surprising. The Mycenaean Epic must have been orally composed, and must therefore have relied upon a formular vocabulary. It must have had noun + epithet formulas for its heroes, and nothing could be more in accordance with the nature of oral poetry than the preservation of such formulas intact over a very long period of time.

Finally there is one piece of information given in the Catalogue which is of special interest,—*the numbers of ships provided by each kingdom*. The places are real; most of the persons are real; but are the numbers of ships fact or fiction?

If they were fact, we should have no means of proving it. In order to establish the reliability of the numbers it would be necessary to prove, first, that they were already in the Catalogue in its Mycenaean phase; and, secondly, that the Mycenaean Catalogue was a reliable source of information more or less contemporary with the event which it describes. Moreover it would be necessary to assume, first, that there was no exaggeration of the truth when the Catalogue was composed; and, secondly, that the numbers have survived unchanged throughout the centuries of oral transmission. These are proofs which we cannot supply, and assumptions which we ought not to make. In particular, it is prudent to allow that a considerable period of time may have elapsed between the Trojan War and the making of the Catalogue: for it is unlikely that an Order of Battle composed at the time of the gathering of the clans, or very soon afterwards, would have distorted the facts so far as to assign the largest and most prominent place to Boeotia and her obscure neighbours. Now, according to Thucydides (I 12), the Boeotians were formerly at home in Thessaly, and later settled in the land "Cadmeis," which is now "Boeotia," in the sixtieth year after the fall of Troy. Evidently this was a commonplace of tradition, accepted by Thucydides; we do not know whether it is true, but we do know that it is consistent with our opinion concerning the Catalogue. For the Catalogue represents Boeotia as it existed *after the migration from Thessaly*,—therefore, according to Thucydides, *at least sixty years after the fall of Troy*. If that period of time has intervened, the picture may well have been distorted, and the immigrants may well have exaggerated the importance of their newly acquired territory. Nevertheless we must remember that the interval is too brief to allow us to regard as fictitious the expedition with which the Catalogue is connected.

I take it as certain that the Catalogue was originally *composed in Boeotia*:[93] not only because of the prominence of Boeotia in the list, but also because Boeotia was the native home of poetry of this type throughout the Dark Ages. This fact is plainly attested by the remnant of a Boeotian catalogue in the Eleventh Book of the Odyssey, and by the catalogues which passed under the name of Hesiod.

We have no reason to believe in the numbers of ships; and the figures themselves discourage all but the sturdiest faith. For example, the figures for Thessalian districts (some of them apparently not maritime) are much too high; the total of 1,186 ships is logistically absurd for a landing in the Troad; and the numbers are to some degree at the mercy of the metre. It is noticeable that the Catalogue includes all multiples of ten up to a hundred, except the only one (seventy, ἑβδομήκοντα) which cannot be fitted into the verse. But can we at least answer the question whether the numbers of ships, reckless exaggerations as they presumably are, existed already in the Mycenaean Catalogue?

In 19 out of 29 places the entries giving numbers of ships can be omitted without leaving any trace; but in the other 10 they cannot easily be disentangled from their contexts. The fact that in a third of the examples the numbers are bound up with the names of persons and places may seem a good reason for supposing that the numbers are as old as the names: but that inference loses its charm so soon as we take into account the language in which the entries are composed. The Mycenaean Greek for "ships" must have been *nāwes*, pronounced νῆες by the Ionians. In twenty places the form νῆες appears; but in the other nine we find the purely Ionian form νέες and in four of these nine it is followed by the verb ἐστιχόωντο,[94] a secondary formation, surely not of Mycenaean pedigree. Moreover one or two of the numbers themselves appear to argue in favour of Ionian composition: it is improbable that the contraction of ὀγδοϝάκοντα to ὀγδώκοντα could be earlier than the Ionian period;[95] and ἐνενήκοντα is surely not replaceable by any conceivable Mycenaean form. We are therefore compelled to admit that about a third of the ship entries are of purely Ionian composition. There is no means of deciding whether the other two thirds are likewise Ionian or inherited from the Mycenaean Epic: it may be thought unlikely that, if ship numbers had been inherited, the Ionians would have preserved two thirds intact and drastically recomposed the other third; unlikely too that the numbers would have been so greatly exaggerated within a generation or two of the Trojan War; but there is no certainty to be attained, and very little value in talk about "likely" and "unlikely."

The rest of the linguistic evidence is sufficiently in harmony with the conclusion that the Catalogues are substantially Mycenaean compositions, rather expanded than altered by the

Ionians. Identification of earlier and later elements in the language is seldom possible, for we do not know what conventions prevailed already in the Mycenaean Epic. Did it admit variety of form in the genitive singular of the second declension? Of augmented and unaugmented verb-forms?[96] τοῖς beside τοῖσι in the demonstrative pronoun? And so forth. Linguistic features of relatively late origin can be discerned here and there, more frequently in the comments[97] than in the lists:[98] but they are rarer than is usual in the Iliad; and are of no special significance, since the whole of the poem has been exposed to Ionian influences for so long a time.

In summary, I take it to be established:

a) that the Achaean and Trojan Catalogues are substantially inheritances from the later Mycenaean period, orally transmitted through the Dark Ages;

b) that both Catalogues are, and so far as we can tell have always been, Orders of Battle; and that their connexion with an overseas expedition must be historically true;

c) that they were preserved independently of the poetical tradition which culminated in the Iliad;

d) that the Iliad, which diverges widely from the lines drawn by the Catalogues, incorporated the Catalogues at a very late stage of its development;

e) that numerous minor additions and adjustments were made within the Catalogues at the time of, or after, their incorporation in the Iliad; but that the lists of persons and places were not much altered;

f) that the numbers of ships are certainly to some extent and may be wholly Ionian additions to the Catalogue.

Whether such "dangerous concessions to human reason"[99] will command universal and immediate assent, I doubt; but I do not wholly despair.

NOTES

[1] I select these as typical pronouncements by persons admirably qualified to judge from different points of view: Gomme, *Historical Commentary on Thucydides* i (1945) 119; Beazley, *CAH* IV (1926) 580; Lorimer, *JHS* 53 (1933) 168; Dunbabin, *The Greeks and Their Eastern Neighbours* (1957) 17; cf. Kraiker, *Antike* 15 (1939) 218.

The picture today is essentially the same as it has always been: see esp. Desborough, *Protogeometric Pottery* (1952) 296 ff., and, for recent statements from widely different quarters, Burton-Brown, *The Coming of Iron to Greece* (1955) 149 ff., 311 ff.; Bury-Meiggs, *History of Greece* (3rd ed., 1955) 57; Matz, *Kreta, Mykene, Troja* [*KMT*] (1956) 145; Lesky, *Gesch. d. Gr. Lit.* i (1957) 19; Finley, *Historia* 6 (1957) 133 ff.; Broneer, *Antiquity* 30 (1956) 15; Dunbabin, l.c.; Brock, *Fortetsa* (1957) 213 ff. Those who maintain that the decadent culture was continuous with the past (i.e., that there was no "archaeological break") must nevertheless admit that the decline in culture was rapid, widespread, comprehensive, and long-lasting. When we are told (as we have been recently) that "the Dorian migration brought about not a cultural but only a political change in Greece," we must not be misled by the phraseology: the new culture may have been continuous with the old, at least in a number of important sites, but the fact remains that the Dorian occupation was followed not only by the abandonment of numerous sites, and not only by a radical subversion of the political and social order, but also by a sudden steep fall in the level of culture, a precipitous descent into a valley of darkness, from which a long slow path led uphill to the moderate heights of Geometric civilization.

[2] Gilbert Murray's translation (*Rise of the Greek Epic* [*RGE*] 82) of Hesiod, *op.* 174 ff.

[3] See further Burr (op. cit. n. 5 below) 36 f., on the Catalogue's omission of the West Locrians; 56 ff., on Achaean and Dorian Lacedaemon; 106 ff., on Thessaly (with Allen, *Homeric Catalogue of Ships* 106 f., 138 ff.).

[4] T. W. Allen, *The Homeric Catalogue of Ships* [*HCS*] (1921), expanding his article in *JHS* 30 (1910), 292 ff.

[5] V. Burr, Νεῶν Κατάλογος: *Untersuchungen zum homerischen Schiffskatalog: Klio*, Beiheft IXL [=XLIX] (N.F., Heft 36), with 43 plates and 9 maps (Leipzig, 1944; the preface is dated 1942, and the author says that his work was virtually finished in 1939; there are references to works published up to 1942). There is an interest-

ing but in some respects eccentric review by A. Heubeck in *Gnomon* 21 (1949) 197 ff.

[6] I.e., 164, not counting *districts*, such as Buprasion, Elis, Arcadia, Phthia, Hellas, ὅσσον ἐφ᾽ Ὑρμίνη, οἱ περὶ Δωδώνην . . . , οἵ τ᾽ ἤπειρον ἔχον . . . , and the like.

[7] Burr himself states a conclusion much more favourable to my argument. He sums up (pp. 111 f.): 60 places archaeologically proved Mycenaean + 31 presumably Myc. by reason of name or connexion with Myc. legend. Considering how insignificant most of the places are, we should have to admit that this is an astonishingly high proportion of identifiably Mycenaean sites in the Catalogue: I personally think Burr's figures very reasonable; but the figures which I give in the text are those which even the most sceptical and reluctant critic would have to concede.

Further information about several places has become available since Burr wrote: see esp. Blegen in *Hesperia*, Suppl. VIII (1949) 39 ff., Hampe, *Die homerische Welt* (1956) 2 ff., on Hyria (the discoveries include a stone pillar engraved with ships; Blegen very naturally raises the question whether there may be some connexion with an expedition overseas); London *Times*, October 12, 1956, and *Illustrated London News*, October 20, 1956, p. 669, on Aulis; London *Times*, December 10, 1956, on Iolcos.

[8] Some subsequent writers have accepted Burr's main conclusion more or less as it stands, e.g. Wade-Gery, *The Poet of the Iliad* (1952) 55, "this authentic list of Mycenaean places," "exact knowledge of Mycenaean Greece"; cf. Lorimer, *Homer and the Monuments* [*HM*] (1950) 46 f.; Bury-Meiggs, *History of Greece* (1955) 20 n. 2, 51; G. L. Huxley, Univ. of London, Inst. of Classical Studies, *Bulletin* 3 (1956) 19 ff.; J. Kerschensteiner, *Münchener Studien zur Sprachwissenschaft* 9 (1956) 34 ff. Others have simply rejected it (Von der Mühll, *Hypomnema*, 1952, 53, "ganz unmöglich") or ignored it (Mazon, *Introduction à l'Iliade*, 1948, 154, "il n'est donc pas absurde d'imaginer que nous avons là le tableau d'une Grèce archaïque, on pourrait presque dire: d'une Grèce pré-dorienne contemporaine de l'expédition de Troie. Mais, à la rigueur, on peut aussi penser que nous sommes ici dans le domaine de l'imagination pure"; but how it can possibly be a work of pure imagination, he does not tell us). Many had already accepted the conclusion as established by Allen, *HCS* (e.g. Bury, *CAH* II, 1924, 479 ff.; Murray, *RGE*, 3rd ed., 1924, 202 ff.; Myres, *Who Were the Greeks?*, 1930, 316 ff.). All I have to say about G. Jachmann's *Der homerische Schiffskatalog und die Ilias* (1958) will be found in the *Classical Review* for 1959.

[9] Valmin, *The Swedish Messenia Expedition* (1938) 12 ff., states a strong case in favour of the identification of Dorion with Malthi. Cf. Burr 67.

[10] Strabo 405: οὐδαμοῦ φαίνεται τῆς Βοιωτίας, ὥς φησιν Ἀπολλόδωρος ἐν τοῖς περὶ Νεῶν. Its position in the list of Boeotian towns is a strong argument against the suggestion—in itself most unattractive—that Nisa is to be identified with Megara (despite Burr 27, with literature n. 5).

[11] Strabo 426.

[12] Ibid.

[13] Strabo 413: οἱ δέ φασι καὶ τὴν Ἄρνην ὑπὸ τῆς λίμνης καταποθῆναι καὶ τὴν Μίδειαν; Burr 26, with notes.

[14] Strabo 373.

[15] Strabo 349.

[16] Strabo 350.

[17] Strabo 388.

[18] Burr 70.

[19] Strabo 440.

[20] It may now be stated with the least possible fear of contradiction by future evidence (*a*) that the Dorian occupiers of Greece never used Linear B; (*b*) that Linear B went out of use among the peoples subject to the Dorians, indeed among all peoples, soon after the Dorian occupation (see Dow, *AJA* 58, 1954, 125 ff.; Ventris and Chadwick, *Documents in Mycenaean Greek* [*DMG*], 1956, 60 f., 110; Bowra, *Homer and His Forerunners*, 1955, 2 f.); (*c*) that the Phoenician alphabet was not adopted by the Greeks much if at all earlier than the middle of the 8th century B.C.: see esp. Albright, *JNES* 10 (1951) 217 ff., *AJA* 54 (1950) 164, and *Archaeology of Palestine* (1954) 194 ff.; Dunbabin, *The Greeks and Their Eastern Neighbours* (1957) 59 f.; Lorimer, *AJA* 52 (1948) 11 f.; Cook, *JHS* 66 (1946) 89 f. with n. 180. Miss Lorimer and Dunbabin argue cogently for c. 780–750; the much later date supported by Rhys Carpenter (*AJA* 37, 1933, 8 ff., and *AJA* 42, 1938, 58 ff.) seems now untenable.

The earliest Greek inscriptions prove the use of the Phoenician-Greek alphabet in the last quarter of the 8th century (see now Buchner, *Rendic. Accad. Naz. dei Lincei*, Ser. 8, Vol. 10, 1955, 221, with n. 2) and imply a period of development, perhaps a few decades long. It seems clearly established that the alphabet was adapted from Phoenician at a stage of development reached by Phoenician in the 9th to 8th centuries (see Albright, *Archaeology of Palestine* l.c.: this conclusion has always seemed to me to follow from the very full evidence set out by Ullman in *AJA* 38, 1934, 359 ff., though the author himself assessed it very differently). Those who would like to believe (as the followers of Schadewaldt must) that writing played any part in "Homer's" making of the Iliad must either push the introduction of the alphabet back further than the evidence will allow it to go, or postulate an 8th-century Homer,— a fashionable opinion (see now Webster, *From Mycenae to Homer* [1958]), but one which seems to me impossible; for if he made any appreciable use of writing, he must have lived in the latter part of that century, and it is inconceivable that the Greeks, knowing the Iliad as they did, should have lost all memory (except the mere name; nobody ever knew his time or place) of its author, if he lived within a generation of the birth of Archilochus, in an era from which quite a lot of less famous and interesting persons were remembered. The name "Homer" came down to the Greeks from their Dark Ages: to them, it was prehistoric,—and that means (Dunbabin, op. cit. 13 ff.) that it must be referred to the 9th century or the first quarter of the 8th; and then there was no question of *writing* poetry, or even of recording in writing a poem orally composed.

[21] This is so generally recognized that I merely assert it without discussion. Indeed I find nothing to discuss, except Burr's suggestion (119 ff.) that a formal and official muster roll of contingents was drawn up at the time of the assembly at Aulis; that this was later versified; and that the versified catalogue was orally transmitted thereafter. There is no doubt that this *could* have been done: Burr compares the Ras Shamra Catalogue (121 ff., with pl. 41, after Gaster, *Palestine Exploration Fund Quarterly*, 1938, 105 ff.), a list of participants in a naval expedition (c. 1400 B.C.) arranged in a series of entries giving name of commander, name of district, number of men; and the Pylos tablets have taught us that the Mycenaeans were methodical and bureaucratic enough. Indeed, the evidence of the Pylos tablets indicates that if there ever was such a Gathering of the Clans as the Iliad asserts, a record of the detail would certainly have been made (see esp. Kerschensteiner, op. cit. [n. 8 above] 44 f., and Mühlestein, *Die Oka-Tafeln von Pylos*, 1956, 41 f.). But whether a poet would have access to it; whether, if he had, he could read it; whether the procedure implied is a likely one for the time,—these are matters of which we know nothing. Few, I surmise, will agree with Burr's suggestion that the Aeolians took their "archives" with them when they migrated to Asia Minor in the Dark Ages, and that interest in this document was then revived as an "important text relating to their own history." It seems very improbable that anybody could still read "Linear B" in the 10th

century: I do not believe in this "pietätvoll mitgeführtes Tonta-felarchiv" (Heubeck, *Gnomon* 21, 1949, 207); and I submit that there is at least one reason why we should reject absolutely the notion that the original versifier had an *authentic* muster roll in front of him at any date. No such authentic document could have given the Boeotians the huge preponderance which they actually enjoy; we should have to suppose that our poet treated with much disrespect the unimpeachable source which he had taken the trouble to consult. But the whole procedure seems to me too im-probable to be worth discussing further.—For Burr, pp. 56, 127, the proof that the Catalogue is based on a *written* document is given by the prosody of Οἴτυλος in B 585. Since the proper form of this place name was ϝίτυλος, the initial O presumably represents digamma (Schwyzer, *Gr. Grammatik* i 224): whoever mistook the οι- for a diphthong must have had a *written* text in front of him. Burr does not notice that this example is not different from a thousand others scattered through the Iliad: it is quite possible that ἠδ' Οἴτυλον replaced e.g. ἰδ' 'Οίτυλον at some time or other in the text; i.e., if Οἴτυλον really is a corruption of 'Οίτυλον, it is easily explicable on the basis of a verse (not *written*) original. The mistake alleged by Burr must of course have been made over a text written *in the Greek alphabet*, i.e., not earlier than the end of the 8th cen-tury,—a consequence intolerable to Burr's own theory.

[22] The following are the most significant features of the place-name epithets in the Greek Catalogue:

 a) Many of them do not recur in the Iliad; of the remainder, many are extremely rare in the Iliad.

Not in Il. or Od.: πολύκνημον, πολυ ταφυλον, πολυτρήρωνα, τειχιόεσσαν, ἔφαλον, ἀγχίαλον, εὔκτιτον, ἀργινόεντα, ἐκατόμπολιν, κλωμακόεσσαν, ἱμερτόν. In Od. but not in Il.: εἰνοσίφυλλον, κητώεσσαν, ὄρος αἰπύ, αἰπὺ πτολίεθρον. In the Doloneia (once) only: ἐσχατόωσαν. Not else-where in Il. attributed to *places*: τρηχεῖαν, ἀγλαὸν (ἄλσος), λευκήν, λευκὰ (κάρηνα). Very rare: πετρήεσσαν (Il. 1: Od. 1), πολύμηλον (1:0), λεχεποίην (1:0), δυσχείμερον (1:0), ἀργυροδίνης (2:0), ἀνθεμόεντα (1:3).

 Relatively commoner in Il. and Od.: εὐρύχορον (2:7), ποιηέντα (3:4), ἀμπελόεντα (3:0), καλλιγύναικα (4:1), καλλίρροον (2:2); com-moner still, εὐκτίμενον πτολίεθρον, ἱερόν, ζαθέην, δῖον, ἐρατεινήν, ἀφνειόν, ἐϋκτιμένην, αἰπεινήν, εὐρεῖαν, ἠνεμόεσσαν, ἠγαθέη, μητέρα μήλων.

 b) There are many metrical equivalents in both Catalogue and Iliad, e.g. for $\smile\smile--$ // after a vowel, the Catalogue has πετρήεσσαν, τειχιόεσσαν, κητώεσσαν, καλλιγύναικα, κλωμακόεσσαν, μητέρα μήλων; the

Iliad has πιδήεσσαν, ποιήεσσαν, παιπαλόεσσα, βωτιάνειρα; after a consonant, Cat. has ἐσχατόωσα, ἠνεμόεσσα, εἰνοσίφυλλος, the Trojan Catalogue adds ἀκριτόφυλλον, the Iliad ὑλήεσσα, ὀφρυόεσσα, αἰπήεσσα, ἀμπελόεσσα, ἠιόεσσα, ἠμαθόεσσα. For the metrical value of εὐρύχορος, Cat. has ὑψηλός, ἱμερτός, ἠγάθεος, αἰπεινός, ἀγχίαλος, ἀφνειός, the Iliad adds εὔπυργος, εὔπωλος, ἱππόβοτος. There are numerous other metrical equivalents, e.g. αἰπὺ πτολίεθρον = ἔφαλον πτολίεθρον; λευκήν // = δῖαν //; πολυστάφυλον = πολύκνημον = Il. πολύχρυσον, βαθύσχοινον; λεχεποίην // = πολύμηλον // = Il. βαθύλειμον, πολύπυρον.

The explanation of the foregoing facts is to be found in the *distinctive* quality of many of the epithets. The same place was always described by the same epithet whenever it occurred in the same case and in the same part of the line; but each place had its own epithet, very often distinctively descriptive of that place and not transferable to many if any other places; if one place was commonly enough mentioned, it had its own set of epithets, to suit its different cases in different parts of the line (cf. the examples of Troy and Ilios quoted on pp. 291–294). The reason why so many of the Catalogue's place epithets are absent from the Iliad is simply that the places themselves do not recur there: if a place does recur, and has an epithet, it will be the same epithet as that in the Catalogue: Β 841 Λάρισαν / ἐριβώλακα, Ρ 301 Λαρίσης / ἐριβώλακος; Β 836 = Φ 43 δῖαν Ἀρίσβην //; Β 750 Δωδώνην / δυσχείμερον, Π 234 Δωδώνης ∪∪ _ / δυσχειμέρου; Β 691 = Δ 378 τείχεα Θήβης; Β 722 Λήμνῳ ἐν ἠγαθέῃ /, Φ 58, 79 Λῆμνον ἐς ἠγαθέην /; Β 615 Ἥλιδα δῖαν, Λ 686, 698 Ἥλιδι δίῃ. The determining factor for each place was meaning, not metre (just as it was for each hero: ποδάρκης δῖος Ἀχιλλεύς is metrically equivalent to πολύτλας δῖος Ὀδυσσεύς, and μέγας Τελαμώνιος Αἴας to μέγας κορυθαίολος Ἕκτωρ): it is only within the scheme of each place (and each hero) that the law of economy is observed.

23 The Catalogue requires some 50 noun + epithet combinations spread over 265 lines: all its needs could have been satisfied by the noncommittal place-name epithets employed in the Iliad, εὐρυάγυια, βωτιάνειρα, εὐτείχεος, ἱερὴ πόλις, πολυήρατος, ἐραννός, εὖ ναιόμενον πτολίεθρον, καλός, βαθυλείμων, ὑψίπυλος, al., none of which is in fact used in the Catalogue, together with a few which do occur in the Catalogue, ζάθεος, δῖος, ἐρατεινός, ἐυκτίμενος, ἠγάθεος, al.

24 The epithet κητώεσσαν, which nobody in historical times understood, is presumably an inheritance from the remotest past.

25 For what follows see esp. Leaf, *Homer and History* [*HH*] (1915) chaps. iii–vi.

26 Boeotians are not mentioned in the Odyssey. In the Iliad, only

E 707 ff.; N 685, 700 (the eccentric little catalogue; see p. 133 above); Ξ 476 (Promachus the Boeotian); N 92, Ξ 487 ff., Π 335 ff., P 597 ff. (Peneleos and Leitos), Z 35 (Leitos), O 329 (death of Arcesilaos), Ξ 450 (death of Prothoenor), O 340 (death of Clonios).

[27] I select these as being the most important: it is well known that the Catalogue differs from the Iliad in numerous other points of less importance, especially in including districts and persons ignored by the Iliad. The Iliad knows nothing of the Arcadians; of the tribes in northern Thessaly; of Nireus, Pheidippos, Antiphos, Epistrophus, Agapenor, Thalpius, Polyxeinos, Gouneus, Prothoos; Eumelos recurs only in Ψ. The Catalogue knows nothing of the Iliad's Antilochus, Patroclus, Teucer. The Iliad has numerous commanders unknown to the Catalogue: Promachos, Orestios, Menesthios, Stichios, Pheidas, Bias; Burr 134 n. 3.

[28] About the beginning of the Dark Ages the lands in question were occupied by "Thessalians," a people from the northwest of Greece, who emerge into the light of history divided into four autonomous districts with their chief towns at Larissa, Pharsalus, Crannon, and Cierion. Of this people, of these places, and of this division of the land (which lasted essentially unchanged throughout the pagan era) the Catalogue knows nothing whatever. The very names, Thessaly and Thessalians, are missing: in their place we find a network of little kingdoms, to which some unsettled tribes are added in the north (for these see esp. Hammond, *BSA* 32, 1931–32, 148 ff.). This evidently purports to be a picture of the territory as it existed in the Late Bronze Age. See Burr 106; Hiller von Gaertringen, *RE* VI A (1937) 111 ff.; H. D. Hansen, *Early Civilization in Thessaly* (1933) 178 f.; Heurtley, *BSA* 28 (1926–27) 158 ff.; T. C. Skeat, *The Dorians in Archaeology* (1934) 61; the period of maximum disturbance was c. 1100 B.C. On the archaeological break between Mycenaean and post-Mycenaean in Thessaly see Desborough, *Protogeometric Pottery* 130 ff., 173 ff.

[29] On the question whether Hellas and Phthia are towns or districts (surely the latter) see Burr 92 f., Hampe 4 f.: the Mycenaean occupation of the site later called "Pharsalos" (first in the "Little Iliad," fr. 19 Allen) is now proved (N. Verdelis, *BCH* 78, 1954, 134 f., and 79, 1955, 268 f.), but whether this place is to be identified with what the Epic meant by "Phthia" remains as doubtful as ever. It looks as though the Epic meant a district, which was contracted to *a single occupied place* (Pharsalos) by the opinion of the Greeks in historical times. For the location of Trechis, Y. Béquignon, *La*

Vallée du Spercheios (1937) 247 ff.; Stählin, *RE* VI A (1937) 1863 f.; Burr 90. For Alope, Béquignon 367 f. Alos remains enigmatic: the identification with Halos, the harbour in the Pagasaean gulf, is (as the ancients observed) intrinsically most improbable, since that harbour lies deep within the kingdom which the Catalogue is about to assign to Protesilaos: Strabo 432 f., περὶ Ἅλου δὲ καὶ Ἀλόπης διαποροῦσι, μὴ οὐ τούτους λέγει τοὺς τόπους οἳ νῦν ἐν τῷ Φθιωτικῷ τέλει φέρονται ἀλλὰ τοὺς ἐν Λοκροῖς, μέχρι δεῦρο ἐπικρατοῦντος τοῦ Ἀχιλλέως ὥσπερ καὶ μέχρι Τραχῖνος καὶ τῆς Οἰταίας· ἔστι γὰρ καὶ Ἅλος καὶ Ἁλιοῦς ἐν τῇ παραλίᾳ τῶν Λοκρῶν, καθάπερ καὶ Ἀλόπη κτλ. There is no means of solving this problem. Burr (89, 106 f.) decides in favour of the harbour Halos, which is to play an important part in his reconstruction of events: but it is all mere guesswork,—"zunächst sei festgestellt: Ἅλος . . . ist die bekannte Stadt am Pagasäischen Meerbusen": *ipse dixit;* and the statement is not strengthened by a highly subjective view of the "structure" of the Catalogue—"an Halos in Lokris zu denken, halte ich für unstatthaft, da der gesamte Aufbau dagegen spricht." The fact remains that the identification with the harbour Halos introduces (what was not there before) a confusion into the Catalogue; and that is and will always be a good reason for doubting whether it is correct. Leaf, whose Catalogue was capable of anything, naturally welcomed the muddle thus created by the moderns; Allen took the opposite view (*Homer and History* 123 f., 343 ff.; *Homeric Catalogue of Ships* 111 f.).

[30] See Leaf, *HH* 110 ff.

[31] Ibid. 139 ff., 161 ff.

[32] The addition of 629, ὅς ποτε Δουλίχιονδ' ἀπενάσσατο πατρὶ χολωθείς, helps to reconcile the Iliad's Epeian Meges with the Catalogue's islander, but leaves untouched the major difficulty of the relation of his kingdom to that of Odysseus.

This is the only point at which there is an inherent confusion in the Catalogue's geography. Odysseus' realm is doubly enigmatic:

a) He rules Ithaca, Samos, Zacynthos, and his power extends (B 635) to the mainland and coast opposite: but the kingdom of Meges lies between him and the mainland; and if "the coast opposite" means (as most suppose) the coast of Elis, it is hard to reconcile Odysseus' claims with those of the Epeians, who are settled on the western coast of Elis (616). I agree with Burr that this line (635) is a relatively late addition designed to rescue Odysseus from the poverty to which the Catalogue condemns him.

I take the poet's Ithaca to be Thiaki, and see no reason for surprise if he is sometimes hazy about details of the geography. The

Leucas theory has no attractions for me; when in doubt, I reread especially Hugo Michael, *Wiss. Beilage zum XII. Programm des Königl. Gymnasiums zu Jauer* (1902), and ibid. *zum XV. Programm* (1905).

b) Much more serious is the difficulty of "Dulichium." The only Dulichium that was ever known is the large island (or part of it) adjacent to Ithaca. But this is a most uncomfortable confusion of kingdoms: Odysseus rules Ithaca, part of Cephalonia ("Samos"), and Zacynthos, but his realm is brutally bisected by the more powerful Meges (40 ships against 12!), king of the rest of Cephalonia ("Dulichium") and the Echinades.

Something is wrong here: and I for one have no confidence whatever in the popular explanations, old or new. The ancients, misled by a bogus etymology, solved the problem by removing Dulichium to Dolicha in the Echinades—a small, miserable, and deserted island, rough living for a goat (Strabo 458, followed by Leaf, *HH* 166). The moderns move it to the mainland (Burr 74 ff.).

The problem is, I believe, to be solved by other methods. In the Catalogue, Meges was king of an important realm in the Western Islands: in the Iliad, he is an insignificant person, not ruler of an *island* kingdom at all. In the Iliad, the great king from the Western Islands is Odysseus: *but in the original Catalogue there was no Odysseus at all.* Just as Ajax had to be inserted into the Catalogue because he was so prominent in the Iliad, so Odysseus had to be inserted because of his great fame not only in the Iliad but also in the Odyssey. But Meges was already firmly established in the Catalogue: so Odysseus must make do with what is left over—Ithaca, never a place of any importance; Zacynthos, not yet claimed by anybody; "Samos," whatever that may mean; the obscure and unidentifiable Neritos, Aegilips, and Crocyleia; and, for good measure —since this is so far a wretched realm—"people on the mainland and on the coast opposite." The kingdom of Odysseus does in fact consist of scraps collected right, left, and centre of Meges' dominion. If Odysseus had no place in the Mycenaean Catalogue, it is likely that he is either a hero of pre-Trojan War poetry (like Ajax) or else a figure rather of folklore than of legend, drawn into the magnetic field of the Trojan Epic.

For the division of realms actually described in the Catalogue see the map (facing p. 124), on which Cephalonia is divided between Samos and Dulichium in a quite arbitrary way; but, whatever division be adopted, the bisection of Odysseus' realm by that of Meges is equally unrealistic.

33 On Ἄργος see Allen, *HCS* 108 ff.; Leaf, *HH* 194 ff.; Ebeling s.v.: Ἄργος may denote (*a*) the town Argos, (*b*) the district of Argos, especially as the home of Agamemnon (the epithets πολυδίψιον, ἱππόβοτον presumably refer specially to the Argive plain); (*c*) Greece in general, sometimes with special reference to southern Greece (the Peloponnese as a whole), sometimes comprising the country entire, the place from which all the Achaeans came to Troy,—this I take to be a usage derived from the paramount importance of the district governed by the great overlord; hence too the usage (relatively rare) of Ἀργεῖοι as a national name (176 examples: Ἀχαιοί 605).

34 There has long been difference of opinion about the importance of Corinth in the Mycenaean period. No great town or fortress and very few other material relics of that period have been discovered; and Corinth plays remarkably little part in the legends inherited from the Mycenaean world.

Nevertheless there is no justification for stigmatizing the reference to Corinth in the Catalogue as a late insertion. It is said that "ἀφνειὸς Κόρινθος fits the eighth century, and, as we judge by the remains, no earlier period" (Dunbabin, *JHS* 68, 1948, 60): but ἀφνειὸς (whatever its derivation may be) in the early Epic signified only, in general, "prosperous"; and it is certain enough that this whole district was populous and productive throughout the Mycenaean era,—indeed the coastal plain dominated by Corinth is "among the most productive areas of Greece," and we can be sure that "at all times there was a considerable population in the district" (Dunbabin, l.c. 59 f.). There is no reason whatever to deny the epithet "prosperous" to this area in the Mycenaean period. Perhaps there was no great palace there: but the Epic never pretends that there was; Corinth was simply "prosperous"—and it is hard to believe that the district in question was ever anything but prosperous. See Blegen, *Korakou* (1921) 124 ff., and other references quoted by Dunbabin l.c.

35 Not that the Iliad is unaware of Diomedes' claim to the kingdom which it assigns to Agamemnon. Allen, *HCS* 66: Δ 372 ff. clearly distinguishes between Diomedes' Argos and Agamemnon's Mycenae; Agamemnon says of Diomedes' father, ἄτερ πολέμου εἰσῆλθε Μυκήνας / ξεῖνος ἅμ' ἀντιθέῳ Πολυνείκεϊ λαὸν ἀγείρων, / οἳ δὲ τότ' ἐστρατόωνθ' ἱερὰ πρὸς τείχεα Θήβης. As Allen says, "That is to say at the time of the first Theban War, in the day of Atreus, Adrastus, King of Argos, sent commissioners round Greece, as Agamemnon in his turn did, to raise an army against Thebes. Among other places

they came 'in a peaceful capacity,' ἄτερ πολέμου, to Mycenae, where they were unsuccessful. . . . Therefore in the body of the poem, as in the Catalogue, Corinth—Sicyon—Mycenae are one state, and Argos—Tiryns—Epidauros etc. another." Allen observes further that φ 108 makes the same distinction berween Argos and Mycenae; cf. Δ 52, and also Ψ 471, where Diomedes is said to be "King of the Argives." That Sicyon was included in Agamemnon's personal dominions is shown by Ψ 296 f. (cf. Pausanias ii 6.7).

36 J. K. Anderson, in a valuable article on Achaea in *BSA* 49 (1954) 72 ff., says that "the boundaries of the Kingdom of Mycenae in the 'Catalogue' are too strange to be accepted." This seems to be the general opinion: I do not believe it can be justified.

37 See esp. F. Schachermeyr, *Hethiter und Achäer* (1935) 156 ff., a lucid discussion of this interesting problem. Leaf, *HH* 208 f., dismisses Tiryns too summarily as a mere "outpost" of Mycenae. Burr, 44 f., seems not to appreciate the difficulties. There is still much of value in Allen, *HCS* 59 ff.

38 So also Schachermeyr, ibid.

39 This last is Schachermeyr's solution.

40 The enigmatic fortress at Gla in the Copaic Lake covers more ground than Mycenae and Tiryns together (the circuit of the great walls is about two miles; of Mycenae and Tiryns together, about one mile): but its size is absolutely dictated by the site,—a low island, for the most part steep-sided, surrounded by the level plain (A. de Ridder, *BCH* 18, 1894, 271 ff., "Fouilles de Gha"; Hitzig-Blümner, *Pausanias* III 461 ff.; Frazer, *Pausanias* V 120 ff.; the four gates were being excavated in 1956. On the more or less contemporary drainage system for the lake see E. J. A. Kenny, *Univ. of Liverpool Annals of Archaeology and Anthropology* 22, 1935, 189 ff.).

The identification of Gla with the Homeric *Arne* was maintained by Noack, *Athen. Mittheil.* (1894) 463 ff., refuted by de Ridder, *BCH* 18 (1894) 446 ff. It is still maintained by Burr (26 f., with literature 26 n. 7), who seems to have overlooked the article by Gomme in *Essays and Studies Presented to William Ridgeway* (1913) 116, which made Leaf (*HH* 93 n. 1) change his mind. If the nature of the ground is taken into consideration, neither Gla nor the reclaimed land around it can ever have been πολυστάφυλος, rich in vines. See also T. W. Allen, *CR* 17 (1903) 239; Nilsson, *Mycenaean Origin of Greek Mythology* (1932) 128.

41 Burr (60 f., approved by Wade-Gery, *Poet of the Iliad* 55 f.) suggests that I 149 ff. originally belonged to the Catalogue and were "transferred" by the poet of Book Nine to their present place. But

why were they then omitted from the Catalogue? It is the practice
of the Epic to repeat passages from one place to another; but the
poets never, so far as we know, *deleted* a passage of this type in the
one place merely because they wished to use it again in another.
Of course no such question of "deletion" arises until after the formation of a more or less standard written text, i.e., not earlier than
the 6th century B.C.

⁴² The whole of this part of the Iliad ("The Embassy") was composed
at a late period in the development of the poem (see Appendix); and
the poet of the Embassy cares nothing about Mycenaean geography.
Ventris and Chadwick (*DMG* 145) say that the cities promised by
Agamemnon to Achilles "must at that time have been an independent area belonging neither to Menelaos nor to Nestor, or some
protest would have been made": it is very much likelier that the
Ionian poet of the Embassy had no idea whom the places belonged
to at that or at any other time.

⁴³ Cf. Il 167 ff.: the description of the five divisional commands in
Achilles' army is wholly independent of anything suggested by the
Catalogue.

⁴⁴ The text gives a selection of the principal points made by F. Jacoby,
"Die Einschaltung des Schiffskatalogs in die Ilias," *Sitzb. d. Preuss.
Akad. d. Wiss.* (1932), phil.-hist. Kl., 572 ff. There is no escape from
the inference drawn from the relation of 446 κρίνοντες to 476
διεκόσμεον, and from the fact that whereas in 457 (ἐρχομένων) the
Greeks are *going to battle*, seven lines later we find that they have
not yet even left their tents (464 f.).

The attempted rebuttal by Burr (7 f.) and Wade-Gery (51 ff.)
ends in total failure. They wish to maintain that the action of
ἡγεμόνες διεκόσμεον in 476 has not been anticipated by βασιλῆες
θῦνον κρίνοντες in 445 f.: that can only be done if you treat κρίνοντες
with violence or disdain. Burr, who goes so far as to assert that "von
einer förmlichen Ordnung der Truppen zur Schlacht mit Hilfe der
Athena . . . ist nirgends die Rede," has no answer to the problem
then posed by κρίνοντες, except to say that it means "*in der
Absicht*, dann dort die eintreffenden Mannschaften zu ordnen,"—
as if κρίνοντες could express a *future* action, and as if the kings
could go darting about (θῦνον) long before their men have even
emerged from their tents (465). Wade-Gery, like Burr, sees that
Jacoby's case is absolutely proved if κρίνοντες here bears its obvious
and normal meaning; he therefore suggests that it may mean
"singling men out" (though on his view the men will not be leaving
their tents until 457),—"To ask the exact purpose of this action

would be (I think) to consider too curiously": but is it really to consider too curiously, to ask what action is denoted by a verb whose normal meaning is being deliberately denied to it? "Perhaps they were directing groups of men, possibly they were collecting their contingents: I think more likely they were hailing individuals, creating an esprit d'élite": but κρίνοντες does not signify directing or collecting or hailing, and there is not one single word—here or elsewhere—about an esprit d'élite. It is very obvious that when the kings are κρίνοντες, "arranging" in some sense, their men are present on parade; they are not still in their tents and ships. (In n. 107 Wade-Gery admits that κρίνοντες may mean *dividing into parties*, but is compelled by his theory to insist that this must be something different from, and preliminary to, the marshalling on the plain. So desperate is the remedy; and it is therefore well that there is no disease.)

The attempt to take ἐρχομένων in 457 as meaning anything but "go to battle" (following κρίνοντες in 446 and ὀτρύνουσ' ἰέναι in 451) needs no discussion (Burr actually takes it as "coming *from the ships and tents*," though they "were assembling" at the command of the heralds as long ago as 444. Wade-Gery also thinks it means "coming *from the camp to the plain*," despite ἠγείροντο in 444, and despite 450–454, which are obviously not said of men still resting in ships and tents).

[45] This invocation is probably a very late addition: note the highly abnormal intrusion of the poet's personality (μοι 484, ἡμεῖς 486, ἐγώ 488, μοι 489 and 490, ἐρέω 493); note also the composer's peculiar knowledge of Asia Minor, 461 the Asian Meadow and River Caÿster, cf. 782 ff. the Cilician volcanoes.

[46] It may be thought likelier that (*a*) 444–458 are an integral part of the Iliad as recited without the Catalogue, (*b*) 459–493 (*minus* 469–473) are the proper introduction to the independent Catalogue; and that when the Catalogue was inserted into the Iliad no attempt was made to harmonize the two. Perhaps: but this modification is of minor importance, and in any case 459–493 are relatively of very late composition. Note especially the form μιγέωσιν for -ήωσιν in 475 (Chantraine, *Grammaire homérique* [*GH*] 1.71; Shipp, *Studies in the Language of Homer* [*SLH*] 122; ἀρέϊ for ἄρηϊ in 479; the un-Epic hyperbole in 489–490; the untraditional phrase νῆάς τε προπάσας in 493).

[47] 469–473 is a possible third: 473 ἵσταντο was never intended for continuous recitation after ἔσταν 467. Jacoby suggests that 467–468 and 469–473 are alternative versions.

[48] It is difficult to know where to draw the line, and I ought to warn the reader that I have deliberately excluded discussion of several topics which, though relevant, are not essential to my principal theme: (a) The question whether there was a Catalogue of Greeks in the *Cypria:* see Jacoby op. cit. (n. 44 above) 575 f., 611 ff.—the evidence both negatively and positively excludes the suggestion. (b) How far the earlier part of the Second Book has been altered in the light of the Catalogue after its addition to that Book: full and to me convincing discussion in Jacoby. (c) Study of the passages which link the Greek to the Trojan Catalogue and which link the Trojan Catalogue to the sequel: the two Catalogues were linked together, at the time of or after their incorporation in the Iliad (769 ff. presuppose knowledge of the First Book: note the untraditional prosody of μηνῖεν in 769; Schulze, *Quaest. Epicae* 349 ff.; Wackernagel, *Sprachliche Untersuchungen zu Homer* [*SUH*], 1916, 140) by a lengthy passage, 761–815, not apparently all composed by one and the same poet. Jacoby ascribes 761–785 to his "Katalogist," 786–802 to "Homer," 803–806 to a later interpolator, 807–815 to "Homer" again; but there is very little firm ground to tread, and opinions will differ about the detail.

[49] So even Jacoby 575: the original was "ein seinem Wesen nach geographisches Gedicht, eine 'Periegese' zunächst von Hellas und den anliegenden Inseln."

[50] O 329, 340.

[51] I 82.

[52] Only four names are repeated in the Achaean list (Alastor, Bias, Menesthios, Schedios); on the Trojan side, twenty (of which two, Melanippus and Thoon, are used thrice).

[53] The Iliad actually knows more about some of the obscurer persons than the Catalogue knows: e.g. who were the fathers of Leitos and Prothoenor (P 601 f., Ξ 450). And the Iliad is familiar with so many as seventy Achaeans who are not named in the Catalogue; about some of them it knows quite a lot (e.g. the story of Echepolos; the genealogies of Alcimedon, Eudoros, Eurymedon, Iasos, Crethon, Menesthios, Polyxeinos).

[54] Leaf, Allen, and Burr all think that the Catalogue is based on a kind of traders' guide (a "list of trade-routes"; a "portulan"; a "Streckenverzeichniss"; an "Abschnitt eines Κατάπλους"). But is it seriously suggested that the alleged mariners *versified* their sailing-directions? If they did not, why *was* it versified?

[55] The foundations for the study of the Trojan Catalogue were laid by Walter Leaf in *Troy: A Study in Homeric Geography* (1912), and

Strabo on the Troad: Book XIII Cap. 1 (1923). Allen's discussion in *HCS* 147 ff. is useful; Burr (137 ff.) has little to add. Jacoby (602 ff.) seems less interested in, and less interesting on, the Trojan than the Greek Catalogue.

⁵⁶ Except the lines interpolated in the 2nd or 1st century B.C., 853–855 (n. 81 below).

⁵⁷ Hesiod fr. 53 Rz.

⁵⁸ Allen, *HCS* 167; ibid. 147 n. 1, 152.

⁵⁹ Burr could not possibly justify the statement (150) that "das Material für den Troerkatalog ist aus der Ilias entnommen"; nothing demonstrably is, much demonstrably is not. Heubeck (*Gnomon* 21, 1949, 209) explains away the discrepancies in a manner peculiar to the school of Schadewaldt.

⁶⁰ Leaf, *Troy* 13, cf. *HH* 75 ff.

⁶¹ *HCS* 166. Forsdyke, *Greece before Homer* (1956) 87, infers from the fact that the Trojan Catalogue ignores the Hittites and associated kingdoms (Assuwa, Arzawa) that "this document . . . must be an Aiolic or Ionian reconstruction of native conditions at the time of the Hellenic colonisation"; but why must a contemporary document mention kingdoms *not* concerned in the matters with which it is dealing? Neither the Hittites nor their subordinates the Arzawans had anything to do with the Achaean siege of Troy (see pp. 108 ff. above).

⁶² The *Cicones* could be added to the list, if it were true that "als gegenwärtig erscheinen die Kikonen nur bei Homer" (Burr 148): but I do not see how this can be maintained in the face of Herodotus VII 110, ἔθνεα δὲ Θρηίκων δι' ὧν τῆς χώρας ὁδὸν ἐποιέετο τοσάδε· Παῖτοι Κίκονες Βίστονες κτλ.

Much more significant is the Τηρείης ὄρος αἰπύ of B 829: Leaf, *Troy* 187 f., *Strabo* 91 f.; Burr 143. Its location was unknown to Strabo, therefore to Demetrius of Scepsis also; i.e., no recollection of the name survived locally into the end of the 3rd century B.C., despite the influence and authority of the Iliad. So presumably its location was unknown from the beginning of the historical era onwards.

In the body of the Iliad, the memory of Κίλλα (A 38 = 452) was preserved only in the Epic: history knew nothing of it (Leaf, *Strabo* 311 ff.: as he says, the context in Herodotus I 149 excludes the identification of that Κίλλα with the Homeric).

⁶³ Miss Gray, in the course of her valuable discussion (*JHS* 74, 1954, 13), says that "the dispute about the position of Alybe, going back to Hecataeus, is surprising if the Greeks discovered it in the seventh

century": to me it seems more than surprising,—it would be incomprehensible.

[64] Ἀλόπη, Ἀλόβη, Ἀλύπη, Ἀλύβων, and even Χαλύβων. For the Alizones see Leaf, *Strabo* 209.

[65] Leaf, *Troy* 307 f.: "Only the mountain Phthires was unknown in ancient days, and the claims of the two conspicuous Carian ranges, Latmus and Grion, were balanced and decided according to individual taste. Whether either, and if so, which, bore the rather unsavoury title may well remain a matter of indifference to us." It is strange that Leaf should have failed to see the critical significance of the point. Strabo 635.

[66] See Leaf, *Troy* 198 ff., 242 ff., and summary conclusion 319 ff.: the reason why the South Coast of the Troad was not included in the Catalogue is because it had been overrun by Achilles early in the war and played no further part therein.

[67] *Lyrnessus:* B 688 ff. (ath. Zenod.), T 59 f., Υ 90 ff., 191 f. *Pedasos:* Z 34 f., Υ 92, Φ 86 ff. Π 151, Pedasus is the name of a horse taken by Achilles from Thebe in the same area.

　　Leaf, *Strabo* 253 ff., 263 ff., 308 ff., also *Troy* 217 ff. with pl. xix, on Lyrnessus–Antandros; *Strabo* 250 ff., 289 ff., 304 f., with pls. xvii–xix and plan p. 293, also *Troy* 221 ff., 246 ff. with pl. xxii, on Pedasos–Assos.

　　According to Strabo, ὑποπλακίη was incomprehensible as an epithet of Thebe (Leaf, *Strabo* 318, cf. 322 ff.).

[68] Thacher Clarke, *Report on the Investigations at Assos* 61 (quoted by Leaf also, *Troy* 222): "An almost direct proof that the citadel at this point, which by nature commands the southern Troad, served as the Lelegian as well as the Greek capital, is further offered by the fact that in following the Satnioeis from the Halesian Plain of its delta to the head-waters of its rugged interior, no other site occurs to which the epithets αἰπεινός and αἰπήεις could be applied."

[69] Strabo 611–612: Pedasos no longer exists; Lyrnessos, like Thebe, is uninhabited. The name of Lyrnessus may perhaps be recorded on the Cretan Linear B tablet KN 1439, cf. 1441, 1442 // *ru-na-so⁻ᵗᵉ*— (the *-te* is smaller and "suspended"), which could represent *Lurnessothen*, "from L."

[70] The Mycenaean origin of the Trojan Catalogue is one of the few subjects on which Leaf and Allen agreed. I cannot find that Burr (150) has any ground for taking the opposite view. He makes two obviously mistaken allegations, (1) that "the material for the Trojan Catalogue is derived from the Iliad": this is the reverse of the truth (p. 140 above); (2) that this material, derived from the

Iliad, *was supplemented by information provided by the colonizing Milesians;* for this there is not a trace of evidence, indeed one of the most remarkable features of the Catalogue is its absolute ignorance of Ionian colonization. "Not until the Milesian colonisation," says Burr (145), "was Sestos controlled from the opposite coast": this is an oversight; the historical (Lesbian) Sestos was never controlled by the historical (Milesian) Abydos, except for brief periods in highly exceptional circumstances (Schol. B on *Il.* B 494). As Leaf says (*Strabo* 125), the conjunction of the two places under one ruler "never recurred after Homeric times,"—except in so far as both fell into common subjection to a foreign power (Persian, Athenian, Spartan).

71 The Trojan Catalogue has very few distinctive epithets for places: the contrast with the Greek Catalogue in this respect indicates that the reason is simply that the poets did not know how to describe the eastern places, and refrained from risky conjecture. They knew Troy, Dardania, Miletus, of course; also a few places in the Troad (Zeleia, Τηρείης ὄρος, al.); further afield, they knew that the. Paeonians were ἀγκυλότοξοι (also Κ 428: contrast the Iliad, Π 287, Φ 205 Παίονες ἱπποκορυσταί); they knew that mules came from Paphlagonia, silver from Alybe.

Immemorially old tradition informed the Ionians that Amphios was λινοθώρηξ (a description which no Ionian was likely to invent for an obscure person); cf. Milman Parry, *L'Épithète traditionnelle dans Homère* 192, on λινοθώρηξ and the Abantes ὄπιθεν κομόωντες, "Par elles ... nous pouvons entrevoir la vieille origine, presque historique, du *Catalogue*." There is no attempt to invent *numbers* of Trojan troops.

72 Burr, 40 ff. with references. For a concise modern survey of Mycenaean Athens see I. T. Hill, *The Ancient City of Athens* (1953) chap. ii; for further detail, Broneer, *AJA* 52 (1948) 111 ff., and esp. *Antiquity* 30 (1956) 9 ff.

It is remarkable that no other place in Attica is mentioned either in the Catalogue or in the rest of the Iliad: the Odyssey mentions Marathon and Sunium. Attica was densely populated in the Late Bronze Age (Karo lists nearly thirty sites, a number appreciably increased since he wrote); but we have no reason to believe that any place except the great fortress of Athens was worth mentioning in the Catalogue. Once more the self-control of the Athenian editors is to be admired: not one single Attic place did they interpolate into the Catalogue or elsewhere. See further Jacoby's interesting note in *Atthis* 393 f. (n. 22).

Hignett, *History of the Athenian Constitution* (1952) 35, says that "the catalogue in the *Iliad* seems to regard Attica as unified under the control of the king of Athens": that seems a risky inference from the fact that no place in Attica except Athens is named; nor is it safer to draw a political conclusion from the fact that an Odyssean poet can call Sunium "the headland *of Athens*."

[73] Δ 328, N 196, 689, Ο 337.

[74] Ο 332 ff.

[75] N 195, 691, Ο 329 (and see Schol. T on line 516).

[76] N 691.

[77] See n. 79 below.

[78] A 265 is a late intruder upon the Iliad, common to Hesiod, *scut.* 182; it is not in the Venetus, or in two third-century papyri, or in numerous other MSS.

Γ 144 is better left out of the picture, indeed out of the Iliad altogether: the mother of Theseus was never a maidservant of Helen at Troy; Bolling, *The Athetized Lines of the Iliad* [*ALI*] (1944) 84.

The sons of Theseus are unknown to the Iliad. Contrast the later versions of the story: Eur. *IA* 247 f., Athenian ships led by ὁ Θησέως παῖς; *Iliou Persis* (108 Allen) Δημοφῶν δὲ καὶ ᾿Ακάμας Αἴθραν εὑρόντες ἄγουσι μεθ᾿ ἑαυτῶν; ibid. 138 f. (=Lysimachus ap. Schol. E. *Tro.* 31), Acamas and Demophon actually went to Troy Μενεσθέως ἡγουμένου, . . . Θησείδαις δ᾿ ἔπορεν δῶρα κρείων ᾿Αγαμέμνων / ἠδὲ Μενεσθῆι μεγαλήτορι ποιμένι λαῶν; ibid. 139 (=Demo. *Epitaph.* 29) ἐμέμνηντ᾿ ᾿Ακαμαντίδαι τῶν ἐπῶν ἐν οἷς ῞Ομηρος εἴνεκα τῆς μητρός φησιν Αἴθρας ᾿Ακάμαντ᾿ εἰς Τροίαν στεῖλαι.

The Tragedians bring the Theseids to Troy: S. *Phil.* 562, E. *Hec.* 123, *Tro.* 31, cf. Schol. *Hec.* 123; Allen, *HCS* 23 ff. It is certain that the older Epic would have done what the Cycle does, namely, put the sons of Theseus in command of the Athenians at Troy, if only it had not been tied by tradition to Menestheus. The whole subsequent history of Menestheus is a struggle to square him with Theseus; and a bad muddle is made of it all (see next note). It is a testimonial to the veracity of the Catalogue that it remains untouched in this respect and makes no allowance whatever for the family of Theseus: its author knew well that the centre of Theseus' activity lay in northern Attica, not in Athens; and that he belongs to an earlier generation.

Theseus is very well and very fully discussed by Hans Herter in *Rhein. Mus.* 85 (1936) 177 ff. and 193 ff. Burr (42) does not appreciate the difficulties: he says that the poet received the names of

Menestheus and Peteos "from some other tradition, which arose at a time when Theseus had not yet made his chief residence in Athens"—but there is no trace of any "other tradition" about M. and P. except that of the Iliad; and if there had been one, it must certainly have been prehistoric, i.e., of Mycenaean origin, for nobody would have invented a "Menestheus the son of Peteos" to rule Athens, in place of the sons of Theseus, from the 8th century B.C. onwards.

79 On Menestheus the son of Peteos:

M. apparently recurs (as is natural, perhaps necessary) in another Catalogue, the list of Helen's suitors in Hesiod fr. 94.43 Rz. ἐκ δ' ἄρ' Ἀθηνέων μνᾶθ' υἱὸς Π[ετεῶο Μενεσθεύς]; cf. Apollod. 3.10.8, Hyginus lxxxi.

The only Attic authors in whom I can find a reference to M. are Aeschines, 3.185, who quotes an epigram (repeated with variants in Plutarch, *Cimon* 7) in which M. is said to have led the Athenians to Troy; and Xenophon, *Cyn.* 1.2, where M. is included in a long list of Cheiron's pupils (M.'s practice in hunting made him the most proficient warrior in Greece, surpassed by none and equalled only by Nestor; evidently an embroidery on the Ionian comment in B 553–555). The only certain representation of him in vase-painting is on a cup by the Codros painter (Ajax and M. leaving home), Beazley, *Attic Red-Figure Vase-Painters* 739 with references, esp. *Jahrbuch des Deutschen Archäologischen Instituts* XIII 70 ff.

Later references fall into the following categories:

I. Allusions to the Iliad, esp. to the Catalogue and esp. to B 553–555: *Peplos* 34 (Diehl); Plut. *Cim.* 7; Hygin. xcvii.11; Max. Tyr. p. 402.10 Hob.; Julian, *or.* ii 53D, p. 67 Hertl.; Liban. *or.* V 57.14, XI 8.13 Foerst.; occasionally with some fictitious addition or embroidery, Alcidamas, *Odyss.* 5, M. δὲ πρῶτος λέγεται κοσμῆσαι τάξεις καὶ λόχους καὶ φάλαγγας συστῆσαι ἡνίκα Εὔμολπος ὁ Ποσειδῶνος ἐπ' Ἀθηναίους ἐστράτευσε Θρᾷκας ἄγων; Philostr. *Her.* 2.16, p. 158 Kays., referring to Homer and praising Ajax as the greatest tactician, Μενεσθέως γὰρ τοῦ Ἀθηναίου τακτικωτάτου τῶν βασιλέων ἐς Τροίαν ἐλθόντος καὶ διδάσκοντος ἐν Αὐλίδι τὴν στρατιὰν πᾶσαν, ὡς χρὴ συνηρμόσθαι, κραυγῇ τε χρωμένοις μὴ ἐπιπλήττοντος οὐ ξυνεχώρει ὁ Αἴας ἀλλ' ἐπετίμα γυναικεῖόν τε ἀποφαίνων καὶ ἄτακτον; Pausan. i 1.2, M.'s port of departure was Phaleron. Allusion to the part played by M. in Book Four, Philodem. *hom.* col. viii 16, p. 35 Oliv.; in the Twelfth, Julian, *or.* ii. 67A, p. 85.21 Hertl. Inclusion of M.'s name in lists of Homeric heroes, Max. Tyr. p. 463.14 f. Hob.; Liban. *or.* V 266.4 Foerst.

II. Attempts to explain his relation to Theseus and the Theseids.

a) By getting him out of the way, to make room for the sons of Theseus in Athens: Apollod. *epit.* vi 15ᵇ (= Tzetz. ad Lycophr. 911), after the fall of Troy, M. sailed with others to Mimas, thence alone to Melos which he ruled as king; Philostr. *vit. Apoll.* i, p. 167 Kays., the people of Gadeira (so already Strabo 3.140) sacrifice to M.; Schol. Thuc. I 12.1, p. 15 Hude, M. was expelled by the Theseids εἰς Ἰβηρίαν; Strabo 6.261, M. founded Skylletion in Bruttium; ibid. 13.622, he founded Elaia, later the port of Pergamon (cf. Steph. Byz. s.v. El., and Head, *Hist. Numorum* 555, coin with head of M. κτιστής; Leaf, *Strabo* 334).

b) By concocting circumstantial stories. The difficulty was that the sons of Theseus ought to have been kings at Athens, and therefore commanders at Troy, at the time in question according to the traditional chronology: but Homer says that M. was in that position. The solution: M. must have ousted Theseus *for a short time;* and the obvious opportunity was provided by the story of Theseus' defeat by the Dioscuri (despite chronology). There was no need to provide M. with descendants, but a halfhearted attempt was made to give him an intelligible ancestor (Erechtheus): Plutarch, *Theseus* 32–35, M. was the earliest democrat; he led the demos against the tyrant Theseus; helped by the Dioscuri and with the people behind him he expelled Theseus, who died in Scyros; M. was succeeded in Athens by the Theseids. Apollod. *epit.* i 23 f., Theseus took Helen from Sparta; the Dioscuri invaded Athens, rescued Helen, captured Aethra, restored M. to power; Heracles rescued Theseus from Hades, sent him to Athens; M. repelled him, he died in Scyros. Pausan. i 17.5 f., a similar story; ibid. i 3.3, the sons of Theseus ruled in Athens after M.; iii 18.5, the Athenians preferred M. to Theseus. Aelian, *v.h.* 4.5, ii p. 62 Herch., essentially the same story as in Apollod. l.c., Pausan. i. 17. Cf. also Liban. *or.* IV 433.11 ff. Foerst.

This is all self-evident fiction of a very late era. The Parian Marble (*Fragmente d. gr. Historiker* 239 A 23 f., ii 996 Jac.) gives M. as king of Athens for the duration of the Trojan War, preceded by Theseus and followed by the sons of Theseus.

III. Yarns and embroideries. There are very few of these. Pausan. i 23.8, a bronze "Wooden Horse" on the Acropolis; "M. and Teucer are peeping out of it, and so are the sons of Theseus"! Cf. Quint. Smyrn. xii 317 ff., M. and Theseids enter the Wooden Horse. Schol. E. *Tro.* 31, M. and Theseids rewarded by Agamemnon. Philostr. *Her.*, 188.20 ff. Kays., Ajax was dead, προύθεντο δὲ

'Αθηναῖοι τὸ σῶμα καὶ M. ἐπ' αὐτῷ λόγον ἠγόρευσεν; cf. Antiphon ap. *Rhet. Gr.* vii 5, 26 Walz, λέγουσι δέ τινες δικανικὸν λόγον εἰρηκέναι πρῶτον M. τὸν στρατηγὸν τῶν 'Αθηναίων ὃς καὶ ἐπὶ Τροίαν ἀφίκετο.

Of his father *Peteos* (Türk, *RE* XIX, 1937, 1130; the name is recorded *Peplos* 34.1, Plut. *Thes.* 32, Apollod. 3.10.8, Pausan. ii 25.6, x 35.8, Aelian, *v.h.* 4.5) nothing was known and very little invented. Diod. Sic. 1.28.6, i 45 f. Vog., reports a ridiculous story that "Petes" the father of M. was an Egyptian who colonized Athens and ruled there. Pausan. x 35.8 says that Stiris (in Phocis) claimed as their founder the son of Orneus, Peteos, who had been expelled from Athens. The sole interesting reference to Peteos is in Athenaeus xi 459ᵃ: Polyidus, sacrificing on behalf of the Seven against Thebes, stopped Peteos as he passed, sat him down, and gave him some of the sacrificial food,—this clearly had some wider context, possibly preserved through the Theban saga. Cf. also Callimachus, *Hecale, Papyr. Oxyr.* 2377.4 'Ορνείδαο, presumably = Peteos the son of Orneus, but the context is unintelligible; as Lobel points out, Menestheus himself may be meant. See also Beazley, *AJA* 45 (1941) 595.

His grandfather *Orneus* (Hanslik, *RE* XVIII, 1939, 1125; Höfer, *Myth. Lex.* iii 1049) is obscurer still: Pausan. x 35.8, father of Peteos; Plut. *Thes.* 32, grandfather of M.; Pausan. ii 25.6, Orneus "son of Erechtheus" was founder of Orneiae in N. Peloponnese; cf. Eust. *Il.* 291.6; Euseb. *chron.* 2.50 Sch.; Steph. Byz. and Phavorin. s.v. 'Ορνειαί. There is one piece of early evidence: a red-figured calyx-crater from the Acropolis; Beazley, *Attic Red-Figure Vase-Painters* 195 with references, esp. *Eph. Arch.* (1885) pls. 11–12, Brückner in *Ath. Mitth.* 16 (1891) 200 ff.; on one side, Theseus killing the Minotaur, on the other "Orneus" and three sons of Pandion. Orneus seems obviously out of place in this company, but we do not know who he was or where he came from. 'Ερεχθεῖ 'Αρνέως in *Inscr. Graec.* II 844 is not helpful.

80 Except their Ionic dialect-dress.
81 On all this see Allen, *HCS* 156 ff.
82 Not quite alone, if I am right about Odysseus, n. 32 above.
83 653–656 may have stood alone as the entry for Tlepolemos; 657–666, the historical digression which first introduces the anachronism, may have been added in the Ionian period, as 667–670 (which first introduce the Dorians) certainly were.
84 Murray, *RGE* 219. See also Robert, *Bild und Lied* 118; Bethe, *Homer* iii 65; Wüst, *RE* s.v. Tlepol.; Von der Mühll, *Hypomnema* 100; Burr 1.

[85] Nilsson, *Homer and Mycenae* 262.

[86] Even Nilsson (l.c.) falls into this error; also Lorimer, *HM* 466 n. 2; Wace, Foreword to Ventris and Chadwick, *DMG* p. xxx, calls Tlepolemos "the son of Herakles, the great Dorian hero": but the great Herakles who was father of T. has not yet any connexion with Dorians. No doubt the Dorian tribes are meant by καταφυλαδόν in 668, but 668–670 are a later addition (Aristarchus athetized 669 only, but it is obvious that all three lines cohere, and 667 surely goes with them). The word πλοῦτον in 670 identifies the line as Ionian: it is not included in the traditional formular vocabulary, and has seldom been admitted to the poem by the Ionians; in the Iliad, only Λ 171, E 708, Π 596, Ω 536, 546, in the Odyssey only ξ 206, ω 486. Nor is φίληθεν ἐκ Διός an old Epic combination (B 32 f., cf. E 653 and Φ 513, not at all parallel; nor is Σ 75 τετέλεσται ἐκ Διός). τριχθὰ δὲ ᾤκηθεν καταφυλαδόν (division into three tribes) following διὰ τρίχα κοσμηθέντες (settlement in three cities) is clumsy.

[87] *HCS* 102.

[88] Cf. Pind. *Ol.* 7.19 ff., with Farnell's Commentary. On Licymnius see now Riemann, *RE* Suppl. VIII (1956) 259 ff.

[89] The Catalogue's remarkable independence is again asserted in its location of Philoctetes' kingdom: later he is known to be at home in Malis, a long way from his Homeric dominion; Leaf, *HH* 127.

[90] Bolling, *AL1* 80.

[91] Allen, *HCS* 56 f.

[92] Von der Mühll, *Hypomnema* 58, with references, to which add esp. Lorimer, *HM* 447 ff. B 549–551 (and therefore perhaps the two preceding lines) are surely a late accretion.

[93] Observe also that, since the Catalogue was created in Boeotia, it may have been continuously preserved there and there only; if so, we can the more easily understand why the main stream of tradition, far away in Ionia, diverged so widely from it, and why it came so late and so reluctantly into the embrace of the Iliad.

[94] Chantraine, *GH* 1.358 f.; Shipp, *SLH* 62.

[95] Chantraine, *GH* 1.35; Shipp, *SLH* 55.

[96] Cf. Ventris and Chadwick, *DMG* 79 (on -oιo, -ojo in the Tablets) and 88 (on variation between *apu-dōke* and *ape-dōke*). It is to be noticed that monstrous forms of the kind we like to ascribe to late rhapsodes existed already in the Mycenaean period: cf. *potniaweios, wanassewiā*, forms inspired by the analogy of βασιλήϝιος.

[97] In the "comments," i.e., apparently Ionian additions to the prehistoric Catalogues:

In the comment on Locrian Ajax, 530 untraditional Πανέλληνας (for Παναχαιούς); on Athens, 550 Ionic μιν, 554 the analogical formation ἀσπιδιώτας (Shipp, *SLH* 68); on Agamemnon, 579 the artificial formation κυδιόων (Shipp 63); on Thamyris, 595 the definite article τόν (Chantraine, *GH* 2.163), 597 f. the un-Homeric εἰ with ἄν and optative (Chantraine 2.278); on the Aetolians, 641 digamma ignored in ἔτ' Οἰνῆος; on Achilles, 686 ἐμνώοντο is an aberration of language (for ἐμιμνήσκοντο), 687 ἔην before vowel (Bolling, *ALI* 80 n. 2), 694 ἀνστη- is untraditional (for ἀναστη-, Shipp 137); on Protesilaus, 700 ἐλέλειπτο, a late formation (Chantraine 1.432), 704 Ionic σφέας; on Philoctetes, 719 ἐν ἑκάστῃ and 720 εἰδότες ἴφι, digamma ignored, 723 μοχλίζοντα is a late creation (Chantraine 1.95); on Merops, 832 ᾔδεε for ᾔδει, and ἔασκε for ἐάασκε (cf. Λ 330; Shipp 38).

98 In the lists: 494 Πηνέλεως is apparently Ionic -λεως for -λαος, but I suppose the name was really Πηνέλεος (-έοιο in Ξ 489); so also Chantraine 1.197; in any case there is no reason to suppose that the -λεως in this name has anything to do with the word which means "people." 506 Ποσιδήιον: ποσι- for ποσει- is exemplified already in the Mycenaean Tablets (Ventris and Chadwick, *DMG* p. 288). 508 and 616 ἐσχατόωσα: a secondary form, presumably not of ancient pedigree; Chantraine 1.358 f., cf. Shipp 62. 521 Ἀνεμώρειαν might have been expected to be -είην in an Ionic text, but there is no need to suppose that it is an Attic spelling (Meister, *Hom. Kunstsprache* 250, against Wackernagel, *Sprachl. Untersuch. z. Homer* 11). 615 Βουπράσιόν τε καὶ Ἤλιδα, digamma ignored; presumably Β. καὶ Ϝάλιδα; on ναίουσι see Chantraine 2.172, and cf. Β 648. 672 Χαρόποιό τ' ἄνακτος: digamma ignored; perhaps an Ionian expansion, or -που τε Ϝάνακτος. 681 τὸ Πελασγικὸν Ἄργος. Chantraine (2.165) thinks this a late use of the definite article; but, if so, the *line* need not be of late composition (τε for τό). 684 καλεῦντο wears an Ionic dress; perhaps formerly κάλεντο, but this may be an Ionic expansion (cf. Ionic νεῶν 685). 750 δυσχείμερον οἰκία: digamma ignored; this must be Ionic, whether composition or alteration; not δυσχείμερα Ϝοικία, for Π 234 shows that δυσχ. was an epithet attached to Dodona. 818 μεμαότες: μεμαοτ- only here and Ν 197, μεμαῶς Π 754; 43 examples of μεμαῶτες, which is according to pattern (βεβάωτες γεγάωτες); Chantraine 1.430, Shipp 140 ("the type [μεμᾶοτες] is probably not old").

On νέες, ἐστιχόωντο, ὀγδώ-, ἐνενή- see p. 153 above.

99 Borrowed from Gilbert Murray, *Rise of the Greek Epic*, Introd., in a similar context.

V

The Documents from Pylos
and Cnossos

BETWEEN the latest of the Linear B documents
and the golden age of Homeric poetry three or four hundred
years elapse. The time is long enough: but it is not the only or
even the opaquest barrier. Near the beginning of this interval
the Mycenaean civilization was overturned and buried: between the documents and the poems lie the Dark Ages of
Greece. The world which the Homeric poets pretend to describe is one which had disappeared from the face of the earth
hundreds of years before: yet there remained one thread unbroken, uniting the memory of past and present,—Homeric
poetry itself, continuously composed and transmitted from the
Mycenaean to the modern age. Surely some traces of the past
may be found in it: though few perhaps and faint, for the Greek
Epic was continually developing; it was reborn and to some extent reattired according to the fashion prevalent in each new
generation. There are indeed certain formular phrases in which
even today the ancient music dwells lingering: but the echoes
become ever fainter, for the Iliad marches on continually,
farther and farther from the past; and the final product, the
poems in their present form, may well reflect much more of the
recent than of that remoter world.

It is worth while to compare the two, poems and documents,
and to notice resemblance and contrast. But as a rule we can
do this only in broadest outlines. We are very seldom able to
make valid comparisons in detail. For it is no good putting
poems and documents side by side and observing, This in the
one is like that in the other. Where the poems agree with the

documents on a point of detail, that detail may have come to the later poets from their own times or from comparatively recent times; it is very seldom possible to prove that it must have come down from the Mycenaean period and could not have been known at first hand in any later period.[1]

I proceed to examine one aspect only of this many-sided Mycenaean world as revealed by the documents,—its relation to the world of the Iliad; and I shall do this in broadest outlines only. It soon becomes apparent that the differences between the two are many and great, the points of contact few and superficial. Here and there we may find that the language of the poem has preserved some relic of its Mycenaean past; and it is likely that the number of such relics identifiable is only a small proportion of the number actually existing. We must constantly remember how scanty and one-sided our information is; and how great the difference between a poem and a taxation-form. The Mycenaean clerk and the Mycenaean poet had different traditions, different purposes, and different audiences; as a rule they talk about quite different things. In general it becomes clear that the tale of Troy, which has a continuous history from the 12th to the 9th century B.C., in its latest phase reflects nothing of its Mycenaean past except misty outlines and a few dim-seen details: but the disparity must not be exaggerated. Much that we learn for the first time from the Tablets may be of a type which was below the level, or alien to the purposes, of Mycenaean poetry.

Let us begin by scanning the outline of the Mycenaean world revealed by the Tablets; first noticing the astonishing fact that the sign-forms, spelling, dialect, phraseology, and tablet-shapes at Pylos on the mainland about 1200 B.C. are almost identical with those at Cnossos overseas 200 years earlier,—this almost incredible uniformity is perhaps the most persuasive of several proofs "that writing was the preserve of specialists trained in a rigidly conservative scribal school."[2] The decipherment of the Tablets[3] has fully confirmed what the intelligible ideograms[4] had already suggested: that the Kingdoms of Pylos and Cnossos were bureaucratic monarchies of a type quite unexpected in Hellas but in many ways similar to some contemporary and earlier kingdoms in the eastern Mediterranean. This is the immediate and enduring impression made by the Tablets: that their world is essentially similar to the societies of Ugarit and Alalakh and Hattusas; it is very unlike anything that we associate with Greeks or anything that ever again existed in Hellas.

These palace archives are the records of a comprehensive and pervasive bureaucracy, administering for hundreds of years a most elaborately organized society. We did not, and could not, know that it ever existed: for suddenly the whole complex system disappeared from the earth, soon to be forgotten, never to be revived. The total extinction of a system so long-enduring, so elaborately constructed, and so rigidly administered, bears eloquent testimony to the depth and darkness of the flood which submerged Hellas when the Dorian peoples settled in the realms of Agamemnon and Menelaus and Nestor.

Observe now these bureaucrats, how wide their scope and how insatiable their thirst for information. They probe into the affairs of people in every gradation of society, from the highest officers of state down to the slave of a manual worker. They have the power to demand, and the duty to record, infinite detail about men and women and children, industrial manufactures and materials, agricultural produce and livestock, all kinds of holdings of all kinds of land, the administration of religious ritual, movements of troops and the manning of ships. There is endless counting and classifying, measuring and weighing, assessing and collecting and distributing. It is as if everything done by everybody was open to official inquiry and subject to official orders. We possess a part only of the archives for a single year at Pylos: they record thousands of transactions in hundreds of places.

Here, for example, are eighteen places, each obliged to make contributions of six commodities, and relative assessments are fixed for each of the places and for each of the commodities within the schedule.[5] Here again is a distribution of bronze, enough to make half a million arrowheads or 2,300 swords, allocated to a large number of places, with a note to say how many smiths in each place are active, how many inactive, and what is the allocation to each.[6] In Crete we count sheep up to 25,051; and again up to 19,000.[7]

But more astonishing and significant is the omniscience, the insatiable thirst for intimate detail. Sheep may be counted up to a glittering total of twenty-five thousand: but there is still a purpose to be served by recording the fact that *one* animal was contributed by Komawens and another by *E-te-wa-no*.[8] Restless officialdom notes the presence in *Pe-se-ro*'s house of one woman and two children;[9] the employment of two nurses, one girl, and one boy, in a Cretan village;[10] the fattening of an insignificant number of hogs in nine places;[11] the existence somewhere of a single pair of brassbound chariot wheels labelled "useless,"[12]—these things and hundreds more of the same type were duly recorded in the palaces of Pylos and Cnossos. A glance at these documents enables you at once to answer such questions as these: How many slaves has Korudallos, and what are they doing?[13] How many sons did the weaving-women from *Ti-nwa-to* bear to the rowing-men at *A-pu-ne-we?*[14] Who is watching over the cattle of Thalamatas?[15] What are the wheat and fig rations for thirty-seven female bath attendants and twenty-eight children at Pylos?[16] What is the acreage of Alektruon's estate, and how much ought he to pay (1) in annual tax, (2) to Poseidon, (3) to Diwieus?[17] How much linen is to be expected from Rhion; what deduction must be made by reason of the exemption of what class of craftsman?[18] In a given room or other space, how many pans, cauldrons, lamps, hammers, brushes, and fire tongs are to be found?[19] To whom, in what amounts, and for what purpose, did *A-ko-so-ta* issue coriander, cyperus, fruits, wine, honey, and what else?[20] How much is due from Dunios to the palace?—Answer: 2,220 litres of barley, 526 of olives, 468 of wine; 15 rams, 8 yearlings, 1 ewe, 13 he-goats,

12 pigs, 1 fat hog, 1 cow, and 2 bulls.[21] What are the personal names of two oxen belonging to *Ta-za-ro?*—Answer: *Glossy*[22] and *Blackie*.

I do not say that these are questions which anyone was likely to ask: the point is that these—and hundreds if not thousands like them—can all be *answered* from the records. They serve to illustrate the omniscience of the bureaucracy. One would suppose that not a seed could be sown, not a gram of bronze worked, not a cloth woven, not a goat reared or a hog fattened, without the filling of a form in the Royal Palace; such is the impression made by only part of the files for a single year.

What was the purpose of this annual amassing of infinite detail about so many activities is so many places? Some of the Tablets are simply inventories,—descriptions of furniture and equipment of various kinds, presumably in use at the Palace or in store near by. But the great majority are records of assessments, deliveries, and distributions,—distributions both of materials for production and of commodities so produced. And now we must ask, what is the political background necessarily implied by this wonderfully elaborate and centralized administrative system? One thing is surely manifest: that whoever controlled this secretariat must to some extent have authorized and controlled the transactions which it records. These archives were not compiled without the exercise of extensive powers, especially the power to extract information about all kinds of activities from all classes in the kingdom. And presumably the source of that power is the same as that which authorized the actions consequent upon the information thus collected,—the fixing of assessments, the exacting of dues, the allocation of rations. From the fact that the archives were found *in the palaces* we naturally infer that the supreme central authority was that of the king himself; though we do not know whether his power was absolute or limited (whether by a council of state or by some other body).[23]

So much is clear in outline. When we proceed to inquire into the structure of this bureaucratic state, we find the detail fragmentary and obscure.

Two characteristics of Mycenaean civilization unfamiliar to the Greek Epic are clearly attested,—slavery, and the specialization of labour. Here are things of which the Homeric poems have no notion,—numerous male and female "slaves of the goddess (or god)"; slaves of a palace official, 32 female slaves of Amphiphoitas; slaves of one man after another, slave even of a bronzesmith.[24] And division of labour is thoroughly systematic: the list of occupational names is a long one,[25] including doctor, herald, goldsmith, potter, forester, baker, carpenter, shipbuilder, bowmaker, flaxworker, carder, spinner, weaver, fuller, stitcher, bath attendant, and unguent boiler.

These at least are hard facts: when we turn to the higher levels of society we enter the realm of theory, if not of dreams.

The Tablets mention (but seldom) a person called *wanax*, apparently "the sovereign," at Cnossos and Pylos and perhaps also at Thebes. There is nothing to contradict the opinion that in each place there was only *one* "sovereign"; but we know very little about him. He has (of course) a *temenos*, a slice of land; he appoints bureaucratic officials;[26] he has "royal servants"— the king's potter, the king's fuller, the king's *e-te-do-mo;* there are textiles "belonging to the king"; his title is recorded in obscure connexions with the places *Pa-ki-ja-* and *Pi-ka-na;* and we are told how much seed he had for condiments at Cnossos.[27] This is a small sum of knowledge; and the rest is guesswork. The comprehensive and centralized administrative system suggests an autocratic monarchic régime: we suppose that the *wanax* was head of the state and supreme in authority, for his palace officials seem to be all-powerful everywhere. I notice in passing one most significant omission in the Tablets: there is not a word about the administration of *justice*, no reference whatsoever to *law.*[28] It is natural to infer that the king, all-powerful controller of the all-seeing bureaucracy, possessed supreme authority also in the region of lawmaking and law enforcement: but it is not a very secure inference, since we know nothing whatever about the king's relation to other great men in his dominions.

Let us leave him, uneasy on doubtful throne, and look to see who comes next. Professor Palmer[29] has reconstructed a feudal hierarchy of alleged Indo-European pattern, with King and Duke and Barons; but the Tablets themselves afford no evidence that such ranks, thus interrelated, ever existed in Mycenaean Hellas. The reconstruction is based on analogies from other societies in combination with the etymologies of certain titles in the Tablets. It is purely theoretical: it might be true, or it might be false,—and we now believe that it is false, for it looks as though the so-called barons must be withdrawn from the system and assigned to religious duties, apparently not in the higher strata of society.[30] In any case it must be admitted that there is nothing in the Tablets to suggest that Mycenaean society was constructed in any such way,—that the so-called duke performed the duties, and possessed the privileges, of a military leader; or that the so-called duke and barons stood in this particular relation to each other and to the so-called king. The whole system is an hypothesis, a pattern not revealed by the Tablets but impressed upon them from outside.

Let us briefly examine the doubtful credentials of the "duke." No. 152 records the *temenê*, slices of land, belonging to the king and to a person called *lawagetas*, in that order; then, after a gap, come the landholdings of certain officials, *telestai* and *worgiones*.[31] It is a safe inference that the *lawagetas*, "leader of the people," was an important officer. The Epic knows nothing of him, and the Tablets tell us nothing about his functions. It is suggested that he was an *army* leader, a duke or Herzog: if it were so, it would be surprising that his title found—or retained —no place in poetry about war. The Epic assigns the military leadership to the king: and the Tablets neither confirm nor contradict it. But in truth the "army command" of the *lawagetas* remains a mere speculation, unsupported by the Tablets; and his claim to the second position in the state, too hastily inferred from his mention next the king in a single document, is vigorously contested by other Tablets.

For somewhere in this exalted sphere we must make room for another great personage, known by name but not by title,—

Echelawon. In no. 171, a record of offerings to Poseidon, he has pride of place, and makes by far the greatest contribution; the *lawagetas* comes third, below even the *damos*, and his offerings are relatively contemptible.[32] Ventris and Chadwick say that the precedence assigned to Echelawon in this record "makes it almost certain that we have here the first contemporarily attested Mycenaean monarch":[33] but this claim is opposed by no. 54, where Echelawon's name occurs near the bottom of a long list of places and persons with numbers of oarsmen attached; and by no. 55, where he is included in a list of authorities responsible for a *deficit* of oarsmen, and again his name is not first in the order. Neither the contents of these lists nor the position of Echelawon in them is easily reconciled with the theory that he was the Great King of Pylos.[34] Yet he is obviously of exalted standing: and we cannot possibly rank him *lower* than the *lawagetas;* for in nos. 55 and 171, when both are mentioned, Echelawon comes in front, and in 171 he makes the *lawagetas* look very small. The hard fact is that we do not know what functions these officers performed, or how they stood in relation to each other and to the king.

Moving downwards (or so we suppose) in the social hierarchy we are soon lost in a wilderness of titles, most of them new to us and all but a few obscure or incomprehensible. They seem to come from a variety of categories. There are titles such as "settler" and "immigrant";[35] there is the volatile term *damos*, a body empowered to lease certain kinds of land and obliged to make certain ritual offerings. There are titles for classes of landholders,—*mo-ro-pa₂*,[36] ktoinoochoi, ktoinetai, kamaeus; there are names for provincial grandees,—*ko-re-te, po-ro-ko-re-te, du-ma, po-ro-du-ma, me-ri-du-ma*. There are titles for religious officers, "priest" and "priestess," "telestai," "keybearers," and a body called "worgiones." There are bureaucrats, both of the palace and provincial, some of the former known by name,—*A-ko-so-ta, We-da-ne-u, We-we-si-jo, A-ke-o, U-ta-jo*, Diwieus, and Amphimedes; others by title,—*e-sa-re-u* in high places, *o-pi-su-ko* and *o-pi-ka-pe-u* in the provinces.[37] There are other obscure titles, such as *hequetas:*[38] this officer is dignified by a patronymic adjective; he accompanies troops of soldiers; he may possess slaves; cloaks and even chariot wheels seem to be named after his title; but we know nothing whatsoever about his relation to other persons or parties in the state.[39]

Among these titles we come at last to one already familiar from the Greek Epic, *basileus.*[40] There are few mentions of him; and there are numerous documents in which his absence is conspicuous. There is one tablet[41] which suggests that in Crete the *basileus* occupied a post in provincial towns comparable with that of the *lawagetas* in the capital: but at Pylos he seems to be one among numerous officials, *ko-re-te-re, mo-ro-pa₂*, and the like, who contribute gold or distribute bronze or receive rations of barley.[42] At first sight he appears rather an insignificant person: a *basileus* may be named low on a list of officials of different types;[43] and his retinue may be lumped together with bakers and leatherworkers and even the slaves of other men.[44] But at least it looks as though he *has* a retinue,[45] and so much cannot yet be said about anyone else in the state. There is a further possibility, at present unconfirmed: that he kept a Council of Elders, *geronsia.*[46] It is prudent to admit that, despite some appearances, the *basileus* may have been a more important official than most: nevertheless it is clear that he and his retinue are subservient to the bureaucrats at Pylos.

Such in briefest outline are some of the most prominent aspects of the world of Mycenaean Greece: how much of all this was remembered in the Ionian Epic? The answer is surely not in doubt. We shall see later that the Epic touches this real world at the surface here and there: but it has no conception of what lay beneath the surface. The Iliad and Odyssey have no notion of a society of this type, an autocratic bureaucratic government, pervasive and penetrating, assessing and collecting and distributing, measuring and counting and recording. They are not even aware that labour was so highly specialized, or that slavery was an integral institution in social and religious life. They have lost, if they ever possessed, almost all the titles of rank in all walks of life: they have forgotten the very commonest terms, *lawagetas*[47] and *hequetas*, *ktoina* and *kama*, *o-pa* and *qe-te-a₂* and *dosmos* and the rest. In Mycenaean Greece the vocabulary was bound up with the system: the system disappeared from the earth,—and with it disappeared the technical terms, for there was no longer any meaning in them or use for them.

Still it remains remarkable that so few of the technical terms survived, where they might have survived, in the Greek Epic. It may be suggested that many of them are of a type unlikely to find a way into poetry designed to glorify a few noblemen at the most exalted level of society: perhaps many of them were; but it is obvious that several of the remainder are words of high dignity, grave import, and widespread usage. The likelier reason why these are wanting in the Homeric poems is that the Epic gradually discarded them: it is not surprising that the Epic could not retain the *words* throughout hundreds of years after the *things* which they signified had vanished from the earth.

But let us not argue about a word or two, or even about a great many. The most important aspect is that of the whole, not of its component parts. What the Homeric poems have lost is not primarily a number of words but *the whole elaborate structure of government, the whole complex system of society, depicted in the Tablets.* Time and again the Iliad and Odyssey show that they have no notion that their Heroic world was in truth a model bureaucracy, a society divided and subdivided and labelled and inspected and rationed and in general controlled in all its phases by a restless and pervasive army of officials. And it is inconceivable that the Epic in the Mycenaean period should not have differed fundamentally in this respect: no doubt it took much for granted, but what it took for granted was something which the Ionian poets never knew,—a complex political and social background, which transmitted to posterity nothing but faint and distorted echoes.

After the lapse of four hundred years (more or less) the memory of the Mycenaean world survived only in certain formular words and phrases; but there at least it did survive, and the Epic words for "king" provide our first example.

The Tablets have two high titles in common with the

Homeric poems, *wanax* and *basileus*. We have seen some reason to believe that *wanax* was the sovereign, the supreme ruler in the central palace. *Basileis*, on the other hand, are manifold, apparently officials—or perhaps governors—in towns or districts beyond the area of the Palace itself. Now Mr Finley has observed an interesting and significant contrast between the Mycenaean and the historical usages of these words: in the Mycenaean period *wanax* is the highest title of state, *basileus* an inferior governor; but already at the beginning of the historical period *wanax* is an extinct or at least obsolete title,[48] and *basileus* may now denote the supreme ruler. The latter has gone up in the world, the former down. It is of particular importance to us to notice that the Mycenaean usage made a lasting impression on Homeric poetry: the older distinction has become confused, for the Epic gives the title *basileus* to men who were clearly—in the Mycenaean sense—*wanaktes*; but the important point is that the title *wanax*, extinct or moribund in the Ionian world, was vivacious in the Ionian Epic. It is used nearly twice as often as *basileus;* and the Ionian poets are still aware (if only subconsciously) that whereas *wanax* is a fit title even for a god, no god is ever to be called by the inferior title *basileus*.[49] The existence of the title *wanax* in the Iliad is a plain proof of the continuity of the Greek Epic from the Mycenaean period onwards; and the restriction imposed on the usage of *basileus* is a striking testimony to the power of tradition. Nothing but the compulsion exercised by a traditional formular language could have enforced the retention of the one word and the limitation of the other throughout an age which cared for none of these things.

The more strictly formular the phraseology, the greater the expectation of Mycenaean relics in the Homeric poems: but the expectation is not always fulfilled, not even where hope is highest. Consider an example or two, significant of much.

There is talk in both Tablets and Epic about tables and chairs, chariots and armour and the like: how do the two com-

pare when they describe such articles? Let the table bear
witness first:

No. 239:

to-pe-za ra-e-ja we-a-re-ja a-ja-me-na a₂-ro-u-do-pi ku-wa-no-qe pa-ra-
  ke-we-[qe ku-ru-so-qe] e-ne-wo pe-[za]
*to-pe-za ra-e-ja me-no-e-ja e-re-pa-te a-ja-me-na qe-qi-no-to *85-de-pi*
  ko-ru-pi-qe
to-pe-za ra-e-ja a-pi-qo-to e-ne-wo pe-za e-re-pa-te-jo po-pi e-ka-ma-te-qe
  qe-qi-no-to-qe to-qi-de

At first sight it reads unlike the Greek language, let alone the
Homeric. But our eyes soon become accustomed to the dusk:
we quickly identify *trapeza, kuanōi te, khrusōi te, en(n)ewopeza,*
elephanti; given time, we recognize *koruthphi*, "with a helmet,"
and *popphi* in the guise of *po-pi*, "with feet." Yet of eighteen
words we have so far given shape to only seven: what is this
majority of monsters, *qe-qi-no-to, we-a-re-ja, a₂-ro-u-do-pi*, and
the rest? We may come to concede that *to-qi-de* may be *tor-*
quidei, "with a spiral," and perhaps also that *a-pi-qo-to* may
be *amphiguotos*, ἀμφίβατος, though its meaning will remain obscure.[50] But of the remainder we can give no proper account:
ra-e-ja, we-a-re-ja are novel and inscrutable adjectives;
a-ja-me-na and *qe-qi-no-to* are evidently standard terms,
whose meanings we can infer, but they come from verbs which
have disappeared from the language;[51] what objects are denoted
by *a₂-ro-u-do, pa-ra-ke-we, e-ka-ma-te*,[52] **85-de*,[53] we do not
know and can hardly guess. And if we turn to other Tablets, we
find no comfort.

No. 214:
pa-we-a e-qe-si-ja re-u-ko-nu-ka pe-ne-we-ta a-ro₂-a

Pawea we recognize as *pharwea*, "cloaks": but all four adjectives seem unfamiliar to us.[54] Look further in this region, and
you move bewildered among such incomprehensibles as *e-ne-ro,*
e-ni-qe, e-ro-pa-ke-je, ko-ru-we-ja, ko-u-ra, nu-wa-ja, o-pi-qi-na,
o-re-ne-ja, pa-ra-ku-ja, to-mi-ka, tu-na-no, u-po-we, wo-ro-ne-ja,
—all epithets for garments or other textiles.

Chariots and chairs are not less obscurely described. The chariot in the Iliad has three names, ὄχος, δίφρος, and ἅρμα: the Mycenaeans used not one of these but a new name, *hiqquiā*;[55] and their descriptions include a distressing number of mysteries or monsters,—the nouns *o-po-qo, ai-ki-no-o, a-re-ta-to, i-qo-e-qe, ki-da-pa, o-pi-i-ja, pe-pa₂-to*, the adjectives *a-te-re-te-a, e-ka-te-re-ta, e-te-re-ta, o-da-ku-we-ta, wa-ra-wi-ta, wo-ra-we-sa*. The chair is called by its Homeric name, only *thornos* instead of *thronos*; here is a sample of its description.

No. 242:
to-no ku-te-ta-jo ku-ru-sa-pi o-pi-ke-re-mi-ni-ja-pi o-ni-ti-ja-pi ta-ra-nu-qe a-ja-me-no e-re-pa-te-jo *85-de-pi
to-no ku-te-se-jo e-re-pa-te-ja-pi o-pi-ke-re-mi-ni-ja-pi se-re-mo-ka-ra-o-i qe-qi-no-me-na a-di-ri-ja-te-qe po-ti-pi-qe

Here are thirteen different words, of which we certainly understand less than half,—*thornos, thranus, kutesos, khrusos, elephas, andrias*. We may well admit that the context is in favour of identifying *o-ni-ti-ja-pi* with *ornithiaphi*, "(decorated) with birds," and *po-ti-pi* with *portīphi*, "with heifers." But the meaning of the standard verbs, *a-ja-me-no* and *qe-qi-no-me-na*, and of the standard nouns, *o-pi-ke-re-mi-ni-ja, se-re-mo-ka-ra-*, **85-de*, can hardly even be guessed; and the Homeric vocabulary will throw no light whatever on them.

From a short survey in this neighbourhood alone we shall soon compile a list of more than thirty adjectives which are incomprehensible, and at least half as many which we understand indeed but which we shall not find in the Homeric poems. Add to these the two or three standard verb-forms; some twenty nouns which we cannot identify with Greek words; and another half-dozen which recur in later Greek but not in the Epic,[56]—it is clear that the Mycenaean clerk and the Homeric poet describe the same objects in very different terms.

The points of contact are slight and superficial; the differences are vast, and must be significant; significant of what? Of one thing certainly, I submit; perhaps of one only. Consider the epithets which the Epic actually applies to chariots, and ask, how many of them would seem at home in the Tablets?— ἄγκυλον, βοήθοον, εὐεργές, εὔξοον, ἐϋπλεκές, εὔπλεκτον, εὔτροχον, θοόν, ἱερόν, καλόν, κάμπυλον, κολλητόν, παμφανόων, περικαλλές, ποικίλον, εὖ πεπυκασμένον. Contrast these with so much as we can understand of the Mycenaean epithets: the distinction is obvious,— the poet employs *general* terms, the archivist *specific* terms. The poet speaks not (as a rule) of *this* chariot, but of *all* chariots; chariots in general may be swift, or shining, or well-made, of wickerwork, angular, with good wheels, and so forth. The civil servant describes *this* chariot, the one in front of him, to be distinguished so far as possible from all other chariots; he must look not for characteristic but for peculiar features; his days in office are numbered, if he is caught recording in the inventory that *this* chariot may be recognized by its swiftness or its beauty. There is indeed a little common ground, and might have been more: the clerk might well have called a chair "silver-studded" or "highly polished," or simply "tall," as the poet does; but the majority of the poet's epithets are out of place in an inventory,—"shining," "beautiful," "imperishable," and the like.

The disparity is much greater in adjectives than in nouns or verbs; these are, as a rule, identical in the Tablets and the poems. Why the verbs *a-ja-me-no*, *qe-qi-no-me-no*, should have been excluded from the formular poetic language we cannot tell; but we recognize that they are exceptional,—a very high proportion of all the verbs on the Tablets will be found again in the Homeric poems.[57] The gulf that divides the poems from the Mycenaean world is wide enough; the Epic has discarded much that became outworn during its progress through the Dark Ages. But the examples of the chair and chariot suffice to account for a great part of the discrepancy between the Mycenaean and the Homeric descriptive vocabularies: the clerk and the poet have contrary purposes, and are looking at quite different aspects of the articles which they describe.

A like tale is told, but darkly and in few words, about the superstitions of the Mycenaean people.[58] We find, what we expected,[59] the names of some of the so-called Olympians,— Zeus, Hera, Athena, Artemis, Poseidon, Hermes; to these we must add Eleuthia, Paiawon, and Enuwalios, perhaps also Erinys.[60] There is no mention of Apollo, Aphrodite, Ares, or Demeter:[61] but they might yet appear in other tablets, whether from Pylos or elsewhere. So far the Ionian Epic is in agreement with the Mycenaean records: but it is nothing more than an agreement over certain names; and from this we learn nothing profitable, for it was already certain enough that these names were not first introduced after the beginning of the Dark Ages, and the quality of their formular phrases had already proved that the principal divinities—or some of them—had played a part in the Epic from the Mycenaean period onwards.

The contact between the Epic and the Tablets is superficial merely: below the surface the Tablets at once disclose a world of which the Homeric poems are unaware. What we observe, however, is not inconsistency but simply difference. The Tablets record details of particular cults at Pylos and Cnossos; neither place of much interest to the Homeric poet. He stands aloof,[62] while the Tablets inform us that the most important divinities at Pylos were Poseidon and a goddess whose name is concealed beneath a title, *Potnia;*[63] behind them is ranged a muster of demons familiar and unfamiliar, ranked in the same list as their priests and priestesses. Zeus and Hera and "Drimios the priest of Zeus" stand on the same level and receive the same tokens of adoration.[64] Above them and below them in the order are Iphemedeia, Diwja, Poseidaeia, and the incomprehensible *Ma-na-sa, Ti-ri-se-ro, Do-po-ta.*[65] Meantime Cnossos goes a different way to heaven, with upturned awestruck eye adoring *Qe-ra-si-ja, Pi-pi-tu-na, E-ne-si-da-on;* invoking "all the gods"[66] in a breath; and respectful toward a strangely entitled female, *"Priestess of the Winds."*[67] The servants of Our Lady of Pylos are not immune from mundane toil: priestesses, and persons unknown to the Epic, "telestai," "keybearers," "worgiones," and "slaves of the goddess," hold leases of land, to some extent under privilege in the name of the divinity.[68] Nothing of all this the Epic knows, perhaps ever knew. Whatsoever part the gods played in the Mycenaean Epic about Troy, not all claims could be satisfied; and there might be no place for the peculiar superstitions practised in districts near the limit of the poet's vision. It is likely that something existed in the Epic and was lost; likelier still that the part of the Olympian Gods was greatly expanded by the Ionian poets, whose latest genius is seen at its most brilliant in the Deception of Zeus and the Revenge of Hephaestus,—but also at its most dismal in the Battle of the Gods. Nothing is quite certain but this: that the Epic tradition preserved little or nothing intact from the Mycenaean world except the names of its principal divinities, inseparably attached to certain epithets, indispensable and ready-made components of the verse. Behind the names and epithets lies a darkness, or at least a density of mist, through which the doubtful eye may penetrate here and there to the outline of something immeasurably old.

A similar lesson is to be learnt from those remarkable documents, the lists of Oarsmen and Troops.[69] And first let us reflect on their historical value, which has been much overrated.[70] The one really important fact, that Pylos was finally destroyed about 1200 B.C., was already proved by the excavations: if now the Tablets inform us that the people put themselves in a state of defence shortly before the catastrophe, we learn nothing but what we must have confidently presumed. It would indeed have been of some interest if the Tablets had proved that the attack came *from the sea;* but in fact they do not prove or even suggest it. No such conclusion can be drawn from lists of oarsmen; and although the troops may be stationed "to guard the coast," there is no reason to suppose that they were expecting a great sea-borne assault. The numbers recorded are small,—perhaps a thousand men, distributed over ten stations; and though this is presumably only part of the evidence, so far as it goes it does not suggest that any great peril impended in this quarter. The number of men recorded in the command of Er-khomenatas at *Ti-mi-to a-ke-e* is only equal to half the number of cowmen available at *Ra-wa-ra-ti-ja*,[71] and the aggregate of all ten commands is only four times the number of carpenters recorded in connexion with the town of *Pa-ki-ja-*.[72] The most important question—whether these tablets record a routine or an emergency transaction—we simply cannot answer.

The lists of oarsmen are in some respects enigmatic documents. No. 53 is a catalogue of "rowers who are to go to Pleuron":[73] five different places unite to provide altogether a mere thirty men,—equivalent to the crew of a single not very large vessel. There is nothing to indicate that the implied voyage is in any way connected with warfare; indeed the sole point of interest is the fact that so many places should contribute toward so small a total. No. 54 throws no light on the historical scene. From its heading we learn that it is a record of oarsmen; but there is nothing to indicate why they are listed,—not even whether they have gone, or are destined to go, on any voyage.[74] The heading introduces a list of diverse entries,—class names, place names, ethnic names, personal names, and other obscure or unintelligible terms, each (except one) with a number of men appended. The aggregate may have been about 700 men,[75] sufficient perhaps for the crews of some fourteen vessels;[76] and for that insignificant flotilla not fewer than twenty-nine places or persons are put under contribution. Whether this record is an act of annual routine, or specially connected with a particular operation, commercial or military, we have no possible means of determining. Nor does the third of these "Oarsmen" Tablets assist us. The first line tells of "oarsmen absent" from a place called *Ro-o-wa*. The sequel, though exceptionally obscure in detail,[77] continues the same theme with reference to other places and persons; but it must be confessed that the thirteen lines which follow the first are almost entirely incomprehensible.[78]

In brief, there is nothing whatsoever to indicate that these

"Oarsmen" Tablets have any connexion with the events which culminated in the final destruction of Pylos. Let us now examine the Military Tablets from this point of view.

The heading consists of three words, of which the first and third are obscure;[79] but the second means "coastal regions," and we are therefore in no doubt about the general purpose of the record,—certain commanders, with their officers and men,[80] occupy certain stations on the coast. Ten different commands are listed. Each entry begins with the commander's name, in half the instances followed by the location of his unit. Then come the names of his principal officers, and then the names of the different companies which compose the unit, and the numbers of men in each company, together with the name of the place whence they have come and often the name of the place to which they are going. Finally the entry closes with the name (and as a rule the patronymic) of some special officer or commissar accompanying the unit. *Mutatis mutandis* this is in form and substance very much like what the Homeric Catalogue of Ships must have been in its Mycenaean phase: but its bearing on the contemporary scene must not be exaggerated. The Tablets give nothing but names and numbers; so the historian who relates the information thus provided to the wider context of the fall of Pylos must content himself with this modest sum of knowledge: that shortly before the destruction of Pylos the coast was watched from ten military stations (none of which can be located on the map), varying in strength from 36 to upwards of 126.[81] He must not fail to notice that all the entries record or imply the *movement*[82] of troops from one place to another; and he may conjecture that the forces were really much greater,—that when he reads of "fifty men *from* A *to* B," he is to understand that the main force was supplied on the spot, and that the bureaucrats are at present interested in nothing but reinforcements and rearrangements involving movement orders. So much, and more,[83] he may conjecture: the limits of his knowledge remain straitly defined; in particular, there is no possible means of determining whether the implied danger from the sea was a great or a small element in the troubles of the time.

Much more significant and interesting is the relation of these Tablets to the Greek Epic. For here again we see the veil lifted from an aspect of Mycenaean life unknown to the Homeric poems. None of the military terms recorded in these documents was hitherto known to us from the Epic or indeed from any other source. The "follower," *hequetās*, seems to have been an officer of some distinction: but there is no trace of his existence in Iliad or Odyssey. The name for a "command" or "contingent," *o-ka*, obscure in itself,[84] is missing from the rich vocabulary of the Epic. And when we meet an officer called *mo-ro-pa$_2$*, and troops called *ke-ki-de* and *ku-re-we*, we are in a world of which the Ionian Epic has preserved not the faintest vestige. The Iliad sees the Mycenaean era through the mist of centuries. It has never quite lost contact, and we can still discern hazy outlines; but the middle distance is dark or distorted, and the deeper background wholly obnubilated.

About two thirds of all the words on the Tablets are the names either of persons or of places.[85] So long a list of names might have afforded useful evidence bearing on the history not only of the Mycenaean Greeks but also of the Homeric poems; but hope is frustrated by various obstacles.[86] Of more than 220 places, fewer than 20 can be located with certainty on the map.[87] And of the thousand (and more) personal names it is impossible to say how many can be identified with Greek or other names already known to us: the ambiguity inherent in the spelling-system obscures all distinction between *Antiphos* and *Artipous*, between *Hagetas* and *Akestas*, between *Charon* and *Kallon*, and so forth. A very high proportion of the total number is thus ambiguous or else wholly unintelligible.

Nevertheless it is certain that the list includes many Greek names; and it is of special interest to observe that the suffix -ε$\acute{v}$s[88] was indeed, as we had expected, common in Mycenaean names. It had long been apparent that names in -ε$\acute{v}$s must be of

Mycenaean pedigree: for this suffix, which is specially character-istic of legendary names,[89] went out of use before the historical period.[90] To the Ionian poets it is a fashion long extinct, never again to be revived: the names *Achilleus*, *Odysseus*, *Atreus*, and the like, survived in the continuous Epic tradition; they would not have been *invented* by any people in Greek lands after the beginning of the Dark Ages.[91]

Of all Mycenaean elements in the Iliad this is (I suggest) the most significant: for the persons and the events are inseparable. The *names* survived only because the *stories* survived. Now there never was a story about Achilles except in connexion with a war against Troy: the name *Achilleus* indicates that the person was the subject of story at least as far back as the 12th century B.C.; and the inextricable entanglement of the person with the event indicates that the story itself must likewise ascend to the Mycenaean period. This is not the only witness to the fact that the Siege of Troy was already the subject of poetry within a generation or two of the historical destruction of Troy VII[a]: a fact which has an important implication to which we shall return.[92]

The Greek names on the Tablets include at least three dozen[93] which recur in the Homeric poems. That was only to be expected, for there was never any reason to suppose that Greek legend employed a unique set of names not borne by living persons in the Mycenaean period. If there was any doubt, it is now resolved: for nothing is more certain than the identi-fication of the names *Alektruon*, *Amphiaraos*, *Deukalion*, *Eteokles*, among others, on the Tablets. The recurrence of Homeric and other legendary names merely fulfils a confident expectation. We may feel satisfaction, but should find no special significance, in the testimony of a Cretan tablet that some per-son bore the name of *Ajax*;[94] and we have no reason to feel aggrieved that the ambiguity of the spelling precludes us for ever from discovering whether *Achilleus* was a common name,— Crete and Pylos both record an *A-ki-re-u*, but he could just as well be *Akireus* (to mention only one of several possibilities), no odder a name than *Akhil(l)eus* itself, or *Aphareus*, or whatever may underlie *A-pa-jeus*, *A-na-teus*, and numerous other obscure names in the Mycenaean list.[95]

More interesting, at first sight, is the question whether the names of Homeric *Trojans* recur on the Tablets. It is natural enough that the rank and file should bear common Greek names:[96] for the Epic required nearly 200 Trojan victims of Achaean slaughter, and nobody will be surprised to learn that Greek names were invented in preference to bogus and probably uncouth barbarians. But what of the leaders, especially the Trojan King and his commander-in-chief? We have seen some reason, and shall see more, to believe that the Greek siege of Troy was an historical event, commemorated by poets soon after its end. If the Trojan King and commander were real persons, their true names must surely have been known at the time, and used by the poets, and transmitted in the Epic down to the Ionian period. What, then, may be the significance of the fact (if it is one) that such names as *Tros* and *Priam* and *Hector* were borne by quite ordinary people at Pylos in or soon after the generation of the fall of Troy?

We might well answer again that this could have been predicted. If, as we believe, Trojans and Achaeans were of the same or similar Indo-European stock, there is no reason why they should not have some proper names in common. But we must pause to reflect upon a fact which invalidates that answer, and indeed frustrates the purpose of any inquiry into this matter. *An apparently Greek name on the Trojan side may be merely an adaptation*, the assimilation of a foreign name to a Greek form. Let the name of *Alexandros* be a warning to us: he looks Greek enough, but we know that he is merely a foreigner in a Greek dress. The Oriental *Alaksandus* has been twisted into a Greek shape; and the name *Hektor* may very well be another of the same type, a familiar Greek form impressed on a similar-sounding foreign name. In that case the appearance of the name *Hektor* in the Tablets would be no more significant or informative than the name *Alexandros* would have been.

For this reason there is little if any interest left in the question whether *Tros* and *Priam* and *Hector* do indeed appear in the Tablets. They have no claim to more than summary judgement. The first of them is merely a guess: *To-ro-o*[97] may just as well be the genitive of Τλώς (to mention only one of the alternatives); *Pi-ri-ja-me-ja* may be *Priameiās*, though a non-Greek *Philiameiās* would be no odder a name; as for *E-ko-to*, he is very likely to be *Hektor*.[98] If the identifications are correct (and we do not know whether they are or not) we may suppose that these were common names in Mycenaean Hellas: and if the King and commander of Troy had foreign names, we should infer no more than that their names *sounded like* "Priamos"[99] and "Hektor," just as *Alaksandus* sounded like "Alexandros."

The place names in the Tablets raise one question of special interest to us. The Catalogue of Achaeans in the Iliad names nine places in the Kingdom of Nestor; and we are at once curious to inquire whether the Tablets tell us of the same places as being inhabited at the end of the 12th century B.C.[100] The bare fact is that of the nine Homeric names the total of those which are and those which may be attested in the Tablets amounts to six.[101] This answer is, so far as it goes, reassuring enough to those who are convinced that the Catalogue more or less truthfully describes the political geography of Mycenaean Hellas; but we are not yet altogether satisfied. We notice, first, that only two[102] of the Homeric nine are at all prominent on the Tablets; and, secondly, that the Tablets present us with an almost entirely different group of nine. Two Tablets[103] have in common a list of nine places in the same order; a third[104] appears to be a fragment of the same list; and a fourth[105] differs only in substituting a new name[106] seventh in the order. In general, most of these nine appear more frequently than most other places on the Tablets;[107] but if we proceed to infer (as Ventris and Chadwick do) that these are "the principal towns of the kingdom,"[108] it would seem to follow that the Homeric Catalogue misrepresents the facts; for the two lists of nine have not more than one name in common. Since this conclusion would be contrary to our well-founded expectation, we shall inquire what claim the Tablets' Nine have to be called "the principal towns of the Kingdom."

It becomes at once apparent that, although several of them are prominent in the Tablets individually, the Nine have no special distinction *as a group*. Even if their names and sequence were invariable, we should not therefore be justified in attributing preëminence to them, for there might well be geographical, economic, or even political reasons for their association. But in fact neither the number nor the sequence is invariable. One place may give way to a newcomer in a list of nine; a majority of them may appear mixed up with a number of other places; and the sequence may be varied. Moreover there is nothing in the nature of the transactions recorded to indicate that the Nine were, as a group, of particular importance. The group-lists record commonplace affairs,—contributions of bronze, distribution of wine, the fattening of an insignificant number of hogs.[109] And when the Nine, or some of them, appear together with other places, most if not all of them are seen to be of moderate account. For example, on the *Ma-* Tablets[110] the Nine recur together with the same number of other places, and the figures indicate that five of our Nine rank among the six *lowest* places in the order of assessment. In a record of contributors of gold,[111] seven of our Nine are listed, but not in the familiar order, and not in one block; they are intermixed with other places (and persons), and their assessments are not above the average. In a list of rowing-men,[112] two of our Nine recur, and contribute numbers about halfway between lowest and highest. And on the so-called "Military" Tablets,[113] where we might expect their importance to be specially manifest, the only one of them which is named among the headquarter towns, *A-ke-re-wa*, has neither pride of place nor any other special distinction;[114] of the other eight, six are not recorded in this context, Charadros is merely a station for a detachment from a more important centre, and *Me-ta-pa* sends a contingent of average size.[115]

The truth appears to be that the Nine were grouped, sometimes alone, sometimes together with other places of similar
type, for certain administrative purposes. Nothing of importance is attributed to them as a group; and when related to
other places they occupy a middle position. It is nevertheless
admitted that several of them appear more often and in more
significant contexts than the others; and the reason may be that
these stood in some special relation to the palace at Pylos. Not
one of the Nine can be located with certainty on the map: but
there are quite strong indications that the two most prominent,
Pa-ki-ja- and *A-ke-re-wa,* were towns in the immediate neighbourhood of the palace;[116] it is indeed perfectly possible that all
nine of them lay close to Pylos.

Now compare anew the Homeric Catalogue with the Tablets:
but first consider that the two things may not be comparable.
The remote Boeotian, compiling his Catalogue, might well differ
from the palace archivists in his selection. He might know the
names of certain key points in the kingdom, such as Dorion
and Kuparissos must surely have been; and he might be quite
unaware that *Pa-ki-ja-* employed a stupendous number of
carpenters,[117] that the Mayor of *Ti-nwa-to* could be assessed
high for gold,[118] and in general that *Ro-o-wa, Me-ta-pa,* and a
dozen other places played a much larger part in the agricultural
and industrial life of the kingdom. We must not forget that the
Tablets, ephemeral and one-sided though they are, have really
gone quite far in support of the Homeric Catalogue, attesting
the existence of perhaps so many as six out of nine places; and
we must now observe what may be a most significant agreement
on a point of detail. The Catalogue, which is interested primarily in ships and soldiers, selects among others the town of
Kuparissos. Now Kuparissos is absent from all but one of the
numerous records of business transactions at Pylos: it is mentioned in two contexts only,—and in both it is specifically the
home of *soldiers.*[119] The coincidence may well be more than
fortuitous. It is at least a clear and stern warning against pre-
mature condemnation of the Homeric Catalogue. The palace

archives are highly specialized documents; we possess only part of the records from a very short period of time, perhaps a single year; and it happens that their interests seldom if ever[120] overlap those of the Homeric Catalogue. But when they do meet for a moment, at Kuparissos, they are in agreement. What the available archives do for Kuparissos, a more extensive set might do for Dorion and Amphigeneia and the rest. In order to pass judgement on the Homeric Catalogue, we should need to know much more than we actually do about the geography and political organization of the kingdom of Pylos; meantime let the example of Kuparissos be a caution against prejudice.

Looking back over the scene, we are satisfied that our first impression has been strongly confirmed by closer acquaintance. The world of the Tablets is one of which the Homeric poems retain only the faintest conception. The whole complex structure of society passed away, and the memory of it faded and perished: only a few points of contact, as a rule slight and superficial, have survived through the Dark Ages. And the next step must be to inquire, how did *anything at all* survive in poetry through the Dark Ages, for three or four hundred years, when the art of writing was lost? If we can answer that question, we shall know how to set about the task of finding, in the Iliad, such relics as there may still be of its Mycenaean past: the method of search, and some specimen of what may still be found, will be the subject of the last of these lectures.

NOTES

In the notes to this chapter I refer throughout to Ventris and Chadwick, *Documents in Mycenaean Greek* (1956), as *DMG*, with number of text therein contained.

[1] Consider, for example, the system of government described in the Iliad, B 48 ff.: King, council of Elders, general assembly of peers.

This may or may not be true of Mycenaean Greece—we simply do not know,—but it is certainly true of Mytilene in the late 7th century B.C. (my *Sappho and Alcaeus* 177 ff.).

[2] *DMG* p. 110; for the uniformity of dialect, pp. 75 f. Mr Finley, in his review of *DMG* in the *Economic History Review* 10 (1957) 134 n. 4, has said what is necessary against the common assumption (cf. Mylonas, *Ancient Mycenae*, 1957, 74) that the tablets from Mycenae indicate that others than professional scribes could write. Schaeffer, *Ugaritica* I (1939) 42, notes the significant contrast between the literate natives and the illiterate Mycenaeans at Ugarit.

[3] The doubts of Professor Beattie (*JHS* 76, 1956, 1 ff.) are shown to be unfounded by Mr. Chadwick (ibid. 77, 1957, 202 ff.); they arise from a misunderstanding of the way in which the decipherment was actually conducted, and of the way in which it can now be methodically checked. Cf. now also Treweek, Univ. of London, Inst. of Classical Studies, *Bulletin* 4 (1957) 10 ff.; Chadwick, *The Decipherment of Linear B* (1958), esp. chaps. 4–6. I have followed Ventris' work with close attention since June 22, 1952, when he sent me a long report of his progress up to date. His system was cryptographically of extreme correctness, and the requisite degree of methodical confirmation was attainable before the end of 1952. Interpretation of the results has gone (I believe) much too fast and far.

[4] *DMG* pp. 48 ff., with fig. 10 (add the helmet-ideogram from no. 300).

[5] Ibid. pp. 289 ff. (the *Ma-* Tablets).

[6] Ibid. pp. 352 ff. (the *Jn-* Tablets).

[7] Ibid. pp. 197 ff., 209.

[8] *DMG* no. 80.

[9] Ibid. no. 24.

[10] No. 17. "Nurses" is a doubtful guess for *a-ke-ti-ra$_2$*: but it makes no essential difference; for if not this, then some other women's occupational name is signified.

[11] No. 75. "Fattening" is another doubtful guess, but there is no doubt that this number of hogs (25) at this number of places (9) is being recorded.

[12] No. 291.

[13] No. 33.

[14] No. 15.

[15] Nos. 31, 32.

[16] No. 9.

[17] Nos. 168 ff.

[18] No. 192.

[19] No. 237. The lamps, hammers, and brushes are very doubtful guesses; but if not these, then other articles of the same general type.

[20] No. 103.

[21] No. 96.

[22] No. 85: *aiwolos*, a clear proof that this adjective might already mean "glittering," "twinkling," "shining" (see pp. 288–289 below).

[23] A case can be made in favour of some kind of *feudalism* in the Mycenaean social system. It looks as though production was in some respects connected with *tribute*, and land tenure with *service*. Important persons were expected to supply *men* for public services (e.g. no. 44; and this is presumably the implication of the records made in nos. 54, 56–60, and of the statement of deficits in no. 55). Various classes of landholder are said to perform (or not to perform) *duties* apparently connected with their tenure (e.g. no. 135.7 *ophelonsa . . . worzeen ou worzei;* nos. 141.2, 148 passim); and the duty of contributing a variety of commodities or artefacts is frequently attested (e.g. nos. 173 ff., with their *dosmos–apudosis–ophelos;* nos. 189 ff., with their [apparent] concessions, *eleuthera, aneta, ou didonsi;* nos. 257 f., the contributions of bronze and gold).

It is to be admitted, however, that the contexts of many of these documents are—or may be—*religious;* and that the nature of the connexion between service or tribute and land tenure is very imperfectly understood. "Feudalism" is a shifty term, useless or even misleading unless defined in its context: in this context we cannot define it, and its use would give the impression that we know much more than we really do about the organization of Mycenaean society.

[24] See esp. *DMG* pp. 123 f. The word δοῦλος and its cognates are very nearly absent from the Iliad (only δούλη Γ 409, in a passage athetized by Aristarchus; δούλιον ἦμαρ Z 463, a passage of purest Ionian poetry); the Odyssey, which has far greater scope for the word, has an isolated δούλη δ 12, δουλοσύνη χ 423, δούλειος in the very late Continuation (ω 252), and δούλιον ἦμαρ twice (ξ 340, ρ 323). Mr Chadwick points out that the Mycenaean trisyllabic form is excluded by the metre in all but two of the Homeric examples.

[25] *DMG* p. 123.

[26] The difficulty of our task and the stark unreliability of our evidence are alike illustrated by comparisons of the versions of the first line of *DMG* no. 235 (= Ta 711) given (*a*) by Ventris and Chadwick: "Thus P. made inspection, on the occasion when the king appointed

Sigewas (?) to be a *dāmokoros*"; (*b*) Palmer, *Minos* 5 (1957) 87: "Inspection carried out by P. when he buried *Sa-ke-wa* Damoklos." Very numerous similar examples could be given.

[27] See nos. 97, 101, 114.5, 120.2, 130, 152, 194; Thebes I, *wanaktero;* KN [Knossos] 73 *wanaka;* KN 976, with *porphure*[in the offing; Py [Pylos] La 622 *wanaktos.*

It is most unfortunate that the verb form in no. 97, *Pa-ki-ja-si mu?-jo-me-no e-pi wa-na-ka-te*, is so inscrutable; and that we cannot tell just what is meant by *wanaka eke* in no. 194 ("*Pi-ka-na:* free allowance, 20 of linen; the king is in possession": as the editors admit, "the place may conceivably have a *wanax* of its own"; but either of the alternative possibilities seems likelier,—that the king is already in possession of his tribute from Pi-ka-na, or that he happens at the time to be resident in Pi-ka-na).

[28] *o-u-te-mi* in no. 207, if it represents οὐ θέμις, would of course not be an exception to this general statement.

[29] The equation of *lawagetas-telestai-hequetai* with duke–barons–counts was proposed by Professor L. R. Palmer in *Trans. Philol. Assoc.* (1954) 18 ff. and in his inaugural lecture at Oxford, *Achaeans and Indo-Europeans* (1955). It is rightly treated with the utmost reserve by the editors of *DMG* and by some others (Finley, *Historia* 6, 1957, 133 ff.; Heubeck, *Gnomon* 29, 1957, 40 ff.; Matthews, *JHS* 76, 1956, 145). It was an interesting and ingenious hypothesis, but unfortunately it finds no confirmation in the Tablets themselves. Within the circle of the Tablets, therefore, it must remain strictly confined to the rank of an unverifiable theory; it must never be allowed to wander outside that circle in the wider world (from which it came) as if it had acquired new strength and independence by contact with the Tablets. We must constantly bear in mind (1) that the Tablets afford no evidence that the *lawagetas* was a *military* officer; (2) that so far from affording evidence that the *telestai* had any status comparable with that of "barons," the Tablets make it probable that they were *religious* officials; (3) that there is nothing whatever to show how the ranks of *lawagetas*, *telestai*, and *hequetai* were interrelated. Certainly there is not a scrap of evidence to show a gradation of class and power comparable with that of a feudal system of the type required by Professor Palmer. The fact that on a single tablet certain landholdings of king, *lawagetas*, and (after a gap) *telestai* and *worgiones* are listed (in that order) is a frail foundation for the inferences that the *lawagetas* ranked next to the king, and that the *telestai* ranked next to the *lawagetas*. It is most imprudent to assume that this list is (in any relevant sense)

complete; or that all four titles are comparable (in fact the last two are presumably religious officials); or that nobody except the king and the *lawagetas* held a *temenos*. We do not know what purpose this document is serving: it may indeed be selective and of very restricted import,—we notice that it mentions only three *telestai*, whereas Pa-ki-ja- (no. 114) could boast of fourteen, and Aptarwa (no. 47) no fewer than forty-five (if sequence in a list were a safe guide, it would be important to notice that the "barons" here are followed by carpenters, and we should have to infer from no. 171 that the *lawagetas* was inferior to the *damos*). (4) If it were true (and we do not know whether it is or not) that the *lawagetas* and *hequetai* originally performed the functions assigned to them by the theory, we should still have no justification whatever for supposing that they retained those functions essentially unchanged down to and throughout the period of the archives.

Similar judgement must be passed on current theories of Mycenaean land tenure. It cannot be too strongly emphasized that almost every stage in every argument is merely guesswork. We do not know what the Mycenaeans meant by *temenos* or *ktoina*; we do not know what *ktimena* connotes; we actually have to *guess* what verb ke-ke-me-na comes from,—then we have to guess what it means, and then we have to guess its relation to *ktimena*. We do not know what o-na-to connotes, or even what root the word comes from (the connexion with ὀνίνημι is far from satisfactory; see especially Édouard Will, *Revue des Études Anciennes* 59, 1957, 27 ff.); we do not know what is meant by e-to-ni-jo or o-ro-jo or ke-ra; we do not know just how a ka-ma differed from a ktoina, and again we have to guess what the word itself means. It is to be presumed that all these words had precise technical meanings: we do not know the technical meaning of any one of them,—indeed we do not know to what Greek words half of them should be related. Guesses at the interrelations of these terms have to be founded on guesses at their meanings, and these in turn have often to be founded on guesses at the very roots from which the words have sprung. It is distressing to find that the results of these exuberant speculations are treated by some with the respect due only to ascertained fact. Few writers on this topic have been so judicious as Bennett in *AJA* 60 (1956) 103 ff.: yet his reconstruction becomes really informative only at the point where the formulas are *interpreted*,—and the interpretations ("baron," "leasehold," "farm," "common land," al.) are for the most part unverifiable conjectures. The review of Hampe's *Homerische Welt* by Heubeck in *Gnomon* 29 (1957) 38 ff.

is in many respects a good corrective. The best treatment of the subject will now be found in Mr Finley's review of *DMG* in the *Economic History Review* for 1957, pp. 128 ff.; and—though the hypothetical elements are (and are admitted to be) all too numerous—there is much of lasting value in Will's article, *Rev. Ét. Anc.* l.c. 24 ff. Palmer replies to Finley in *EHR* 11 (1958) 87 ff., but Finley's fundamental criticisms seem to me unshaken.

[30] See Chadwick, l.c. in n. 63 below. Notice that in no. 120.1 a *telestas* has more than a sporting chance of being at the same time a beetroot collector, *teutlagoras* (by means of a series of risky conjectures A. Tovar, *Münch. Stud. z. Sprachwiss.* 10, 1957, 77 ff., presses the claims of seaweed against beetroot).

[31] The editors of *DMG* (pp. 264 ff.) call no. 171 (and also 152) a "hierarchical division," but they are so different that if one of them is hierarchical the other cannot be; there is therefore no reason to suppose that either is. No. 152 gives *wanax–lawagetas–telestas* (after a vacant space)–*worgioneio–e-re-mo.* no. 171 gives Echelawon–*damos–lawagetas–worgioneio–ka-ma.* The only points in common are the *worgioneio*, and the *lawagetas*,—though he comes after the king in one, below Echelawon and the *damos* in the other. Echelawon cannot be identified with the king (see p. 185); and the suggested equation of *telestai* and *damos*, improbable in itself, is contrary to the available evidence; Ventris and Chadwick admit that it is "surprising, after the apparently sharp contrast between these entities on the other land-tenure tablets." If both tablets had offered king–*lawagetas–telestai–hequetai*, in that order, we might have learnt something; let us learn something else from the fact that they do *not.*

[32] Echelawon offers "480 l. wheat, 108 l. wine, one bull, 10 cheeses, one sheepskin, ?6 l. honey"; the *lawagetas* contributes a miserable couple of rams, 72 l. flour, 24 l. wine.

[33] *DMG* pp. 120, 265.

[34] Mr Chadwick points out that in no. 54 Echelawon is the first man named, and that his contribution is comparable with that of whole towns, larger than most; moreover in no. 55 he is concerned with 5 men, Menuwas and the *lawagetas* with one man only. True, and I agree that these facts support the opinion that Echelawon was a person of great importance (greater than the *lawagetas*, certainly). But I still think it most improbable that the great king would be listed below another man (as in no. 55), or so low in a list of classes and places (as in no. 54); and why was he not simply called *wa-na-ka?*

[35] Or whatever is meant by *ktitas* and *metaktitas;* cf. Kerschensteiner, *Münch. Stud. z. Sprachwiss.* 9 (1956) 39.

[36] See *DMG* p. 400: *mo(i)ro-ppas,* "owner of a portion," is an ingenious guess (it would be a serious mistake to consider it more than that).

[37] A-ko-so-ta: nos. 50, 103, 154, cf. 249; We-da-ne-u: 54.14, 62.6 ff., 167.6, 169, cf. 77 We-u-da-ne-u (perhaps a different person); We-we-si-jo: 70, al. (255 a different person); A-ke-o: 63; U-ta-jo: 66, al.; Diwieus: 169.4 (the same name also 59.9, 76.2, see n. 39 below); Amphimedes: 62, Ep 03.11–12 (has slaves), 146.

The *e-sa-re-u:* nos. 189, 190; the *da-mo-ko-ro:* no. 235.1 (where he is named, and so is an "inspector" Pu_2-ke-qi-ri).

The principal tasks of these people seem to be inspection, allocation, and distribution.

o-pi-su-ko and *o-pi-ka-pe-e-we-:* no. 257.2.

[38] I have much doubt about the *harmost,* possibly implied in *DMG* no. 235.2; cf. Py Ea 25; but see Palmer, *Minos* 5 (1957) 70 f.

[39] It seems likely that a *hequetas* was a palace official (not a "military feudal" rank): Diwieus, who in no. 169 receives a contribution of wheat from Kopreus, is probably the same person as the official whose name stands in the heading of no. 76 and also in no. 59.9, where he is described as *hequetas.* See further esp. Mühlestein, *Die Oka-Tafeln von Pylos* (1956) 33 n. 1.

[40] We ought to exclude from the evidence both no. 39.2, where pa_2]-*si-re-u* is an unlikely supplement ("prob. *not,*" *DMG* Vocab. p. 404), and no. 43 (with 44), where the mention of *basileis* depends on a doubtful reading combined with a speculative supplement—pa_2-]*ṣi-re-wi-jo-te:* if this really were equivalent to βασιλεύοντες, we should learn from this document that a *basileus* might be a *mo-ro-pa_2* and *ko-re-te* (Klumenos, Perimos), and that he might serve as a subordinate officer in the *o-ka* of another person (Poikilops, cf. no. 58.11). The principal remaining texts are nos. 38.12, 91, 232, 258, and Jn 02, 03, 845 (cf. *DMG* p. 353).

[41] No. 38.

[42] Nos. 91, 258, Jn 02 etc.

[43] No. 258.

[44] No. 91.

[45] pa_2-*si-re-wi-ja* = βασιληϝία: the contexts decidedly favour "retinue" against "palace" (let alone "kingdom"); but it is to be emphasized that "retinue" is only a plausible guess.

[46] *ke-ro-si-ja,* which could be *gero(n)sia,* occurs only in the Pylos Tablets An 23 and no. 40. In the latter place the *ke-ro-si-ja* of four men are mentioned, and the name of one of these recurs in Jn 03

as *basileus* (at A-pe-ke-e, wherever that may be). The connexion of a *geronsia* with a *basileus* thus depends on the assumption that the same person is denoted by the same name in both texts: but this is a very risky assumption, for the name in question (A-pi-qo-ta) recurs at Knossos (KN 915), and may well have been common.

[47] His title lends itself readily to formular versification: λαϝαγέτᾰ (like ἱππηλάτᾰ), λαϝαγεσίας ἐϋ ϝειδώς, sim.

[48] On the survival of *wanax* in the historical period see Bechtel, *Gr. Dial.* i 447 f.; Finley, *Historia* l.c. 141 n. 2; Ruijgh, *L'Élément achéen dans la langue épique* (1957) 112 ff.

[49] The fact was observed and discussed by Wackernagel, *Sprachliche Untersuchungen zu Homer [SUH]* (1916) 210.

[50] See Palmer, *Minos* l.c. 67: I agree with his objections to earlier renderings, but am not attracted by his own suggestion (ἀμφίβατος could surely not mean "splay-legged").

[51] I do not see how *qe-qi-no-to* can be explained in terms of Homeric δινωτός (Ventris and Chadwick, *DMG* p. 341, confess the difficulties; Palmer, *Minos* l.c. 62 f., offers without much apparent confidence what seems to me a far-fetched explanation. One of the difficulties is the reduplication in the form *qe-qi-no-to:* Mr Chadwick tells me that Professor D. M. Jones has suggested that it may be third person sing. indic. perfect passive; in no. 239.3, however, it seems clearly adjectival).

For *a-ja-me-na* and other words in these contexts see esp. Chantraine, *Minos* 4 (1956) 52 ff., Palmer, l.c. 58 ff. Some of the identifications which are apparently becoming generally accepted (e.g. λαεία, "of stone," for *ra-e-ja; ϝεαλεία*, "of crystal," for *we-a-re-ja*) seem to me very doubtful.

[52] *e-ka-ma-te* is confidently equated with ἔχματι in *DMG*, both text and Vocabulary; the equation seems to me far from certain, and if it were true we should still not know just what was meant.

[53] See *DMG* p. 338.

[54] *e-qe-si-ja* might mean "associated with the official called *hequetas*"; but our confidence is shaken when we find the same epithet applied to chariot wheels (no. 288); *re-u-ko-* is presumably *leuko-*, but *(-o)nu-ka* is very obscure; the connexion of *a-ro₂-a* with ἀρείων seems hazardous and is not yet confirmed in any context.

[55] *hiqquiā* was most inconvenient to the Epic metre; its genitive and accusative (which the Epic would need much more often than its nominative) were quite unmanageable. It is possible, as Mr Chadwick points out to me, that *ἱππία survives in ἱππιοχάρμης (whence the extravagant ἱππιοχαίτης).

[56] Incomprehensible adjectives applied to various artefacts, especially

textiles, domestic furniture, and chariots: *a-te-re-e-te-jo, a-te-re-te-a, e-ka-te-re-ta, e-ne-ro, e-ni-qe, e-ro-pa-ke-ja, e-te-re-ta, e-wi-su-zu(?)-ko, i-to-we-sa, ko-ni-ti-ja-ja, ko-u-ra, me-no-e-ja, nu-wa-ja, o-da-ku-we-ta, -o-nu-ke, o-pi-qi-na, o-re-ne-ja, pa₂-ra-de-ro, pe-ne-we-ta, po-ro-e-ke, ra-e-ja, so-we-ne-ja, to-mi-ka, to-qi-de-we-sa, tu-na-no, u-po-we, wa-ra-wi-ta, we-a-re-ja, we-je-ke-a₂, wi-so-wo-pa-na, wo-ra-we-sa, wo-ro-ne-ja;* more or less comprehensible but not Homeric, *akaranos, amphiguotos* (?), *elephanteios, enaliptos, ennewopeza, khalkodetos, konkhuleios, koronowessa* (?), *kresiowerges, kuteseios, miltowessa, pedwessa, phoinikeos, ptilowessa.* Incomprehensible nouns, especially in contexts relating to tables, chairs, garments, chariots: *ai-ki-no-o, a-re-ta-to, a₂-ro-u-do-, i-qo-e-qe, ka-ru-we, ki-da-pa, ko-no-ni-, ne-pa₂-sa-, o-pi-i-ja-, o-u-ka, pa-ra-ke-we, pe-pa₂-to, po-ka-ta-ma, sa-pa, se-re-mo-ka-ra-a-, to-mi-ja, to-u-ka;* more or less comprehensible but not Homeric, *epikelemnia* (?), *hiqquia, opaworta, paltaia, opoquon* (?).

I must make it very clear that I have not the least intention of casting doubt on the decipherment; and that I fully recognize the progress which has been made and is being made (see esp. Palmer, *Minos* 5, 1957, 58 ff.) towards the interpretation of these difficult texts. It is tenable that quite a number of those terms which I personally at present find "incomprehensible" ought rather to be labelled "already doubtfully comprehended."

[57] Including those implicit in proper names and compound words, I count more than 50 verbs, some 170 nouns, and some 70 adjectives, common to the Homeric poems and the Tablets. See now especially Mr Chadwick's in the Festschrift for J. Sundwall (1957), *Mycenaean Elements in the Homeric Dialect.*

[58] The evidence is assembled and discussed in *DMG* pp. 125 ff.

[59] The Tablets "unexpectedly reveal the worship of many of the gods and goddesses known from classical sources," *DMG* p. 275: but surely it is the contrary which would have been unexpected,—it would have been a shocking surprise if the Tablets had indicated that Zeus, Poseidon, and others were *not* worshipped by the Greeks before the beginning of the Dark Ages. So also Heubeck, *Gnomon* 29 (1957) 43: the Tablets are in this respect "eine erfreuliche Bestätigung des zu erwartenden Sachverhaltes." There are special reasons why the worship of Dionysus by the Mycenaeans should be unexpected: but there is not yet any evidence that he was worshipped; *DMG* p. 127.

[60] *e-ri-nu*, between "all the gods" and "the priestess of the winds" on a ritual tablet, has a good chance of being *Erinys*. The addition of

Hephaestus and Dionysus to the list of attestations is at present speculative (*DMG* p. 127).

[61] I see no reason to believe that her name is connected with the obscure term *da-ma-te* in no. 114.1.

[62] Though there might be exceptions to the general rule, cf. Od. γ 6 ff.: it is possible, though it cannot be proved, that this Odyssean poet knew that Poseidon was in fact the chief god of Pylos. Cf. also *DMG* p. 310 on Od. τ 188 ff.

[63] Mr Chadwick has very kindly allowed me to read the typescript of an article on *Potnia*, to be published shortly in *Minos*. *Potnia* is discussed by Luria also in *Minos* 5 (1957) 45 ff.

[64] No. 172, obverse, 9–10.

[65] I find the suggested interpretations of these names (Mnasa, the thrice-hero, the lord of the house) excessively speculative; not more acceptable is the identification of *Ma-na-sa* proposed by Luria, l.c. 41 ff.

[66] See the comment in *DMG* p. 303.

[67] Cf. Pausanias, ii 12.1, with Frazer's note; Luria, l.c. 48 f.

[68] No. 135.5: *i-je-re-ja e-ke e-u-ke-to-qe e-to-ni-jo e-ke-e te-o*, "the priestess holds it, and declares that she holds it for the god" (or "declares that the god holds it") "as an *e-to-ni-jo*." I take it that when we are told (as so often) that a "slave of the divinity" holds certain land, we are being indirectly informed that the slave holds it *qua* slave of the divinity.

[69] Nos. 53–60. Very full discussion by Mühlestein, *Die Oka-Tafeln von Pylos*; he seems to me to have thrown a great amount of light on the detail of these documents.

[70] See Palmer, *Minos* 4 (1956) 122; *DMG* p. 138; Kerschensteiner, *Münch. Stud. z. Sprachwiss.* 9 (1956) 39 f.; Mühlestein rightly speaks only of *conjecture* ("lassen also vermuten, dass die Invasion von der See her erfolgt ist"), but I find nothing convincing in his attempt to show that these tablets record something more than routine movements.

[71] No. 45.11.

[72] No. 51.11–12.

[73] Fragments of accidental verse abound in all Greek prose writing; there is nothing new to be learnt from the fact that ἐρέται Πλευρῶνάδ' ἰόντες forms half a dactylic hexameter. *Entire* dactylic hexameters occur quite often: witness the following, casually noted thirty years ago in my text of Demosthenes,—iv 6 καὶ προσέχειν τὸν νοῦν τούτοις ἐθέλουσιν ἅπαντες (and, just before it, πάντα κατεστράπται καὶ ἔχει, τὰ μὲν ὡς ἂν ἑλών τις). xviii 114 οἷς ἐπέδωκε τετίμηται, σχέτλιον γὰρ ἂν εἴη ;

143 τὸν γὰρ ἐν Ἀμφίσσηι πόλεμον, δι' ὃν εἰς Ἐλάτειαν ; ibid. τὴν ἰδίαν ἔχθραν ἐπάγειν μ' ὑπελάμβανον αὐτῶι, / ἥτις δ' ἡ φύσις, ἄνδρες Ἀθηναῖοι, γέγονεν του— ; 192 ἢ τὸ παρὸν τὴν τοῦ συμβούλου τάξιν ἀπαιτεῖ ; 198, a splendid line, Ἑλλήνων ἀτυχήματ' ἐνευδοκιμεῖν ἀπέκειτο ; 251 οὐδεμίαν γὰρ πώποτ' ἐγράψατό μ', οὐδ' ἐδίωξε ; 258 συμβεβίωκα τύχηι, καὶ πόλλ' ἂν ἔχων ἕτερ' εἰπεῖν. xix 174 αὐτοὶ δ' οὐδ' ὁτιοῦν ὑγιὲς γράψαντες ἔπεμψαν. xx 60 προξενίαν εὐεργεσίαν ἀτέλειαν ἁπάντων ; 67 καὶ γὰρ τἄλλ' ἀγάθ' εὐξαίμην ἂν ἔγωγε παρ' ἡμῖν ; 121 ἢ μὴ τοῦτο ποιοῦσα χάριν τισὶν οὐκ ἀποδώσει ; 125 οὗτοι ποιήσωσιν, ἐὰν ἄρα ταῦτα λέγωσι ; 149 μηδ' αὐτὸς φαίνου τά τ' ὀφειλόμεν' ὡς ἀποδοῦναι. xxi 146 ὄντων ἰσχυρῶν τότε καὶ Δεκέλειαν ἑαυτοῖς ; 179, a very neat verse, ταῦτ' ἔλεγεν μὲν ἐκεῖνος, ἐχειροτονήσατε δ' ὑμεῖς.

Demosthenes' avoidance of hiatus and of runs of more than two short syllables explains the frequency of such lines (and innumerable part-lines); but part-lines are common in all Greek prose writing, and it would have been astonishing if a few had not occurred in the Tablets.

[74] "man darf also [viz. because the men are called "rowers"] annehmen, dass auch diese Gruppe ein auswärtiges, zur See erreichbares Ziel hatte," Kerschensteiner, *Münch. Stud. z. Sprachwiss.* 9 (1956) 39: one may indeed *assume* it, but there is nothing whatever to show whether the assumption is true or false.

[75] Actually 443, but there are numerous gaps.

[76] Assuming about 50 rowers to a vessel; but it is really very doubtful what allowance should be made.

[77] Sense in general could be restored by altering Echelawon's name from dative to nominative: "Menuwas has discharged one man; Echelawon has discharged five men; the *lawagetas* has discharged [x] men, etc."

[78] Specially puzzling in this context (of "absent oarsmen") is the detail about the landholding of a hequetas in vv. 11 ff., "and the hequetai have the *e-to-ni-jo* of the *ka-ma*": the editors suggest that "the connecting link must be the holding of land in return for feudal service"; possibly, but it is awkwardly phrased and hard to relate to the immediate sequel.

[79] *o-u-ru-to o-pi-a₂-ra e-pi-ko-wo*: the third word presumably means "overseers," "lookouts," or the like; the first word is most ingeniously (but very far from certainly) interpreted as *hō wruntoi*— ὧ(δε) and ϝρῦσθαι,—"thus they guard."

[80] See esp. Mühlestein, *Die Oka-Tafeln von Pylos* 41 f.

[81] These figures include commanders, officers, and *hequetai* as well as "men." The numbers of "men" bear no apparent relation to the

number of "officers": To-ro-o's command includes 4 (or 5) officers and 110 men; Ma-re-u's, 4 (or 5) and 50. The commands vary greatly in strength both of officers and men; and we do not know why some should have *hequetai* and others not. The location of the *o-ka* is given in about half the examples but not in the other half: possibly the unplaced units are included in the places last mentioned (e.g. Nedwatas' unit is posted with Ma-re-u's at O-wi-to-no); so Palmer, *Minos* 4 (1956) 123, but there may have been some other reason (cf. Mühlestein, op. cit. 8).

The total number of combatants listed is 808, but allowance must be made for three missing numbers which might bring the total to 1,000.

[82] This point is particularly stressed by Mühlestein, whose penetrating study has greatly clarified the detail of these documents. Specially valuable is his recognition of *i-wa-so* and *o-ka-ra₃* as appellatives of army units: treated as *places* they made unsatisfactory sense (*DMG* p. 189: Maleus has 50 men *of O-wi-to-no at O-ka-ra₃*, while Nedwatas moves 50 men *from O-ka-ra₃ to O-wi-to-no;* a similar difficulty arises if *i-wa-so* is treated as a location). I find Mühlestein's exposition in general convincing, and suspend belief only on one or two points of importance: (*a*) I doubt the equation of *o-ka* with ὁλκάς, and do not think the case at all strongly supported by what seems a risky interpretation of *anagein ophellontes* in *DMG* no. 44; (*b*) I find nothing solid or seductive in his argument (30 ff.) that these tablets are necessarily connected with a particular emergency and could not be the routine record of normal troop movements.

Since our geographical knowledge is so deficient, it is worth stressing (as Mühlestein does, op. cit. 30) that all the *o-ka* places are presumably more or less *coastal* (as two of them, Ro-o-wa and A-ke-re-wa, almost certainly were); so also are places which supplied rowers on the Oarsmen Tablets (Za-e-to-ro, Po-ra-i) and places which are clearly *destinations* of troops here (Nedwon, E-ra-po Ri-me-ne, presumably A₂-ru-wo-te, Ai-ta-re-u-si, U-wa-si). Ethnics, especially if they recur in more than one unit, seem as a rule to represent places *from which* troops came to coastal stations (though this would not imply that such places were not themselves coastal). But I have to confess that after prolonged effort I cannot make sense of the *relative* geographical positions (the best attempt is that of Mühlestein, op. cit. 31 f.); of the *absolute* positions we know not a single one, except presumably that of the Kuparissioi.

[83] For instance, it is an easy conjecture that these lists are records of

feudal services rendered; i.e. *X*, whose fief is conditional upon the sending of so many men at royal command, has in fact sent so many.

⁸⁴ The interpretation of *o-ka* as *ὀρχά = ἀρχή must be regarded as extremely speculative; ὄρχαμος says a word, or at least a whisper, in its support. There is no quite clear example of ἀρχ- in the Tablets, but it looks as though this (not ὀρχ-) was the spelling, for one or more of the identifications A-ke-wa-to = Ἀρχέϝαστος, A-ki-wo-ni-jo = Ἀρχιϝώνιος, A-ke-ra-wo = Ἀρχέλαϝος, A-ke-ti-jo = Ἀρχετίων, may well be correct. The editors, *DMG* p. 401, prefer the equation with ὀχά; Mühlestein (*Oka-Tafeln* 36 ff.) argues hard for ὀλκάς.

⁸⁵ See esp. *DMG* pp. 92 ff., 139 ff.

⁸⁶ Ibid. p. 93.

⁸⁷ Outside Crete and the Kingdom of Pylos: Zacynthos, Cnidos, Cythera, Cyprus, Pleuron, and (unless it is the Cretan town) Miletus. In Crete: a dozen towns (including a few speculative identifications). In the kingdom of Pylos not a single place can be put on the map except the royal seat of Pylos itself and presumably Kuparissos. Ro-u-so is not to be identified with Lousoi (Sudhena) in remote central Arcadia; Ventris and Chadwick themselves draw attention to the fact that Ro-u-so is in the singular number (*DMG* p. 199), not plural, and it is highly improbable that the Tablets are referring to this remote spot, on the far side of Mount Chelmós.

Professor Palmer, in *Minos* 4 (1956) 120 ff., offers a highly speculative reconstruction of Pylian geography: a consistent whole is built up of hypothetical parts, based on the major hypothesis (or rather series of hypotheses) that Pi-*82 = Pi-jai = Φ(ε)ιαί = the port of Olympia = the northernmost point of a geographical sequence,— the last a particularly hazardous element in the equations; "the parallel of the Athenian tribute lists shows that purely arbitrary orders may be adopted in such cases," *DMG* p. 142. From this point onwards the path is beset by equal or greater hazards: there is nothing approaching certainty (cf. Mühlestein, op. cit. 29) in the theory that A₂-ru-wo may be ὁ καλούμενος Αὐλών—yet "this important 'fix' is the hinge on which all that follows turns" (p. 134); we do not know (and may think it by no means likely; cf. Mühlestein, op. cit. 16 n. 1, 21) that O-ka-ra₃ = Oikhalia; we have to guess at the identity (let alone the location) of U-ru-pi-ja-jo, O-ru-ma-si-jo, and numerous others.

Professor Palmer says that "the new documentary information will enable scholars . . . to reach a new assessment of the reliability of the [Homeric] Catalogue": I disagree in principle. The concatenation of hypotheses may serve a purpose (to me, it serves the the purpose of proving very clearly how impossible it is, on this evidence, to attain a profitable conclusion) provided that it is strictly confined to the circle of the Tablets: its conclusions being hypothetical, and based on hypothetical premisses, they should never be allowed for one moment to roam outside those limits.

The sketch of Pylian geography by Miss Kerschensteiner (n. 70 above, 48 ff.) is much less speculative, but still essentially dependent on a number of uncertain identifications.

88 The opinion that -εύς is non-Greek is no longer tenable; see especially Leroy, *Mélanges Henri Grégoire* (1951) 223 ff., "À propos des noms en -εύς et de quelques traits communs au grec et à l'iranien"; Schachermeyr, *RE* XXII (1954) 1518 f., agrees.

89 See esp. E. Bosshardt, *Die Nomina auf -εύς* (Zürich, 1942).

90 In nouns other than proper names, -εύς was operative in the Epic and remained in fashion during the historical period; see Leroy, Bosshardt, and Buck-Petersen, *Reverse Index* p. 27.

91 There is a further remarkable fact: that most of the principal mythological hero names have non-Greek stems,—Ἀχιλλεύς, Ὀδυσσεύς, Αἴρας, Νέστωρ, Μηριόνης, Τυδεύς, Θησεύς, Σαλμωνεύς, and dozens more. I am not persuaded by recent attempts to relate these stems to the Greek language (cf. Palmer, *Eranos* 54, 1957, 7 ff.); nor do I take seriously the conventional derivations of less obviously foreign names such as Ἀγαμέμνων, Μενέλαος, Διομήδης, for the apparent Greek elements are linguistically objectionable and do not really make sense. I notice (and so did Bittel, *Grundzüge* p. 52; cf. Krahe, *Antike* 15, 1939, 187) that the same phenomenon is apparent in the names of the (presumably Indo-European) Hittite kings *Suppiluliumas, Muwattallis, Tuthalijas,* and the rest.

92 See p. 253 below.

93 *DMG* 103 ff. gives a list of 58, with the warning that "not all of these may be correctly identified; but at least the majority are likely to be right." That is a very fair statement, and opinions will differ on the question just how many of the 58 are acceptable. *A-ta-no* is equated with *Antanor* but might as well be *Athanor; Pa₂-da-ro* (*Pandaros*) may be *Pardalos; Po-te-u* (*Ponteus*) may be *Portheus; Pe-keu* (*Phegeus*) may be *Perkeus; Pu-ra-ko* (*Phulakos*) may be *Pularchos; Pu-ri* (*Puris*) may be *Pulis; Te-se-u* (*Theseus*) may be *Therseus;* and so forth.

94 Αἴρας: KN Np 973, Ai-wa.

[95] *DMG* pp. 100 f.: 106 names in -ευς are listed; 26 of these are unidentifiable, the majority of the remainder are obscure or ambiguous.

[96] Ibid. p. 104: a list of 20 names which coincide with those of Trojans in the Epic; but some of them (e.g. Antenor, Ilos, Pandaros, Phegeus, Phylakos, Puris, Tros) are merely possibilities, alternatives being admitted by the ambiguous spelling.

[97] Note also the feminine name in no. 143, *To-ro-ja*.

[98] The termination in -ōr is indicated by *E-ko-to-ri-jo* in PY Cn 45.

[99] The Lesbians called Priam Πέρ(ρ)αμος; the Ionians, Πρίαμος: that is all very comprehensible if his name really sounded something like *Periamos*.

[100] See Kerschensteiner (n. 70 above) 46 ff. with n. 39.

[101] Πύλος: the Tablets passim. Ἀμφιγένεια: Xa 12, *a-pi-ke-ne-a*. Θρύον: no. 40, Tu-ru-we-u (Θρυεύς?). Αἰπύ: *A-pu₂*, frequently. Κυπαρισσήεις: no. 187 *Ku-pa-ri-so*, no. 56 *Ku-pa-ri-si-jo*. Ἕλος: nos. 257, 258 *E-re-i* (or *E-re-e*). Ἀρήνη, Πτελεός, Δώριον do not occur in the Tablets.
    Contrast with this the list compiled by the relatively late poet of the Embassy in Iliad IX (pp. 297 ff. below): not one of his seven places recurs in the Tablets.

[102] Pylos and (if the equation is correct) Aipu.

[103] *DMG* nos. 75 and 250: the Tablets' Nine are (in order) *Pi-*82*, *Me-ta-pa*, *Pe-to-no*, *Pa-ki-ja-*, *A-pu₂*, *A-ke-re-wa*, *E-ra-to*, *Ka-ra-do-ro*, *Ri-jo*. The fifth may well be *Aipu*, the eighth and ninth *Kharadros* and *Rhion*; the identifications of the other six are all very doubtful or else wholly unknown. Not one of them can be located on the map.

[104] Vn 05.

[105] *DMG* no. 257.

[106] *Ro-u-so* for *E-ra-to*.

[107] *A-ke-re-wa* and *Pa-ki-ja-* are specially prominent; *Pe-to-no* and *E-ra-to* occur no more frequently (indeed less so) than numerous other places (e.g. *I-wa-so*, *Ro-o-wa*, *Ro-u-so*); the other five are named more frequently than most other places except *A-ke-re-wa* and *Pa-ki-ja-*.

[108] *DMG* p. 142.

[109] Ibid. nos. 75, 250, 257.

[110] Ibid. pp. 290 f.

[111] Ibid. no. 258

[112] Ibid. no. 54.

[113] Ibid. nos. 56–60.

[114] Unless there is some special significance in the fact that the *o-ka*

at A-ke-re-wa has three *hequetai* whereas the others have two, one, or none at all.

[115] Charadros, 60.5; Me-ta-pa, 58.3.

[116] No. 172 (reverse) 2 shows a particularly close connexion between Pylos itself and Pa-ki-ja- (*Pu-ro: i-je-to-qe Pa-ki-ja-si* etc.). No. 97 mentions Pa-ki-ja- in immediate connexion with the *wanax*; the special importance of the place is manifest in no. 114 also. A-ke-re-wa is the centre of a military (no. 59.11) and naval (54.7) force, and it heads the list of what appear to be places officially inspected (no. 154) by A-ko-so-ta, evidently an important palace functionary (n. 37 above).

[117] No. 51.11.

[118] No. 258.21.

[119] No. 56.8, twenty Kuparissian *ke-ki-de* (a *Truppennamt:* Mühlestein, op. cit. 18) under the command of Nedwatas; no. 56.10, another ten of the same; no. 187, "at Kuparissos, the *ke-ki-de* are in possession."

[120] Only (if at all: pp. 193 ff.) in nos. 53–60.

VI

Some Mycenaean Relics in the Iliad

THE SEARCHER for historical fact in the Homeric Iliad must begin by finding the answer to two questions. First, how far back does the Greek Epic tradition extend? It is obvious that the Iliad presupposes poetry of the same type over a long period of time: but *how* long? Does the tradition go back beyond the Dark Ages into the period when the glory of Mycenae was still great? Secondly, if the answer to that question is affirmative in general, how far back does this particular theme of poetry go, the story of the Achaean siege of Troy? Was it already sung by poets in the royal or noble courts of Greece in the 12th century B.C.?

The answer to the first of these questions may be stated with the utmost brevity. It has long been known that the pedigree of Greek Epic poetry ascends into the Mycenaean era. The proofs of this have been stated so often before that I do no more than repeat them summarily.

The one proof is provided by comparison of certain passages in the Iliad with objects discovered by excavation. *The Iliad and Odyssey describe in accurate detail places and objects which never existed in the world after the Mycenaean era.* The boar's-tusk helmet in the Tenth Book of the Iliad is one of the best examples: here is a distinctive and complex object, accurately described in the Iliad at the latest stage of its development, known to have been fashionable so far back as the 16th and 15th centuries B.C., obsolete in the 13th and extinct in the 12th century.[1] In the words of Martin Nilsson, "such an object, the

[1] For notes to chapter vi see pages 265–296.

containing parts of which were of perishable materials, . . . would not have survived the centuries separating the Mycenaean Age from the beginning of the historical period. There is no explanation left but the one that the description was preserved through the lapse of time by the epic tradition."[2] There are several other such examples:[3] each singly and all together they testify, beyond the possibility of confutation, that the memory of certain material objects survived from the Mycenaean era into the Iliad, hundreds of years after the objects themselves had disappeared from the world. This is one of the most certain and most important discoveries ever made in the field of Homeric scholarship.

The second proof is provided by the Homeric dialect. The language of the Epic is predominantly *Ionic:* but deeply embedded within it are forms and features alien to Ionic but familiar to the *Arcadian* and *Aeolic* dialects. Many but not all of these non-Ionic features are irreplaceable: that is to say, the corresponding Ionic forms are excluded by the metre.

Now the Arcadian and Aeolic dialects, as we know them, are descendants of the dialects predominant in southern and northern Hellas (respectively) in the Mycenaean period: and their presence in the Ionian Epic has generally been regarded as good evidence that the Epic must have a continuous history from the Mycenaean period onwards, when those dialects were predominant. Until recently it seemed reasonable to infer the following series of events: the Epic was originally created in Hellas by peoples who spoke the Arcadian and Aeolic dialects; when these peoples migrated to Asia Minor under pressure from the Dorians, they came into contact with other emigrants, speakers of the Ionic dialect, in Asia Minor; and these Ionians adopted the Aeolic-Arcadian Epic, made it their own, gradually transformed it both in language and in spirit into an Ionian poetry, but retained within it numerous indispensable forms and phrases, essential constituents of the verse, irreplaceable by Ionic counterparts. This account of the phenomena has recently been challenged, and the new outlook has at least in one aspect an advantage over the old.

The new theory maintains, in briefest summary, the following position:[4] The dialect which we call *Ionic* is fundamentally akin to *Arcadian;* the peculiar features which differentiate it from other dialects as *Ionic* are all (or most) of relatively late development. In the Mycenaean period *one* dialect was predominant in southern Greece: when the Dorians occupied the Peloponnese, part of the Mycenaean population stayed at home, part emigrated; the stay-at-homes, to be called "Arcadians," retained their dialect with comparatively little change through the Dark Ages, while the emigrants, to be called "Ionians," developed a number of new characteristics in their new homes. This theory has yet to stand the test of time;[5] if it should prove to be true, we shall have to change our opinion about the origin of the apparent mixture of dialects in the Epic. There will be this advantage, that it will no longer be necessary to postulate a transference of the Epic from a people of one dialect to a people of another dialect. Arcadian features in the Epic will be heirlooms from the past of the Ionian people themselves; and we shall now suppose simply that the Mycenaean emigrants from the Peloponnese took their own poetry with them to Asia Minor,[6] where it developed in the course of time, without change of owner, into the Ionian Epic.

We shall still have to insist, however, that the Ionian Epic itself does not reveal or represent the alleged *evolution* from Mycenaean into Ionian dialect. The phenomena in the Epic remain what they were,—heirlooms from a remote past, not stages in an evolutionary process; they are still strange and isolated, apparently alien elements embedded in up-to-date Ionic. Let these elements be *not* (after all) alien, but simply "Old Ionic": they are nevertheless of immensely greater antiquity than the "New Ionic." They are (many of them) forms and features which had long been extinct or obsolete in the language at the time when the Epic flourished in Ionia: they go back to a time when the South Mycenaean dialect had not yet ramified into its two divergent branches. The new theory is thus not essentially incompatible with the old in this respect: the *origin* of the Arcadian elements is differently explained, but their *significance* remains what it was,—they still carry the Epic back to the Mycenaean past. And the existence of specifically *Aeolic* forms confirms this conclusion: they are relics of a time—the Mycenaean period—when Aeolic was spoken in the north, Arcadian in the south of Greece, and poetry was composed in both, each admitting the influence of the other.[7]

Now for the second question. We know that the Greek Epic extends back into the Mycenaean era: do we also know that this particular theme, the Achaean siege of Troy, was the subject of poetry at that time? The answer will be given in the present lecture. It will (I hope) become apparent that the Iliad preserves facts about the Trojans which could not have been known to anybody after the fall of Troy VII[a], and facts about the Achaeans which are intelligible only against the background of the Trojan War. This is my principal theme; but I introduce it with the reminder that Martin Nilsson, in his Sather Lectures for 1932, proved that Greek mythology in general is of Mycenaean origin. The Ionians inherited little if any mythology from their own past, apart from the foundation legends of a few cities: all the great legends of Greece are connected with centres of Mycenaean civilization,—"a constant correlation" which "cannot be considered as accidental." Moreover "a close inspection shows that the mythical importance of a site corresponds to its importance in the Mycenaean civilization":[8] Oedipus at Thebes, Heracles at Tiryns, Agamemnon at Mycenae, the Argonauts at Orchomenos and Iolcos,—the celebrated stories revolve around the most important centres of Mycenaean culture and power, most of which lapsed into long obscurity after the 12th century B.C. Thus the story of Troy is seen against a much broader background: it is one of many subjects of poetry which all have this in common, that they are indissolubly linked to the great palaces of Mycenaean Hellas in the days of their glory. And after hundreds of years have elapsed the Iliad still displays the story of Troy in its Mycenaean setting; the events and persons have nothing whatever to do with Ionians of the 10th or the

9th or the 8th century B.C. For this reason alone we could be fairly confident that the story and its setting have been transmitted to the Ionians by their Achaean predecessors in the art of Epic poetry. But now let us look at a different source of information, the formular phrases in the Iliad itself.

The Epic has a continuous history from the Mycenaean era to the making of the Iliad. But the Iliad is a late, indeed the latest, version of the story, refashioned and told afresh by the genius of Ionia in the 9th century B.C.: surely it may well be that few traces of its Mycenaean past survive? Certainly there are no extensive "Mycenaean passages" remaining in the Iliad (excepting, with many reservations, the Catalogues in the Second Book). But there is a special reason why the Iliad might nevertheless preserve many a relic from Mycenaean times, continuously transmitted through the centuries: I mean *the formular character of its language*, which confirms the high antiquity of the Epic and at the same time guarantees the preservation of many a fact and fancy from the remotest past.

It is not easy at first to grasp the full significance of Milman Parry's discovery[9] that the language of the Homeric poems is of a type unique in Greek literature,—that it is to a very great extent a language of traditional formulas, created in the course of a long period of time by poets who composed in the mind without the aid of writing. I shall briefly describe some of its principal characteristics.

The Greek Epic is (to use a convenient term) *oral* poetry. Its language differs from that of all other Greek poetry inasmuch as its units are not words, selected by the poet, combined by him into phrases, and adjusted by him to his metre: its units are *formulas*,[10] phrases ready-made, extending in length from a word or two to several complete lines, already adapted to the metre, and either already adapted or instantly adaptable to the limited range of ideas which the subject-matter of the Greek Epic may require him to express. The oral poet composes while he recites; he must therefore be able to rely upon his memory. He makes his lines out of formulas which he knows by heart, and which he has learnt to use in this way as one learns to use an ordinary language. Whatever he needs to say next is immediately supplied, not by words which he must combine and versify, but by phrases already complete and metrical. "Unlike the poet who writes out his lines . . . he cannot think without hurry about his next word, nor change what he has made, nor, before going on, read over what he has just written. . . . He must have for his use word-groups all made to fit his verse."[11] He must be a craftsman before he can become a poet: there is an immense stock of traditional formulas, to be learnt only by long apprenticeship; and experience may then assist him to use them with any degree of skill from competence to consummate artistry.

That the language of the Greek Epic is, in this sense, the creation of an oral poetry, is a fact capable of proof in detail; and the proofs offered by Milman Parry are of a quality not often to be found in literary studies. It is now a securely established fact, that the Iliad reveals the traditional formular language of an oral poetry in a very advanced phase of its development. Its treasury of formular phrases is distinguished by three virtues over and above their high poetic quality,—multitude, complexity, and thrift.

About the multitude of formulas in the Greek Epic, let it suffice for the moment to say that about one-fifth of the Homeric poems is composed of lines wholly repeated from one place to another, and that in some 28,000 lines there are some 25,000 repeated phrases. It is repetition which turns a phrase into a formula, and repetition is the child of utility and time; if there were no other evidence, we should be obliged to postulate a very long period of time to account for the development of so gigantic a treasury of formular phrases.

And we have to reflect not only upon multitude but also upon complexity. "Each formula is . . . made in view of the other formulas with which it is to be joined";[12] and many formulas have an internal flexibility, such that the formula is not a completely stereotyped phrase, but one of a group of phrases differing (it may be) by a single word of equivalent metrical value but radically different meaning; and such groups of phrases in turn "fall into groups which have a larger pattern in common."[13] The interrelations of formulas, their internal flexibility and external dovetailings, are developed in the Homeric Epic to an astonishing height of efficiency.

The third characteristic of Homeric formulas is their economy. Generally speaking, for a given idea within a given place in the line, there will be found in the vast treasury of phrases one formula and one only. The Epic language is to a very great extent "free of phrases which, having the same metrical value and expressing the same idea, could replace one another."[14] An illustration of this "law of economy" (as I shall call it) was given by Milman Parry in the following words: "All the chief characters of the Iliad and Odyssey, if their names can be fitted into the last half of the verse along with an epithet, have a noun-epithet formula in the nominative, beginning with a simple consonant, which fills the verse between the trochaic caesura of the third foot and the verse-end: for instance, πολύτλας δῖος Ὀδυσσεύς. . . . In a list of 37 characters who have formulas of this type, which includes all those having any importance in the poems, there are only three names which have a second formula which could replace the first."[15] And this is only part of a much more elaborate system of formulas for these proper names, in which the law of economy is operative: "if you take in the five grammatical cases singular of all the noun-epithet formulas used for Achilles, you will find that you have 45 different formulas of which none has, in the same case, the same metrical value." . . . "When one multiplies the case of the single formula by all those which are to be found in the two poems, and which require the 250 pages of C. E. Schmidt's *Parallel-Homer* for their listing, one has the statement of a thrift of expression which it is rather hard, perhaps, for us to understand."[16] What the poet has in memory is a stock of many thousands of interrelated formulas already adapted to his verse; and it may be stated as a general rule that none of these formulas can replace any other to express the same meaning in the same part of the line. Common sense insists that the time required for the development of this vast, intricate, and highly economical phraseology is to be reckoned in generations, perhaps in hundreds of years. And since a formula, once it has outstripped and outlived all competitors, is (as a general rule) irreplaceable and immortal, it is to be expected that many phrases created for the Mycenaean Epic, having become formulas in the course of time, must have survived unchanged into the Ionian Iliad. In particular, the epithets in the Iliad traditionally linked with certain names are likely to be informative in this respect. I begin with a few observations on the formular epithets for "the sea," which offer a good illustration of the oral poet's technique.

The sea.—Four names for "the sea," πόντος, ἅλα, θάλασσα, and πέλαγος, occur altogether in 384 places; and in 143 of these an epithet accompanies the noun. A study of these noun + epithet combinations[17] (which constitute only part of a wider formula-vocabulary for "the sea") provides a vivid illustration of the oral technique in poetry: it becomes at once apparent that a very high proportion of the verse is composed of traditional formulas supplied ready-made by the memory. The 143 noun + epithet combinations are almost entirely made up of a small number of repeated phrases,—πολιὴν ἅλα, οἴνοπι πόντωι, πολυφλοίσβοιο θαλάσσης, and the like. There are seventeen[18] of these formulas, accounting for all but 15 of the 143 passages. Moreover, in the Iliad, excepting a single line in the Fifteenth Book, the law of economy is strictly observed: each formula is unique, in the sense that it cannot be replaced by any other formula in the same part of the line. In this example, then, we find that the traditional formula-system accounts for more than nine-tenths of the composition: we have a glimpse not into the poet's mind but into his memory. For this one idea, "the sea," and for its expression in noun + epithet phrases only, he relied upon his memory to provide him with a ready-made formula for almost every requirement; and the traditional vocabulary was now so highly developed, so refined and reduced, that for each requirement he found never, or hardly ever, more than one single formula. He has no freedom to select his adjectives: he must adopt whatever combination of words is supplied by tradition for a given part of the verse; and that traditional combination brings with it an adjective which may or may not be suitable to the context.

It is immediately obvious that the art of the Homeric poet, and the history of the development of the Homeric poems, can only be appreciated in the light of this peculiar technique of verse-making. I offer a few primary observations.

1) Some formulas are of more recent creation than others. Those which include obsolete adjectives—ἀτρύγετος for example, a word obsolete and unintelligible in the heyday of the Ionian Epic—are likely to be much older than those which include artificial forms, created by analogy out of metrical convenience (such as εὐρέα πόντον, for εὐρύν, on the analogy of εὐρέι πόντωι). The creation of formulas presumably continued over a long period of time: so long as oral poetry remained a living art, new phrases were invented; utility, tested by time, would confirm some and reject others.[19] The greater the combination of complexity with economy in a formula-system, the older it is likely to be: but in each example we must look to see whether there is in the epithet (or occasionally in the noun) some particular quality which proves or indicates that the formula is very ancient. Such quality may be observed in more than one aspect of a formula: in some special peculiarity of language (for example, the obsolete syntactical relation typified by βοὴν ἀγαθός, πόδας ὠκύς); in the facts that a word is moribund in the Epic itself[20] and utterly extinct thereafter (for example, ἀμφίφαλος; μελίη in the sense "spear"); in restriction of usage (for example, the limitation of φαίδιμος to a very small number of nouns and to a single position in the line); in its intrinsic meaning (σάκος ἠύτε πύργον, the shield that is carried "like a tower," an object which never existed after the Mycenaean era). One or more of such characteristics, in conjunction with complex and economic formular usage, may testify that a particular noun + epithet

combination ascends to an age very much remoter than that of the Ionian Epic.

2) The law of economy is not quite strictly observed. In most of the larger samples a few breaches of the law occur. "The sea" admits a single exception to the rule: in one place in the Iliad and in two in the Odyssey θαλάσσης εὐρυπόροιο stands where πολυφλοίσβοιο θαλάσσης could stand:[21] since neither epithet occurs elsewhere, we are not free to suppose that the one has been transferred to the sea from some more familiar attachment; and we must certainly not suppose that εὐρυπόροιο was deliberately chosen by the poet as being the more suitable to its context. In the Iliad passage it is much less suitable than πολυφλοίσβοιο would have been; and, in general, what is selected by the poet is not the epithet but the combination of noun + epithet, and his criterion is not suitability to the context but metrical convenience.[22]

We have to recognize the fact that alternative formulas, though relatively very rare, do yet exist: δῖοι Ἀχαιοί is competing with κοῦροι Ἀχαιῶν, Ἕκτορος ἀνδροφόνοιο with ἱπποδάμοιο, ἐΰξοον with ἐΰτροχον ἅρμα, χρυσήνιος with χρυσόθρονος Ἄρτεμις, πτερόεντες with στονόεντες ὀϊστοί, among others. In some cases, it may be, the selective process which has established the law of economy throughout the poet's language is not yet quite complete; in others, an epithet is transferred from one traditional phrase to another under the influence of analogy; in others, the poet's memory or training may be at fault; in a very few the variant epithet may have been deliberately selected by the poet. The most significant and interesting feature of these duplicates is their rarity: the value of the law of economy as evidence for the high antiquity of the formula-systems is emphasized by this striking contrast of the innumerable traditional with the mere handful of equivalent phrases.

3) A further type of economy is imposed on the formula-system by the long process of natural selection. For "the sea" there are three common nouns[23] and about a dozen traditional epithets. Each of the common nouns might conveniently be

used in all of its four declension-cases: but in fact the process
of selection has so restricted the formula-system that noun +
epithet combinations in the dative case are supplied with πόντος
only, and in the genitive with θάλασσα and ἁλός only. Moreover
the epithets are for the most part restricted each to its own
noun: only πολιός and ἀτρύγετος are used with more than one of
the nouns. Nouns originally distinct in meaning may become
more or less synonymous in the course of time: for example,
πόντος and ἁλός may be used in the Epic without distinction of
meaning; yet their usages preserve the memory of a time when
πόντος signified the deep sea, ἁλός the sea around the coast.[24]
Adjectives applicable to the one might at that time be excluded
by the other: and indeed it is the original distinction of meaning
which explains why the formular language excluded ἁλὸς
ἰχθυοέσσης, ἁλὸς εὐρείης, and why εἰς ἅλα, ἐξ ἁλός are common
whereas ἐς πόντον, ἐκ πόντου are not.

4) Such contrast between an older restricted sense and a
more recent freer one is quite often to be observed; and here and
there we discern a most interesting fact. Take a noun which has
certain formular epithets but also a number of nonformular
epithets scattered through the poems; look at these two classes
of epithets, and you may see that the same noun is being quite
differently described by the two classes; for example, the shields
described by the recurrent phrases are fundamentally different
from those described by the nonrecurrent phrases.

5) It must not be supposed that the formular language was
ever limited to the extent observable in the Iliad and Odyssey.
These two poems are the only survivors from a much larger
number, and their formular language is only a fraction of the
whole.[25] There is only a single instance of θάλασσά τε ἠχήεσσα:
but there exists no metrical equivalent, and this phrase, which
has a traditional ring, may well have been a common formula;
the same is to be said of the isolated ἀνεμοτρεφὲς ἔγχος in Λ 256.

Whereas the law of economy excludes such a formula as
κορυθαίολος Αἴας, the need being already supplied by Τελαμώνιος
Αἴας; and whereas original distinction in the meaning of the

nouns accounts for the absence of ἁλὸς εὐρείης; it is *mere chance* which has suppressed such convenient formulas as πολιὸν κατὰ πόντον, πόντον ἐπ' εὐρύν, and hundreds of others.

6) The few individual phrases attest as a rule no desire to create anything novel or picturesque or otherwise effective. Some are merely variations of traditional phraseology;[26] others are inspired by analogy; others owe their existence simply to forgetfulness or ignorance of the traditional phrascology,— there was no excuse for putting γλαύκη . . . θάλασσα in the room of πολιὴ . . . θάλασσα in Π 34; and μείλανι πόντωι in Ω 79 was a monstrous lapse of memory.[27] The composer of ἅλα πορφυρέην, ἁλὸς πολυβένθεος, βαθείης ἐξ ἁλός, εἰς ἅλα . . . βαθεῖαν, was merely serving the convenience of the moment by transferring traditional epithets from other objects to "the sea."[28] The question whether such novel phrases might one day become respectable formulas depends entirely on their utility. There remains in this category only one combination, ἅλα μαρμαρέην, which can be identified as a new flight of fancy, owing nothing to tradition or analogy, inspired by the desire to create a picturesque phrase.[29]

7) In the great majority of formular phrases, noun and epithet are juxtaposed.[30] This is natural, since they were designed to fill a given section of the verse; and it is in general true over the whole extent of the Epic formulas: κορυθαίολος Ἕκτωρ occurs 38 times, κορυθαίολος divided from Ἕκτωρ only once; πόδας ὠκὺς Ἀχιλλεύς 31 times, divided never; φαίδιμος 70 times, never separated from its noun. Hundreds of similar examples may be readily accumulated. The epithets for "the sea" thus illustrate a general rule: of the 17 formular combinations, 14 (with 114 occurrences) have noun and adjective juxtaposed; only 3 (with only 17 occurrences) have them separated. The commonest form of separation is that exemplified by κυμαίνοντα, ἰχθυόεντα, at the end of the line, where a stock epithet is conveniently added to fill the end of a line of which the sense is already complete.

This coherence of noun and epithet is highly significant. It means that where an epithet can be proved to be very ancient, a noun (or name) with which it is specially associated must be very ancient too; and this is specially probable where the epithet is of an absolutely restricted type,—in the Iliad, πόδας ὠκύς is never used of anybody but Achilles, κορυθαίολος of no hero but Hector. If it can be shown that these epithets are of very high antiquity, the names with which alone they are associated must likewise go back to the remote past; for the survival of the epithets in the Epic depended upon their connexion with the names.

8) In the example of "the sea," formular phrases accounted for about nine-tenths of all the noun + epithet combinations. A similar study applied to dozens of other themes and objects in the Epic shows, as a general rule, that this example is typical of the whole,—not merely of noun + epithet phrases, but of any other sort of phrase. This very high proportion of the Iliad, between four-fifths and nine-tenths of the whole, is composed of ready-made phrases, remembered from the past, not created for the present. This is the extent of the limitations upon the Homeric poet. He has no interest in originality of expression, or in variety. He uses or adapts inherited formulas. When these fail to serve the need of the moment, then—and as a rule then only—he makes a new phrase: but that happens relatively seldom, and through compulsion, not choice. The primary requirement of this poetry is that its language should be fixed and familiar. It differs from written poetry, inasmuch as its language is created not by choice and arrangement of words, but by use and adaptation of words already chosen and arranged. I am very far from suggesting that there is *less* scope for poetic art in oral than in written verse. Our appreciation of the Greek Epic begins with the recognition of its formular technique of oral composition: let nobody suppose for a moment that I think it ends there.

The sky.—The sky gives another example, very briefly and clearly, of the Homeric poet's dependence on a small stock of formular phrases. The noun οὐρανός, which occurs about 100 times, is combined with an epithet in 53 passages; 48 of these 53 are repetitions of only three formular phrases, μέγαν οὐρανόν, οὐρανὸν εὐρύν, and οὐρανὸν ἀστερόεντα. The law of economy is never broken, and the phrases have fixed positions in the line.[31]

Wine.—Wine is mentioned under the name οἶνος in 137 places, including 72 in noun + epithet combination. Three formular phrases account for 20 of the Iliad's 22 examples; and of the remaining two, one is evidently traditional and the other may be also. In this example, then, tradition supplied the poet with the whole of what he needed. The Odyssey, which has 50 noun + epithet combinations, offers much greater variety: but nine recurrent phrases account for 45 out of 50 passages, and two of the remainder are simple variations of formula; of the remaining three, two are special cases where the adjective is a predicate, and the third may be traditional. The law of economy is maintained in all but one out of 72 places.[32]

Φαίδιμος *and* ὄβριμος.—These two epithets vividly illustrate the severity of the laws and limitations imposed by tradition on the oral poet in the composition of the Iliad. Both are potentially of a most useful type, easily adaptable to three or four places in the line, and broad .enough in meaning to be applicable to a great variety of subjects. Yet both are in practice absolutely confined to one and the same position in the line (the fifth foot), and both are restricted to an exceptionally narrow range of subjects. All 50 examples of φαίδιμος are made up of five recurrent phrases: no other subject has this epithet except Ajax, Achilles, Hector, "son," and "limbs." The epithet ὄβριμος is not less austere in behaviour: four phrases account for all but one of 25 examples; only Hector, Ares, Achilles, and "spear" receive it, with a single exception. So imperative is the restriction to the fifth foot that, when ἔγχος requires an epithet of this metrical value elsewhere in the line, ἄλκιμον is invariably used instead of ὄβριμον.

The Odyssey, as so often, differs: it has very nearly forgotten the word ὄβριμος, which occurs thrice within a short space in the. Ninth Book and nowhere else; it has no idea of any restriction to particular subjects or to a particular place in the line.

Its usage of φαίδιμος is much more conventional, but here too is a characteristic innovation,—the antitraditional dative case combined with an antitraditional subject, "the shoulder."[33]

The shield of Ajax.—The noun + epithet combinations for "the shield" in the Iliad are of exceptional interest. In general, they are obviously a product of the oral technique in poetry: of 84 examples,[34] all but 18 are, or include, repetitions of ready-made phrases.[35] But here we observe, not for the last time, two illuminating facts. First, the recurrent phrases differ fundamentally from the nonrecurrent phrases in the types of shield which they describe; secondly, one of the recurrent phrases provides the clearest possible example of a Mycenaean relic embedded in a Homeric formula.

The difference between the types of shield described by the recurrent and the nonrecurrent phrases admits an obvious explanation. The Ionian poets inherited a stock of formulas which as a rule they employed in composing their verses, but on the few occasions when no formula was available or convenient they invented epithets of their own. Now their own epithets naturally describe the shields with which they themselves were familiar; and it happens that these were fundamentally different from the shields described by the ancient formulas. Thus arose the distinction which we observe in the Iliad. The traditional epithets describe two kinds of shield:[36] σάκος, a large, strong, broad shield made of layers of leather; and ἀσπίς, a round shield with a boss (or bosses) on the face. Now the traditional epithets account for about four-fifths of the passages in which noun + epithet combinations occur: and it is noticeable that not one of them says anything about the only aspect of the shield that is normally visible,—*the outer surface.*[37] There can only be one reason for this reticence: that there was nothing worth saying about it; at least, the outer surface cannot have been the most interesting feature of the shield. But here is a violent conflict between the old formulas and the new individual epithets: for the outer surface is the one part of the shield which interests the Ionian poet; and the few individual epithets sharply contradict the many formular epithets, putting the emphasis on *an outer face of bronze*, "which, when it existed at all, must have been far the most conspicuous feature." The Ionian poet is familiar with a bronze-faced shield: yet he has not a single formula-phrase at his command to describe it. The force of tradition compels him regularly to describe a shield with no bronze face: from time to time, but seldom, the formulas leave him a loop-hole for the insertion of an adjective of his own, and then at once the shield becomes brazen, of beaten metal, flashing, gleaming, beautiful, and variegated.[38] What he knows, and what he would describe if he could, is very different from what his formular vocabulary compels him to describe; and he has not yet attempted, or has failed in the attempt, to create new formulas to describe new objects.[39]

This is a satisfactory proof that the formulas must be very old; but can we say how old? The shield of Ajax gives an answer. It is very large; it is carried "like a tower"; and in two passages[40] it has a strap which passes *over the left shoulder*,— "a position only possible with a body-shield which was used as a stationary defence to be set in place when both hands were free from wielding weapons." Periphetes[41] trips over the rim of his own shield; Hector's thumps against his neck and ankles.[42] Now, to find a shield of this type—a huge shield, without metal surface, a shield which you set up in front of your body "like a tower"—we must go far back into the Minoan-Mycenaean era. This type is seen on dagger blade and signet ring from the shaft graves at Mycenae, and on other works of art down to, but not after, the third Late Helladic period.[43] The traditional description of the shield of Ajax, together with one or two episodes in the Iliad, preserves the memory of an object which was common in the Mycenaean era but never existed in the world afterwards. And there is no way by which that memory could have been preserved through the Dark Ages into our Iliad except through the medium of Greek Epic poetry, orally composed and continuously transmitted. These traditional phrases, φέρων σάκος ἠΰτε πύργον and the like, are and always have been constituents of dactylic hexameter verse; their form and their matter teach us that the Greek Epic was being composed already in the Mycenaean era; the history of the Iliad, in which these phrases are preserved, must be continuous from the time of the fall of Troy or thereabouts, and may be much older.

Consider further that the shield which is "of seven oxhides," which is carried "like a tower," and which has a strap passing over the left shoulder, is not just anybody's shield: it is *the shield of Ajax;* and the name of Ajax is embedded in the formulas together with the prehistoric epithets. Nobody else is allowed to supplant him.[44] Shields are mentioned in 170 passages, and more than a hundred Achaeans are named, in the Iliad: but nobody else has a shield that is ἑπταβόειον or is carried ἠΰτε πύργον. This remarkable consistency is not fortuitous: what the traditional phrases have preserved is not only the Mycenaean shield but also the name of the Mycenaean hero with whom alone it is associated. Ajax has played his part in the Greek Epic since the Mycenaean era. So, perhaps, has Periphetes. His shield, described by a unique epithet, "reaching to the feet," was long enough to trip him up: it is either a tower shield or a figure-of-eight; and its bearer is actually called *"the man from Mycenae,"* Μυκηναῖος Περιφήτης,—the only person in the whole Greek Epic so described: the uniqueness and aptness of his description indicate again that tradition has preserved not only the Mycenaean shield but also the name of its owner, a pair indissolubly compacted.

But it is not enough to say simply that the tower shield of Ajax is an heirloom in the Iliad from its Mycenaean past. This type of shield is first seen in Hellas on dagger blade and signet ring from the shaft graves at Mycenae, made in the 16th century B.C.: but an entirely different type of shield is portrayed on the monuments from the 13th century onwards,—a relatively small shield, more or less round, wielded by a central handgrip; and the shields described by the formulas in the Iliad are also entirely different from the tower shield, one being a broad leather σάκος, the other a round bossed ἀσπίς, both wielded by hand and both very much smaller than the tower shield. What Miss Lorimer writes of the body shield in general applies with special force to the tower shield: "Homer's body-shield perpetuates the memory of those current in LH I and II [i.e., c. 1600–1400 B.C.], and probably still remembered in the early part of LH III [i.e., in the 14th century]. . . . The poet's knowledge cannot be accounted for by assuming the survival through so many disturbed centuries of objects made of perishable material; it can only have come to him by poetic transmission."[45] Thus the Epic formulas, which as a rule describe shields of the late Mycenaean era, here preserve also the memory of a type obsolete if not extinct already at that time.

If Ajax and his shield are inseparable, it follows that the person of Ajax was celebrated in poetry when the tower shield was in vogue; and that is long before the Trojan War. The magnet of the Trojan War has attracted this hero of earlier adventures: The evidence enforces this conclusion: and confirmation comes from an unexpected source,—from the fact that of all the great heroes Ajax alone had no place in the immemorially old Catalogue of Ships; a deficiency made the more obvious by what was intended to correct it, the addition of a single line to insert his name.[46] It is surely not by mere chance that the Catalogue omitted from its list of combatants the one great hero whose equipment anyway removes him to an era earlier than the Trojan War.[47]

Among many things that might be said about the antiquity of Ajax, one is of particular interest.

There are two Ajaxes in the Iliad: the great Ajax, son of Telamon, and a smaller Ajax, son of Oileus, commander of the Locrians from the north of Hellas. Of these two the Iliad often speaks, or appears to speak, in the dual number, Αἴαντε: we understand by that term "Ajax the son of Telamon and Ajax the son of Oileus"; and that is certainly what the Ionian poet himself understood. But the life of the tradition is immensely long; and the Iliad has not quite obliterated a much earlier meaning of Αἴαντε,—one so old that there is hardly another trace of it even among the most ancient linguistic relics preserved by the Greek Epic.

Wackernagel observed, so long ago as 1877,[48] a number of remarkable and related facts. First, since nothing but their name, "Ajax," connects the two persons in question, the coupling of them in the dual number is an abuse of language. The primary function of the dual in Greek is to couple *pairs*,—two eyes, or ears, or knees; two parents, and the like. Its usage was soon extended to include couples which are not, strictly speaking, *pairs;* but it was not intended to stretch so far as to cover two completely unrelated objects or persons who merely happen to have the same name. Secondly, the following power was inherent in the Indo-European dual: if two different words were capable of being united in a dual number (for example, "father" and "mother"), then *one* of the pair alone, acting for both of them, might take the dual ending. Thirdly, Ajax has a brother, very closely associated with him in the Iliad,—Teucer; and (this was Wackernagel's astonishing discovery) the Iliad preserves clear traces of the use of the dual Αἴαντε in the manner just described, meaning "*Ajax and his brother.*" Ajax and Teucer, the pair of brothers,[49] might regularly be given dual adjective or verb when mentioned together, and the *name* of one, *in the dual number*, might stand for both. If Αἴαντε was a very ancient term, it cannot have meant "the two persons who happen to be called Ajax"; but it could have meant "Ajax and his brother"; and the Iliad indicates that this is just what it did mean at an earlier period. This usage of the dual has disappeared even from the Epic except in a single other example: Μολίονε, which originally meant "Molion and his twin brother." Once more, it is not by mere chance that *Ajax* is the person associated with a relic of exceptionally remote antiquity.

There is one place in the Iliad where it is very obvious that Αἴαντε means "Ajax and his brother Teucer," not "the two Ajaxes." In the Fourth Book, from verse 223 onwards, Agamemnon reviews his army, visiting one contingent after another. He inspected the Cretans and spoke to their leader

Idomeneus. Then he passed on and came to "the Ajaxes," who were already at the head of their infantry, formed in dense companies, bristling with spears and shields; to them also he spoke, and passed on. Now pause a moment, Agamemnon, and tell us, what contingent it is that you have visited. "The two Ajaxes', of course." But do you not see that there is no such possibility? The two Ajaxes have nothing in common but the name: they are not joint commanders of one regiment. And do not plead that no harm is done if two different regiments are for the moment combined into one. Remember those "dense companies, bristling with spears and shields": but the only thing that anyone knows about the regiment of the smaller Ajax is just this,— that it has no spears or shields, and that it never takes the field beside any other regiment; it does not join in pitched battles, but keeps its distance, and its only weapon is bow and arrow,[50] a thing despised by the Achaeans ih the Iliad. Only a poet who had no clear vision, indeed no vision at all, of the scene which he is describing could combine this exceptional and indeed unique contingent of semi-savage Locrians with the highly conventional[51] troops of another chieftain,—merely because the two leaders happen to have the same name. Certainly the poet, if asked, would say that Αἴαντε means "the two Ajaxes"; and would admit that he has made a bad mistake. But he has not made a mistake, except in his interpretation of Αἴαντε: he has preserved an almost obliterated truth, the usage of Αἴαντε in the sense "Ajax and his brother." Tradition supplied him with a formula for addressing Ajax, Αἴαντε 'Αργείων ἡγήτορε, in which Ajax's brother was included: in the early Epic this formula had been employed correctly; and the force of immemorial tradition has preserved it in a few contexts up to the end. It is very natural that the later poet should fail to notice the occasional confusion which is caused by the difference between the old and the new meanings of a word or formula; but no poet would of his own free will, as a positive and creative act, describe the two Ajaxes as joint commanders of an army comprising the regular Salaminians and the highly irregular Locrians.

There is at least one other place where the original meaning of Αἴαντε, "Ajax and his brother," is deeply embedded in the Iliad. In N 177 ff. Ajax and his brother Teucer are fighting side by side. Teucer kills Imbrios: he therefore has the right to strip the body of its armour; and he sets out to do so. Hector intervenes, but is repelled by Ajax; *and the* Αἴαντε *proceed to drag and despoil the body of Imbrios.* Here it is very obvious that Αἴαντε means "Ajax and Teucer": nobody else took part in the killing of Imbrios; nobody else has any interest in, or claim to, the spoils. It is indeed so obvious, that the later poets were inspired to correct what they thought to be a mistake. If the term Αἴαντε was used, the smaller Ajax *must* have been engaged in the action; let us proceed at once to say "that the head of Imbrios was now cut off *by Ajax the son of Oileus*." This we shall certainly not tolerate: what, we shall ask this bounding intruder, are you doing with a head which belongs to us? Imbrios was our victim, not yours: Teucer killed him, Ajax helped to secure the body; you had nothing whatever to do with him. The smaller Ajax pops into the scene suddenly, and out of it again immediately, having done his simple duty; which was, to bring the term Αἴαντε into line with modern opinion.[52]

The spear of Achilles.—Some of the commonest words in the Greek language are of unknown origin, apparently not of Indo-European stock: ἀγαθός and κακός, εἰρήνη and πόλεμος, φρήν and σῶμα, ἄνθρωπος and παρθένος. It is a peculiar feature of the Greek Epic vocabulary, that it includes pairs of words, used more or less synonymously, of which the one is of Indo-European origin and the other is not: the sea may be θάλασσα or πόντος; the land γαῖα or χθών; a shield ἀσπίς or σάκος; a bow τόξον or βιός; a spear ἔγχος or δόρυ; a sword ξίφος or φάσγανον. In each pair the former noun is of unknown origin, the latter[53] is Indo-European; and in each except the penultimate it is the word of unknown origin which is commonly used in later Greek, both prose and poetry, whereas its Indo-European partner has no further existence except within the conventions of poetic vocabulary. In the example of ἔγχος and δόρυ the position is reversed: ἔγχος, the alien word, has no further life except so far as poetry preserves it; δόρυ, the Indo-European, remains at all times the common word.

The Epic use of the words for "spear" is a typical product of the oral technique in poetry. The words ἔγχος and δόρυ occur in nearly 500 places, and in 225 of these they are combined with adjectives. But these 225 noun + epithet combinations consist almost entirely of a few formulas repeated over and over again: twenty-three formulas account for 211 of them;[54] and so firmly are the traditional phrases attached to particular places in the line that only 17 out of 211 examples show any variation in this respect. The law of economy is maintained in general not only within the sphere of each word but also throughout the large group formed by both together: there is a single exception to the rule that no δόρυ formula can take the place of any ἔγχος formula in the same case and number in the same part of the line.[55]

I make no apology for the flood of statistical facts. There is no other way of establishing beyond question what we want to know. It is absolutely certain that the Iliad is an "oral" poem, composed in a vocabulary designed to fulfil the requirements of poets who were not familiar with, or at least did not practise, the art of writing. But not every need was supplied; and we must ask, what proportion of the language of the Iliad comes from the trained memory, how much scope was left over for the individual's creative mind? The answer is the same for the spear as for most other matters which can be tested: about nine-tenths of the Iliad's language was supplied by memory in ready-made verses or parts of verses. It is to be remembered that the noun + epithet combinations are only part of a much wider traditional phraseology for "spear"; that the whole of this is only part of the whole for weapons in general; and that this in turn is only a fraction of the whole for all subjects.

The need for a word meaning "spear" is very great. It is supplied as a rule by δόρυ and ἔγχος, with some assistance from χαλκός and ἐγχείη;[56] and one of these occurs, on the average, every fifty lines throughout the Iliad and the Odyssey. In these circumstances there must be some particular reason why *one* man's spear, especially in *one* episode, has a different name. The fact is that for Achilles' spear, and for his only,[57] especially in the episode of the death of Hector, there is an exceptional name,—μελίη, "an ash-tree," an ash-wood spear. It occurs in ten places only; it is always the spear of Achilles; and it carries a traditional epithet, Πηλιάδα μελίην, whether that originally meant "from Mount Pelion" or (as the Iliad has it) "belonging to his father Peleus."[58]

It is doubtful whether anything but the force of immemorial tradition could have maintained this exceptional word in so restricted an employment; and there are other facts which confirm the impression of extreme antiquity. The word itself, μελίη, in the sense "a spear," is not only rare, restricted, and obviously moribund in the Iliad: it is a usage which henceforth has no existence whatever in the Greek language, except in a few later reminiscences of the old Epic. The Ionian poets themselves make no use of it, except in this one context; for them, it is not a living word. Yet there must have been a time when it was alive, and that time can only have been in some period much earlier than that development of the Greek Epic language which is represented to us by the Homeric poems. Formally, μελίη bears a token of notable antiquity in its initial double consonant: μελίη lengthens a preceding short vowel in 11 out of 13 places;[59] and the same feature is manifest in the compound ἐυμμελίης; that this feature was archaic and obsolete in the Ionian Epic is shown by the fact that it is ignored in the adjective μείλινος.[60]

It is certain that this moribund and severely restricted "ash-tree" is a survival from a very remote past; and it has a good companion in the epithet ἐυμμελίης.[61] This compound is of a type which has almost disappeared from the Epic language, if indeed it was ever common therein. The Ionian poets created no more of the kind: ἐυ- in combination with a weapon has no parallel in the Epic; there is no εὔασπις, εὐσακής, εὐεγχής, εὐάωρ, or other monster of that sort. But if ἐυμμελίης has no brother, it has a single interesting and congenial cousin, ἐυκνήμιδες, another very old traditional epithet, unique of its kind: for ἐυ- in combination with a piece of armour is equally isolated. Moreover, ἐυμμελίης is most narrowly restricted in usage: there is no ἐυμμελίην Ἀχιλῆα or Ὀδυσῆα, no Αἴαντος or Ἰδομενῆος ἐυμμελίω, no Ἕκτορ' ἐυμμελίην or the like. It is absolutely confined to *two Trojans*, Priam and the son (or sons) of Panthous. Rarity of word; rarity of type of word; formular usage; restriction to one or two persons; disappearance from the language after the Epic and deadness within it,—all these characteristics combine to proclaim the high antiquity of ἐυμμελίης.

And again we must take the further step. The words μελίη and ἐυμμελίης are restricted to particular persons. The noun is linked with Achilles, the epithet with Priam. What the old formula-vocabulary has preserved is not only the ash-wood spear but also the names of the persons with whom alone it is associated. I do not suggest that the episode in which the ash-wood spear is so prominent is, as it stands in the Iliad, an heirloom from the remote past. Indeed I am certain that it is not: it is, in its present form, a relatively late Ionian composition. What the ash-wood spear suggests is that its owner, Achilles, has played a part in the Greek Epic from a very remote period; and that the episode of which it is a permanent feature, the killing of Hector by Achilles, is of very great antiquity. But the story was told over and over again for hundreds of years, and the version in the Iliad is simply the latest version, bearing in its language innumerable and unmistakable tokens of its lateness. It may well be that the detail of the story changed together with the language: but among all the changes made in the long course of time some elements remained unalterable,— the names of the heroes, and also one other thing: from the beginning of the tradition to the end it was remembered that the weapon used by Achilles in this episode was, exceptionally, "an ash-tree," and at this stage of the story was regularly so called.

And what of Priam[62] with his "fine spear of ash-wood"? His epithet carries him also far back into the past, surely beyond the dismal night of the Dark Ages into the Mycenaean world. For some reason—presumably because it was true—it was customary to distinguish certain Trojans, in particular their king, as possessors of fine spears of ash-wood. Neither the idea nor the word-formation would ever have occurred to the minds of the Ionian poets to whom we owe the making of an Hellenic out of a Mycenaean Epic.[63]

The Achaeans.—The Achaeans are named in more than 720 places, and the behaviour of their noun + epithet phrases is wonderfully regular. Five formulas alone account for 168 out of 224 occurrences; and seven other formulas bring the proportion of traditional usages up to about nine-tenths of the whole.[64] It is a striking example of the technique of oral poetry: the poets have no choice, do not even think in terms of choice; for a given part of the line, whatever declension-case was needed and whatever the subject-matter might be, the formular vocabulary supplied at once a combination of words ready-made.

Most of the epithets in the traditional formulas are of a general type; but four of them, including three of the commonest, tell us something of interest about the Achaeans: they were long-haired and dark-eyed; they wore fine shin-guards and "tunics of bronze."

That these descriptions are *true* is not seriously to be doubted. The formulas are fossilized. The Epic tradition is continuous from the Mycenaean era onwards, and that was the great age of the Achaeans: it is perverse to suppose that the Epic had no epithets for them in their own time, but invented some later, in the Dark Ages, when the Achaeans had relapsed into obscurity.

The first pair tell us what the Achaeans looked like: κάρη κομόωντες, they wore their hair long; and the picturesque fact is reported in a phrase of extreme antiquity. The language of the Greek Epic is, as a whole, antiquated in comparison with that spoken and written from the 8th century B.C. onwards: but some of its features are antiquated in comparison with the rest of the Epic itself. There are words and constructions which are evidently obsolete, some indeed almost extinct, within the Epic,—features which had long ceased to be part of the living tradition of creative poetic art. In reading the Iliad we become so accustomed to the phrases βοὴν ἀγαθὸς Διομήδης, πόδας ὠκὺς Ἀχιλλεύς, κάρη κομόωντες Ἀχαιοί, that we fail to recognize how odd they are. The practice of attaching nouns to adjectives (or adjectival participles), πόδας ὠκύς, κάρη κομόωντες, had died out of the language long before the Ionian period. The living Epic does not create any more of this obsolete type;[65] but it still preserves a few embedded in immemorially old formulas, just as it preserves many another word and phrase which the makers of the Iliad themselves did not understand,—ἀκάκητα, προμνηστῖνοι, νυκτὸς ἀμολγῶι, πτολέμοιο γεφυραί, and their like; including the egregious ἰόμωροι, whose stem and termination alike were unrecognizable fossils; nobody in the heyday of the Ionian Epic or ever afterwards knew what the one or the other meant.[66]

There is still something very odd about this epithet. "Longhaired" is a relative term, implying a standard of comparison. And there is a special reason for asking the question, *with whom* is the comparison here? For it happens that the only foreign people with whom the Mycenaeans were really well acquainted were the longest-haired people in the whole history of the Aegean, *the Cretans*, who wore their hair so long as to reach below the waist. Some of our portraits of Mycenaeans show the hair worn quite long; and the epithet may perhaps be justified in itself.[67] But it is certainly not justified in comparison with the Cretans. There are (so far as I see) two possible explanations: either the Mycenaeans wore their hair long because they were "*taboo* while on the warpath,"—a common practice, attested in many places from remote antiquity up to the present day;[68] or the Mycenaeans adopted from the Cretans this fashion together with so many others,—the fashion of wearing the hair to an extraordinary length; and the epithet was created by their poets at the time when the fashion was adopted, and survived long after it had been abandoned.

The signs of extreme old age are manifest again in the second of our epithets, Ϝελίκωπες Ἀχαιοί. This was an obsolete word, hardly surviving into the Iliad, extinct before the Odyssey.[69] It is not even certain that the Homeric poets knew what it meant: the learned men of a much later era tell us what they thought it meant; but it is fashionable nowadays to say that they were mistaken.

According to Liddell and Scott, who summarize a standard doctrine, Ϝελίκωψ means "with rolling eyes, quick-glancing"; and they add, "as a mark of youth or high spirits,"—an unfortunate addition, for the word describes Achaeans in general, and there is nothing to suggest that they rolled their eyes because they were young or in high spirits. It is obvious that the word describes and distinguishes the Achaeans as a people: it is not intended to distinguish young and high-spirited Achaeans from old and depressed ones. Nor is the alleged meaning in itself tolerable: the Achaeans, we are asked to believe, "rolled their eyes" as a matter of course; and this habit was so marked that their own poets described them, as a people, by the name "the eye-rollers." You will therefore find special comfort in the assurance that Ϝελίκωψ could not possibly bear this meaning: ἑλικο- in compound regularly signifies the *shape* of an object,— ἑλικοβόστρυχος means "having curly, or wavy, hair," not "rolling your hair"; ἑλικοκέρατος means "having curly horns," not "rolling its horns." So ἑλίκωψ, if it has anything to do with ἑλικο-, should refer to *the shape* of the eyes; and this seems a likelier thing to be mentioned as a racial characteristic.[70] But there remains a great obstacle: a *helix* always implies *more than one bend;* it means not "curved" but "curly," "undulating," "spiral"; and although the large eyes of the Greeks with their strongly marked curves might well be distinguished as a racial feature and called "curved" eyes, it does seem odd to call them "curly" eyes.

The doctrine of the ancients is more comfortable. They believed that Ϝελίκωψ meant *"black-eyed,"*[71] and had no relation to the root which means "curly." They must have had some reason for this belief,—a reason solid enough to outweigh the temptation to connect the epithet with that familiar ἑλικο- which meant "curly." We cannot prove or disprove their opinion: but we cannot deny that it makes good sense, and that it may have been well-founded. If we adopt it, we have an added consolation: we are no longer obliged to believe that the poet, when he wished to refer to cows with crumpled horns, could call them "crumpled cows"; they are nothing but *black* cows.

Let us turn to the next epithet, ἐυκνήμιδες. It seems odd, that this article of attire, the shin-guards or leggings, should take the limelight. There are more obvious attributes that might have been chosen: but the choice fell on this one,—"the Achaeans wore fine shin-guards." Not a word about bronze or any other specific distinction:[72] they were simply "good greaves." What made these relatively humble garments so significant?

We know the answer; and it affords us further evidence that facts about the Mycenaeans may be fossilized in the formulas of the Iliad. First we observe that the description is *true:* leggings are worn by Mycenaean fighting-men on the Warrior Vase and stele, on a frieze from the megaron at Mycenae, on two sherds of pottery,[73] on a fresco at Pylos,[74] and on an ivory relief from Delos,[75] all of the third Late Helladic era. But there is something much more significant: the description is not only true, it is *distinctive,*—the Achaeans did wear greaves, the Trojans did not.[76] This article of attire distinguished the Greeks "from every other contingent on the field of battle . . . in the Eastern Mediterranean regions in the thirteenth and early twelfth centuries";[77] it was "not worn by the Egyptians or by any of their foes who appear on their monuments." You could tell a Greek by his greaves:[78] and we may be confident that the formula which embodies this truth about the Mycenaeans began its life in the Mycenaean era, destined to survive through the Dark Ages into the Iliad.

Now, finally, the "tunics of bronze," Ἀχαιῶν χαλκοχιτώνων. These are troublesome objects. Let us consider two different questions: did the Mycenaeans in fact wear tunics of bronze; and does the Iliad (apart from its use of this epithet) represent them as wearing tunics of bronze? The answers are, they did not and it does not.

Metal shirts of more than one fashion were commonly worn at the other end of the world, in the east, from the 15th century B.C. onwards; and one kind especially, the scale corslet, might well have been described as a "bronze tunic."[79] But no trace of such a thing has ever been discovered in Hellas; and excavation has been so extensive and in other respects so successful that the argument from silence would be a strong one even without support. As it happens, there is positive evidence to confirm it: we possess a few pictures of Mycenaean warriors of the third Late Helladic period, and observe that they wear not simply tunics, whether of bronze or not, but *corslets over tunics*;[80] and when a corslet is worn, nothing of the tunic but skirt and sleeves will be visible,—the corslet is much the more prominent, and of course the more important, article of attire. Thus the old formula, "Achaeans with bronze tunics," appears to be inconsistent with the evidence, both negative and positive, provided by archaeology.

We turn to the Iliad; in vain, for it supports the archaeologist against its own epithet, "bronze-shirted." The Iliad's tunic is not of bronze;[81] and the Iliad's fighting-men, like those of the Mycenaean paintings, wear corslets over their tunics. How then are we to explain the fact that the traditional formula insists that "bronze tunics" were characteristic of the Achaeans?

I see no other likely explanation but that suggested by the Warrior Vase. There we find fighting-men clad in corslet over tunic: both corslet and tunic have what appear to be metal attachments; but the skirt of the tunic is much the more thickly spangled, and I agree with Miss Lorimer that this is "the one chiton . . . which meets the case." A thickly spangled kilt is a picturesque garment: it may have been a *distinctive* garment, specially associated with Achaean armour; it is worthier of mention than the drab leather corslet, here sparsely and earlier perhaps not at all so decorated. It may be more than mere co-incidence, that a reasonable explanation of an epithet which we believe to be Mycenaean is provided by one of the few Mycenaean pictures in our possession.

The explanation would be the more persuasive if it were possible to show that the corslet in the early Epic was indeed a drab and inconspicuous object; it would then be so much the easier to understand why the metal-plated kilt took all the limelight.

Some of the problems presented by the corslet, *thorex*, in the Iliad[82] seem insoluble; but this point at least is clearly established,—the corslet was indeed, as we were hoping, an unspectacular object in the early Epic. The corslet is a very important piece of armour: and it must therefore be significant that it is relatively seldom mentioned in the Iliad, and very seldom combined with an epithet in a formular phrase. The noun, *thorex*, occurs only 35 times, with an epithet in only 18 places; and these 18 combinations are distributed over so many as 13 different adjectives. Only one noun + epithet combination, and only one or two other phrases, have any claim to be recognized as formulas of high antiquity.[83] In so long a poem, among so many descriptions of arming and fighting and wounding and stripping, one would expect much talk of corslets: but in fact the corslet seldom plays any part in scenes of fighting,[84] and has only the smallest foothold in the traditional formular phraseology.[85] There must be a reason why it should differ from shield and spear and helmet and the rest: why is it so rarely mentioned? why is it so seldom included in old formular phrases? The obvious answer is: because it played very little part in the early Epic; the traditional language provided the Ionian poets with very little to say about the corslet, and most of what they do say is their own invention.

Can we take the further step, and deny that the corslet had any place at all in the Mycenaean Epic? It is obviously possible (indeed it seems to me the likeliest explanation of the epithet "bronze-shirted") that the metal-plated kilt is a rudiment of a metal-plated tunic,—that the epithet in question reflects an earlier fashion, before the more efficient corslet overlay the more picturesque tunic. But still it seems certain that the corslet had begun to establish itself in the Epic already in the Mycenaean period.[86] Although very few mentions of the corslet in the Iliad can claim a pedigree of high antiquity, the verb θωρήσσεσθαι comes to the rescue of the noun θώρηξ. The verb differs from the noun in three respects: it is much more firmly embedded in the poem; it has much more formular quality,[87] *and it is obsolete,*—it is surely a relic from a remoter past, not an Ionian invention, for it has no further life after the Epic, except in reminiscences or imitations.[88] It regularly means "to put on armour" in general, not specifically "to put on a corslet": the verb was formed after the noun,[89] and developed a more extended meaning; if the verb is old, the noun must be still older.

In summary we must conclude that the corslet was worn by Mycenaean warriors, and was mentioned—though seldom—by Mycenaean poets, who envisaged a dull inconspicuous garment, presumably of leather. And we guess that the epithet "of bronze tunics" refers to a tunic metal-plated, whether on the skirt only, as on the Warrior Vase, or (more probably) over its whole surface, at a time before the adoption of the leather corslet.[90]

Hector.[91]—The formular vocabulary is alone enough to refute the theory, still dear to some, that the person of Hector was invented by "Homer." The descriptive phraseology for Hector in the Iliad is remembered, not invented. It consists of a small number of fixed patterns of words, covering all five declension-cases, each already adapted to its place in the line in accordance with the law of economy. Noun + epithet combinations occur in 183 passages, and thirteen fixed formulas account for about 84 per cent of them; of the remainder, all but 8 are slight variations of these traditional patterns. This wonderfully efficient and economical system of automatic phraseology for Hector is the creation of a long process of selecting and rejecting,—of an evolution which might be summarily called "survival of the fittest formula." But when we proceed to inquire whether his formulas include anything which can be identified as a characteristic of the Mycenaean world, there seems at first sight to be nothing so significant as the shield of Ajax or the ash-wood spear of Achilles. And yet we shall not dismiss Hector without a keen glance at one article of his equipment, *the helmet.*

There must have been a reason, however far back in the past, why certain epithets which might theoretically be applied to many persons are in practice restricted to one person only. Now the adjectives κορυθαίολος, "with glittering helmet," and χαλκοκορυστής, "with helmet of bronze," which together account for a quarter of all the occurrences of noun + epithet for Hector, were not used in the traditional language[92] of any person except Hector. Why not? Why is there no 'Οδυσεὺς κορυθαίολος, Διομήδεα χαλκοκορυστήν, and the like? Had nobody except Hector a bronze helmet, a glittering helmet? The answer, I believe, is precisely this; the fact is that the Greek helmet in the traditional language was a nonmetallic helmet, and no Greek had a glittering bronze helmet like Hector's. These epithets make a distinction, which is very likely to have been a true distinction, between the Greeks and their Trojan opponent.

First let us make sure that we know what the epithets mean. You may think there can be no question: but look at the dictionaries. According to Ebeling, κορυθαίολος means *"shaking* the helmet," and χαλκοκορυστής *"armed* with bronze." Bechtel agrees, and can prove to you that κορυθαίολος really does mean *"having a mobile helmet."*[93] Frisk thinks that this may have been the original meaning; Trümpy makes no objection;[94] and Liddell and Scott render it *"moving the helm quickly."* Here are authorities enough: but they must all be wrong,[95] for the simple reason that their epithet corresponds to nothing that ever existed either in the world of warriors or in the imagination of poets. Not even the helmeted head, let alone the helmet, was ever so habitually and noticeably *shaken* as to call for a special descriptive epithet, "Hector the helmet-wagger." The *crest* of a helmet might shake: but nobody supposes that κόρυς ever meant "the crest"; nor was a restricted epithet ever inspired by so commonplace a sight as the nodding of a plume. κορυθαίολος means "with flashing helmet," and χαλκοκορυστής is nothing but a synonym of different metrical value, meaning "bronze-helmeted."[96] The helmet of Hector was made of, or fortified with, bronze: *and therein it differs from all other helmets in the old formular language of the Greek Epic.* For if you look at all the noun + epithet phrases for helmet, a curious distinction is apparent: the recurrent phrases describe nonmetallic helmets; the nonrecurrent phrases describe metallic helmets. That is to say, the Ionian poets inherited a set of traditional formulas in which the helmet—excepting only Hector's—was not made of metal; but whenever it was convenient for them to *select* epithets, instead of using ready-made formulas, they inclined to choose words which meant or implied that the helmets were of bronze.[97]

The helmet and the shield were treated alike. The Ionian poets thought of both as being metallic, and added to them the gleam and glitter of bronze whenever they could,—but that was not very often, for most of their phrases were taken ready-made from formulas which excluded bronze. They are not aware that the shield and helmet which they envisage, and which they describe when they have the chance, are fundamentally different from those which are consistently portrayed in the traditional formulas which compose the greater part of the poems.

The formulas preserve the memory of a world unfamiliar to the Ionian poets; and what is certain in a few examples is probable in many others,—that the older world is the Mycenaean. The oldest formulas for "helmet" go back to a period when the helmet was not of metal; and before the end of the Dark Ages the language of those formulas included elements already obsolete[98] or even unintelligible.[99] There is not much room for doubt that here again the world of the formulas is earlier than the Dark Ages: it is much likelier to be a fact known before the Dark Ages than one merely imagined during them, that the Trojan's helmet was different from that of the Greeks.

The question remains, was it *really* different? Is it *true* that Trojan helmets were of metal and Mycenaean were not? For the Trojan we have no evidence whatever; we can only say that the metal helmet was worn by remoter Orientals during the third Late Helladic era.[100] As for the Mycenaeans, it may be significant that, with a single exception, no metal helmet from any period has ever been found in Mycenaean Hellas. The exception, which comes from a royal grave at Dendra,[101] is an embarrassed and surely transient phantom. Like the equally isolated example from Crete,[102] it was probably made to gratify the pride of a particular chieftain;[103] manufactured a couple of hundred years before the fall of Troy VII[a], it bears no resemblance to any other Mycenaean helmet at any date, and may well be of foreign origin.[104] The rest of our evidence is pictorial; and the only picture[105] which suggests the use of metal in connection with a Mycenaean helmet is that on the Warrior Vase. Here are two types of helmet, both apparently of leather but studded with small discs which may be of metal.[106] These are by no means enough to upset the alleged distinction between Greek and Trojan: it would be very natural, that the sight of a real bronze helmet should awaken a lively interest in the wearers of these halfhearted hybrids; and we must remember that we are asking not "What did the Mycenaeans wear at Troy?"[107] but "What did the Mycenaeans wear when the formular vocabulary was in the making?"—a process which goes back into a remoter past, when the leather helmet was yet unadorned with metal discs; and beyond that into a past from which the boar's-tusk helmet might begin its long voyage down the stream of oral poetry into the Iliad.[108]

The Trojans.—The Trojans are deeply embedded in the old formular language: 55 out of 67 noun + epithet combinations reveal their traditional character.[109] A peculiar feature of the adjectives is monotony of meaning: so many as nine out of sixteen are more or less synonymous words denoting "a proud temper,"—ἀγαυοί, ἀγέρωχοι, ἀγήνορες, μεγάθυμοι, μεγαλήτορες, ὑβρισταί, ὑπέρθυμοι, ὑπερφίαλοι, ὑπερηνορέοντες: early and late the Epic poets never wearied of saying that the Trojans were a stiff-

necked, arrogant caste. This persistent emphasis on a single
quality is abnormal and surely not fortuitous. It goes far back
in the language, and may well represent what the Mycenaeans
thought about their enemy: the Trojans were an arrogant people, just as later all Cretans were liars and all Lydians effemi-
nate.

But there is one other epithet, the commonest of them all,
which is much more interesting,—ἱππόδαμοι, "tamers of the
horse." Here is an adjective which might conveniently be applied to many peoples, but is in fact restricted to one only, the
Trojans. Individuals might be famous for their skill in manag-
ing horses (though in fact no Greek except Diomedes was distinguished by this epithet in the early Epic),[110] and a particular
place, like Argos, might be described as *good pasture* for horses:
but it is quite a different matter to apply this description to a
whole people as if it were a well-known national characteristic;
and indeed it is never so applied—except to the Trojans. This
restriction is evidently not fortuitous: for the epithet εὔπωλος,
"having excellent foals," is attached to the name of the Trojan
city Ilios, *and to no other city whatsoever.*[111] There must be some
reason why the Greek Epic distinguished the Trojans and their
town from all other peoples and places in this respect: *what*
reason? Either the poets invented the distinction, not knowing
or not caring about the truth; or they were recording a fact
known about the historical Trojans. And when we come to
choose between these alternatives, let us remember what we
learnt from the excavations of Troy VI, *that the founders of the
last great fortress, our Trojans, were the first to introduce the horse
into that region.*[112] The epithets ἱππόδαμος, εὔπωλος, do reflect an
historical fact about the Trojans,—a fact which could not have
been known to anybody living later than the fall of Troy,
except by oral report; and that means by way of the Epic tradition. These adjectives for Troy and the Trojans carry the Epic
back into a time before the fall of Troy VII[a], and reassure us
that the Trojan War was among the subjects of the Mycenaean
Epic.[113]

It is an established fact that some of the Iliad's formular phrases, including names of persons, have been continuously preserved from the Mycenaean era onwards. Ajax and his shield, Achilles and his spear, Hector and his helmet, were the subjects of Epic verse already at that time,—that is to say, within or almost within living memory of the actual destruction of Troy VII^a. Let us now draw the most obvious and interesting conclusion: that the subject of the Iliad, the siege of Troy by the Achaeans, is not fictitious but historical; and that the names of some of the principal persons[114] must be the true names of persons engaged in the Trojan War. *For the events and the poetry are nearly contemporary: and it is inconceivable that the Mycenaean Epic should have celebrated Achilles and Agamemnon at that time if there were no such Kings; it is inconceivable that it should have celebrated their expedition against Troy if there was no such expedition.*

It is most important to recognize the fact that only about one hundred years divide the fall of Troy from the fall of Mycenae. The wrath of Achilles, the death of Patroclus, the combat with Hector, in brief, the framework of the story and the detail of its episodes,—let all this be imaginary, as most of it surely is: but the names of the great kings must be the true names of men who lived in Mycenaean Greece and fought the Trojans. We know that the Epic existed during (and for some time before) the critical period, from 1250 to 1150 B.C.: and the extent of time is much too brief to allow, what otherwise might well have been allowed, the possibility that an imaginary expedition has been ascribed by the poets to more or less legendary kings. The poet in the 12th century B.C. could not possibly have told his audience of a fictitious war conducted by a fictitious king almost if not quite within living memory. The early Greek Epic was designed for recitation to kings and noblemen, who took great interest in their pedigrees and in the deeds of ancestors near and remote: who can imagine a poet at the court of Mycenae reciting to the son or grandson of an earlier king the story of an expedition conducted by that king, when his audience knew very well that there was no such expedition and no king so named?

There is no possibility that the whole story might have been concocted during the Dark Ages after the fall of Mycenae: the Greek Epic reaches far back beyond that time, and knows facts about Trojans and Achaeans which could not have become known to anybody after the Dark Ages began. The Achaeans did fight the Trojans, and Agamemnon was the name of Mycenae's king.

Achilles is certainly not less historical. Indeed it is probable[115] that the Mycenaean Epic about Troy, of which the Iliad is the final development, was created in the north of Hellas, to glorify Achilles. It is inconceivable that the court poets of Mycenae should have composed, for recitation to their King, a version of the story in which that king is portrayed in a generally unflattering light; is roundly abused and insulted by an inferior chieftain from the north; must yet make humble apology to him; and play a part of much less distinction than that assigned to Achilles or Patroclus or Ajax or Diomedes. Achilles is preeminent in this story: for that reason, coupled with the fact that the events and the poetical record of the events are so nearly contemporary, he must have been a real person and he must have fought at Troy. It is, I repeat, not to be imagined that the Trojan adventures of Achilles were sung by poets in the 12th century B.C. to an audience who knew from their own or their fathers' experience that there were no such adventures and no such person.

Study of the traditional formula-vocabulary shows that the names of Agamemnon, Menelaus, Diomedes, and numerous others are deeply embedded in the story and mount to a very high antiquity; they are certainly not creations of the Dark Ages. The formular descriptions of Patroclus give him a strong claim to the status of Mycenaean, though his part in the story (like that of Aeneas) has been greatly expanded in later times. As for Nestor, his place in the Mycenaean Epic is certified by the story which he tells at the end of the Eleventh Book of the

Iliad: it is a tale of border warfare between the kingdom of Pylos and its neighbours in the north, two generations earlier than the Trojan War; and it is told against a geographical background which existed in the Mycenaean era but never existed in the world again. There is no practical means, except the tradition of oral poetry, by which the knowledge of this vanished world could have survived through the Dark Ages into the Iliad.[116] In its present form it is a brilliant piece of late Ionian composition; but it has a continuous pedigree ascending to the Mycenaean era.

There is another aspect of this theme at which I merely glance in passing. The heroes' names have epithets, of which some are distinctive and inseparably attached: if the names are truthful, what are we to think of the epithets? They tell us something about the persons, during or soon after the lifetime of those persons: but is what they tell us fact or fiction?

First we must distinguish between universal and individual epithets: δῖος, ἀντίθεος, and the like could not be (and are not) restricted to particular persons. But other epithets are so restricted. The most obvious class is the patronymic, Τελαμώνιος Αἴας, Menelaus and Agamemnon Ἀτρεῖδαι, and so forth. But in addition to the patronymic some other epithets, which might theoretically be universal, are in practice restricted: only Achilles is ποδάρκης and (except in ν 260) πόδας ὠκύς; only Odysseus is πολύτλας, πολύμητις; only Hector is κορυθαίολος; only Agamemnon is εὐρὺ κρείων; only the smaller Ajax is ταχύς; only Patroclus is ἱππεῦ and ἱπποκέλευθε. In general we shall judge that such distinctive epithets, applied (and restricted) to real people within or soon after their own lifetimes, are likely to have some truth in them; the epithets must have been, or must have been believed to be, true descriptions of those people. In the example of Agamemnon the fact is self-evident: he was the overlord; and he alone is described as "ruling far and wide." If Hector alone is distinguished as wearing a bronze helmet, the likeliest reason for the distinction is that it reported a truth, a matter of common knowledge at the time. As for Achilles "the swift runner," it is possible that the epithets reported a known fact; but possible too that they had their origin in a single particularly celebrated episode,—the pursuit of Hector round the walls of Troy, whether that episode had any foundation in fact or not. Observe in passing that the origin of some of the distinctive epithets lies outside the story as told in the Iliad: there must have been episodes, whether fact or fiction, whether connected with the Trojan War or not, in which Patroclus had much to do with horses, and Ajax the son of Oileus was a fast runner. Observe also that some of the obscurer persons have rare and distinctive epithets: why is Amphios called λινοθώρηξ, "linen-corsleted"; why is Deiphobus "white-shielded," λευκάσπιδα? These are not conventional, merely ornamental, epithets: they describe specific objects of exceptionally uncommon types. And they are not likely to be late poetic fictions, for the technique of oral poetry would have automatically suggested μενεχάρμης (or μεγάθυμος) for the one and μεγαλήτορα for the other. Whatever else is said about such persons may well be fiction: but it is doubtful whether these extraordinary epithets could ever have come into existence except as true descriptions of real objects.

That the war and most of the principal names are historical is (I take it) proved beyond reasonable doubt by the solid argument that the record is nearly if not quite contemporary with the events recorded; and the special conditions governing the recitation of the Greek Epic preclude the possibility of fiction, at least so far as the principal names and the outline of events are concerned. But if we proceed to ask how far the poets embroidered the story already in the 12th century B.C., and how much truth was left in the detail of the story when it culminated in the Iliad after three or four hundred years, then we are on difficult and dangerous ground which lies beyond the limits which I have set myself.[117] Nevertheless I mention two factors in the calculation. First, the close study of the language of the Iliad shows that the story in its present form is a thoroughly Ionian version of the traditional theme. There is certainly no passage of twenty lines—I should rather say that there is no passage of ten lines—on which the relatively late Ionian poet has not left the mark of his own peculiar dialect. It is therefore imprudent to assume that the story itself has escaped extensive modification. Secondly, the relation of the plot of the Iliad to that of other stories suggests that the *Wrath of Achilles* (together with much that depends upon it) is representative of a *type;* the tremendous wrath of a great hero was a common motif, a favourite of the storytellers. The Iliad itself tells of the wrath of Meleager, of Aeneas, of Alexander;[118] and the wrath of Achilles has no special claim to be considered less fictitious than these.

This fact, that important elements in the story may be *typical*, common motifs—and therefore, it would appear, fictitious,—weighs heavily in the balance when we proceed to estimate whether *Helen* was a real person, and whether she eloped with Paris and so became the cause or occasion of war. The two questions are connected: for one of the principal witnesses to her name in the formular vocabulary implies at the same time her prominence in the story,—δῖος ᾿Αλέξανδρος, ῾Ελένης πόσις ἠυκόμοιο: her name is bound up with Alexander's in a formular phrase. The fact that the man is described as being merely the husband of the woman is proof enough that she played an important part in the story; and the description itself shows that that part was the elopement. But here again the theme is *typical;*[119] it is the common story of the beautiful princess stolen from her husband or lover, who must win her again by force or guile. It is evidently possible that this element in the Iliad is the creation of the Ionian poets, a storyteller's motif woven into the texture of the Trojan War at a time when the royal house of Mycenae was extinct and the past no longer vivid in memory but merely a theme for poetry. At the same time let us admit that there is much room for doubt. The story is not in itself impossible or even unlikely: such things have happened, and have been the occasion of wars. We do not know whether this element was or was not present in the Mycenaean

Epic. If it was, it must have been historical; for no poet in any court in Hellas could found his true story of the Trojan War on a fictitious tale of the Great Queen's elopement, if the whole world knew that nothing of the sort had happened.

It has taken time and labour enough to lay the foundations of our subject; and that is all we have done, if indeed so much. Hittite documents, Trojan excavations, and the Homeric Catalogues of combatants have given us good reason to believe that the siege and sack of Troy by Greeks, from the mainland of Greece, was an historical event, something which really happened in the world and was remembered for all time through the continuous tradition of Epic poetry. This being so, it was proper to look further, to see how far the picture could be filled in,—how far we may discern persons, and facts about persons, traceable back to the Mycenaean period of the Greek Epic. The tablets from Pylos and Cnossos afforded not much assistance in our search; but we found a source of information in the old formular phraseology of the Iliad itself. The principle of the argument was this, that in the language of the Iliad there are certain systems of formular phrases distinguished by a high degree of frequency, complexity, and thrift; these systems must be the product of a long process of poetic creation and selection, and it is within them that we should look for relics of the very remote past. We have applied this principle to a few test cases; and in some we have seen it confirmed by independent evidence from archaeology. It adds something to the appeal of Homeric poetry, to know not only that its subject is historical, but also that its leading people are, for the most part, real people, remembered and idealized figures of men and women who played no small part on the stage of history, living brilliantly and richly on the verge of the darkest night that was ever to fall over ancient Greece. It is nevertheless to be emphasized that the Iliad in its present form is substantially the work of poets who lived during the Dark Ages: I close with a very brief summary of what I suppose to be the principal stages in its history.

i) Poetry of this type was continuously composed and recited in Greece from (at latest) the 15th century B.C. onwards, the period of the boar's-tusk helmet and the shield of Ajax. It was from the beginning, and remained to the end, oral poetry, composed in the mind and preserved in the memory, without the aid of writing. This particular theme, the story of the Trojan War, was already the subject of poetry at the time of that war or very soon afterwards.

ii) From the 12th century B.C. onwards, the greater part of Greece was submerged for several hundred years under the flood of Dorian invaders: but in Athens and the eastern Aegean the descendants of the Mycenaeans preserved their independence; and the old poems were recited at the courts of Ionian kings throughout the Dark Ages.

iii) Towards the end of the Dark Ages, probably in the 9th century B.C. and certainly not later than the earlier part of the 8th, there was a new flowering of the poetic genius of the people: the old poems were developed, expanded, and transmuted into a new idiom and a new spirit; though the main outline of the stories never changed, and many of the old Mycenaean phrases—formulas indispensable in the making of oral verse on these subjects—were used perpetually, more or less unaltered.

iv) From the end of this period survived a great name, Homer. We do not know, and can hardly guess, what it was that distinguished him from others. Hundreds of poets over hundreds of years had contributed to the making of a great treasury of verse on many themes: yet Homer did something which made his name for ever famous. The obvious explanation may well be part of the truth,—simply that he was a greater poet than the rest. But the nature and history of the Greek Epic render it very improbable that this is more than part of the truth. It may very well be that, before Homer, poetry about the Trojan War consisted of relatively short lays, interconnected only in so far as they described parts of the same story against the same background; and that Homer first combined these into a continuous story on a single main theme, the story of Achilles and Hector. Homer could recite (over a period of days, I suppose) not merely whatever episode you asked for, but a series of related episodes in a definite order, making a connected narrative with a beginning, a middle, and an end. We have no possible means of determining how far the lays may have been already suitable for this purpose,—whether Homer himself composed much or little. In general the structure of the Iliad is loosely knit: there is the sharpest contrast between the excellence of the narrative art *within* an episode and the weakness of the connexion (very often) *between* episodes. Patroclus is sent to deceive the Trojans, especially Hector, who will suppose him to be Achilles because he is dressed in Achilles' armour; that is one episode, brilliantly narrated. Then Patroclus fights the Trojans and is killed by Hector; another episode brilliantly narrated. But the connexion between the two episodes is wonderfully feeble,—in the second episode the poet actually forgets that Patroclus is supposed to be masquerading as Achilles. Again, nothing in the Iliad is of higher quality than the Embassy to Achilles in the Ninth Book: yet in the following episodes Achilles is unaware that any such embassy was ever sent to him. The unity of the Iliad exists in broadest outlines only: the connexions between the chief structural features are usually rather loose and sometimes very weak.

v) There is another reason why we cannot hope to discover what Homer himself composed: the fact that we do not know what relation our Iliad bears to his Iliad. Our Iliad is the descendant of a written version, a standard text made at Athens in the 6th century B.C. and widely circulated thereafter. What happened to the Iliad between Homer and the 6th century? We simply do not know. We do not even know whether any written copy of the poem was ever made before the 6th century: if there was one, we do not know that the Athenian standard text was based on it,—and we shall not assume that it must have been, for the more natural development was the making of the first written text from contemporary oral versions, the versions offered by the best professional reciters of the day. The Iliad of the early 8th century may have been considerably expanded and in other ways altered by later poets for a couple of hundred years: but we lack the evidence on which even a judgement in principle might be founded. An oral poem must to some extent change from recitation to recitation and from poet to poet: but it is certain that a particular poem, even of this length, can be committed to memory by professional reciters, and transmitted through generations from master to apprentice with a high degree of fidelity. There is no doubt that some large additions were made to the Iliad much later than the latest possible date for Homer, a person prehistoric to the Greeks themselves in the archaic and classical periods: but there is no means of determining the extent of the alterations in the body to which the additions were made.

vi) The history of the Iliad culminates at Athens in the making of a written text, destined to become the standard text, though it was still possible to add a new episode to it so late as the 4th century B.C. Our own text of the Iliad and Odyssey shows here and there the operation of a rather perfunctory editorial process (especially in the addition of the Catalogues and Doloneia to the Iliad and in certain passages of the Odyssey) which must be ascribed to the first makers of the written text at Athens. In the 2nd century B.C., Aristarchus at Alexandria made a revised edition of this ancient vulgate,—an edition most faithfully transmitted from copy to copy, until we find its true portrait in our own earliest complete manuscript of the Iliad, Venetus A, more than a thousand years later.

ADDENDUM TO CHAPTER VI

IT IS convenient to summarize under a single heading the evidence of the Mycenaean Tablets concerning names, shapes, and materials of military equipment, so far as it is relevant to the present inquiry.

1. *Names.*—The common Mycenaean noun for *spear* was ἔγχος (*DMG* nos. 257, 263); for *sword* φάσγανον (261, 262, etc.),

but also apparently ξίφος (247); for *bow* τόξον (52); for *arrow* neither ἰός nor ὀιστός but a new word, *pa-ta-jo* (257, 264), evidently *paltaion;* the *helmet* was κόρυς (239, 292, 300; much the commonest of the Epic terms), its cheekpiece was *parāwaion* (292, 299); corslets were *to-ra-ke,* θόρρακες (or whatever the pronunciation was). There is nothing here that was not in accord with expectation except the word for *arrow.*

2. *Shapes.*—Sword, spear, arrow, helmet, and corslet are portrayed in ideograms at Cnossos; corslet and helmet, at Pylos. The drawings are of interest at present principally because of the evidence which they may afford about materials.

3. *Materials.*—Our immediate purpose is to inquire whether *bronze* was used in the making of shields and helmets; and it soon becomes evident that the Tablets do little or nothing to assist us. Bronze was used in the making of arrowheads (257), spear points (257, 263 ἔγχεα χαλκάρεα), chariot wheels (278 χαλκόδετα, al.), and presumably swords. Whether it was used in connexion with helmets and corslets we cannot tell: the shapes depicted in the ideograms suggest to me (though others may judge differently) nonmetallic materials; and there is no actual mention of bronze with reference to either corslet or helmet. But there are complications:

a) An obscure term, *qe-ro₂*, occurs in no. 299 in connexion with something "on the helmet" and with "cheekpieces." In another place, no. 230, sixteen *qe-ro₂* are included in a list of vessels, between 31 pots (δέπας) and a tripod amphora, together with a bronze-ideogram and another ideogram which bears some—not, I think, very much—resemblance to the corslet-ideogram. Ventris and Chadwick (p. 376) suggested that this may be evidence in favour of the use of bronze in corslets: "the object *qe-ro₂* (which appears to be part of a corslet . . .) is once qualified by the bronze-ideogram." Yes, but in that context (no. 230) it is obviously some kind of pot or cauldron. Suppose that the same word was used to signify some part of a corslet: it would not at all follow that it was made of bronze for that purpose too; the transference of usage would more probably be suggested by *shape* than by *material*. At the most, we should learn nothing about the corslet itself, but only something about an unidentified object, *qe-ro*$_2$, which may have had some connexion with a corslet (note that the QE which is sometimes included in the corslet-ideogram may stand for *qe-ro*$_2$).

b) In a number of Tablets from Cnossos (*Documents in Mycenaean Greek* [*DMG*] p. 380; e.g. Cnossos nos. 246, 247) a corslet-ideogram has been erased and an ingot-ideogram sub stituted. But if some necessary connexion between corslet and metal is inferred, it is still neither certain that the inference is correct nor possible to say what the connexion would be if it were correct. Moreover, those Tablets are exclusively concerned with corslets in association with chariots and horses: as Ventris and Chadwick say, "such body-armour may have been re stricted almost entirely to charioteers, for whom the absence of a shield made it a necessity; which would help to explain its absence from chieftains' graves." This seems to me a likely explanation, and we may go so far as to recognize a probability that bronze was used in connexion with the corslets of chariot eers at Cnossos; so far, but not a step further.*

c) A difficult problem is set by certain objects called *o-pa-wo-ta*, presumably *epaworta*, ἐπ-αϝορτά, "things fitted on." These articles provide the Mycenaean clerk with his most pressing need,—something to help him distinguish one corslet from an other. They are never said to be metallic, so the inquiry into their nature may well be irrelevant to our purpose; but let us look at no. 292: "Five pairs of old corslets, with 20 larger equal [   ] and 10 smaller *opaworta*; of the helmet, 4 *opaworta* and 2 cheekpieces." Whatever these articles "fitted on" may be, they are attached not only to the corslet but also—though in much smaller numbers—to the helmet. The word itself sug gests that they are not integral parts of the garment, but superficial attachments; it seems therefore unlikely that they are to be identified with the horizontal bands shown on the

* I doubt the relevance of *DMG* no. 222 (=KN J 693), where a chiton, apparently "of fine linen, seems" to be *valued* or *weighed* in terms of bronze.

corslet-ideograms, for those are surely *segments of the corslet itself* (stitched rows of padding, I suppose; so also Matz, *Kreta, Mykene, Troja* 67, "jerkins of leather or of several layers of linen"; Ventris and Chadwick, pp. 395 f., suggest that metal plates may have been "sewn *into* wadding of this kind, and thus not appear as separately identifiable plates on the exterior,"— if so, they would have been of no use to the describer, whether clerk or poet; but stitched-in plates would surely not have been called *opaworta*). It is conceivable that *opaworta* signify metal discs or plates of the type—though not necessarily of the size— depicted on both helmet and corslet on the Warrior Vase: these are indeed "things attached"; they fulfil the condition of applying to both garments; and they account for the rather large numbers. But the inquiry has perhaps gone far enough: it is time to remind ourselves that we do not know what the *opaworta* were, and have no information that they were metallic.

[New evidence about *qe-ro₂* and *opaworta* is provided by a tablet from Cnossos, to be published by Mr Chadwick in collaboration with G. Huxley (*BSA* 1958: Mr Chadwick has generously permitted me to see and refer to the contents of the tablet in advance of publication). This Tablet lists "a helmet (with ideogram), *opaworta* on the helmet, *x* cheekpieces" (the number is lost); then on the line above (presumably a continuation of the contents of the main line) "2 *qe-ro₂*, 2 shoulder pieces, *x opaworta*" (the number is lost). Chadwick and Huxley show reason to identify *qe-ro₂* with armlets, or arm-guards, and contend that the ideogram in no. 230 (KN 740) is consistent with this identification; they propose also an etymological explanation (*qe-ro₂* = *squelio; ψέλιον*, Aeol. *σπέλιον*. A special reason has to be found for the form *qe-ro₂* in no. 230, where the number of objects is plural, not dual).

This is a valuable document: but it throws no light on the meaning of *opaworta* or on the question whether *qe-ro₂* might be of bronze. If the editors' interpretation is accepted, *qe-ro₂* will have no bearing on the question at issue for me,—whether the Tablets refer to *corslets* made of, or fortified with, bronze.]

NOTES

[1] See Nilsson, *Homer and Mycenae* 138; Lorimer, *Homer and the Monuments* [*HM*] 212 ff.; Agnès Xenaki-Sakellariou, *BCH* 77 (1953) 46 ff. For an apparent boar's-tusk helmet of relatively late date see the *Illustrated London News*, February 2, 1957, 181.

[2] Nilsson, l.c.

[3] See for example Nilsson, op. cit. 137 ff.; Lorimer, *JHS* 49 (1929) 145 ff. and *IIM* 95 ff., 272 f., 324, al.; Gray, *JHS* 74 (1954) 1 ff., with summary p. 14, and (on the Homeric house) *CQ* n.s. 5 (1955) 1 ff.

[4] See esp. Porzig, *Indogerm. Forsch.* 61 (1954) 147 ff.; Risch, *Mus. Helv.* 12 (1955) 61 ff.; Chadwick, *Greece and Rome*, n.s. 3 (1956) 38 ff.; Ruijgh, *L'Élément achéen dans la langue épique* (1957) 11 ff.

[5] In the argument so far developed there is, as Risch is careful to confess, "much that is still provisional." The relation of Aeolic to Doric in the Mycenaean period is particularly obscure, and the new theory may well have to be modified on this point. But what primarily concerns us at present is the relation between Ionic and Arcadian: and here it may be admitted that the case in favour of their identity in the Mycenaean period is deserving of most serious consideration. There is inevitably much that is speculative and undemonstrable in a reconstruction of Mycenaean dialects from evidence provided by the dialects as they existed more than half a millennium later; and unfortunately the Linear B Tablets afford very little help. But the facts displayed in Risch's *Uebersichtstabelle* (p. 75) demand explanation, and the new theory does go far towards explaining them.

[6] In order to account for the relation between Attic and Ionic, we should have to suppose that the Mycenaean emigrants (the future Ionians) stayed a considerable time in Attica before proceeding overseas (a supposition altogether in harmony with the tradition concerning the relation between Athens and the Ionian cities overseas), and that during that time began the differentiation of the dialect, which thereafter developed on slightly divergent lines in Attica and in the new homes founded by the emigrants overseas. Attica must then have been the second home of the Epic, Ionia the third,—and the last, until it returned to Athens in the 6th century B.C., when the standard text was established.

[7] The whole question of Aeolic forms in the Epic will have to be re-

considered in the light of the new theory. It may be that some of what we call Aeolic forms were, in the Mycenaean period, common to Aeolic and Arcadian: but there will remain a residue which can be referred to no other dialect but Old Aeolic, and it is very improbable that these first made their way into the formular language of the Epic after the diaspora which followed the Dorian occupation of Hellas.

Ruijgh (op. cit. n. 4 above) shows in great detail how the antiquity of a considerable number of alleged Arcado-Cypriot words in the Epic is proved by their complex and economic formula quality (see pp. 223 ff. above). Thus he performs a long-needed double service,—positively, establishing the survival of numerous Mycenaean formulas; negatively, exposing the limitations of that *méthode leumannienne* which had proved seductive to many.

⁸ Nilsson, *The Mycenaean Origin of Greek Mythology* (1932) 27 f.

⁹ I say "discovery" because, although Parry had some predecessors in this region, nobody before him understood how to use the evidence to enforce the conclusion that the Homeric poems are products of the oral technique; Parry did understand this, and did prove it with a variety of exceptionally solid arguments. Parry's Homeric writings are listed by A. B. Lord in *AJA* 52 (1948) 43 f. Leif Bergson, in his *Épithète ornementale dans Éschyle, Sophocle et Euripide* (Uppsala, 1956), shows a profound appreciation of the significance of Parry's work and proposes some interesting additions to and subtractions from the detail.

¹⁰ I hope I have used the words "formula" and "traditional formula" consistently: a *formula* is "an expression which is regularly employed, in the same metrical conditions, to express a certain essential idea" (Parry, *L'Épithète traditionnelle dans Homère* 16); the proof that formulas are *traditional formulas* "lies in the fact that they constitute a system characterized at once by great extension and by great simplicity" [i.e., by the law of economy] (ibid. 19); such systems must be the result of a long process of evolution.

¹¹ Parry, *Harv. Stud. Class. Phil.* 41 (1930) 77.

¹² Ibid. 43 (1932) 6.

¹³ Ibid. 7.

¹⁴ Ibid. 41 (1930) 86.

¹⁵ Ibid. 86 f.

¹⁶ Ibid. 89 and *Épith. trad.* 116.

¹⁷ See Miss Gray's article in *CQ* 41 (1947) 109 ff.; the extent of my obligation will be at once apparent.

¹⁸ [In this and the following notes, ∥ signifies the end (or beginning) of

a line, / signifies the middle caesura.] εις αλα διαν ∥ 11; / πολιης αλος
and accus. 15; αλος πολιης / 6; / αλος πολιοιο 3; αλος ατρυγετοιο ∥
7. πολυφλοισβοιο θαλασσης ∥ 8, metrically equivalent to θαλασσης
ευρυποροιο ∥ 3; / πολιης ◡◡◡ θαλασσης ∥ and accus. 4. ευρει ποντωι ∥
and accus. 8; οινοπι ποντωι ∥ and accus. 16; ηεροειδει ποντωι ∥ and
accus. 11; πολυκλυστωι ενι ποντωι ∥ 3; ποντον ◡◡◡ ιχθυοεντα ∥ incl.
dat. 7 κυμαινοντα ∥ 6; ∥ ποντον επ᾽ ιχθυοεντα 5; ∥ ποντον επ᾽ ατρυγετον 7.
/ πελαγος μεγα 2. The same phrases recur in apparently untraditional positions in the line as follows: ∥ _ πελαγος μεγα 1; / αλος
ατρυγετοιο 1; ποντωι / εν ιχθυοεντι 1; ευρεα ποντον ◡_ ∥ 1; οινοπα
ποντον / 1; ατρυγετον / ποντον 1; εις αλα διαν / 1. For the residue of
15 phrases see n. 27 below.

[19] Since the emphasis in this section falls so heavily on certain
formulas which may be of Mycenaean pedigree, I ought here particularly to stress my belief that these are relatively few in number,
and that a very large part of the Homeric formula-vocabulary is of
more recent development. So long as the oral tradition lasted, each
generation increased and adapted the inherited stock; quite a number of common formulas are shown by their content or language to
be creations of the Ionian poets.

[20] Mr Chadwick has kindly shown me a copy of his contribution to
the forthcoming Festschrift for J. Sundwall, on Mycenaean elements in the Homeric dialect: here we find a most useful list (37
items) of a specially interesting category of obsolete or obsolescent
words in the Epic, those which are actually attested in the Linear
B Tablets.

[21] θαλ. εὐρυπόροιο, O 381, δ 432, μ 2. In the Odyssey there is a further
breach, since πέλαγος μέγα when accusative (as in γ 179, 321) duplicates πολιὴν ἅλα; in Ξ 16 it is nominative and has no duplicate.

[22] πολυφλοίσβοιο would suit the sense much better in O 381; in δ 432
(a line of doubtful pedigree) εὐρυπόροιο seems pointless, but in μ 2
there may be a contrast with ῥόον Ὠκεανοῖο.

[23] πέλαγος is excepted here, being convenient only in nom. and accus.

[24] Gray, l.c. 112.

[25] As Milman Parry was careful to emphasize (L'Épithète traditionnelle 85, and elsewhere).

[26] See n. 18 above.

[27] γλαύκη in Π 34 is not justified by the γλ-, since the preceding
syllable needs no lengthening; the adjective itself does not recur
in the Epic. μείλανι for μέλανι is a unique monster. The other untraditional phrases are: ε 56 εκ ποντου βας / ιοειδεος (πόντος has no
noun + epithet formula in the genitive); Ξ 204 ατρυγετοιο θαλασσης∥

(ἀτρύγ. never elsewhere of θάλασσα, or in this position in the line); δ 406 / αλος πολυβενθεος, unique; N 44 / βαθειης εξ αλος (see next note); A 532 // εις αλα . . . βαθειαν / (see next note); Ξ 273 // ‿◡◡‿ αλα μαρμαρεην; Π 391 // ες δ' αλα πορφυρεην.

There remains some doubt about the following: λ 107 ιοειδεα ποντον //, γ 158 μεγακητεα ποντον //: these two look like a pair, allowing for preceding consonant (ϝιο-) or short vowel (μμεγα-); there is no alternative phrase for "the sea," accus., in this position. A 350 επ' απειρονα ποντον //: there is no duplicate. A 157 θαλασσα τε ηχηεσσα //: there is no duplicate, and the whole line has a traditional ring.

If λ 107, A 350 are traditional, the following are merely variations of position: Λ 298 / ιοειδεα ποντον, δ 510 ποντον / απειρονα.

²⁸ The attachment of βαθειης (-αν) to ἁλός (ἅλα) would never have been made in the early Epic: it may be by chance that βαθύς is never applied to πόντος; it is not by chance that it has no formular attachment to ἅλα, *the sea around the coast*.

²⁹ This phrase (Ξ 273) occurs in the Διὸς 'Απάτη, where it is in harmony with its surroundings,—a brilliant and highly unconventional composition, evidently very late in the Ionian period.

³⁰ There is therefore no value in a recent attempt to draw inferences from the fact that ἄναξ is used of certain divinities but not of others in the Epic. The question whether a divinity is to be called ἄναξ depends almost entirely on whether name + ἄναξ can cohere in a formula: and it is apparent that ἄναξ, ἄνασσα in juxtaposition with the various cases of Ζεύς, 'Αθήνη, 'Αφροδίτη, and others are for the most part impossible or highly inconvenient. Where name and attribute in combination are metrically convenient, a formula is made (Ποσειδάωνι ϝάνακτι, 'Απόλλωνι ϝάνακτι); coherent Διὸς ϝάνακτος, sim., ἀνάσσης "Ηρας, sim., are intractable.

³¹ / μεγας ουρανος and accus. 4; ουρανος ευρυς and accus. 33, in the following positions: / (◡)‿◡◡‿◡ 25, ‿◡◡‿‿ // 7, ‿◡◡‿ / 1; ουρανον αστεροεντα // and gen., dat., 11. The residue is // ουρανον ες πολυχαλκον 2 (perhaps traditional); / σιδηρεον ουρανον 2 (Odyssey only), // χαλκεον ουρανον P 425.

³² Iliad: αιθοπα οινον // 10, αιθοπα οινον / 1; / μελιφρονα 4; / μελιηδεα incl. gen. 3, μελιηδεα οινον // incl. gen. 2.

Δ 259 / γερουσιον αιθοπα οινον, which recurs in Od., is presumably traditional; Γ 246 οινον / ευφρονα fulfils a need and has no duplicate.

Odyssey: αιθοπα οινον in three positions, 12; οινον ερυθρον // incl. nom. 7; μελιηδεα οινον incl. gen. in two positions, 6; / μελιφρονα 4; ηδει οινωι // incl. gen. 4; μελανος οινοιο // 3; ηδυποτοιο in two positions,

3; // ἡδυν incl. gen. 3; // οινον ερισταφυλον 2; / γερουσιον αιθοπα οινον (also Iliad) 1. Variations are β 340 οινοιο /παλαιου ηδυποτοιο; φ 293 // οινος . . . / μελιηδης; γ 46 μελιηδεος οινου // is antitraditional for μελανος οινοιο //, but was suggested by the traditional μελιηδεα οινον. δ 622 ευηνορα οινον // is isolated, but has no duplicate.

The law of economy is broken only by γ 46 (see above); in ι 205 ακηρασιον (= ερισταφυλον) is predicative, so presumably is ακρητωι in ω 73.

[33] φαίδιμος: Il. 50 + Od. 20 = 70. Iliad: φ. Αιας // 6; φ. Εκτωρ // 29; φ. υιος // 4; φαιδιμα γυια // 7; φαιδιμ' Αχιλλευ // 4. Odyssey: φ. υιος // 12; φαιδιμ' Οδυσσευ // 5; φ. Αχιλλευ // 1; φαιδιμωι ωμωι // 2.

ὄβριμος: Il. 25 + Od. 3 = 28. Iliad: ο. Εκτωρ // 6; ο. Αρης // 4; ο. Αχιλλευ // 1; ο. εγχος // 13; ο. υδωρ // 1 (Δ 453). Odyssey: ο. αχθος // ι 233; / λιθον ο. ι 305; / θυρεον μεγαν . . . // οβριμον ι 240 f.

φαίδιμος, ὄβριμος are a pair, providing for antecedent vowel and consonant. ὄβριμος is obsolete, very nearly extinct in the Odyssey (it is remarkable that there should not be a single example of ὄβριμ' 'Οδυσσεῦ //).

From among other examples I select, as being characteristic, ἀγλαός and ἄλκιμος:

ἀγλαός (Il. 43 + Od. 28 = 71) in 52 of 71 places is restricted to two subjects, δῶρα and υἱός with its plural τέκνα. A variant of ἀγλαὰ δῶρα is ἀγλά' ἄποινα (3); αγλαα εργα (4, Odyssey only) may well be traditional, so also αγλαον υδωρ (4). The residue is comprised of ιστον (2), αλσος (2), γυια, εγχος, αεθλα, κεραι αγλαε (once each). See further Ruijgh, L'Élément achéen 143 f.

ἄλκιμος, potentially applicable to a considerable variety of persons and things, is narrowly restricted in practice: four subjects (Ajax, son, heart, spear) account for all 35 noun + epithet combinations; four of the five phrases used in the Iliad are absolutely restricted to a particular place in the line.

ἄλκιμος, like ὄβριμος, is clearly moribund in the Odyssey: Il. 35, Od. 12 (including 28 + 7 noun + epithet). One might have expected ἄλκιμον ἦτορ to suggest itself in the course of the Odyssey; but it never appears. Further, the obsolete epithets in -οψ: though potentially useful and adaptable to a variety of positions, these occur only in coherence with a very limited range of nouns in a particular part of the verse. νῶροψ, ἤνοψ only of bronze, always fifth foot; μῆλοψ of grain, fifth foot; μέροψ only of men, always after fourth long syllable; οἶνοψ only of sea and oxen, 16 out of 19 in fifth foot; αἴθοψ only of wine and bronze (with one exception: κ 152 καπνόν), 30 out of 35 in fifth foot; νώρ-, ἤν-, αἴθ-, μῆλοψ appear in no case except accusative and dative; so also οἶνοψ, except βόε οἶνοπε (2). μέροψ was confined in the tradition to gen. plur., μερόπων ἀνθρώπων (9), whence later Σ 288 μέροπες ἄνθρωποι, Β 285 μερόπεσσι βροτοῖσι. For the suffix -οψ in the Mycenaean Tablets, see Ventris and Chadwick, *Documents in Mycenaean Greek* [DMG] 99 (Αἰθίοψ, Ποικίλοψ; ϝοίνοψ of an ox, cf. Ν 703 = ν 32).

I add a single illustration of a different sort of traditional epithet, ἴφθιμος. Allowing for a single exception (the formular κρατὶ δ' ἐπ' ἰφθίμωι κυνέην εὔτυκτον ἔθηκεν, 4), it has no formular connexion with any particular noun; yet it is subject to severe restrictions in usage and in position. It coheres not with particular words, but with a particular class of words,—persons, or parts of persons (42 out of 44 examples; the only aberrants are Ρ 749 ἰφθ. ποταμῶν, Ψ 260 βοῶν τ' ἴφθιμα κάρηνα): ἴφθιμον Μενέλαον, Μελάνιππον, Διὸς υἱόν βασίλεια, παράκοιτις, ἄλοχος, Λύκιοι, Λυκίων ἡγήτορες, al. It is confined to the positions ‖ ___, ___ /, / και ___ (the only aberrants are Λ 373 ἰφθίμοιο ‖, Ψ 260 quoted above; the forms -οιο and -α occur nowhere else).

The epithet (27 Il. + 17 Od. = 44) is obsolescent already in the Iliad and extinct after the Epic except in imitations thereof. Its meaning is unknown to us; and was evidently unknown to the Ionian poets, for in Ρ 749, Ψ 260 it is probable that "powerful" was intended, as if the word were connected with ϝίς,—wrongly, for ἴφθιμος has no initial digamma (excluded in 25 places), and its frequent application to *women* (one-fifth of all examples) rules out the conventional "validus, robustus, viribus pollens."

δαιδάλεος, φαεινός, and others behave in a manner generally very similar.

[34] Eighty-four passages, in which 101 epithets occur (102 according to Miss Gray, but I take μέγα in Υ 260 to be adverbial).

[35] σάκος: Il. 67 + Od. 12 = 79, including Il. 32 + Od. 2 = 34 in noun + epithet combinations.

Traditional: μεγα τε στιβαρον τε ‖ 5; σακος ευρυ / 4; επταβοειον ‖ 4; Αιας δ' εγγυθεν ηλθε φερων σακος ηυτε πυργον 3; αμφ' ωμοισι / σακος θετο τετραθελυμνον 2 (placed among "individual" phrases by Miss Gray, but admitted to be "almost certainly an obsolescent traditional phrase," 119 n. 1. I suppose that επταβοειον and τετραθελυμνον were once a pair for the verse-end, allowing for preceding vowel or consonant).

In untraditional position: Η 220 επταβοειον /.

Individual: Η 220 (σακος ηυτε πυργον) ‖ χαλκεον (επταβοειον); Η 222 σακος αιολον (επταβοειον) ‖; Π 107 / σακος αιολον; Η 245, 266 / δεινον σακος (επταβοειον) ‖; Λ 572 σακει / μεγαλωι; Ψ 820 σακεος μεγαλοιο //; Υ 259 εν δεινωι / σακει . . . // σμερδαλεωι; Ξ 9–11 σακος ειλε / τετυγμενον . . . // χαλκωι παμφαινον; Σ 608 / σακεος πυκα ποιητοιο; Κ 149 ποικιλον . . . / σακος; Τ 380 Χ 314 (nom.) σακεος . . . // καλου δαιδαλεου; Ρ 268 σακεσιν / χαλκηρεσιν; Ν 552 σακος (ευρυ) / παναιολον; Θ 272 / σακει . . . φαεινωι //; Ν 342 σακεων τε φαεινων //.

Ν 130 σακος σακει προθελυμνωι //, though isolated, rings traditional (cf. Gray, l.c. 119 n. 1). Only nom. and accus. singular in traditional formulas; the individual phrases add gen. and dat. plural as well as singular. Five traditional phrases account for 19 occurrences; the individual phrases add as many as 14 new epithets spread over only 17 places.

For the compounds of σάκος see Ruijgh, L'Élément achéen 95.

ἀσπίς: Il. 93 + Od. 3 = 96, including Il. 49 + Od. 1 = 50 in noun + epithet combinations.

Traditional: παντοσ' εισην // incl. dative 17; ασπιδος ομφαλοεσσης //, incl. nom. and accus. pl. 12, + ομφαλοεσσαν // without preceding ασπιδα 1; // ασπιδος ευκυκλου incl. accus. pl. 4; // ασπιδος αμφιβροτης 3; φαεινην incl. gen. 6.

In untraditional position, Ν 715 // ‿∪∪ ασπιδας ευκυκλους; Λ 32 αμφιβροτην / ∪∪‿∪∪ ασπιδα.

Probably traditional: Ο 646 / ποδηνεκε' ερκος ακοντων; Ν 163, Π 360 (dat.) // ασπιδα ταυρειην, cf. Ν 161 (ασπιδα παντοσ' εισην) // ταυρειην.

Individual: Λ 32–33 (αμφιβροτην) / πολυδαιδαλον ασπιδα θουριν // καλην (special case of a famous shield); Μ 295 // καλην χαλκειην / εξηλατον; Γ 349, Ρ 45 // ασπιδ' ενι κρατερηι; Π 803 τερμιοεσσα //; Ν 406–407 (ασπιδα παντοσ' εισην) // . . . ρινοισι . . . // δινωτην; Ν 804 (ασπιδα παντοσ' εισην) // ρινοισιν πυκινην; Υ 162 ασπιδα θουριν //.

Of 50 occurrences, all but half a dozen are or include traditional formulas.

The law of economy prevails in general over the whole group. Exceptional is ευκυκλος = αμφιβροτης (see Gray, l.c. 120). The individual phrases add ασπιδ' ενι κρατερηι (= εν ευκυκλωι, εν αμφιβροτηι); τερμιοεσσα = παντοσ' εισ η; χαλκειην = ταυρειην; ποικιλον = χαλκεον.

ηυτε πυργον and επταβοειον are not alternatives: the latter is an epithet descriptive of the shield itself, the former is an adverbial simile describing not the appearance of the shield but the manner of its carrying (φερων σάκος ήυτε πύργον = "carrying his shield as if it were a sort of defensive tower erected in front of him").

[36] Here I follow Miss Gray, whose important discovery appeared in *CQ* 41 (1947) 109 ff.; from this article the verbatim quotations in the next paragraphs are taken.

[37] Except of course the bosses on the ἀσπίς; there is nothing to indicate

that these were metallic. φαεινός does not necessarily imply metal; see n. 97 below.

38 Miss Gray draws attention also to the significant facts that the individual epithets, "unlike the traditional phrases, . . . make no distinction between ἀσπίς and σάκος, and . . . do not unite organically with their nouns."

39 There are more examples than usual of the addition of new epithets to old formulas; the Ionian poet cheerfully combines "bronze" even with the seven oxhides of Ajax's shield (H 219–223, with much circumstance).

40 Ξ 402 ff., Π 106.

41 Ο 646 ff.

42 Ζ 116 ff.

43 Lorimer, HM 134 ff., with figs. 1, 2, 5, 7, 8 (fig. 2 is now very well seen in Matz, Kreta, Mykene, Troja [KMT] Taf. 90); Nilsson, Homer and Mycenae 143 ff.; Karo, Schachtgräber von Mykenai 181 ff. Representations in art continue long after disuse in practice (see now Hampe, Die homerische Welt [HW] 12 f.); but the Epic descriptions come from life, not from pictures.

44 Notice too that the antique τετραθέλυμνον (once only in the Iliad) is applied to the shield of Ajax's brother; Ο 478 f.

45 HM 166.

46 See p. 147 above; Bolling, The External Evidence for Interpolation in Homer (1925) 16.

47 Moreover (it has often been pointed out) Ajax is the only one of the principal Achaeans who never wears a corslet in the Iliad; this fact may well be more than fortuitous, since there is reason to believe that the corslet was introduced at a relatively late period into Mycenaean armour; see pp. 247 f. Ajax never carries the shield called ἀσπίς; neither does Achilles, except in Σ 458 (see Trümpy's list, Kriegerische Fachausdrücke p. 30).

48 Kuhns Zeitschrift 23 (1877) 302 ff.; cf. Kühner-Gerth, Ausführliche Grammatik d. gr. Sprache II i 70.

49 I do not argue at length whether they were brothers or half brothers; probably brothers, as in Ο 439, cf. Schol. T on Μ 371; Wilamowitz, Ilias und Homer 49 n. 1; Robert, Gr. Heldensage iii 2 1049.

50 Ν 713 ff.

51 Δ 280 ff.

52 This is part of a larger context in which, as Wackernagel observed, the new interpretation of Αἴαντε has been roughly superimposed upon the old. The trouble begins in Μ 343 ff.: Menestheus sent a

herald to fetch Ajax, "*both*, if possible, otherwise Telamonian Ajax alone." In order that "both" might signify "both Ajaxes" instead of "Ajax and Teucer," a line was added, 350 "*and let Teucer come with him*" (repeated 363); the addition was properly athetized by Aristarchus as wanting in MS authority. When he hears the message, Telamonian Ajax tells Oilean Ajax to stay where he is: he himself and Teucer go to help Menestheus. Thus in M 400 ff. Telamonian Ajax and Teucer fight side by side, having left Oilean Ajax in another quarter. And now Poseidon (N 46 ff.) speaks to the Αἴαντε: who are they? Obviously Ajax and Teucer, for the poet has just gone out of his way to tell us that the two Ajaxes are *not* together. But once again the occurrence of the term Αἴαντε leads to a jack-in-the-box intrusion by Oilean Ajax (N 66 ff.), just as it does in the later passage (197 ff.); in this case the confusion is great and obvious, since we were told a moment ago in so much detail that the one Ajax had separated himself from the other.

Wackernagel detects traces of the original sense of Αἴαντε in H 161 ff. (plausibly) and in Θ 261 ff. (not quite so plausibly). It is to be observed that Αἴαντε in most of its occurrences—there are 22: its dative is Αἰάντεσσι, 5; Αἴαντες (-ας) only 6 times, including some fluctuation between dual and plural in MSS—is neutral, i.e., there is no indication whether it is Teucer or Oilean Ajax who is included with Telamonian Ajax. Passages which *exclude* Teucer (N 313 Αἴαντές τε δύω Τεῦκρός θ', thoroughly untraditional phraseology) are very rare. Ajax the son of Oileus plays very little part in the Iliad (except in B, Ψ) apart from the places where the term Αἴαντε has inspired a mention of him.

[53] Except perhaps in the example of φάσγανον.
[54] ἔγχος: nearly 250 examples, of which 117 in noun + epithet combinations.

Traditional: nom. and accus., δολιχόσκιον εγχος ∥ 23; ∥ ‿∪∪ αλκιμον εγχος (6 times followed by ακαχμενον οξει χαλκωι) 8; εγχος ∥ βριθυ μεγα στιβαρον 6; μειλινον εγχος ∥ 6; replaceable by χαλκεον εγχος ∥ 22; οβριμον εγχος ∥ 13; / πελωριον εγχος 2; / δολιχ' εγχεα 3. gen., no example. dat., εγχεσιν αμφιγυοισιν ∥ 8; εγχει οξυοεντι ∥ 7; εγχει μακρωι ∥ 7; ∥ εγχει χαλκειωι 7.

These phrases occur in different positions or cases as follows: ∥ εγχει οξυοεντι Π 309, cf. τ 33; εγχεα οξυοεντα ∥ E 568; / εγχεσιν αμφιγυοισ' Ο 386; ∥ εγχος . . . / δολιχοσκιον χ 97; ∥ εγχος . . . ∥ χαλκεον Ο 126; εγχος ∪‿‿ ∥ χαλκεον Χ 285; ∥ χαλκεον εγχος Φ 393; αλκιμον εγχος ∪‿‿ ∥ φ 34, χ 25.

Individual: P 296 εγχει τε / μεγαλωι; Γ 135 εγχεα μακρα ∪__ //; Φ 397 / πανοψιον εγχος. Φ 72 εγχος / ακαχμενον is a fragment of a traditional phrase (see above); Λ 256 ανεμοτρεφες εγχος is unique but may be traditional (forming a pair with δολιχοσκιον, if initial vowel required by metre).

I.e., 127 combinations, comprising 112 examples of 12 traditional phrases in fixed positions and 10 more examples in variable position. Only three or four individual phrases. The law of economy is broken by the pair μειλινον εγχος = χαλκεον εγχος (see below), and by the individual phrase / πανοψιον εγχος = / πελωριον εγχος. (On the position of ἔγχος in the verse, see now Ruijgh, *L'Élément achéen* 91.)

δόρυ: nearly 250 examples, of which 98 in noun + epithet combinations.

Traditional: nom. and accus., δορυ μακρον // 6; / δολιχον δορυ 4; / δορυ μειλινον 5 = / δορυ χαλκεον 5; // οξυ δορυ 2; αλκιμα δουρε / 3; οξεα δουρα / 3; μειλινα δουρα // 2; οξεα δουρα // 3; χαλκηρεα δουρα // 2; δουρε / δυω κεκορυθμενα χαλκωι // 3. gen. φαεινου δουρος ακωκη // 3. dat. δουρι φαεινωι // 22; οξει δουρι // 11; δουρι τε μακρωι // 3; χαλκηρει δουρι // 5.

Variety of position: δορυ μακρον / N 168, 830; οξεα δουρα ∪__ // Π 772; δουρατ' ∪__ // οξεα (παμφανοωντα) Ε 618; δουρε / δυω κεκορυθμενα χαλκωι // οξεα Λ 43; δορυ χαλκεον__ // N 247, Π 608. Individual: K 373 / ευξου δουρος ακωκη; M 444, P 412 / ακαχμενα δουρατ' εχοντες; λ 532 δορυ χαλκοβαρες /; Ξ 443 δουρι / ... οξυοεντι //; Ε 618 δουρατ' ∪__ // (οξεα) παμφανοωντα; N 260 // δουρατα ... // ... παμφανοωντα //; Ε 656 δουρατα μακρα //; χ 148, μ 228 (δουρε), δουρα // μακρα.

I.e., 98 combinations, comprising 82 examples of 11 traditional phrases (counting χαλκηρεα, -ει, sim., as one phrase) in fixed positions and 7 more in variable position. Only 10 individual phrases, of which several are based on traditional models. The law of economy is again broken by the alternative χαλκεον for μειλινον; moreover Ε 656 δουρατα μακρα = N 715, T 361 μειλινα δουρα; and οξεα δουρα (and dual) = αλκιμα δουρα (and dual αλκιμα δουρε).

In all the traditional phrases the plural is δουρα: δουρατα occurs only in the few individual phrases. The Epic declension is δόρυ δουρός δουρί δοῦρε δοῦρα: it has no gen. or dat. plural, and no variety of form is permitted despite the potential usefulness of δορί δούρατος δούρατι etc.

It is significant that ἔγχος, the obsolescent word, is more regular in its behaviour than δόρυ, the Ionians' own word for "spear."

[55] οξει δουρι // and εγχει μακρωι // are metrical equivalents.

⁵⁶ ἐγχείη is rare: 23 examples, highly formular in usage. χαλκός may denote bronze, armour, spear, sword, knife, axe, arrow, cauldron, hook. When used of the spear, sword, knife, or axe it appears in noun + epithet combination in 60 places: clearly traditional are οξει χαλκωι ∥ 38, νηλει χαλκωι ∥ 18, ταναηκει χαλκωι ∥ 4; probably also χαλκος ατειρης ∥ 2 (+1 when used of armour), cf. χαλκον / ατειρεα 1 (+2 when used of the metal or of armour).

Thus 63 of 65 occurrences are traditional formulas. The only individual phrases are E 75 ψυχρον δ' ελε χαλκον οδουσιν ∥, and Δ 511 ∥ χαλκον ... / ταμεσιχροα, where the tradition would have suggested / ταναηκεα (see above); / ταμεσιχροα χαλκον recurs in Ψ 803.

The use of χαλκός as "spear" creates a couple of breaches in the law of economy: οξει χαλκωι in this sense could have been οξει δουρι (or εγχει μακρωι); νηλει χαλκωι could have been δουρι φαεινωι; and χαλκος ατειρης ∥ could have been χαλκεον (μειλινον) εγχος.

αἰχμή is occasionally used more or less synonymously.

⁵⁷ Except in the Catalogue, B 543, of the Abantes: a welcome excep- ⁻ tion, since the Catalogue is fundamentally of Mycenaean date.

⁵⁸ Μελίη: the tree, N 178, Π 767; the spear, B 543 (see previous note), and Π 143 = Τ 390, Υ 277, 322, Φ 162, 169, 174, X 133, 225, 328 of Achilles' spear. In Υ 273 f. Zenodotus read μελίην ιθυπτίωνα, rejected by the vulgate.

Μείλινος: μειλινον εγχος ∥ E 655 (Tlepolemus); Z 65 (Agamemnon); N 597 (Menelaus, but v.l. χαλκεον cf. 595); Υ 272 (Aeneas, but v.l. χαλκεον); Φ 172 (Achilles, μμειλινον possible); X 293 (Hector). δορυ μειλινον E 666, 694 (Tlepolemus); Π 114 (Ajax); Π 814 (Euphorbus); Φ 178 (Achilles). και μειλινα δουρα N 715 (the Locrians do *not* possess μ. δ.); Τ 361 (Greeks generally). The Odyssey contributes an isolated individual, επι μελινου / ουδου. The adjective is almost restricted to contexts concerning Tlepolemus (3), Achilles, persons engaged in fighting him (4), and Euphorbus (1),— one of the two persons to whom the epithet εϋμμελίης is restricted (see below).

⁵⁹ Though in 3 of the 11 places movable ν might have served.

⁶⁰ It is to be observed further that μελίην carries with it also the epithet ιθυπτίωνα (Φ 169, cf. Zenodotus on Υ 273 f.), unique and of highly antique appearance.

⁶¹ εϋμμελίης: ευμμελιω Πριαμοιο ∥ 4 (Π 738 αγακληος Πριαμοιο is a novelty, in breach of the law of economy); P 9 Πανθου υιος / ευμμελιης, P 23 Πανθου υιες / ευμμελιαι, P 59 Πανθου υιον / ευμμελιην Ευφορβον. The Odyssey, which cares for none of these things—and which shows

how wide the scope was for doing what is not in fact done—contributes its isolated abnormality, γ 400 εὐμμελιην / Πεισιστρατον, a new name-connexion and a new position in the line.

The combination εὐμμελίω Πριάμοιο requires special comment; see Schulze, *Quaestiones Epicae* 118; Boisacq, *Dict. étym.*, 3rd ed., p. 624; Chantraine, *Grammaire homérique* [*GH*] 1.65, 200 f.; Schwyzer, *Gr. Grammatik* [*GG*] i 252; Shipp, *Studies in the Language of Homer* [*SLH*] 125 n. 2. The adjective μείλινον and the duplication of the initial letter in μμελίη, εὐμμελίη, indicate original *σμελϝιjᾱ, developing μμελϝίᾱ. We must then explain (i) the apparent short syllable in μελίη, εὐμμελίω (contrast μειλινον); (ii) the difference between μελίη, which normally lengthens a preceding short syllable, and μείλινον, which does not; (iii) the -ω in εὐμμελίω; for εὐμμελίᾱς must have had genitive -αο, and -ω looks as though it can only be explained in terms of Ionic -εω, therefore a relatively late form.

I do not think that any of these questions presents serious difficulty. (i) μμελϝίᾱ is a highly inconvenient form, admissible in this metre only before a vowel (and only at the beginning of the line or after a long syllable); its genitive and accusative cases (which are likely to be needed in the Epic much more frequently than the nominative) are not admissible in this metre at all. But a word for "spear," especially one associated with Achilles, is likely to have been a common word, which the early Epic poet must force to fit his metre if possible; and it is possible, by pronouncing it μμελjᾱ instead of μμελιᾱ—I suppose that λϝ had already been assimilated to λλ. Similarly the intractable εὔμμελλῑᾱς can be pronounced εὔμμελλjᾱς. The adjective μμελϝινον, μμελλινον, Ionic μειλινον, needed no such special treatment. (Compare the Epic ὀϝῑλῆjος, which replaced the intractable ὀϝῑλῆϊος in the phrase Ὀιλῆιος ταχὺς Αἴας; our tradition has turned the old patronymic adjective Ὀιλήιος, cf. Πηλήιος, Τελαμώνιος, simm., into the genitive of the father's name, Ὀιλῆος, contrary to the old Epic convention). (ii) μείλινον is disappearing from the Epic vocabulary, yielding place to χάλκεον: χάλκεον ἔγχος, δόρυ χάλκεον 27, μείλινον ἔγχος, δόρυ μείλινον 11 (including two variants, χάλκ. for μείλ.); this is much the most remarkable of all exceptions to the law of economy in the formular language, and there must be some special reason for it. καὶ (μ)μείλινα δοῦρα occurs twice (χάλκεα δοῦρα does not occur, and the only metrical equivalent, if such it be, is the "individual" phrase δούρατα μακρά in E 656). The facts indicate that this adjective survived into the Ionian period in connexion with δόρυ and ἔγχος, presumably in such phrases as καὶ (μ)μείλινα δοῦρα, καὶ (μ)μείλινον ἔγχος; and that the Ionians, who were not sensible of the double consonant, extended the formular phraseology to / δορῠ μειλινον, ανεσχετὄ μειλινον εγχος; but since the adjective itself was obsolescent, the popular χάλκεον replaced it more and more as time went on,—had the formation of the Epic lasted another century or so, it is quite likely that μείλινον would have disappeared altogether from the Iliad. (iii) The correct explanation of ἐυμμελίω is surely the simple one,—that the Ionians inherited the word only in this genitive form, probably enough only in the formula ἐυμμελίω Πριάμοιο, and wrongly thought that its nominative would be ἐυμμελίᾱς, Ionic ἐυμμελίης, whereas in truth its nominative was ἐυμμέλιος; the man with a good μελίη may be called ευ-μελι-ος, just as the man with an enduring καρδίη was called ταλα-καρδι-ος, the man who has no ζημίη is a-ζημι-ος. Indeed the -ᾱς (-ης) termination would be among the rarities in the Epic vocabulary. It is noteworthy that in all three places where the MSS offer the genitive (Θ 552 is not in any MS) an unusual variety of spellings is attested: Δ 47 -ίω, -ίωι, -ίου, -ίοο, -οίο; Δ 165 -ίω, -ίωι, -ίοο, -οῖο; Ζ 449 -ίω, -ίωι, -ίου, -ίοιο, -οῖο; two of these offer what I take to be the "correct" spelling (within the conventions of our texts), ἐυμμελίου (for -ῐ̄ο). The formula can then be as ancient as the alternative -ου for -οιο allows; and the Epic vocabulary at large suggests that it was allowed in the remotest past, back beyond the Dark Ages.

[62] Priam's name occurs in 137 places, of which 36 in Ω (a book distinguished by manifold and astonishing novelties in language). Noun + epithet combinations occur in only 44 places, of which 16 in Ω. Despite the aberrations of Ω, the combinations show much formular quality, but less than usual fixity of position in the line, excepting / ευμμελιω Πριαμοιο (4) and Πριαμοιο ανακτος // (8; not in Ω). γερων Πριαμος / 2; γερων / Πριαμος 2, / γερων Πριαμος, / γερον Πριαμε 5 (Ω only); // Δαρδανιδης Πριαμος and dative 3, Δαρδανιδης / Πριαμος and accus., voc., 4; Πριαμοιο / . . . Δαρδανιδαο // 2; Πριαμος θεοειδης // and accus. 6; Πριαμωι / μεγαλητορι 3; Πριαμοιο / δαιφρονος 3.

There is a small miscellaneous remainder: / Πριαμος μεγας Η 427, Ω 477; / αγακλητος Πριαμοιο Π 738 (antitraditional for ευμμελιω Πριαμοιο); / Πριαμωι . . . διωι // Ν 460; Πριαμον βασιληα // Ω 680 (but θεοειδεα // 483); in Η 366 θεοφιν μηστωρ αταλαντος is added to the formula Δαρδανιδης Πριαμος.

[63] I add a few more notes in illustration of the formular technique:

The sword.—The principal weapon in Homeric fighting is the spear: the sword plays a much smaller part. The spear is mentioned under one name or another about 600 times, the sword about 120. The sword may be called χαλκός (in the only certain examples, always οξει χαλκωι ∥ or νηλει χαλκωι ∥) or specifically by one of the names ξίφος (62 including 39 noun + epithet), φάσγανον (25 incl. 12 n. + e.), and ἄορ (23 incl. 10 n. + e.).

ξίφος behaves in a highly traditional manner: two formulas (ξίφος ὀξύ, ξίφος ἀργυρόηλον) account for 27 out of 39 noun + epithet occurrences; the residue of 12 includes several which may be traditional (especially / μεγα ξιφος, 2; ξιφει/μεγαλωι 2; ξιφος αμφηκες / 2, + 1 in a different position; / ξιφει . . . κωπηεντι ∥ 2; the other three are N 576 / ξιφει . . . ∥ Θρηικιωι μεγαλωι; Ο 712 ξιφεσιν μεγαλοισι /; χ 443 ξιφεσιν / τανυηκεσι,—these last two alone use the plural, a further token of their nontraditional character).

ξίφος ἀργυρόηλον is of special interest, since the epithet describes a sword of Mycenaean craftsmanship (Lorimer, *HM* 273 f.; Gray, *JHS* 74, 1954, 14, "ἀργυρόηλος points to Myc. I–II").

φάσγανον and ἄορ (both of which belong to the Mycenaean element in the vocabulary: Ruijgh, *L'Élément achéen* 89 f.) occur so seldom in noun + epithet combination that no useful conclusion can be drawn. It looks as though 9 out of 12 in the former and 6 out of 10 in the latter are traditional: φάσγ. ὀξύ ∥ 6, φάσγ. ὀξύ / 1; φάσγ. ἀργυρόηλον ∥ (incl. gen.) 2; αορ οξυ / 3, τανυηκες / αορ 3.

The law of economy is upheld throughout the whole group formed by the three nouns (and also χαλκός).

The bow and arrows.—Bow and arrows are used in the Iliad by Trojans, but on the Greek side only by Teucer, by the rank and file, and by the eccentric Locrians. The Greek heroes despise this weapon, which therefore plays a small part in the poem. Nevertheless the evidence of formular usage is sufficient to carry the bow and arrows back to a remote past. Both for bow and for arrows there is a pair of nouns, one already obsolete in the Iliad (βιός, ιός), the other in common use (τόξον, ὀιστός); and the noun + epithet combinations for both common and obsolete words are almost entirely confined to a few formular phrases.

For τόξον, five formulas account for 30 out of 32 combinations (Il. 47 + Od. 67 = 114 incl. 32 n. + e). The Iliad has only καμπυλα τοξα ∥ 5; αγκυλα τοξα in two positions 2; τοξον / ευξοον 1; / παλιντονα (-ον) 3; μεγα τοξον (preceded by κυκλοτερες) 1; aberrant is Ο 463 εν αμυμονι τοξωι. The Odyssey has μεγα τοξον (in three positions) 7; καμπυλα τοξα (in two positions) 3; αγκυλα τοξα 1; / ευξοον 8; / παλιντονον 1. Thus five epithets—καμπυλα αγκυλα παλιντονα ευξοον μεγα—account for all but one (Ο 463). There are no individual phrases even in the Odyssey, where much variety of location in the line is allowed.

This is presumably the residue of a much larger system. καμπυλα τοξα ∥, αγκυλα τοξα ∥, τοξα / παλιντονα, τοξον / ευξοον, and μεγα τοξον in several positions are all that is left over from the past; these five account for all but one example, but the fixity of location has been relaxed. The Homeric Hymns, which freely apply φαίδιμον κρατερόν εὔκαμπές to the bow, illustrate by contrast the rigidity of the older formular vocabulary.

βιός (Il. 7, Od. 9) survives in the Iliad in two presumably traditional phrases: Λ 49, Ω 605 αργυρεοιο βιοιο ∥ (of Apollo's bow); Λ 387, Ο 472 (accus.) βιος και ταρφεες ιοι ∥. Of its other three occurrences in the Iliad Δ 125, though isolated, has a traditional ring, λίγξε βιὸς κτλ.; and K 260 βιον ηδε φαρετρην ∥ was probably a stereotype (cf. ζ 270, φ 233, χ 2). In the Iliad, βιός occurs nowhere outside this narrow range of expression except in Ο 468. In the Odyssey, βιος και ταρφεες ιοι ∥ recurs once, βιον ουδε—or ηδε—φαρετρην ∥ 3, and there are a couple of repeated phrases, εντανυσηι βιον εν παλαμηισι ∥ 2, ετανυσσε / βιον 2; only φ 173 has βιός outside these narrow limits. The antiquity of βιός is attested by the facts that it is very rare in the Epic, that it is preserved there almost entirely in a few formular phrases, and that it has no life of its own after the Epic.

ὀιστός (Il. 40 + Od. 14 = 54 incl. Il. 19 + Od. 6 = 25 n. + e.) draws a less clear picture, again apparently the disintegrating relic of a much wider and stricter system: traditional are πικρος οιστος ∥ incl. accus. 11, ωκυς οιστος ∥ incl. accus. 2 (+ ωκυν οιστον / 1); / ταχεες ... οιστοι ∥ 3; probably also χαλκηρε᾿ οιστον ∥ 2, and either στονοεντες οιστοι ∥ 2, or πτεροεντες οιστοι, 1; perhaps traditional phrases are to be found in, or under the surface of, E 393 / οιστωι τριγλωχινι, Θ 297 / τανυγλωχινας οιστους. The only obviously individual phrases are Δ 125 οιστος ∥ οξυβελης, and whichever of πτεροεντες and στονοεντες is responsible for the breach of the law of economy (since πτ. recurs with ιός and στ. does not, the latter looks guilty).

ιός (Il. 28 + Od. 10 = 38 incl. Il. 10 + Od. 4 n. + e.) is an obsolete word (Ruijgh, L'Élément achéen 94; in Υ 68 the poet even mistook its gender, ἰὰ πτερόεντα—I do not believe that he was avoiding the "surallongement" of ιοὺς πτερόεντας). ταρφεες ιοι ∥, 3, is traditional; 116 ιον ∥ αβλητα πτεροεντα is isolated but has a traditional ring. The residue is nondescript: ∥ ιωι τριγλωχινι, ∥ ιοι τε πτεροεντες, ταχυν ιον ∥, / πολυστονος ... ιος ∥, ∥ ιους ... / χαλκηρεας (cf. χαλκηρε᾿ οιστον), once each; ∥ ιος χαλκοβαρης, ιων ∥ ωκυμορων twice each. (Miss Gray observes that τριγλωχίς, describing the three-barbed Scythian arrowhead, can hardly have come into the Epic much earlier than 700 B.C.) I do not repeat the evidence (which is very lengthy) for the *chariot*: ὄχος is very ancient (see Shipp, *SLH* 1, 9 on ὄχεσφι); in the Iliad, half a dozen fixed phrases in fixed positions account for 48 out of 59 appearances; in the Odyssey the word is very nearly extinct (δ 533 only); only two noun + epithet combinations occur (E 745, Θ 389 ∥ ες δ᾽ οχεα φλογεα, obviously untraditional; neither the adjective φλογεος nor the plural οχεα is used elsewhere in the Epic; Λ 160, Ο 453 ∥ κειν᾽ οχεα κροταλιζον, κροτεοντες)—with οχεα agaiη, and with the late intrusive word κεινός—is the only other instance of an epithet with this noun). ἅρμα (Il. 57 + Od. 9) behaves normally; most of the poet's needs were supplied by half a dozen formulas,—but there are two breaches of the law of economy: P 448 και αρμασι δαιδαλεοισι = κολλητοισι (of which 4 examples), and B 390 / ευξοον αρμα = / ευτροχον αρμα (2). Formular quality is shown by the remarkable restriction of the form ἅρμασι to the fourth foot. δίφρος (Il. 65 + Od. 6), though otherwise highly traditional in its behaviour, appears more relaxed in its noun + epithet combinations (which, however, number only 20). In general, it looks as though ὄχος is on its way out, ἅρμα firmly established, and δίφρος on its way in, in the heyday of the Ionian Epic.

64 'Αχαιοί. About 723 occurrences in Il. and Od., including about 224 in noun + epithet combination (not counting πάντες 'Αχαιοί, πολλοί ἄλλος κάρτιστος 'Αχαιῶν sim.).

The examples being so numerous, the fixity of the traditional formula-system is specially remarkable:

‿∪∪‿‿ ∥: consonant precedes, nom. and accus. υιες (-ας) Αχαιων ∥ 61; vowel precedes, nom. κουροι Αχαιων ∥ 9, with competition from διοι Αχαιοι ∥ 7, in breach of the law of economy (note that δῖος is not applied to peoples in the older Epic; contrast K 429, τ 177); accus. λαον Αχαιων ∥ 18 (and λαον / Αχαιων 2).

∪∪‿∪∪‿‿ ∥: consonant precedes, nom. and accus. ηρωες (-ας) Αχαιων ∥ 9; vowel precedes, nom. and accus. ϝελικωπες (-ας) Αχαιοι (-ους) ∥ 6, with breach of the law of economy in A 123, 135, ω 57 μεγαθυμοι Αχαιοι ∥, though this may have been the traditional phrase following a short vowel. The genitive is supplied by Δαναων ταχυπωλων. There is no formular dative: the relatively late form of the dative 'Αχαιοῖς (for 'Αχαιοῖσι) alone would fit the verse-end.

∪‿∪∪‿∪∪‿‿ ∥: consonant precedes, nom. and accus. ευκνημιδες Αχαιοι ∥ 36, with breach of the law of economy in Δ 66, 71 υπερκυδαντας Αχαιους ∥; vowel precedes, nom. and accus. καρη κομοωντες Αχαιοι ∥ 27; genitive: Αχαιων χαλκοχιτωνων ∥ 24; and the following may well be a traditional pair for genitive + preposition, αρηιφιλων υπ' Αχαιων ∥ 3, φιλοπτολεμων υπ' Αχαιων ∥ 1. There is no dative formula, Αχαιοισι(ν) ∪∪__ ∥: αριστηεσσιν Αχαιων ∥ 8, of which the nominative is αριστηες Παναχαιων ∥, is not relevant here, for "*the chiefs of* the Achaeans" has a restricted meaning.

∪∪_∪∪_∪∪_∥: μενεα πνειοντες Αχαιοι∥ 3, with breach of the law of economy in H 41 χαλκοκνημιδες Αχαιοι ∥, γ 104 μένος άσχετοι υίες Αχαιών ∥. The common υιες Αχαιων is in seven places expanded to αρηιοι υιες Αχαιων, which begins to compete with ευκνημιδες Αχαιοι. Apart from this, and from the other breaches of the law of economy noted above, there are very few individual phrases: Z 255 δυσωνυμοι υιες Αχαιων ∥ (another expansion of the traditional υιες Αχαιων); Κ 287 χαλκοχιτωνας Αχαιους ∥; Ο 326 Αχαιοι/αναλκιδες; and the absurd Τ 248 (cf. 193) κουρητες Αχαιων ∥ (as if κουρητες = κουροι), antitraditional for ϝελικωπες Αχαιοι. It should be mentioned that παντες Αχαιοι ∥ (in nom. and accus.) is sometimes in competition with κουροι Αχαιων ∥ and its accus. λαον Αχ. ∥. The foregoing constitutes only part of the formular phraseology for the name Αχαιοί.

The economy—and therefore the antiquity—of the traditional phraseology is well illustrated by the fact that *five* phrases alone (λαον Αχ., υιες Αχ., καρη κομοωντες Αχ., ευκνημιδες Αχ., Αχ. χαλκοχιτωνων) account for so many as 168 out of 224 examples. Three more certainly traditional phrases bring the total up to 192. And of the small residue, nearly half have some claim to formular status. The proportion of the whole covered by only eight phrases is 86 per cent.

Αχαιοί is much commoner than Αργέιοι and Δαναοί (Cauer, *Grundfragen der Homerkritik*, 3rd ed., 1923, 281: Αχ. 605 Il. + 118 Od. = 723; Αργ. 176 Il. + 30 Od. = 206; Δαν. 146 Il. + 13 Od. = 159): the latter two have very few formular noun + epithet combinations:

Δαναοί: traditional: Δ. ταχυπωλων ∥ 9 (Δ. ταχυπωλοι by analogy Θ 161, antitraditional for ϝελικωπες Αχαιοι); ω φιλοι ηρωες Δαναοι θεραποντες Αρηος ∥ 4, with Δαναους θεραποντας Αρηος ∥ 1; Δαναων / ∪∪_∪∪ αιχμηταων ∥ 4, with breach of the law of economy in Ν 680 Δαναων / ∪∪_∪∪ ασπισταων ∥. Isolated: αιχμηται / Δαναοι Μ 419; ∥ ηρωες Δαναοι Β 256; ∥ ιφθιμων Δαναων Λ 290; Δαναοισι / φιλοπτολεμοισι Τ 351.

Αργέιοι: only Δ 285 = Μ 354 Αργειων / ∪∪_∪∪ χαλκοχιτωνων; Φ 429 Αργειοισι/ ∪_∪∪ θωρηκτησι; Θ 472 Αργειων/∪∪_∪∪ αιχμηταων; Τ 269 Αργειοισι / φιλοπτολεμοισι; the obscure epithet argues for antiquity in Ξ 479 ∥ Αργειοι ιομωροι (+ απειλαων ακορητοι), Δ 242 ∥

Αργειοι ιομωροι (+ ελεγχεες; cf. Θ 228 Αργειοι / κακ' ελεγχεα ειδος αγητοι).

It is surprising that 'Αργέιοι should be so deficient in epithets. Note also that since the dative plural Αχαιοις ‖ is excluded by the early Epic (Αχαιοις for -οισι only seven times), one would expect Αργειοισι ‖ to be a common verse-end; in fact it is very rare (only six times, of which two in K). Δαναοισι ‖ also is exceedingly rare.

65 Schwyzer, *GG* I 148 n. 1, 386, 446, II 430.

66 Among other antiquated formulas in the Homeric poems the following are presumably to be reckoned: μήστωρες ἀυτῆς and μήστωρι φόβοιο (Fraenkel, *Gesch. d. gr. Nomina agentis* i 15); ἀτάλαντες 'Ενναλίωι ἀνδρειφόντηι; πάρος μεμαυῖαν 'Αθήνην and ἄμοτον μεμαυῖα; ἴσας δ' ὑσμίνη κεφαλὰς ἔχεν; ταλαύρινον πολεμιστήν; εἰς ὦπα ϝιδέσθαι (ὦπα not used except in this phrase; Chantraine, *GH* 2.103); the old masculines in -α, ἱππότα κυανοχαῖτα νεφεληγερέτα ἀκάκητα μητίετα (Chantraine, 1. 199); the types ὁμοίοο πτολέμοιο, κακομηχάνοο κρυοέσσης, Ιλίοο προπαροιθεν(ibid. 1. 45); several phrases inclusive of duals, τὼ δ' οὐκ ἀεκόντε πετέσθην, μεμαῶτε μάχεσθαι. And of course a large number of words; see especially Ruijgh, *L'Élément achéen*, chaps. ii, iv.

67 Cf. Helbig, *Hom. Epos* (1887) 236 ff.; Bremer, *RE* VII 2 (1912) 2110; Matz, *KMT* (1956) 125: "Die 'haupthaarumwallten Achaier' Homers sind also nicht der dichterischen Phantasie entsprungen" (he rightly observes that young Greeks wore their hair long "bis weit in die archaische Zeit hinein": but the high antiquity of this Homeric formula is attested by its linguistic peculiarity and by its position within an exceptionally complex and economical formula-system). Mylonas, *Ancient Mycenae* (1957), reproduces a wonderful intaglio portrait of a Mycenaean's head from the recently discovered grave circle B, and draws attention to the "long hair, reminiscent of the long-haired Achaeans" (p. 139, with fig. 49). Among other recent examples notice especially the long thick hair of the warrior's head in ivory discovered by Wace at Mycenae in 1953 (first in *Illustrated London News*, November 14, 1953, p. 792, fig. 10, also in Hampe, *HW*, 1956, Taf. VII^b; compare also the man's head in Taf. XV^a).

68 Murray, *Rise of the Greek Epic* 132 f. See especially Frazer, *Golden Bough* III 196 ff., 258 ff.: cut hair may come into your enemy's possession and may be used (by contagious magic) against you (ibid. 268: how the enemy deals with your clippings).

I do not know whether Nilsson has found any supporters for his suggestion (ap. Persson, *New Tombs at Dendra near Midea* 199) that the reference is to the crest of the helmet: κάρη κομόωντες =

"with upright crest," contrasted with ὄπιθεν κομόωντες, "with crest hanging down at the back."

[69] Later it occurs only in imitations of the Epic style. In the Iliad itself, three different phrases were invented by the Ionians to replace it,—Δαναοὶ ταχύπωλοι (from the traditional Δ. ταχυπώλων), μεγάθυμοι Ἀχαιοί, κούρητες Ἀχαιῶν.

[70] This is Düntzer's interpretation, approved by Bechtel, Lexilogus s.v., "ἑλίκωψ described a man with arched eyes, the reference being to the arched βλέφαρον or eyeball." But "curved, arched, domed" is not the meaning of ἑλικο-.

[71] See the evidence assembled by Pfeiffer on Callim. fr. 299.1. (I suppose that νέες ἀμφιελίσσαι and νέες ἀμφιμέλαιναι meant much the same thing.)

[72] Trümpy (19), like others before and since, holds that the epithet εὐκνήμιδες in itself suggests *metal* greaves: on the contrary, the fact that the material is never mentioned suggests that it was not worth mention. He adds that "because greaves in the Iliad are always associated with the *thorex*, we must suppose that they were of metal,"—an obviously invalid argument, even if there were much better evidence for a metal *thorex* in the Early Epic.

[73] Lorimer, *HM* 251 with pls. II, III, XII.

[74] *Illustrated London News*, January 16, 1954, p. 89, fig. 13.

[75] Hampe, *HW* 14 with Taf. X.

[76] Except in Γ 330, where that arming formula is applied to Paris.

[77] Lorimer, *HM* 252.

[78] Whether the greaves were made of metal or not. The Epic formulas say nothing about their material, except that they might have "silver ankle-pieces" attached to them, ἀργυρέοισιν ἐπισφυρίοις ἀραρυίας. Indeed the Epic ignores the greave altogether except in the epithet εὐκνήμιδες, one repeated line (in the arming-scene, Γ 330 = Λ 17 = Π 131), and three references to the exceptional pair made by Hephaestus for Achilles. The makers of the formular vocabulary envisaged an unspectacular object, presumably made of leather; and it is noticeable that the Ionian poets only once allowed a *metal* greave to intrude (Η 41, χαλκοκνήμιδες Ἀχαιοί, where the older style would have given μένεα πνείοντες Ἀχαιοί; cf. Gray, *JHS* 74, 1954, 6 n. 36).

That metal greaves were not wholly unknown in Mycenaean Hellas has recently been proved by the discovery of a pair at Callithea, south of Patras: N. Yaluris, *BCH* 78 (1954) 125 with Abb. 25; Hampe, *HW* 14 with Taf. VIII[b]. Previously no metal greaves had ever been found on the Greek mainland earlier than the 7th century, though they have been found at Enkomi in Cyprus (Lorimer, *HM* 251 with fig. 29; Hampe, *HW* 13 with Taf. VIIIᵃ; Catling, *Opusc. Athen.* 2, 1955, 21 ff.); and there is some doubt about the material of the greaves worn by the man on the Pylos fresco and the falling warrior on the megaron fresco from Mycenae (Lorimer ibid.; Gray, *JHS* l.c. 6 n. 36. Similar are the leggings of a man on a fresco from Mycenae, House of the Oil Merchant, published by Wace in *BSA* 48, 1953, 14 f. with pl. 9 a: "white gaiters fastened with red garters below the knees"). The silence of the Epic and of the excavations is a reason for doubting whether the metal greave was familiar in Hellas in the 13th and early 12th centuries (Hampe suggests that the Callithea pair may be a specimen imported from the north); and Miss Gray points out to me that the *tin* greaves of Hephaestus suggest a poet not familiar with *bronze* greaves.

79 Lorimer, *HM* 197 ff., 209.

80 Ibid. pls. ii, iii, xii.

81 Except the χιτών χάλκεος of N 439 f.,—but that is worn by a Trojan; Lorimer 209 f. The epithet χαλκοχιτώνων has spread from the Achaeans to a few other contexts: of the Greeks under the name 'Αργέιοι Δ 285, M 354; of the Epeians Δ 537, Λ 694 (unique nominative); of Boeotians O 330; of Cretans N 255 (a line wanting in Aristarchus' text, in several papyri and numerous MSS); and of the Trojans E 180, P 485.

82 The available evidence is to be found in Miss Lorimer's *Homer and the Monuments* 196 ff. and in Miss Gray's penetrating study, *JHS* 74 (1954) 6 ff.; cf. Trümpy 9 ff., 14 ff., Valeton, *Mnemos.* 47 (1919) 187 ff. θώρηξ occurs 35 times (Iliad only); in compound (αἰολο-, λινο-, χαλκεο-) 6; θωρηκτής 5; θωρήσσομαι 39 (+ 3 in Od.). The root is of unknown origin.

83 The formular arming-description (Γ 332 = Λ 19 = Π 133 = Τ 371) is likely to be very old: δεύτερον αὖ θώρηκα περὶ στήθεσσιν ἔδυνεν //, without epithet except in Π 133, ποικίλον ἀστερόεντα (which suggests a *thorex* spangled with metal discs), and Λ 20 ff. (a special case): Gray, 8, "Agamemnon's corslet has several connexions with the 'lobster' type seen on the Enkomi Griffin-slayer [=Lorimer, *HM* pl. 11.4]; it comes from Cyprus, it is made of bands of metal, and it covers the body above the belt (Λ 234). It seems certain that the poet is drawing on Late Bronze Age epic,"—this is an Oriental, not a Greek, corslet; and mention of the corslet in connexion with other easterners may be very early (Τρώων ... θωρηκτάων, Λυκίων πύκα θωρηκτάων). The only other θώρηξ phrases which show old formula

quality are (1) καὶ διὰ θώρηκος πολυδαιδάλου ἠρήρειστο, Γ 358 = Η 252 = Δ 136 = Λ 436: in the first two of these places the line is absurd, in the third inconvenient; all the more reason for regarding it as a stereotype automatically suggested by certain contexts, regardless of the requirements of a particular sequence. πολυδαιδάλου implies elaboration, perhaps metal discs attached as on the Warrior Vase. (2) I agree with Miss Gray (9 n. 48) that the phrase καὶ διπλόος ἤντετο θώρηξ (two occurrences) "may be a misunderstood formula."

84 About once a book on the average.

85 I have gone over this ground again, but find nothing to add to Miss Gray's principal conclusions: (1) θώρηξ "tends to appear in the least traditional contexts"; (2) it possesses very slight formular quality, see n. 81 above; (3) the numerous individual epithets (αἰόλος, παναίολος, δαιδάλεος, λαμπρὸν γανόωντες, ποικίλος, ἀστερόεις, φαεινός, χάλκεος) indicate—as they did for shield and helmet—that the Ionian poets found in the traditional vocabulary a dull and inconspicuous object, which they freely adorned with new epithets intended to stress the use of *metal;* (4) the six places where θώρηξ is connected with γύαλον have probably come into the Epic at a late phase of its development: Miss Gray's explanation of γύαλα seems to me to have the advantage over Miss Lorimer's (*HM* 205); see also Trümpy 11 ff.

86 There is of course no doubt that the *thorex* was in fact familiar to the Mycenaeans: see n. 82 above, and add the evidence of the ideograms on the Linear B tablets. I notice that Matz (*KMT* 127) agrees that the *thorex* is relatively a latecomer to the mainland.

87 συν τευχεσι θωρηχθεντες // 6 (thrice preceded by // πρωι δ᾽ υπηοιοι, twice by the antique // αυτοι δε πρυλεες); ες πολεμον / θωρηξομαι (-ησσεο, -ησσετο) 4. High formular quality is revealed in the limitation of the number of verb-forms in use, and of locations in the verse: θωρησσοντο (-εσθαι, sim.) // 13; θωρηχθηναι (-εντες, sim.) // 12; / θωρηξομαι 8; θωρησσοντο / 2. There remain only the aberrant θωρηξεν ᴗ __ // Π 155 and // θωρηξαι Β 11 (=28=65), the only examples of the active voice and of these positions in the verse.

88 And in the peculiar sense "to get drunk"; Weber, *Anacreontea* 62 f., Lorimer *HM* 204.

89 "To arm yourself" may be θωρήσσεσθαι (originally "to put on a corslet"), or κορύσσεσθαι (originally "to put on a helmet"). I suppose that the latter word reigned supreme until the corslet was adopted.

I see nothing to recommend the suggestion that *thorex* may originally have meant "armour" in general, later limited to one particular piece of armour, the corslet. The Epic—our only source—provides no evidence in favour of this, so far as I see; we know that θώρηξ meant "corslet" in the late 13th century (Linear B, with ideograms), and do not know that it ever meant anything else.

Trümpy (15) is not justified in saying that θωρήσσεσθαι presupposes *metal* corslets, "denn ein Stoffpanzer wäre für eine derartige Verallgemeinerung des Sinnes nicht bedeutend genug": the corslet is one of the most important pieces of defensive armour, larger than any other (except the shield); it is very natural that the verb for "arm yourself" should be derived from this prominent garment, whether it was made of metal or not. (I presume that no sort of corslet was worn in the era of the figure-of-eight shield and tower shield.)

90 Some individual Achaeans: the evidence of noun + epithet combinations:

Patroclus and Helen—

Πάτροκλος: the name occurs in the Iliad 152 times, including 35 in noun + epithet combination.

Probably traditional: Πατρόκλοιο / Μενοιτιαδαο 5 (+1 Odyssey); Πατροκλεες ιππευ ∥ 4; Πατροκλεες ιπποκελευθε ∥ 3; διογενες / Πατροκλεες 5 (διογενης is not of very general use: common of Odysseus, of Ajax five times, of four others only once each).

The residue contains nothing of interest except the highly unconventional type of epithet seen in Πατροκληος δειλοιο ∥ (4).

It is certain that the part of Patroclus was greatly expanded in the Ionian period. But the unique epithets ἱππεῦ, ἱπποκέλευθε (both confined to Patroclus, the latter nowhere else in the Greek language) indicate that Patroclus had a story and a career independent of, and antecedent to, the part which he plays in the Iliad. It may well be that his integral part in the Wrath of Achilles is an Ionian contribution to the Epic: but the peculiar epithets contradict the notion that he was "invented" for the sake of the Iliad. The high antiquity of Patroclus is indicated also by the peculiar word ἐνηής (cf. Bechtel, *Lexilogus* s.v.: = *ἐν-ᾱϝ-ης, "in favour"): this adjective is obsolete, indeed very nearly extinct; apart from the late composition which includes Ψ 648, it is restricted in the Iliad to Patroclus (P 204, 670 ἐνηείη, Φ 96, Ψ 252). The word, and the person with whom it was exclusively associated, came down together from a very remote past.

Bechtel, op. cit., s.v., thinks ἱπποκέλευθε a late and highly artificial formation, for ἱπποκελευθοποιός. I see no reason for this: *κέλευθος may well have meant "one who exhorts," ὁ κελεύων, cf.

Ω 326 (ἵππους) κέλευε κατὰ ἄστυ; in effect, "a driver"; for the ţermination cf. ἔρι-θος.

'Ελένη: Il. 40 + Od. 26 = 66, including Il. 26 + Od. 10 = 36 in noun + epithet combination. Probably traditional: Αργειη Ελενη in two positions, 13; Ελενης (ποσις) ηυκομοιο ∥ 7; δια γυναικων ∥ 5. These three phrases account for 25 out of 36 examples. In quality too they are traditional: 'Αργείη is an epithet restricted to Helen; δῖα γυναικῶν is an antique phrase; and the place of Helen in the early Epic is guaranteed by the fact that she cannot be detached from Alexander,—διος Αλεξανδρος Ελενης ποσις ηυκομοιο; she is embedded in one of his formular phrases, and about his antiquity there is no doubt whatever.

There may well be further traditional phrases in the residue: Διος εκγεγαυια ∥ 3; Ελενη τανυπεπλος / 3; ευπατερειηι ∥ 2; καλλικομοιο ∥ 1, a likely partner for ηυκομοιο. More probably—in most cases certainly—individual,/ λευκωλενωι 2; κουρη Διος αιγιοχοιο ∥ 1 (usually = Athene); καλλιπαρηιος ∥ ο 123, antitraditional for δῖα γυναικῶν; Τ 325 ριγεδανης Ελενης, one of the few examples in the Iliad of an epithet specifically chosen for the sake of a particular context.

91 "Εκτωρ (Iliad only)—

Noun + epithet combinations (including 4 examples of Πριαμίδης without "Εκτωρ) occur in 183 passages; 156 of these are (or include) repetitions of 13 formulas. The traditional formula-vocabulary as represented in the Iliad was as follows:

Nom.: vowel precedes, φαιδιμος Εκτωρ ∥ 29; consonant precedes, οβριμος Εκτωρ ∥ 4. κορυθαιολος Εκτωρ ∥ 25, + 1 / κορυθαιολος ‿∪∪ Εκτωρ ∥; μεγας κορυθαιολος Εκτωρ ∥ 12. / διφιλος 4; Πριαμοιο / παις 1; ∥ Εκτωρ Πριαμιδης 7.

Gen.: Εκτορος ανδροφονοιο ∥ 8 = Εκτορος ιπποδαμοιο ∥ 4 (+ Η 38 ∥ Εκτορος . . . / . . . ιπποδαμοιο ∥), an exception to the law of economy.

Dat.: Εκτορι διωι ∥ 11; Εκτορι χαλκοκορυστηι ∥ 4; ∥ Εκτορι Πριαμιδηι 3.

Accus.: Εκτορα διον ∥ 19; Εκτορα χαλκοκορυστην ∥ 3; / θρασυν Εκτορα 6; υιον Πριαμοιο / δαιφρονος 3; ∥ Εκτορα Πριαμιδην 5.

Voc.: ∥ Εκτορ υιε Πριαμοιο 3.

Thus 13 formular phrases,—φαιδιμος, οβριμος, (μεγας) κορυθαιολος, διφιλος, Πριαμοιο παις, Πριαμιδης -ηι -ην (perhaps originally Περραμίδης), ανδροφονοιο, ιπποδαμοιο, διωι -ον, χαλκοκορυστηι -ην, θρασυν, υιον -ε Πριαμοιο, account for 156 noun + epithet combinations in 183 passages.

The residue is insignificant:

Ten more or less untraditional uses of Πριαμιδης: Τ 76 (Εκτορος) . . . ∥ Πριαμιδεω; Ξ 364 Μ 437 Ο 596 (Εκτορι) . . . ∥ Πριαμιδηι; Ψ 182

(Εκτορα) . . . // ᴗᴗ Πριαμιδην; Β 816 (Εκτωρ) // Πριαμιδης; and, without Εκτωρ, Ε 684 // Πριαμιδη, Η 258 // Πριαμιδης, Γ 356 = Η 250 // ᴗᴗ Πριαμιδαο.

Eight examples of the traditional Εκτορα διον in untraditional positions: ᴗᴗᴗ / 4, // ᴗᴗᴗ 2, / (ᴗ)ᴗᴗᴗ 2; one example of traditional / θρασυν Εκτορα divided (Θ 90 / θρασυν ηνιοχον ᴗᴗ‒‒ // Εκτορα).

Individual phrases only in Ν 123 Ο 671 (accus.) // Εκτωρ ᴗᴗᴗ / βοην αγαθος; Κ 406 Χ 277 Εκτορα ποιμενα λαων //, conflicting with traditional χαλκοκορυστην; Ω 789 / κλυτου Εκτορος; Ο 440 Εκτωρ μεγαθυμος /; Λ 57 // Εκτορα τ᾽ αμφι μεγαν; Λ 820 / πελωριον Εκτορα, conflicting with traditional / διφιλον (on this see Parry, *L'Épithète traditionnelle* 197 ff.).

(Independent formulas are seldom added to Hector-formulas: // Εκτωρ Πριαμιδης + αταλαντος Αρηι // 1, + βροτολοιγωι ισος Αρηι // 2; // Εκτορ υιε Πριαμοιο + Δια μητιν αταλαντε // 1; Εκτορ᾽ . . . + θοωι αταλαντον Αρηι // 1).

[92] κορυθαιολος is applied to Hector in 39 places: elsewhere only of Ares, in the late Ionian composition *The Theomachia* (Τ 38; / κορυθαιολος, an untraditional position in the verse); χαλκοκορυστής 7 times of Hector, elsewhere only Ζ 199 of Sarpedon (in a genealogy).

[93] In vain Bechtel (*Lexilogus* s.v.) quotes Ν 805 σείετο πήληξ, Ο 608 f. πήληξ . . . τινάσσετο; what he cannot quote is κόρυς σείετο or the like. κόρυς is *the helmet*, and that is not a mobile object; πήληξ in the places quoted means *the crest*, and that is what is "shaken." In Euripides, *Hypsipyle* 16 (18) 4, πήληκα σείων, the dragon shakes its crest, not its helmet. (It may well be that the Greeks thought that πηλ- in πήληξ was connected with ἔπηλα, "shook," a derivation very different from that of the moderns.—Bechtel s.v., Boisacq s.v. πέλλα II.)

It is commonly held that "mobile," "nimble," or the like is the root meaning of αἰόλος (Buttmann, Ebeling, Bechtel, Boisacq s.v.): this meaning appears in the Epic in the verb, αἰόλλω (ν 27 only), and in the adjective in πόδας αἰόλος ἵππος, cf. αἰολόπωλος (whether also in αἰόλον ὄφιν, αἰόλαι εὐλαί, is quite uncertain). Much commoner in the Epic is the secondary—if indeed it is secondary—meaning, "*versicolor*," "sparkling," or the like. The idea of *mobility* is excluded for αἰολοθώρηξ, αἰολομίτρης, αἰόλα τεύχεα, σάκος αἰόλον (despite Ebeling and Bechtel, "quod saepe movetur"), ζωστῆρα παναίολον, σφῆκες μέσον αἰόλοι (= τὸ μέσον εὐκίνητοι διὰ τὴν ἐντομήν, Schol. absurdly); cf. Hes. *scut.* 399 ὄμφακες αἰόλλονται. αἰόλος applied to κόρυς can only bear this (alleged) secondary meaning, just as it does when applied to other pieces of armour, θώρηξ μίτρη ζωστήρ σάκος τεύχεα; and just as it does in the Cretan Tablet *DMG* no. 85, where an ox has the name *Aiwolos* (*Glossy*, or the like; nobody ever yet named his ox "quick-darting" or "nimble" or the like).

On the accentuation of κορυθαίολος (-αιόλος codd. Ven., Hesych., Eust.) see esp. Frisk, *Eranos* 38 (1940) 36 ff.

[94] Frisk l.c.; Trümpy 47.

[95] But the Dindorfs' Thesaurus has it correctly: "variam habens galeam, i.e. variegatam" (however puzzled the reader may be by what follows, and by their accentuation).

[96] See esp. Frisk l.c. 37 ff. ἱπποκορυστής surely meant "with horse (-plume) helmet," not "marshaller, arranger of chariots" (LSJ, cf. Ebeling). Schwyzer, *GG* i 430 n. 3, 448. But the expression θεοί τε καὶ ἀνέρες ἱπποκορυσταί remains odd.

[97] See Miss Gray's article in *CQ* 41 (1947) 114 ff., with full statistics and discussion, leading to the conclusion that "Homer . . . found in the tradition a helmet which was fundamentally nonmetallic, ornamented by a horsehair crest and reinforced by various attachments, the meaning of which had already become obscure; this he overlaid lavishly with the colour, brilliance and elaborate decoration which now leave the most vivid and lively impression on the reader." This most interesting and important conclusion is firmly established by exceptionally precise and penetrating argument. It is tenable that the nonmetallic helmet had bronze cheekpieces attached even in the oldest tradition. (χαλκοπαρήιου 3 Il., 1 Od.; and this might be the implication of χαλκήρεος, 2 Il., 2 Od., though Miss Gray shows that χαλκήρεος has slight claim to a traditional connexion with words for "helmet." χαλκοβάρεια—once only, with στεφάνη—has no claim to a place among traditional phrases; χαλκείη—twice with κόρυς, once with στεφάνη—has no claim to a traditional connexion with the helmet. φαεινή in the formular vocabulary does not necessarily imply "metal," cf. μάστιγα φαεινήν, al.) Miss Gray does not include κορυθαίολος, χαλκοκορυστής in her discussion.

[98] τρυφάλεια, ἀμφίφαλος, τετράφαλος, τετραφάληρος. κόρυθ' αἰόλος itself is a formation of the same obsolete type as πόδας ὠκύς, κάρη κομόωντες.

[99] αὐλῶπις: it is very doubtful whether the Ionian poets knew what this meant; guesses ancient and modern incline to the fantastic, and there is something to be said for Miss Lorimer's suggestion (*HM* 242) "that both αὐλῶπις and αὐλωπός represent Greek efforts to reproduce a non-Greek word."

¹⁰⁰ Lorimer, *HM* 231 ff., cf. 198 fig. 16; Hood and De Jong, *BSA* 47 (1952) 257 f.

¹⁰¹ A. W. Persson, *New Tombs at Dendra near Midea* 43 and 119 ff. with fig. 114 and pl. ɪ. Cf. Lorimer, *HM* 225 ff., with pls. xɪɪɪ, xɪv. The helmet is dated by its discoverer not later than the first half of Late Helladic II.

¹⁰² Beyond the mainland we have to consider only (*a*) a single bronze cheekpiece from Ialysus in Rhodes (Lorimer, *HM* 211 with pl. xɪɪɪ.1); (*b*) the bronze helmet from Crete, dated just before the final destruction of the palace at Cnossos, discovered by Hood (*BSA* 47, 1952, 243 ff.)—this, like the Dendra helmet, was a metal casing, to be attached to a thick padding; but unlike the Dendra helmet it is "of the shape that appears to have been most character-istic of Aegean helmets during the Late Bronze Age" (l.c. 257).

If Hood is right in detecting Aegean influence on the bell helmets from Beitzsch, Oranienburg, and Lucky, and in dating the alleged influence to the (Aegean) Late Bronze Age (l.c. 259 f.), we should of course have to suppose that such helmets were common in Greece too at that period; the fact remains that only one (and that of the sub-Mycenaean period) has yet been found.—See *JHS* and *BSA Archaeol. Reports* for 1957, pp. 8 f.

¹⁰³ "The aspect of prestige must not be overlooked," Hood, l.c. 257.

¹⁰⁴ Lorimer, *HM* 226.

¹⁰⁵ I do not think it is possible to use the evidence of the Linear B pictograms in this connexion; see pp. 261 ff.

¹⁰⁶ The helmets on the Warrior Vase are especially well described and discussed by Miss Lorimer, *HM* 227 f.; her pl. ɪɪɪ 1 *b*, which I have compared with the original in the National Museum at Athens, is a much better reproduction than most.

For possible relics of metal plates or discs for body armour in the Mycenaean period see *BSA* 47 (1952) 260 f. with notes 98–101.

¹⁰⁷ The date of the Warrior Vase seems to be in the neighbourhood of 1200 B.C.

¹⁰⁸ Some other Trojans: the evidence of noun + epithet combinations:
 Ἀλέξανδρος: the name occurs in 45 places, and two phrases ac-count for all but one of his 21 noun + epithet formulas. A. θεοειδής (incl. 2 accus.) ∥ 12; A. / Ελενης ποσις ηυκομοιο (incl. 1 accus.) ∥ 6,— this formula begins διος (-ον) A. in 4 of the 6; and ∥ διον A. without the sequel occurs once, also again in untraditional position, Γ 403 διον / Αλεξανδρον. The only individual phrase is Δ 96 A. βασιληι ∥.

(The name Πάρις is very rare: nom. 7, gen. Γ 325 only, accus. 3. Never in noun + epithet combination; presumably an old title, not a proper name; itself quasi-descriptive, therefore not qualified by epithets. Evidently a very old word, hardly surviving into the Iliad.)

There is in general a probability that a common name whose noun + epithet combinations are frequent but fixed and economical played a larger part in the early Epic than another common name whose noun + epithet combinations are few and very diverse. The contrast between Alexandros and Aeneas must have some significance.

Αἰνείας: the name occurs in 83 places, but of these only 15 are in noun + epithet combination, and the 15 are scattered over so many as 9 different phrases. ‖ Αινεια Τρωων βουληφορε 4; / μεγαλητορος Αινειαο 4 (Φ only; μεγαλητορος is a stereotype, and has no necessary connexion with the name); the rest once each, Ρ 754 Αγχισιαδης, Ε 468 υιος / μεγαλητορος Αγχισαο, Μ 98 f. / ευς παις Αγχισαο, Ε 217 Τρωων αγος, Ε 311 αναξ ανδρων, Υ 267 δαιφρονος, Ν 482 ποδας ταχυν, cf. Ε 272 codd.

Alexander has played his part in the Epic from a very early period; Aeneas was little more than a remembered name, whose part has been greatly expanded by the Ionian poets at a relatively late period.

None of these names recurs in the Odyssey.

[109] Τρῶες (Odyssey not included). The formular system shows some signs of disintegration: there are one or two breaches of the law of economy, and the noun tends to float about in the line. Though there is more than usual variety of position for some of the adjectives, the underlying pattern is distinctly visible, and new creations are very few:

ἀγέρωχος: Τρωων αγερωχων ‖ 5

ἀγαυός: Τρωες αγαυοι ‖ 3

ἱππόδαμος in several positions: ‖ Τρωων ιπποδαμων (+ dat., accus.) 12; Τρωσι / μεθ' ιπποδαμοις 2; Τρωεσσι / ⏑‒⏑⏑ ιπποδαμοισι ‖ 3; ιπποδαμοι / Τρωες 2.

ὑπέρθυμος in two positions: ‖ Τρωες υπερθυμοι (+ accus.) 6; / υπερθυμοι 1.

ὑπερφίαλος is in competition with ὑπέρθυμος, involving a breach of the law of economy: ‖ Τρωες υπερφιαλοι 1; / υπερφιαλοι 3 (in Φ only). Of these two, ὑπερφίαλος is presumably the more recent: it is an adjective which elsewhere has hardly secured a footing in the Iliad (4 examples), whereas in the Odyssey it is very common (21).

μεγάθυμος in three positions: ‖ Τρωες δε μεγαθυμοι 3; / μεγαθυμοι (+ gen.) 5; μεγαθυμους ‖ (+ gen.) 3.

φιλοπτόλεμος: ‖ Τρωσι φιλοπτολεμοισι 3; this may well be the traditional dative formula in this position. ‖ Τρωσιν υπερθυμοισι, which would have suited the metre as well, does not occur. Just so, whereas Ἀχαιῶν χαλκοχιτώνων ‖ is a formular verse-end, Ἀχαιοὺς (-οὶ) χαλκοχίτωνας (-ες) is not found.

ἀσπιστής and αἰχμητής are in competition for the end of the line: Τρωων / ∪∪ ‿∪∪ ασπισταων ‖ 4, αιχμηταων ‖ 1. Similarly where an initial consonant is required, Τρωων / ∪∪ ‿∪∪ θωρηκταων ‖, 3, competes with χαλκοχιτωνων ‖, 2. But these are not old noun + epithet formulas: that is to say, there is not in these examples a fixed traditional coherence between name and epithet; the use of αιχμ., θωρ., etc. at verse-end is in itself a formular element, applicable to diverse needs.

The residue is small, and may include traditional phrases: Τρωες / μεγαλητορες 2; once each, Τρωων / ευηφενεων, Τρωων υπερηνορεοντων ‖, Τρωας / αγηνορας, ανδρεσσι / ∪ ‿∪∪ υβριστηισι ‖ Τρωσιν (this last phrase is relatively modern: ὕβρις and its cognates are very rare intruders upon the Epic vocabulary).

[110] ἱππόδαμος of individuals: Diomedes 8, his father Tydeus 2; elsewhere only Atreus, Antenor (twice each), Castor, Hippasus, Hyperenor, Thrasymedes (once each), and the alternative Ἕκτορος ἱπποδάμοιο for ἀνδροφόνοιο.

It is not at all the same thing to say that a place is *good pasture* for horses, ἱππόβοτον Ἄργος and the like; or that the horses of a people were particularly *swift*, Δαναῶν ταχυπώλων.

[111] Ἴλιος, Τροίη: The land and fortress of Troy are described by the epithets "steep, broad, holy, fertile, windy, frowning, of good walls, good towers, good foals, high gates, broad streets." Most of these are well applied to the fortress resurrected by excavation; and there was a time when it was thought that "Homer" must have seen Troy before the earth concealed it. It is obvious, however, that most of these epithets apply just as well to other fortresses: a poet who had never seen Troy would not be at a loss for epithets suitable to fortresses in general; and in fact all these epithets except the significant εὔπωλος are applied to other places.

But if the Ionian poets did not see the broad streets and high gates of Troy, it is possible that their predecessors did, and that the epithets were originally inspired by the sight of Troy VI or VIIᵃ before its fall. One of the most important tests of antiquity in the Homeric poems, that of *formular usage*, indicates that this is indeed so. The name Ἴλιος in the Iliad is among the most rigidly traditional and formular in usage in the poem. Out of 106 examples, 95 are repetitions of formular phrases; and 41 of its 45 noun + epithet combinations are made up of repetitions of only 5 formulas. The formula-system has been so reduced and refined that a very great utility is attained with a very small vocabulary; and the law of economy prevails not only here but also throughout the wider group formed by Ἴλιος and Τροίη together. So narrow a limitation of the potentially extensive usages of this common word can only have been created by a long process of natural selection; in the time of the Ionian poets, almost the whole of what they need to say about Troy in 28,000 lines is supplied ready-made in some twenty formular phrases, the end-product of an immemorially old tradition.

Ἴλιος: Il. 106 + Od. 19 = 125 (including -οφι, -οθι, -οθεν); of these, Il. 45 + Od. 5 = 50 in noun + epithet combination.

Traditional: // Ἴλιος αιπεινη (+ gen., accus.) 6; Ἴλιος ιρη // (+ gen., accus.) 24; // Ἴλιον εις ευπωλον 5; // Ἴλιον ‿υυ‿ / ευτειχεον 4; προτι Ἴλιον ηνεμοεσσαν // 7.

Individual: // Ἴλιος οφρυοεσσα X 411 (οφρ. here only in the Epic; tradition would have suggested ηνεμοεσσα); // Ἴλιον εις ιερην H 20; // Ἴλιον αιπυ O 71 (the only example of the Attic neuter Ἴλιον); Ἴλιον εις ερατεινην //, E 210, has no alternative in fact (though in theory ευπωλον would have served), and may be traditional.

Other formular phrases: Ἴλιον ‿υυ‿ εν ναιομενον πτολιεθρον; if ‿υυ‿υ is required after Ἴλιου, ευκτιμενον replaces ευ ναιομενον. The formulas are used both wholly and in part: Ἴλιου εκπερσαντες ευκτιμενον πτολιεθρον, and simply Ἴλιον εκπερσαντες; Ἴλιου εξαλαπαξαι ευκτ. πτολ., and simply Ἴλιον εξαλαπαξαν. Thus one formula dovetails into another: Ἴλιον εκπερσαντ' ευτειχεον απονεεσθαι.

The other formular phrases (without epithet) are: / οτε (πριν, οι) Ἴλιον εισανεβησαν (-βηναι, αμφεμαχοντο, εισαφικεσθαι); // Ἴλιον εις αμ' επιοντο (επευθαι); / ορεων εις Ἴλιον ιρην; Ἴλιοθι προ //; / ες (οτε) Ἴλιον ειληλουθα (-θει); / προτι Ἴλιον απονεοντο (-εσθαι, -οιμην, ηγεμονευειν); / τοι Ἴλιωι εγγεγαασιν; //αψ εις Ἴλιον ηλθε; εις ο κε τεκμωρ // Ἴλιου ευρωσιν; επει ουκετι δηετε τεκμωρ // Ἴλιου; υπο Ἴλιον ηλθε (-ον) //; // Ἴλιοο προπαροιθεν (with its immensely archaic genitive form); προτι (κατα) Ἴλιον, very often + ιρην; Ἴλιον εισω //, often preceded by νηυσι or νηεσσι κορωνισι. Ἴλιος ιρη // four times leads to // και Πριαμος και λαος. . .; // Ἴλιον εις ευπωλον thrice leads to / ινα Τρωεσσι μαχοιτο (-οιμην).

These few formular phrases account for all but eleven of the Iliad's 106 examples of Ἴλιος in all its forms.

Τροίη: Il. 50 + Od. 25 = 75 (excluding -ηθεν, -ηδε); including Il. 17 + Od. 5 = 22 noun + epithet combinations.

Traditional: εν(ι) Τροιηι / εριβωλακι 3; ενι Τροιηι ευρειηι // 4; //

Τροιηι εν ευρειηι 5; / Τροιην εριβωλον 2; Τροιην / ∪∪‿∪∪ ευρυαγυιαν 2 (despite the separation of name from epithet, the two have a traditional connexion: πολιν ευρυαγυιαν ∥ Τρωων 5, Τρωων πολιν ευρυαγυιαν 1, Πριαμου πολις ευρυαγυια 1; χ 230, antitraditional, Πριαμου for Τρωων); Τροιην / ευτειχεον 2; υψιπυλον / Τροιην 2.

In I 329, κατα Τροιην εριβωλον ∥, the use of this adjective at the end of the line may well be traditional: κατα Τροιην ευρειαν ∥ may seem the natural counterpart to ενι Τροιηι ευρειηι ∥, but it is noticeable that ευρεια with Τροιη is never in fact found in the accusative case.

Individual: only Η 71 / Τροιην ευπυργον, for εριβωλον, a breach of the law of economy.

Troy is also called άστυ μέγα Πριάμοιο, Τρώων πόλις, πόλις . . . Τρώων, Πριάμου πόλις.

Notice that ήνεμόεσσα and εὐρυάγυια, metrically equivalent, are restricted, the former to Ίλιος and the latter to Τροίη. Similarly Τροιηι εν ευρειηι, never αιπεινηι, but Ιλιου αιπεινης, never ευρειης. Τροιην εριβωλον, Ιλιον εις ευπωλον, never Τροιην ευπωλον, Ιλιον εις εριβωλον. And so forth.

Strictly speaking, Ilios is the fortress, Troy the land; but Troy is quite often used to signify the fortress.

112 See pp. 57 f. above.
113 See further E. Delebecque, *Le Cheval dans l'Iliade* (1951) 232, where an interesting inference is drawn from an original distinction between *goading* (κεντέω Ψ 337 only; κέντρον Ψ 387, 430; κεντρηνεκέας Ε 752, Θ 396; κέντορες ίππων Δ 391 Kadmeians, Ε 102 Trojans) and *whipping* (πλήσσω, πλήξιππος): the extreme rarity of references to *goading* is explained by the fact that horses in the Iliad are almost always harnessed to chariots; one may *whip* a horse in harness, but not *goad* or *prick* it. "The whip is the instrument of the charioteer, the goad is that of one who guides (on foot or on horseback) a horse or a herd of horses." The suggestion is that the formulas κέντορες ίππων, κεντρηνεκέας . . . ίππους—"legends in epitome," as Delebecque calls them—may reveal a trace of their origin: "Epithets like κεντρηνεκής attributed to horses, or κέντορες ίππων to men or peoples, may carry within themselves a faded but faithful image of an epoch when a pastoral people used the goad to control their large roaming herds." This seems a probable inference: and I do not see how to avoid the further conclusion that the making of such a phrase as κέντορες ίππων, as a distinctive epithet of the people, must ascend to the time when it was true of the people,—a time when they still lived in their remote "Indo-European" home. The same conclusion,

however surprising it may be, would be indicated also by the traditional formula μώνυχες ἵπποι (Delebecque 149 f.; 33 times in the
Iliad, only in nom. and accus. plural, and always in the same place
in the line), if this epithet really means "single-hooved," i.e., with a
hoof that is a single solid whole, not divided like that of cattle,
sheep, goats. That description distinguishes the horse from the
other common domestic quadrupeds, and it is hard to conceive that
such a distinction should have asserted itself at any time *except
when the people in question first became familiar with the horse,*—
and that time lies far back in the "Indo-European" past of both
Achaeans and Trojans. It is in itself rather a farmer's than a
poet's description; it does seem unlikely that any people would
have thought of this way of describing a horse after they had been
familiar with the horse for a generation or two, let alone after 500
years.

In the old formular language μώνυχες is invariably preceded by
a short syllable: its use in this metre must therefore date from a
time when *σμώνυχες had already lost its first consonant. But I
wonder whether this word is not among the incomprehensibles,
bearing an illusory resemblance to a derivative from the roots of
semel and ὄνυξ.

114 Some, not all, of the principal persons: if Ajax was ever a real person, he lived much earlier than the time of the fall of Troy VII[a];
his fighting was done in the day of the tower shield, an object
which the Achaeans at Troy had probably never seen and certainly
never used.

115 Probable, not certain: it is theoretically conceivable that the
glorification of Achilles at the expense of Agamemnon is the work
of the Ionian poets; I cannot imagine why they should wish to do
so, and think it infinitely more probable that the preëminence of
Achilles in this story is an heirloom from the Epic's Mycenaean
past.

116 See especially F. Bölte, *Rhein. Mus.* 83 (1934) 319 ff.; also R.
Hampe, "Die homerische Welt im Lichte der neuen Ausgrabungen:
Nestor," in R. Herbig, *Vermächtnis der antiken Kunst* (1950)
11 ff. I cannot find that Wade-Gery (*AJA* 52, 1948, 115 ff.) pro-
duces satisfactory evidence for his theory that the "Pylian Epic"
refers to events of the Protogeometric period; nor is there anything
persuasive in Meyer's suggestion (*Gesch. des Altertums* iii 262 f.)
that it refers to the struggle of Achaeans against Dorian invaders.
Schadewaldt's treatment (*Iliasstudien* 83 f.) of the passage seems
to me wholly mistaken: in particular, his contrast of the chrono-

logical with the narrated series of events includes some very special pleading: there is no excuse for splitting off 671–672ᵃ from 672ᵇ ff. (specially connected as they are by ὅτε in 672); 688–689 are not out of place chronologically, being merely a comment on the whole subject-matter of 672–687; it is arbitrary to split up the coherent incident 696–704 into three chronological phases, and to separate 703–704ᵃ from 704ᵇ–707. The real order is as follows: (1) 671–688 Itymoneus-raid and consequent division of spoils; (2) 689–693 background; weakness of Pylos through Heracles' visitation; (3) 694–707ᵃ resumptive; detail about division of spoils; (4) 707ᵇ ff. attack by Epeians on Thryoessa, and so forth to the end.

· [117] I might have written, if Leaf had not, this: "Between the general fact that the war took place, and the most fanciful incidents described as occurring in it, such for instance as the battle of the gods in Il. XX, there is every gradation of actuality. The larger part of the incidents we shall of course dismiss at once as mere invention. . . . We shall not conclude that because Achilles was a historical person, the same may be said of the dog Argos" (*Homer and History* 28).

[118] Meleager, I 527 ff.; Aeneas, N 460; Alexander, Z 326.

[119] See now C. H. Gordon, *Riv. d. Stud. Orientali* 29 (1954) 164 ff., and *Minos* 3 (1954) 130 f.

The same distinction, between the typical and the individual, may help us to answer another question: whether the episode of the Wooden Horse is founded on fact or not. In summary, it does not appear that this belongs to the stock-in-trade of the storyteller; the Wooden Horse is likely to be, in Professor Rose's words, "a confused reminiscence of some Oriental siege-engine" (*Greek Mythology* 252 n. 50); cf. Murray, *Rise of the Greek Epic* 33, it has "a special air of verisimilitude"; and Leaf (*Homer and History* 31), "It is highly probable that Troy was in fact taken in this way." The ancients supposed it to be a siege engine: Pausanias i 23.8, Vergil *Aen.* 2.151, Pliny *NH* VII 202; cf. Robert, *Gr. Heldensage* 1225 ff.

See further Schachermeyr, *Poseidon* 190 ff.

APPENDIX
Multiple Authorship in the Iliad

I. THE EMBASSY TO ACHILLES

THE FACT that the Iliad is a work of multiple authorship is perhaps most easily recognized in the example of the Embassy to Achilles in the Ninth Book, one of the most important and memorable episodes in the poem.

Agamemnon took the girl Briseis away from Achilles. Achilles, enraged at the insult put upon his honour, withdrew from battle and remained in his tent. The Trojans won a great victory in his absence: the time has come for Agamemnon to offer apology and compensation. And that is the subject of the Ninth Book: Phoenix, Ajax, and Odysseus are appointed ambassadors; they go to Achilles and plead with him, but he rejects their plea.

Here the unprejudiced will quickly recognize two facts: first, that the large part played by Phoenix in this embassy has been superimposed upon an earlier version in which only Ajax and Odysseus were sent to plead with Achilles; secondly, that this earlier version was itself superimposed upon an Iliad which knew nothing of any such embassy at all. The observations which lead to these conclusions are simple and straightforward: they require common-sense judgements on matters of fact. They are not new: they were observed (and the natural judgements were passed upon them) by the earliest Homeric critics. But now we seem to be losing sight of them: some of the most popular books on Homer do not so much as mention them. I begin with Phoenix:

I 163 ff. Nestor says to Agamemnon: let us summon persons who shall go to Achilles and offer compensation, *"Phoenix first, and he shall take the lead;* then Ajax and Odysseus; and two heralds shall follow together with them."* Prayer and libation are offered and the ambassadors depart. The sequel is now described thus:

"So *the pair of them* went along the seashore, *both* praying to Poseidon; and *the pair of them* reached Achilles' tent, and they found him singing ballads; and *they both* advanced, *and Odysseus was the leader,* and they stood in front of him. And Achilles leapt up in astonish-

ment, and addressed *the pair of them*: 'Welcome to you *both*; friends
are you that visit me, *the pair of you*, the dearest friends I have, *both
of you*.' With these words he led *the pair of them* forward, . . ."

I said that the point at issue would be simple and straightforward.
You will already be asking yourselves, "What has happened to
Phoenix?" A moment ago we were told that there would be three
ambassadors, Phoenix, Ajax, and Odysseus; and that Phoenix was to
be the leader. Now at once *the pair of them* go to find Achilles, and we
are reminded over and over again that it was *a pair of them*. And now
we are told that not Phoenix but Odysseus was the leader. What has
happened to Phoenix? Later we are to learn that Phoenix is Achilles'
oldest friend; and he is to play the longest and most important part in
the embassy. But that is very awkward, because according to our poet
he did not go to Achilles. He did not even start to go: from the moment of his appointment to the leadership of the embassy onwards,
Phoenix mislaid himself.

Since he is to lead the embassy, he might be expected to be the first
speaker when the time comes: and indeed, when the time comes, Ajax
nods to Phoenix, prompting him to begin. But Odysseus noticed, and
anticipated him. We are reassured: Phoenix was there, after all. But
how and when did he get there? Why, above all, did the poet go out
of his way to exclude him from the company of those who did go
there? Why that unending "*both*" and "*pair of them*"?

Let nobody think that this could be a momentary lapse into
negligence. Phoenix is a person of whom we had not heard before.
He was specially introduced at this time to be the leader of an embassy to Achilles, in which he is to play the most important part; and
many a reader has testified that in the whole of Homer there is no
more wonderful poetry than here; this is the star of the Greek Epic at
its brightest.

What is the explanation? There is only one way out: the text is a
combination of two things, *an embassy without Phoenix, and an embassy with him*. The special introduction of Phoenix is immediately
followed by a passage which presupposes that no such person has
been mentioned at all. An embassy of two and an embassy of three
stand side by side in the text: but the one is incompatible with the
other; and the only way of producing such a result is by superimpos-
ing the one upon the other, and then omitting to make the proper
adjustments. A serious omission, no doubt; but an inconceivable com-
mission. Our first proposition is securely established: Phoenix has
been introduced at a later stage into an embassy which consisted of
Ajax and Odysseus only.

It would be natural to comment at once, "Is there no other possible explanation of the facts? Is not the Homeric Question still at issue? And how can it be at issue still, how can it not be determined already in favour of multiple authorship, if there is no acceptable answer on this point?" Listen, and perpend.

Some do not even mention these matters at all; them we securely ignore. Among their number the ancient critics are not to be counted: the Alexandrians, who could make no sense of the composition here, tried to explain what is said in terms of what is not said, and what is done in terms of what it was impossible to do:

1) It was maintained that the dual numbers ("both" and "the pair of them") might stand for plural numbers; in short, that in Greek, when you say "two" you may mean three or more. Since this is simply false, I say no more about it. It was a natural development, that the plural should come to replace the dual number; but there is no reason why duals should ever come to be used of more than two subjects,— and in fact they never did.[1]

2) The popular explanation in antiquity, ascribed to Aristarchus, and repeated in more or less elaborate forms,[2] runs as follows: that Phoenix was not (after all) a member of the embassy; his business was to go ahead and prepare Achilles' mind for the interview; and that is why he is not mentioned in the company of the other two when they set out.

About this explanation it will suffice to say three things. First, it is pure fiction; not a word of it is in, or is suggested by, the text. Secondly, that it is obviously false, instantly contradicted by 193 ταφὼν δ' ἀνόρουσεν Ἀχιλλεύς,—when Ajax and Odysseus arrived, Achilles *leapt up in astonishment:* it is very obvious that the picture in the poet's mind is not of an Achilles who has just received a preparatory visit from Phoenix. Thirdly, that the verb used of Phoenix in 168, ἡγησάσθω, could not mean that he went on in advance of the others, but only *that he was their leader.*[3] It is seldom granted us in this sort of inquiry to say that something is absolutely impossible: we are so fortunate as to be able to say it about both these ancient explanations of our problem. And we can say it also about a modern refinement of the second one:

3) Schadewaldt in 1938, Mazon in 1948, and Focke in 1954[4] agreed in principle that Phoenix is not to be considered a member of the embassy. He holds, it is said, "a special position," not on the same footing as Ajax and Odysseus. He is rather a confidant of Achilles than an ambassador for Agamemnon; and this is the reason why the poet

[1] For notes to Appendix see pages 324–340.

makes no mention of him when the embassy sets out. Now I have learnt by long experience that what appears feeble and false to me may bear to others the aspect of great and prevalent truth. But here at least the ground is surely firm enough under our feet: what the poet said is that ambassadors should be sent to Achilles, and that the persons summoned should be, first, Phoenix, and then Ajax and Odysseus. Not a word about "special positions," except that Phoenix is to have the special position of leading this embassy. Such a position might be a good reason for giving prominence to him: to give it as a reason for excluding him from the company of the ambassadors is, I suggest, an absurdity. I leave you to pass what comment you will on the state of mind of Schadewaldt's Homer: "We shall now send an embassy to Achilles. Its members shall be Phoenix, Ajax, and Odysseus. Its leader shall be Phoenix. Now, off they go, and we shall describe it thus, '*So Ajax and Odysseus went to find Achilles, and Odysseus was the leader, and Achilles said how glad he was to see Ajax and Odysseus.*'"

Unhappy Phoenix, Achilles' oldest friend, not one single word of you; and as if that were not enough, your leadership is instantly and silently taken from you; we shall go out of our way to say that Odysseus was the leader.

Let the consequences be clearly understood: the position is not, and cannot be, defended in depth; if this front line does not hold—if it is broken, as it obviously is, without more than formal resistance,—then there is an end of the battle. We have here, in the very heart and soul of the poem, in one of the great masterpieces of all Greek literature, irrefutable proof of multiple authorship. We are now free to turn to a different point, significant in the light of what we have already established.

Phoenix addresses these words to Achilles (I 496 ff.): "Nay, Achilles, subdue your great spirit: you ought not to keep your heart without pity. Not even the gods are inflexible, they who are greater than you in nobility and honour and strength. Them with burnt sacrifice and gentle prayers, with libation and savour, men turn aside supplicating, whenever one transgresses and does wrong. For these too exist, the Spirits of Prayer, daughters of great Zeus, limping and wrinkled and with eyes asquint. It is their task to follow on the track of Madness: but Madness is strong and swift, therefore it far outruns them all, and over all the earth it wins the race to injure men, while the Prayers come behind with healing. The man who venerates the daughters of Zeus when they come near, to him they give great blessings and they listen to his entreaty. But he who disdains and stubbornly denies them,—they go to Zeus the son of Kronos and pray that Madness walk together with him, that he be hurt and punished."

The point of interest here has long been recognized for what it is.[5] Look first at 501, the words ὑπερβήη καὶ ἁμάρτῃ, "transgresses and does wrong"; and notice that these are words which imply a conception of moral conduct entirely foreign to the rest of the Iliad. Then look at 512, "Let *Atê* walk with him, that he be hurt and punished"; nowhere else in the Iliad is the infliction of injury regarded as a punishment for wrongdoing. I do not linger over the detail: the fundamental idea is what matters here. Phoenix warns Achilles against certain consequences of rejecting Agamemnon's apology: if he does reject it, he will be putting himself in the wrong, and the wrath of heaven will smite him in return. That is to say, the responsibility lies with Achilles, and he can make up his mind to do the one thing or the other; but if he decides not to accept the apology, he will have made a wrong choice, and the gods will hold him solely responsible and will punish him for it.

We are so familiar with this way of thinking—and so were the Greeks of the archaic and classical eras—that it costs us an effort to recognize and admit that it is not merely strange to, but also incompatible with, the rest of the Iliad. The notion of man's responsibility and heaven's retribution is here introduced into a world which opposes and rejects it. We have wholly misunderstood the Iliad if we suppose that the original offence of Agamemnon was entirely his own doing, that Achilles' persistence in his wrath was wrong, that the death of Patroclus was his punishment, that the release of Hector's body made amends. None of these ideas has any place in the poem,—except in this speech by Phoenix. The Greek Epic has a fundamentally different conception of the relation of man to god: that conception has been so often and so fully explained that I merely summarize the result.

In most of the transactions of his life Homeric man felt no need to philosophize about causes and effects. It was only in exceptional circumstances, and especially when things went wrong, that questions of responsibility arose; and the question was answered in uncommonly clear and consistent terms. There were obvious reasons why man could not be held accountable for unwise actions, for conduct contrary to his own interest, such as might involve breach of the code of honour or law. Such things are done under the influence of emotions which take possession of the mind, destroying the judgement; and if you ask, who put the madness into the mind, who created those emotions, the answer must be that it was not man who was the creator of his mind. Thoughts and emotions come into the mind, whether suddenly or slowly, as if from outside; man does not acknowledge, because he does not feel, any personal responsibility for their coming. There is therefore no choice but to assign to supernatural agency what cannot be explained in rational terms. There are in the world so many things which man did not create and does not control: in the sphere of human conduct, for example, the results of an action often turn out to be different from what the action was designed to achieve; responsibility for the actual results, in such a case, cannot be assigned to the human agent, whose intention has been frustrated. What no man has done must be ascribed to superman. Man does not create his own madness: nor can he foresee the consequences of what he does, however sane. The creator and foreseer must be outside and beyond him: in the last resort, they are embodied in the supreme power of the universe, in the will of Zeus. It is only Zeus who can foresee the results of all or any actions; and foreknowledge of course implies prearrangement. This is the heart and soul of Homeric thought: that the life of man proceeds in conformity with a prearranged plan; each has his *Moira*, his share in the scheme of things, his allotted portion. He can only do what destiny has predetermined for him; and only Zeus knows what that is, or whither it will lead. The ultimate responsibility for all actions lies not with man but with the agency which assigned his destiny to him; and the workings of his destiny within the individual may be uncomfortable and inconsistent,—even the wisest is exposed to the sudden access of supernatural passions which invade his understanding and take possession of it. Agamemnon's dishonouring of Achilles at the beginning of the Iliad is a striking example of this philosophy: "It was not I who caused it," he says, "but Zeus and Moira and Erinys, who put blindness into my heart" (T 86 ff.); and Achilles himself agrees that this is true. When Achilles rejects the apology of Agamemnon, nobody (except Phoenix) dreams of blaming Achilles: as Ajax is the first to assert, it is the gods who put him into that frame of mind (I 636 f.). The code of honour may—and probably does—require that Achilles accept the apology: if he does not accept it, it must be because the gods have put Madness into his heart, just as they had put it into Agamemnon's. But nobody ever supposed that Agamemnon or Achilles was to blame for what the gods have done to them. The saner man may argue with them, may point out to them their folly, may try to persuade them to fight against the emotions in their hearts, perhaps not in vain (for who knows what the gods have decreed?): but everybody must admit that the folly was implanted by the gods, that the wrongdoer acts as he does because the gods have disturbed his understanding,—it would have seemed absurd that a man would of his own free will unhinge his own mind and act contrary to his own interest. "Homeric man does not possess the concept of will, . . . and therefore cannot possess the concept of free-will."[6] It would be hard to think of anything much more shocking to Homeric sentiment than the notion that man, not god, is responsible for what happens in the world.

That, in broad outline, is the philosophy which is consistently maintained in the Iliad throughout all its transactions; the Odyssey seldom shows anything in advance of it. And nobody has succeeded, or could succeed, in showing how the speech of Phoenix might be reconciled with it. Here and here alone is the expression of a totally different outlook on life, including such modern terms as "transgress" and "sin" and "make amends," the familiar language of the new philosophy of Crime and Punishment, of man's responsibility and Heaven's retribution. There is nothing halting or tentative or transitional: an entirely novel outlook on the universe is here expressed in elaborate poetic allegory, a highly sophisticated presentation of ideas which must have been long familiar when these lines were composed, but which stand in absolute contradiction to the whole of the Iliad before and after it.

It is likely that this great poet interpreted the action of the Iliad as a whole in conformity with the new outlook. In particular, the death of Patroclus must have assumed a novel colour in his eyes. Achilles' rejection of Agamemnon's apology is now to be regarded as a sin, an action freely willed despite warning, contrary to the pleasure of the supreme god. He must therefore be *punished*,[7] and his punishment will be the loss of his dearest friend. This poet has at least partly turned Epic into Tragedy; he has inserted a layer of guilt-culture into the fabric of shame-culture. The rest of the Iliad regards the death of Patroclus as a link in the chain of events, a natural cause of later effects; there is no suggestion that it might have been avoided, that the blame lies with Achilles for his obstinacy here,—*indeed the embassy to Achilles is never again so much as mentioned in connexion with the death of Patroclus*. The moment this speech by Phoenix is over, we are back again in the world of immutable destiny, of Zeus almighty, of man at the mercy of the supernatural; and in that world we remain to the end of the poem.

We are now no longer astonished if Hell should rival Heaven for novelty. If Phoenix tells the truth, the House of Hades—hitherto dim-seen and desolate—has been reconditioned, its government re-organized. Hades himself, elsewhere in the poem a shadowy person (if indeed a person at all),[8] emerges plumper and more prosperous, newly entitled "the Zeus of the Underworld"; and here for the first time (and the last) in the Iliad we hear the name of Persephone, his female consort. Among their ministers are the Furies, *Erinyes*, who will hear you if you beat upon the ground and utter curses; they will come up to the light and exact retribution from those who spill the blood of kins-men. Here, as before, we are much closer to Aeschylus than to Homer. The Epic at large knows nothing of any "Zeus of the Underworld," of a consort Persephone, of Furies who walk the earth in search of victims. There are indeed a few other places where the reformed Hades and the Furies have crept into the poem: but the part which they play is insignificant compared with the part which they do not play; the ghosts of the Homeric dead pass in their dozens over to a vague intangible afterworld, unrewarded and unpunished, bodiless and voiceless and witless: *that* Hades needs no wife or servants, and indeed he has none; there is not even anything for *him* to do,—and indeed he does nothing.

Not even Earth, our familiar land, is quite the same. I suppose that no Epic poet of an earlier age could have forgotten, among other things, this—the name of Achilles' native country. We all know it: he lived ἀν' Ἑλλάδα τε Φθίην τε, in the districts called Hellas and Phthia in the south of Thessaly. Only one person does not know this, and that is his oldest friend, Phoenix; for he tells us that Hellas was the realm of his own father, Amyntor; and when he quarrelled with his father and fled from home to the court of Achilles, he says (and we must be-lieve him) that Hellas was the land he left and Phthia the land he came to. He has no notion that Hellas, like Phthia, was in fact the kingdom of Achilles' father.

Heaven, Earth, and Hell are our witnesses: their testimony has not been refuted, though it has often been ignored. It remains only to ob-serve that the story of Meleager, as told by Phoenix, is composed in a style of Greek very different from that which prevails in the Iliad at large.[9]

The part of Phoenix was superimposed upon an already existing embassy to Achilles. We turn to the question whether that earlier embassy was itself superimposed upon an already existing Iliad. The principal arguments are neither numerous nor complex.

1) Allowing one or two exceptions (to which we shall return), we may assert that the remainder of the Iliad reveals no awareness that this embassy to Achilles ever occurred.[10] It is, however, much in the

manner of the Greek Epic to narrate a more or less self-contained episode and then to proceed without further reference to it; we shall therefore draw no immediate conclusion from the silence of the Iliad.

2) *In the immediately following action of the Iliad Achilles himself on two distinct occasions appears to deny that any approach has yet been made to him by Agamemnon.* This fact, if indeed it proves to be one, will of course put the case for multiple authorship beyond question. Minor inconsistencies and self-contradictions abound in the Iliad: Pylaemenes, who died in the Fifth Book, is resurrected in the Thirteenth; and nobody cares. Schedios is killed by Hector not once but twice; we do not weep for him. Chromios is killed three times, and innumerable eyes are dry. There are scores of such trivialities, which no ordinary reader or listener would notice. But what we are now considering is different in kind: the embassy to Achilles, once included in the poem, becomes one of the most important structural features of the whole; moreover, it was held in antiquity, as it is today, to be one of the most memorable passages in all Greek poetry. Not one single person who ever heard or read the poem through has ever forgotten in the immediate sequel (if indeed at all) that Agamemnon sent an embassy to Achilles and that Achilles rejected it. *Only the poet, the alleged creator of the Iliad, apparently forgot it:* not once but twice he proceeds to make Achilles insist that no approach has yet been made to him.

This position is so obviously absurd that the unitarian has no choice but to deny the alleged facts; and that is what he does. I too have tried as hard as most, harder than some, to find an alternative explanation. The attempt has ended in failure; and I now present the case, as follows.

a) Λ 607 ff. Achilles, inactive in his tent, observes the Greeks hard-pressed by the Trojans. It is his first appearance in the poem since the embassy, and this is what he says: seeing that the hour is at hand when the Trojans will reach the Achaean ships, the hour when all is lost unless he intervenes, he cries to Patroclus, *"At last I think the Achaeans will stand about my knees in supplication;* for a need past endurance has come upon them." Now it seems very obvious that these words were not spoken by an Achilles about whose knees the Achaeans were in fact standing in supplication on the previous evening; an Achilles who had rejected their prayers, who had made it clear that he would never accept apology or compensation, but would wait until Hector was killing the Greeks in their tents and burning their ships. Listen to the strong voice of common sense uplifted by George Grote in 1837: "Heyne, in his comment, asks the question, not unnaturally, '*Paenituerat igitur asperitatis erga priorem legationem, an homo arrogans expectaverat alteram ad se missam iri?*' I answer—neither the one nor the other: the words imply that he had received no embassy at all. He is still the same Achilles who in the first book paced alone by the sea-shore, devouring his own soul under a sense of bitter affront, and praying to Thetis to aid his revenge: this revenge is now about to be realized, and he hails its approach with delight. But if we admit the embassy of the ninth book to intervene, the passage is a glaring inconsistency; for that which Achilles anticipates as future, and even yet as contingent, had actually occurred on the previous evening; the Greeks *had* supplicated at his feet,—they *had* proclaimed their intolerable need—and he had spurned them." That is, and will always remain, the obvious implication of Achilles' words. What else could they possibly mean?

i) I had thought of trying to explain the words thus: Achilles is saying, with grim humour, "Now is the time for the Greeks to come to me on bended knees (as they did last night)"—that is to say, their need now is even greater than it was then; and this he might say however many fruitless embassies there had been in the past. To myself, however, this appears a desperate remedy. For, first, if this is what the poet meant, let him know that nobody ever understood him to mean it in the next three thousand years: it simply is not the obvious meaning of the words in their context. And, secondly, it is out of harmony with what has actually happened,—*he had rejected the embassy absolutely;* he had made it clear that he would not accept apology or compensation; from that time onwards there is no question of his expecting a renewal of Agamemnon's offer. The passage would therefore have to be understood as being heavily ironical; and nothing could be farther from the spirit of Achilles at this time. The voice here is not one of irony, but of triumph. The suggestion would not be worth mentioning, if what follows were not on a much lower level of probability.

ii) The best that the modern defenders of unity of composition can do is to plead that the words of Achilles be very strictly examined and interpreted. When he says that "Achaeans" shall now come and implore his intervention, he means (though he does not say it) "*the whole Greek army.*" And when he says that they shall "stand about his knees," he means that they shall implore him very much more earnestly than the previous embassy did: for in the embassy it was not "the Achaeans" who came to him; it was only Phoenix, Ajax, and Odysseus, and a couple of heralds; and it was not said that they took their duties so seriously as actually to "stand about his knees." The suggestion is that Achilles here distinguishes between what happened last night and what is to happen now. Last night only five persons came, and they did not "stand about his knees."[11] One interpreter actually goes so far as to say that the words of Achilles here presuppose a simpler form of embassy, the form described in the Ninth Book.[12]

I do not think this is worth discussing at length. It is wrong to examine the words so microscopically; and the resulting forced and narrow interpretation is in fact wholly incorrect. It is absurd to say that the conduct of the ambassadors in the Ninth Book could not fairly be described as "standing about the knees of Achilles in supplication"; a humbler apology, a more earnest prayer, could hardly be made. At the very least, it is fantastic to suppose that what happened in the Ninth Book was such that a distinction can be drawn between this passage and that on the ground that, although the ambassadors earnestly implored Achilles, they were not actually *said* to "stand about his knees." As for "the Achaeans," nobody can deny that Ajax, Odysseus, Phoenix, and the heralds are Achaeans; so, if you wanted to draw a distinction between the deputation intended here and that described in the Ninth Book, it would be well, or even necessary, to say here "*all* the Achaeans" or something of that sort. It will be generally agreed that this sort of explanation is very farfetched: it is now, I hope, also clear that the required meaning is not to be found in the text. This passage is obviously, in effect, a denial that any approach has yet been made to Achilles.

b) The crisis has come. The Trojans are among the Achaean ships. Achilles decides to send Patroclus to the rescue.[13] He addresses to him a long speech (49–100); and twice, perhaps thrice, in the course of it he uses terms which appear to deny that Agamemnon has yet made any apology or offer of compensation. The first passage is much less conclusive than the other two, but it serves well as an introduction:

    i) Π 52–61:*

"But this thought comes as a bitter sorrow to my heart and my spirit,—
When a man tries to foul one who is his equal, to take back
a prize of honour, because he goes in greater authority.—
This is a bitter thought to me; my desire has been dealt with
roughly. The girl the sons of the Achaians chose out for my honour,
and I won her with my own spear, and stormed a strong-fenced city,
is taken back out of my hands by powerful Agamemnon,
the son of Atreus, as if I were some dishonoured vagabond.

* The translations are by Richmond Lattimore: *The Iliad of Homer* (Chicago: University of Chicago Press, 1951).

Still, we will let all this be a thing of the past; and it was not
in my heart to be angry for ever . . ."

It may be thought natural that the insult to his honour should still
distress Achilles even after compensation has been offered and rejected: but it must surely have been contrary to the code of good behaviour, that he should then continue to talk in these terms. Nobody
would have guessed that this speaker has recently rejected the
amende honorable; but there is no means, in this instance, of refuting
the man with a special case to plead.

ii) Π 83–87:

"But obey to the end this word I put upon your attention
so that you can win, for me, great honour and glory
in the sight of all the Danaans, *so they will bring back to me
the lovely girl, and give me shining gifts in addition.*
When you have driven them from the ships, come back . . ."

Nothing could be much more explicit than this. Patroclus is to repel
the present attack, but is not to follow up his success; the final defeat
of the Trojans is to be reserved for Achilles. And the object of these
instructions is definitely stated: Achilles is determined that the Greeks
shall require his intervention, *that they shall restore to him the beautiful
Briseis and give shining gifts in addition.* But that is precisely what
was offered in the embassy, and what Achilles rejected once for all,—
he said that he would not accept that compensation or any other
compensation; he would not intervene to save the Greeks; he would
not fight until his own life was threatened. These are the words of a
poet for whom the Ninth Book of the Iliad does not exist in the world.
You may be curious to know how the true believer in unity of composition deals with this difficulty; for it would seem that there could
not possibly be any way round it or out of it. Let it suffice to examine
a single example of the defence's pleading,—a fair enough example, for
it stands in Schadewaldt's book, and was approved by Focke so
recently as 1954. It runs as follows:
"Achilles did not, on that occasion [viz. in the Ninth Book], agree
to the compensation, because at that point of time he was wholly unwilling to render any kind of service. On the other hand, he did not
even with a single word resign his claim to the woman and to the true
satisfaction which, in this heroic world, is assumed as a matter of
course. Now the situation is altered. Hector stands before the ships,
which are about to be set on fire. Achilles is still unwilling to fight in
person; he remains obstinate enough, but Patroclus shall give the

Achaeans a breathing-space. Is it so unheard-of, if, in this altered situation, hard by the goal which Achilles had set, towards which the action looks and presses forward, the return of Briseis comes back into the field of vision?"[14]

You will notice at once the prime fallacy,—the statement that in the Ninth Book Achilles "*did not by so much as a single word resign his claim to the woman and the gifts.*" That is simply false, and the whole argument based upon it must follow it into limbo. I see no meaning in Schadewaldt's words unless it be this: that Achilles did not reject the compensation offered in the embassy, and is therefore free now, "in the altered situation," to raise the matter afresh. That would be a satisfactory conclusion if the premise were true: but the premise is obviously false,—how *could* Schadewaldt say that Achilles "did not renounce his claim to the woman and the compensation, no, not by a single word"? Listen to some of the words in which he *did* renounce his claim:

I 378 ff.:

"I hate his gifts. I hold him light as the strip of a splinter.
  Not if he gave me ten times as much, and twenty times over,
  as he possesses now, not if more should come to him from elsewhere,
  or gave all that is brought in to Orchomenos, all that is brought in
  to Thebes of Egypt . . .
  not if he gave me gifts as many as the sand or the dust is,
  not even so would Agamemnon have his way . . . "

and much more to the same effect. The defence lies in the dust. Achilles *did* renounce the woman and the gifts,[15] *and he renounced them for ever, unconditionally.* He openly recognized (I 602 ff.) that whatever action he might take in the future would now have to go unrewarded, ἄτερ δώρων, as in the example of Meleager,—the making of that point was indeed the whole purpose of the parable of Meleager. And let us have no special pleading about "altered situations": *the present "altered situation" is precisely the one which Achilles envisaged and hoped for at the time when he rejected the embassy.*

iii) There remains a third reference (Π 71–73),[16] which I shall expound with all possible brevity. "Soon," says Achilles, "the Trojans would be filling the ditches with their dead, *if Lord Agamemnon were well-disposed to me.*" Once more the implication is obvious: Agamemnon has remained obdurate, he has not relaxed his hostility towards Achilles. There is only one way in which Agamemnon could show himself "well-disposed" towards Achilles, and that is by apologizing and offering compensation: that is just what he did in the embassy, yet

Achilles here complains that there has been no change in Agamemnon's disposition towards him.

The current explanation[17] here seems to be that $ἤπια\ εἰδείη$ signifies *a disposition in general*, just as $ἄγρια\ οἶδε$ refers to the permanent quality of the lion's temper, and $ὅτ'\ ἄγγελος\ αἴσιμα\ εἰδῇ$ denotes the rightmindedness characteristic of heralds. Therefore it is argued that Achilles here refers to the fact *that Agamemnon is, generally speaking, no friend of his;* and this he might say at any time, even if a dozen reluctant embassies had been wrung out of Agamemnon. The meaning will then be: "the Trojans would fill the ditches with their dead, if only Agamemnon and I (generally speaking) got on well together." One needs only to look at the words in their context to see that this is not what Achilles means:[18] he is talking not in general but in specific terms,—of his quarrel with Agamemnon, of the estrangement between them since Agamemnon insulted him at the beginning of the story, of the compensation due to him. Here he gives a reason why the Trojans have a breathing-space: if Agamemnon has offered to restore Briseis and to make full compensation, that reason is now simply the refusal of Achilles to come to terms with Agamemnon despite an offer of good-will on Agamemnon's part. Achilles might well say, "the Trojans would suffer, if only I were well-disposed towards Agamemnon"; he no longer has the right to put it the other way round,—for according to the poet of the Ninth Book Agamemnon has gone to the extremest possible lengths to show a change of heart towards Achilles.

These are the principal facts, and this is the only possible judgement on them: that this long speech of Achilles, like the shorter speech in the Eleventh Book, was composed by a poet who knew nothing of any embassy. For him, no approach has yet been made by Agamemnon to Achilles; what he says would be nonsense if there had been. I conclude with the simple and cogent words of Walter Leaf: "This is not a mere superficial inconsistency such as may be due to a temporary forgetfulness . . . it is a contradiction at the very root of the story, as flagrant as if Shakespear had forgotten in the fifth act of *Macbeth* that Duncan had been murdered in the second. To suppose that the same intellect which prepared the embassy to Achilles by the eighth book, and wrought it out in such magnificence and wealth of detail in the ninth, could afterwards compose a speech, so different and yet so grand, in entire oblivion of what had gone before, is to demand a credulity rendering any rational criticism impossible."[19]

Is there any further step to take? Is this as far as we can go on firm ground? Clearly it cannot be the end: for if the embassy to Achilles was introduced into an Iliad which actually denied that there ever was an embassy, there is no escape from a further inference about the Nineteenth Book. In that Book, Achilles accepts at last apology and compensation; and the scene of reconciliation is based on the assumption that the embassy in the Ninth Book did take place. It follows that this part of the Nineteenth Book was composed later than the Ninth, and is (like the Ninth) a later addition to the continuous story of the wrath of Achilles. Thus another large piece must be withdrawn from the original design—if there was an original design.[20] Let us look into one or two byways along this road.

1) The Reconciliation (Book XIX) presupposes the Embassy (Book IX): but does it presuppose the embassy *with* Phoenix or *without* him? The reconciliation recalls the events of the embassy in some detail: now Phoenix plays far the most important part in the embassy, but in the reconciliation his part is not mentioned at all. We can therefore affirm that the reconciliation shows no awareness of the embassy with Phoenix:[21] but it does not follow that its author possessed no such awareness, and we shall presently see reason to believe that Phoenix had indeed been already added to the embassy when the reconciliation was composed.

2) The embassy was added to an Iliad which neither had it nor allowed for it; the reconciliation was added later still. Can we tell whether both of these additions were, or could have been, made by the same poet? How multiple is our authorship? Is there anything which prompts or even obliges us to infer that these two episodes are the work of different poets, each in his own time expanding a basic Iliad?

Let us begin by observing an apparent fact about the reconciliation considered as part of the general structure of the Iliad. A reconciliation was offered and rejected in the Ninth Book. Achilles was determined not to intervene until the last possible moment; then he sent Patroclus to relieve the pressure on the Greeks. But Patroclus was killed, and from that moment onwards the heart of Achilles was possessed by a single thought—to fight again, to avenge his friend whatever the cost might be. On this point we shall be agreed: that there is now no question of Achilles not fighting; we know for certain that he will fight, that he will kill Hector and drive the Trojans from the field. The death of Patroclus has done what the embassy failed to do: for the purpose of the embassy was simply this, to persuade Achilles to fight. The last thing we expect to happen now is that Agamemnon shall renew his apology and his offer of compensation, at the very moment when the whole purpose of apology and compensation has ceased to exist. The reconciliation is not only unnecessary to the structure of the poem: it is also an actively disturbing feature of it,—it does not occur in the poem until the object which it is designed to achieve has already been achieved by other means, the death of Patroclus.

The reconciliation is a flaw in the fabric of the Iliad: but it would be imprudent to infer multiplicity of authorship from this particular type of imperfection, since it is possible to discern a special motive for it. The theme of the Iliad is the Wrath of Achilles—*his wrath against Agamemnon:* and a poet may ask himself, is that theme to be left incomplete at the end of the poem? Subtract the reconciliation, and the grounds for Achilles' wrath will be exactly the same in the Twenty-fourth Book as they were in the First; the only difference will be that there is now no hope that the quarrel can ever end, since in the meantime Achilles has rejected an apology. It may very well be that this was the primary reason for the reconciliation in the Nineteenth Book, the desire to settle the matter between Achilles and Agamemnon in the course of the poem, and to settle it *at this time* in order that the limelight may now fall wholly on what replaces the Wrath of Achilles as the main theme—the Death of Hector. You may think that it would have been much better not to adopt this course; but that is a matter for dispute to which there is no end.

I turn now to a quite different point. Phoenix, in the course of the embassy, warned Achilles of what may happen to men who reject compensation for injury. He quoted at great length the example of Meleager: Meleager, like Achilles, withdrew from battle in anger; he too rejected prayer and compensation. But in the end danger came home so close to him that he was compelled to fight; and so he fought, and defeated the enemy. But then of course nobody was going to renew offers of compensation: he had lost his chance of fighting in return for gifts, and in the end he had to fight unpaid, τῷ δ' οὐκέτι δῶρα τέλεσσαν. Now the whole point of this parable is that this is what will happen to Achilles if he rejects the compensation offered; and Achilles does reject it. The story of Meleager tells us what was in the poet's mind; it openly informs the listener what he is to expect. Achilles, like Meleager, is going to be compelled to fight (and so he is), and he will then find that it is too late to ask for this or any other reward. The parable of Meleager loses all its colour and significance if it is addressed *to a man to whom it does not apply,*—a man who is going to get the full compensation after all. The composer of the parable, the Phoenix-poet, was looking forward to an action in which the death of Patroclus compelled Achilles to fight without compensation. So much I take to be very obvious: and then the reconciliation must have been composed not only later than the introduction of Phoenix into the embassy,[22] but also by a different poet. And we shall have identified four different poets,—the poet of the reconciliation, the Phoenix-poet, the original embassy-poet, and the poet or poets of the Iliad into which all these matters were introduced.

It is relevant here to say something about the style and contents of the reconciliation. The Greek Epic is uneven in quality: it rises to great heights, and occasionally it sinks to considerable depths. The distance between the extremes might fairly be illustrated by comparison of the embassy with the reconciliation,—the one outstanding for excellence, the other a long way below.

T 28–338: The start is unpromising. Achilles has lost his friend; he is distraught with grief and rage; Hephaestus has made him a suit of Olympian armour; his mother Thetis brings it to him. Now surely he will rush into battle intent upon the killing of Hector? And so he might: only his mother unexpectedly and very abruptly tells him that he must first make friends with Agamemnon,—though she does not explain (and we cannot guess) why on earth he must do so at this time or indeed at any time. Moreover, Achilles is to make the first move. The cause of his quarrel with Agamemnon is exactly the same as it has always been; and no reason is given or guessable why he should now climb down, ask Agamemnon to be friends again, say that a woman was not worth all this trouble. What he now specially desires is that the Greeks should start fighting again,—not only a penitent and down-looking Achilles, it appears, but also a mighty prudent one; I imagine that an earlier and better tale described his rushing into battle alone and without delay to settle his score with Hector; not waiting to make speeches in the Marketplace and inviting the co-operation of the regular army.

There follows the reply of Agamemnon, beginning thus: "Agamemnon spoke from the place where he sat, *not standing up in the midst of them:* 'O Greeks, *when a man is standing up as I am,* it is right to listen to him and wrong to interrupt.' " He proceeds to assign the whole blame to divine influences: Zeus put *Atê* into his mind; and what could he do, seeing that even Zeus was once at the mercy of *Atê?* There follows a long description of the deception of Zeus by Hera; and in the course of it, contrary to the custom of the Greek Epic, Agamemnon is made to repeat verbatim what the gods said to each other. He knows what words the gods used in Olympus on that occasion, and we are grateful for the disclosure, while the laws of the Epic art lie in fragments about our feet. Agamemnon ends this uncommonly long oration (67 lines) with the surprising statement that he will make abundant compensation to Achilles; though there is now no obligation upon him to do so, nor has he been asked to do so, nor is there any longer a purpose in doing so. He ought to give Briseis back, no doubt: but that is the one thing that he forgets to mention; though it soon appears that he really meant to mention her, and indeed he does restore her.

Achilles briefly replies that he has no interest in compensation. He is eager to go to battle; but repeats that he is not going alone, the whole army is to support him. Now at last, let us hope, the action will begin. But hope is to be long deferred, and the heart to be made moderately sick. Odysseus has a word to say, indeed he has a great many words to say, mostly about food. You cannot expect the army to fight before breakfast: no doubt Achilles is in a hurry, but the men must have their meal. Meantime Agamemnon can be sending for Briseis and the abundant gifts. Agamemnon agrees: everything[23] that was promised in the embassy shall be brought and given to Achilles. Achilles would rather postpone these dealings: he reluctantly agrees that the army shall eat, though he himself has no such desire. This gives Odysseus a second innings: Achilles must learn to treat this question of food more seriously. Let him take the advice of a wiser and older man: it really is a great mistake for soldiers to go about with empty stomachs. More than 180 lines have now passed since luncheon stole the limelight, and nothing has been achieved. Now at last Briseis and seven other women and splendid gifts are brought to Achilles, and Agamemnon swears a great oath that he has never laid hands on Achilles' concubine. This oath is accompanied by the ritual slaughter of a boar; a thing contrary to tradition, if we were not past caring.

The public meeting is now over, but the tempo is no quicker: nothing is not mentioned—removal of the gifts to Achilles' tent; lamentation of Briseis over Patroclus' body; a renewed attempt to make Achilles eat his dinner; a long lament by Achilles over his dead friend; and finally the intervention of Zeus, who has evidently been listening to Odysseus, for he concentrates wholly on this matter of dinner,—everybody else, he observes, is at table; only Achilles refuses meat and drink. Athene is to go at once and drip some nectar and ambrosia into him, otherwise he will find himself very hungry later on.

When Athene has done this, Achilles may at last put on his armour and go to battle. The story has been held up for about 320 lines; and I am not the first to suggest that it would be very much better without them. The reconciliation is out of place in the story and ill-executed in its context; it is none the better for being padded as it is with lec-

ture upon lecture about food.[24] Food supply was presumably a matter
for anxiety to Ionian campaigners in the Dark Ages and later; no
doubt also to armies abroad in the Mycenaean period. But it was not
a good subject for heroic poetry; and nowhere else does the Epic poet
make so loud a song and so long a dance about it. It is not as if there
were any special reason why he should do so here: for the crisis of the
Iliad is now to come, and this is a sorry introduction to it, composed
in a novel and untraditional style.[25]

II. The Achaean Wall

Thucydides prefixes to his history of the Peloponnesian War a short
synopsis of the past, from Minos of Crete down to his own time. In the
tenth chapter he is at pains to refute a misleading impression con-
veyed by the Iliad. The army of Agamemnon may have been larger
than any before it: but it must have been smaller than the armies of
the present day. The Catalogue of Ships in the Second Book affords
evidence for this conclusion:

"If we strike the average of the smallest and largest ships, the numbers of those who sailed will appear inconsiderable, representing as
they did the whole force of Hellas. And this was due not so much to
scarcity of men as of provisions. Difficulty of subsistence made the
invaders reduce the numbers of the army to a point at which it might
live on the country during the prosecution of the war. Even after the
victory which they obtained on arrival—and a victory there must
have been, or the fortifications of the naval camp could never have
been built,—there is no indication that their whole force was employed; on the contrary, they seem to have turned to cultivation of
the Chersonese and to piracy from want of supplies. This was what
really enabled the Trojans to keep the field for ten years against them,
the dispersion of the enemy making them always a match for the detachment left behind. If they had brought plenty of supplies with
them, and had persevered in the war without scattering for piracy and
agriculture, they would easily have defeated the Trojans in the field,
since they could hold their own against them with the division on
service. In short, if they had stuck to the siege, the capture of Troy
would have cost them less time and less trouble."[26]

Let us focus our attention on the sentence in the middle: "After
they had won a victory on arrival—and this is proved by the fact that
they could not otherwise have built the fortifications for their camp,—
they did not apparently employ all available forces even in the field of
operations" (understand: "any more than they had done when mo-
bilizing in Hellas").

Here is one of the most important articles of external evidence in the whole Homeric Question. Consider the two following facts. First, in the Iliad the fortifications round the Greek camp take the full limelight for the first and last time in the Seventh Book, when they are actually built. That is the one question which everybody could answer about the wall: In what year was it built? *It was built in the tenth year*, during the course of the Iliad's story. Secondly, Thucydides quotes the presence of the wall as proof of his statement *that the Greeks won a battle on arrival at Troy*. The one thing which the Iliad says very clearly about the wall is that it was built in the tenth year: Thucydides goes out of his way to quote the Iliad as evidence that the wall was built at the beginning, in the first year, of the war. It follows that the Iliad current in Thucydides' day did not include the extensive passage in the Seventh Book of which the building of the wall in the tenth year is the principal theme.

Is there any escape from this obvious inference? Let us first dispose of two easily refutable rejoinders:

1) Nobody, so far as I know, argues that Thucydides simply forgot all about the Seventh Book,—that at the very beginning of his History, in an otherwise carefully considered argument, looking to the Iliad for proof of a point about the wall, he forgot the only passage in which the wall is the principal theme, and stated by way of proof something which is flatly contradicted by that passage. If he needs evidence from this source on this point, there is only one passage in the whole of the Iliad which will provide it: yet that is the one passage which he does not remember; and it makes nonsense of what he does remember (whatever that may have been). If this were what happened, rational criticism would be at an end; but I waste no more time talking about what nobody believes, indeed what nobody even asserts.

2) It has been suggested that Thucydides refers not to the Iliad but to some other branch of the Epic tradition.[27] This I believe to be demonstrably incorrect. The argument which he began in his tenth chapter, and of which this controversial passage is the immediate sequel, explicitly refers not to some other branch of the tradition but to the Second Book of the Iliad. Right up to the controversial passage Thucydides is still dealing with the inference which he draws from the numbers of ships and men given in the Homeric Catalogue: he now quotes the evidence of the wall round the ships at Troy; and it would indeed be a desperate remedy, to plead that he might now suddenly switch over to some other source,—a source flatly contradicted by the Iliad on the point at issue. Suppose there was another source,

in which the wall was built at the beginning of the war:[28] what is the good of referring to it here, when everybody knows that according to the Iliad the wall was not built until the tenth year?—especially if you have just told your reader that you are talking about the Iliad, not about "some other source." "The Iliad," wrote Professor Robertson, "is clearly Thucydides' main authority"; I do not think that the matter needs any further discussion.

Is there any other way of escape? One only has been found: by alteration of the text of Thucydides. But before we consider the proposed alterations it is proper to inquire whether there is any *intrinsic* fault in the text. I agree with what appears to be the general opinion, that there is no intrinsic fault in it. Granted certain presuppositions, Thucydides' argument is lucid and cogent enough, both in general throughout the whole section and in particular in the controversial passage.

The presuppositions are, briefly, as follows: In general, Thucydides believes that there really was an Achaean siege of Troy, and that the Homeric facts and figures afford evidence, though not necessarily reliable evidence, for the historian. In detail, he accepts the ten years' duration of the siege, and he takes it for granted, or as a well-known fact, that when the Achaeans arrived at Troy their landing was opposed by the Trojans. This was a natural, I think inevitable, assumption: for it was common sense to suppose that the Trojans resisted the invasion, and the one full account, that of the *Cypria*, told of a great battle on the beaches in which first the Trojans repelled the Greeks and then Achilles put the Trojans to flight. Moreover, everybody knew one fact about the landing,—the death of Protesilaus when he leapt ashore, the first casualty of the war. So far as I know, these presuppositions are outside controversy; I say no more about them. Let us now follow the argument stated by Thucydides.

He begins by observing that if you accept the figures given in the Catalogue of Ships you will find that the number of Greeks who sailed to Troy was smaller than might have been expected; and he suggests that the reason why it was not larger is to be found in the problem of supply. No more men could be enlisted than could live off the country during the war. He then observes that the same explanation, shortage of supplies (not of men), would account for another problem: why did the Greeks take so long to conquer the Trojans? Contrast (he says) what happened when they arrived with what happened for the next ten years: when they first arrived they defeated the Trojans in a battle; but from that time onwards for ten years the Trojans were a match for them. Not only were they never able to invest the city, let

alone to storm it: they were not even more than equal to the Trojans
in the field. Thucydides infers that after the initial victory they must
have dispersed their forces: part were engaged in providing supplies,
and that is the reason why the Greeks took so long to conquer Troy,—
the Trojans were a match for that part of the Greek army which was
left to oppose them in the field. If the Greeks had been free to concentrate the whole of their forces against the Trojans, they would have
taken the city in less time and with less trouble.

This may not be the only possible explanation of the alleged facts,
but it is certainly a reasonable one. The argument in general is clear
and coherent, and the controversial passage is entirely free from intrinsic fault whether of matter or of form.

Thucydides infers the limitation of the Greek numbers, and the dispersal of the limited numbers, from facts which are simple and commonplace, with one exception: how does he know that the Greeks defeated the Trojans on arrival at Troy? The whole of this part of his
argument depends upon it: if there is no such contrast between initial
superiority and subsequent parity, the reasoning in this whole section
collapses. From that contrast you could properly infer that the Greeks
must have diverted part of their forces to other occupations. But
without the contrast how would you know that they *did* disperse their
forces after arrival at Troy? It would be a mere guess, exposed to
obvious objection: but Thucydides could refute any objection by
pointing to the relative weakness of the Greeks for ten years in the
field, contrasted with their superiority at the time of arrival.

It was therefore necessary for Thucydides to prove that the Greeks
did defeat the Trojans on arrival: how does he do it? You may say,
surely he might take it for granted; the Greeks did establish themselves in their beachhead, and held their position for ten years. The
landing was opposed, and the very fact that the Greeks formed a
camp on shore proves that they must have been successful in the
battle for the beaches. I do not at all dispute this. Thucydides might
very well have taken it for granted; and, if he had been thinking of the
Cypria, he *would* have taken it for granted, for the *Cypria* actually
described the victory on landing,—there would have been no point in
deducing from the presence of a wall what was explicitly described by
the source. The fact, however, is that Thucydides does not take this
matter for granted: he has ready to hand an indisputable proof; and
naturally he includes the proof.

Its essence is simple. Perpend two facts: (i) the Greeks and Trojans
fought a battle on the shore; (ii) the Greeks built a fortification on
the shore. Now draw the obvious conclusion,—the Greeks must have

won the battle on the shore. The army which, having fought the enemy on the shore, concedes to him the territory and the leisure to build walls and towers and trenches, is an army which failed to win the battle. It is no good saying that it might have been a drawn battle; or that the Trojan casualties might have been the less; or that the Trojans might have been ready to resume the offensive the next day. If the day's fighting has earned room and freedom to construct fortifications, the Greeks have won what they fought the battle for. There, says Thucydides, is the solid and spectacular monument of a successful landing-operation, the fortification around the Greek camp. That is in fact his argument: and it is beyond cavil—*provided that he is free to suppose that the wall was built at the beginning of the war.* If his Iliad contained the passage which describes at length the building of the wall in the *tenth* year, he could not possibly quote the Iliad in support of his *first-year* wall; but if it did not contain that passage, he would naturally assume (as we also should have done) that the wall was built at the beginning of the war. And he might have noticed a passage in the Fourteenth Book which supports that assumption:

Ξ 30 πολλὸν γάρ ῥ᾽ ἀπάνευθε μάχης εἰρύατο νῆες
θῖν᾽ ἐφ᾽ ἁλὸς πολιῆς· τὰς γὰρ πρώτας πεδίονδε
εἴρυσαν, αὐτὰρ τεῖχος ἐπὶ πρύμνῃσιν ἔδειμαν.

*"Far from the fighting the ships were hauled up on the
beach on the gray sea: they hauled the first ships
to the plain, and built a wall by their sterns."*

In the Iliad of Thucydides there is only one thing that this could mean,—that the wall was built when the ships were hauled up; that is to say, at the very beginning of the war. And there is a further reason why Thucydides must suppose that the fortifications were constructed immediately upon arrival: the fact that this was normal practice in his own day. There are several good illustrations in his own History.[29] I am speaking now not of occasional brief raids, or of immediately successful attacks on relatively small targets, but of more or less protracted operations on a hostile coast. If the invader intended to stay for any length of time on a foreign shore, and if he met or expected opposition, then he fortified a beachead at the earliest possible moment,—at once, if the actual landing was unopposed; after initial victory, if it was opposed. Thus the existence of fortifications is the obvious token of a successful landing whether opposed or unopposed; and, if opposed, it is proof positive of a victory in the first encounter with the enemy. *It could never in any circum-*

stances be evidence of a defeat in the initial encounter: the invader who loses the first battle finishes the day in the sea or on his ships. Only if the enemy retires can the invader build fortified camps; and the enemy who retires has lost the battle for the beachhead. We can therefore dismiss without further ado the conjecture, ἐκρατήθησαν for ἐκράτησαν. For this reason, and for one or two others,[30] it would not make sense.

　• We have now reached this position: that there is no intrinsic fault in the text of Thucydides at the controversial point; alteration of the text cannot be (and indeed has not been) justified on its own merits; it is imposed upon the text from outside, by reason of a particular opinion—itself highly speculative—about the composition of the Iliad and the history of the transmission of its text. Such a procedure starts under a heavy handicap: nevertheless, if a likely conjecture could be made to bring Thucydides into harmony with the Iliad, we ought to give it very serious consideration. If there were any such conjecture, the case for multiple composition of the Iliad at this point would not be materially weakened: it would still be founded on the text, not upon a speculative alteration of it. But the unitarian would at least have what at present he lacks,—an answer to the charge.

Not many conjectures have been made, and only one calls for serious consideration,—Professor Robertson's ἔτει ῑ ἐτειχίσαντο for ἐτειχίσαντο. He translates: "That they did win a victory is obvious, for otherwise they would not have built the fortification round their camp in the tenth year of the war." And he comments: "The building of the Greek wall was a confession that the offensive had passed to the Trojans; its postponement till the tenth year was (as Thucydides saw) a proof that up to then the offensive had lain with the Greeks." Professor Gomme rejects this conjecture primarily because the idea that an unwalled camp might afford evidence of a successful landing is one which would not have occurred to Thucydides: for him, it is the fortified camp which is the immediate sequel and visible token of a successful landing in the given conditions.[31] To me, the decisive point is much more fundamental: the proposed conjecture breaks an indispensable link in the chain of Thucydides' argument.

In his translation Professor Robertson takes ἐκράτησαν to mean "they did win a victory": agreed, but then what becomes of the argument as a whole? "After they arrived they won a battle: this is obvious, *because otherwise they would not have fortified their camp in so late a year as the tenth*"? It seems an odd way of proving *a victory at the time of arrival.* The only thing proved by a camp left unfortified for ten years would be the conclusion *that the Greeks were superior to the*

Trojans throughout that period; but that, as we have seen, is the exact opposite of what Thucydides is arguing,—Τρῶες τοῖς ἀεὶ ὑπολειπομένοις ἀντίπαλοι, the Trojans were always a match for the Greeks in the field throughout the ten years. When we pass from Professor Robertson's translation to his comment we find that ἐκράτησαν is taken to mean not "they won a battle," but "they were masters in the field": the postponement of the fortification till the tenth year is a "proof that up to then the offensive had lain with the Greeks." But even if the aorist (in ἐκράτησαν) were replaced by an imperfect tense (and this would surely be necessary; cf. Thuc. VI 2.5), the alleged meaning still cannot be reconciled with Thucydides' argument in this passage as a whole. He is explaining *that the Greeks dispersed their forces, and that the Trojans were therefore a match for them, and this is why the war lasted so long:* what could be the point of starting with the statement, and proving it by a special argument, *that the Greeks were masters in the field up to the tenth year?* The emended text actually contradicts the main argument of this whole section: for if the offensive lay with the Greeks for ten years, there is no longer any evidence that they *did* disperse their forces. The point to be made is that they were *not* masters in the field: they were only equal to their opponents; that is why they took so long to conquer Troy, and that is how we know that they dispersed their forces.

The contradiction of Thucydides by our Iliad remains absolute, and there is now no means of avoiding the conclusion *that the Iliad as known at Athens in Thucydides' day did not include the latter part of the Seventh Book.* Let us now turn from external to internal evidence.

Consider first the speech of Nestor (H 327–343); and notice above all the enormous fault in the structure of the poem. *"We have suffered heavily,"* says Nestor; *"it is time to stop fighting, to collect and cremate our dead, and to build high towers and a trench to protect our army from being crushed by the attack of these proud Trojans."* Suppose that you did not know what has happened in the Iliad up to this point: you would of course infer that the Achaeans must have been hard pressed, that they are on the defensive, the Trojans attacking. For the first time in ten years the Achaeans must build a defensive wall. At the very least, then, you would laugh to scorn the notion that what has happened up to this point is an unbroken run of success for the Achaeans.

But that is what really has happened. The wonderful successes of Diomedes are the principal theme of the Fifth Book and the earlier part of the Sixth. The fortress of Troy is in utmost peril (Z 73 ff.); not even Achilles had ever shown such prowess or been so terrible to the

Trojans (Z 98 ff.); only the gods can save the city now. Hector checks the Achaean attack for a moment, and goes into the city to arrange special prayers for deliverance. It is no exaggeration to say that by the end of the Sixth Book the Trojans are harder pressed than they have ever been, or ever will be again before the death of Hector. But perhaps there is something in the earlier part of the Seventh Book,—something to mitigate the absurdity of building a defensive wall for the first time in ten years at the very moment when you have won your greatest success in ten years? Let us look. At the beginning of the Seventh Book Hector and Paris emerge from Troy, to the great relief of their distressed army. Each kills one Greek, the Lycian Glaucus kills a third. But still the Trojans are in great peril, and Apollo intervenes to rescue them (H 26 f.). It is decided that there shall be another duel, Ajax against Hector; and all that happens between this point and the proposal to build a wall is a single combat in which the Greek is the superior.

Such is the background for the building of a defensive wall round the Achaean camp in the tenth year,—a wonderful success, followed by momentary relief of pressure on the Trojans, followed by a duel divinely ordered to give the Trojans a breathing-space; and in that duel the Greek gets the better of the chief Trojan hero. Not even the utmost skill of the modern psychological interpreters can cure the malady. If this manner of composition is held to be consistent with the idea that the Iliad was planned, as a whole and in its major parts, by a great or even a competent artist, then common sense and criticism have no foothold in this region. It is not surprising that Nestor's untimely speech has been widely quoted as clear evidence of multiple authorship by many who have not so much as noticed the conflict of testimony between the Iliad and Thucydides.[32]

There remains a last matter of importance. It has long been held, and was finally proved in great detail by Wackernagel, that the Alexandrian text of the Iliad, the source of our own, was an Athenian text. The spelling in our manuscripts is Attic more or less throughout; a large number of specifically Attic forms and features of dialect appear in the text, some of them irremovably embedded in the verse. It is therefore not open to us to say that our Iliad is Homer's, whereas Thucydides and his compatriots must have had some other (and inferior) version. The Iliad at Athens in the 5th century B.C. is a lineal ancestor of our own. Now the latter part of the Seventh Book, being as it was in the Alexandrian Iliad, must have been in the Athenian Iliad; though we have already learnt that it was not included in the Athenian Iliad in the time of Thucydides. Does it not follow that this large addition to the Iliad must have been the work of an Athenian poet? If not, how did it come to be included in the Athenian vulgate? I am not sure that the consequence is inevitable, but it is obviously probable, and there is one point in Nestor's speech which seems to suggest that it is true (H 332): *"We shall gather ourselves (?) together,*[33] *and with oxen and mules we shall wheel the dead bodies hither; then let us burn them, at a little distance from the ships, so that each man may carry the bones home to his children when we return to our native land."*[34] Professor Felix Jacoby, in a widely quoted article (*JHS* 64, 1944, 37 ff.) distinguished by a depth and breadth of learning beyond the scope of most of us, established the following propositions: that the practice of bringing the bodies (or ashes) of the fallen warrior back to his native land was peculiar to Athens; and that it was not instituted there until the year 464 B.C. It was uniform Hellenic custom to bury the fallen in a *polyandrion* on the battlefield. The practice to which Nestor alludes is not merely unknown to the Greek Epic: it is unknown to Greek history—except at Athens in this late period. It is, says Jacoby, "a speciality of Athens," a "custom . . . known only for Athens."

The coincidence is striking enough. Thucydides has proved to us that the speech of Nestor was not included in the Iliad much if at all before the end of the 5th century: now we learn that this part of it cannot have been *composed* until (at earliest) a little before the middle of that century. Moreover the history of our text had suggested that the composer of this passage was likely to have been an Athenian: now we learn that nobody but an Athenian would have been likely to compose this part of it. There is other detail in the text which confirms or is consistent with our general conclusion.[35] That conclusion must now be frankly accepted. The history of the development of the Iliad before the Alexandrian recension is a subject about which we have large prejudices but hardly any factual information. The poem includes numerous other passages composed by speakers of the Athenian dialect: but most if not all of them may have been composed so far back as the 6th century or even a little earlier. There are a few other passages which we know to have been added to the vulgate in the 4th century and later:[36] but the speech of Nestor remains by far the largest and most important example of its kind.

It is vain to assert that nobody any longer composed this sort of thing in the 4th century B.C.; and that, if anybody did, such a composition could not have become part of the standard text. Such assertions have no foundation in reason. They have no value as intuitively apprehended axioms; and there is no factual evidence to

support them. These are questions to which we simply did not know
the answers: we must not prejudge them. And now we do know the
answers: such passages were composed, and did enter the vulgate, in
the 4th century B.C.

NOTES

I. I have read much, by no means all, that has been
written on the subject of this essay. I have found the greatest help in
M. Noé, *Phoinix, Ilias, und Homer: Untersuchungen zum neunten
Gesang der Ilias* (Preisschriften, gekrönt und herausgegeben von der
Fürstlich Jablonowskischen Gesellschaft zu Leipzig, 1940) pp. 1–124.
(See now also G. Jachmann, *Der homerische Schiffskatalog und die
Ilias*, 1958, 56 ff., published when my book was already in proof.)

[1] On the question whether the dual number is ever used of more than
two persons see esp. Noé 12 ff.; based on Ohler, "Ueber den Ge-
brauch des Duals bei Homer," *Programm des grossherzogl. Gymn.*
(Mainz, 1884), Cuny, *Le Nombre duel en grec* (1906), and Boll,
Zeitschr. f. Oesterr. Gymn. 68 (1917) 8 ff., 69 (1919–20) 414 ff.; cf.
also Schwyzer, *Gr. Grammatik* ii 48 f.

The plain fact is that there is nothing in the Homeric poems remotely comparable with what is alleged here. Of course the plural
may be used instead of the dual: that is very natural. But it would
be a most unnatural development, if the dual ever came to replace
the plural; and in fact there is no such example—with a single
exception which nobody is likely to use as an argument in the
present debate. E 487 μή πως ὡς ἀψῖσι λίνου ἀλόντε πανάγρου: it would
be difficult for a phrase of this length to behave in a manner more
disrespectful to Homeric convention: ἀψῖσι, πανάγρου are newcomers
to the Epic vocabulary; and the ridiculous dual is not more offensive than the prosody of ἄλοντε. Such a passage is not comparable with I 182 ff.: "für die Menge von Dualen im I eine solche
Verständnislosigkeit des Dichters anzunehmen, dass er nämlich die
Formen nicht etwa mit Pluralen verwechselt, sondern sie gar be-
wusst als Dualformen für den Plural gebraucht hätte, geht nicht
an" (Noé 15). Θ 70 is not relevant to our problem: it does not offer
an example of a dual representing more than two subjects; the

dual κῆρε does not mean more than two κῆρες,—the number of Fates is two (70) and the fault lies in applying both κῆρες to each of the two parties. The composer's mind here was obsessed by words rather than thoughts, and δύο κῆρε above induced him to put κῆρες ἐξέσθην in 73 f. instead of κῆρ ἕξετο. It is a comfort, that we are not required to believe that 73–74 were an integral part of the ancient vulgate (athetized by Aristarchus).

No useful evidence is forthcoming from Λ 566 f., Δ 452 f., Θ 185 f., al.; Noé 14 f.

[2] See esp. Scholia A on I 168, 169, 180, 182, 192, 197, Scholia BT on I 168.

[3] Elsewhere in the Homeric poems (there are 44 occurrences in addition to I 168, 192) ἡγεῖσθαι is confined to contexts in which two or more persons are in movement, and the verb is applied to that one of the persons who takes the lead; and it is always apparent or to be presumed that the other person or persons referred to in the context are subordinate (in respect of the action described) to the subject of the verb ἡγεῖσθαι, unless the context plainly dictates otherwise. In I 168 the context dictates nothing, and we must suppose that Phoenix is intended to be (as indeed he turns out to be) the principal person in this company of ambassadors; otherwise there could be no conceivable purpose in saying that he is to "take the lead" of them.

In what respect may a context "plainly dictate otherwise"? It may show by implication that the action signified by "lead the way" is in effect "*show* the way," "act as guide." This implication is present in a single passage of the Iliad (Λ 71) and in five passages of the Odyssey: in all the examples the meaning is "go in front," and the idea "show the way" is an inference from the context. In I 168 there is nothing in the context to impart this color to the verb: the notion that Ajax and Odysseus and the heralds needed to be *shown the way* to Achilles' tent (after ten years) is in itself absurd; it is now seen to be inconsistent with the phraseology.

Nothing relevant to our purpose can be inferred from the difference in tenses between ἡγησάσθω and ἡγεῖτο. I wondered for a time whether the aorist in Φοῖνιξ ἡγησάσθω might denote "let Phoenix take the lead," i.e., simply "*go in front*" (a suitable position for Achilles' friend), whereas the imperfect in ἡγεῖτο δ' 'Οδυσσεύς might mean "Odysseus *was in command.*" But no such distinction can be drawn in view of the synonymity of ἡγεῖτο and ἡγησάσθην in the Epic at large (e.g. Β 567, 638, 851, 870, al.). Note further that nothing can be made of the distinction between πρώτιστα and αὐτὰρ ἔπειτα: Ν 491 οἳ οἱ ἅμ' ἡγεμόνες Τρώων ἔσαν, αὐτὰρ ἔπειτα λαοὶ ἕπονθ', Β 405 Νέστορα μὲν πρώτιστα καὶ 'Ιδομενῆα ἄνακτα, αὐτὰρ ἔπειτ' Αἴαντε: there is no suggestion that any interval of time elapses between the "first" and the "then"; it is a matter of precedence, not of sequence in time; cf. the formular ἡγήσατο . . . ὁ δ' ἔπειτα μετ' ἴχνια βαῖνε. Schadewaldt's note, *Iliasstudien* 138 n. 3, was injudicious.

⁴ Schadewaldt, op. cit. 137 ff.; Focke, *Hermes* 82 (1954) 260 ff.; Mazon, *Introduction à l'Iliade* 176 f.

Schadewaldt's usual remedy (the theory of a "stufenweise eigene Arbeit" by Homer himself) fails him here: he has to admit that the Phoenix problem cannot be solved by any appeal to *Bearbeitung* of that type; it lies *im Wesen der ganzen Erfindung* (an important admission). What he finally asks his reader to believe is this (p. 139): "The poet may well have 'excepted' Phoenix, just because of his exceptional position in the Embassy, when he turns his attention to the journey of the official ambassadors and their greeting by Achilles." *Num his auribus fidam?* Just what was the "exceptional position" of Phoenix? It was—there can be no dispute about this—*that he was to be the leader;* and the very introduction of him here, so unexpected (we have never heard of him before), concentrates attention upon him much more than upon the others. Notice that the distinction of the others as "official ambassadors" is nowhere even remotely suggested by the Iliad, which in fact makes Phoenix far the most important of the ambassadors; it is a distinction introduced in support of an unstable edifice of conjecture.

⁵ See Jaeger, *Sitzber. d. Preuss. Akad. d. Wiss.* (1926) 69 ff.; Pfeiffer, *Philologus* 84 (1928) 137 ff.; Snell, *Philologus* Suppl. XX 1 (1928) and 85 (1930) 141 ff.; Noé, op. cit. 32 ff.; Voigt, *Ueberlegung und Entscheidung bei Homer* (1934); Dodds, *The Greeks and the Irrational* (1956) 7, 20 n. 31.

⁶ Dodds l.c. 20 n. 31.

⁷ "The notion of *Atê* as a punishment seems to be either a late development in Ionia or a late importation from outside: the only place in Homer where it is explicitly asserted is the unique Λιταί passage in *Iliad* Book Nine, which suggests that it may possibly be a Mainland idea, taken over along with the Meleager story from an epic composed in the mother country," Dodds 6.

⁸ Hades appears in the Iliad as a person only in the following places (apart from the Embassy): Ε 395, in Dione's account of gods who suffered at mortal hands; Θ 367 f., in Athene's account of the labours of Heracles; Ο 185 ff., in Poseidon's tale of the tripartite division of the world. That is to say, the Iliad never presents Hades *as a person* in its own story: it merely includes a few *other* stories in

which he was so presented. In harmony with this fact is the extreme rarity of noun + epithet combinations for Hades: in 46 occurrences of the name, only Ἄιδι κλυτοπώλῳ thrice, with N 415 πυλάρταο κρατεροῖο, cf. Θ 367 f. πυλάρταο . . . στυγεροῦ. The Odyssey adds nothing of importance (except that the *Nekuia*, like the Iliad at large, has no personal "Hades"). Υ 61 ff. (Aidoneus) stands right outside the main tradition.

It may be argued that the common phrase "House of Hades" indicates that Hades was regarded as a person: perhaps so, but the fact remains that nothing is said either about him or about his house (δῶμα once, no epithet; δῶ once, with the misbegotten adjective εὐρυπυλές; δόμος commonly, without epithet always in the Iliad and, except once, εὐρώεντα, in the Odyssey).

The normal Epic conception of the afterworld practically excludes the possibility of a colorful "Hades"; O 185 ff., Υ 61 ff., the few other references to a personal Hades quoted above, and the creation of the phrase Ἄιδι κλυτοπώλῳ, are surely the work of Ionians at a relatively late stage in the tradition.

Persephone is unknown to the Iliad elsewhere (Odyssey κ, λ only). The Erinyes are confined to the Embassy and Reconciliation, with O 204 and Φ 412 (also five places in the Odyssey). For the un - Homeric Ζεὺς καταχθόνιος see Noé 60 ff.

[9] The speech of Phoenix is on the whole very conventional in phraseology up to 527, except where new ideas introduce new language ('Ερινῦς accus. plur.; ἐπαράς unique in the Epic, so is καταχθόνιος; ἐπαινὴ Περσεφόνεια 457 and 569 only in the Iliad); the most remarkable features are 468 φλογὸς Ἡφαίστοιο, where Hephaestus stands for "fire," cf. P 88; μέθυ for "wine," a modernism (Η 471 only in Iliad, common in Od.); 484 the Dolopes, a people unknown to the Iliad (including the Catalogue); 501 λισσόμενοι, unique usage of this verb for prayer by man to god; 503 the dual ὀφθαλμώ, only N 474; 505 οὕνεκα "therefore," elsewhere always "because"; 521 Ἀχαιικόν, a rarity; 522 μὴ . . . ἐλέγξῃς, a rare use of μή with second pers. aor. subj. in prohibition (6 in Iliad, 3 in Od.); there are numerous unique or very rare words, apparently not from the traditional formula-vocabulary: παρατρωπῶσι, ῥυσαί, παραβλῶπες, σθεναρή, ἀρτίπος (θ 310 only), φθάνει (Φ 262 only), στερέως (Μ 267, Ψ 42, ψ 103), ἐπιζάφελος (ζ 330 only), δωρητοί, al.

In 527–605, the Meleager story, strange and surprising phenomena cluster much more thickly than usual:

531, 577 ἐραννῆς: a useful adjective, absent from the Iliad's vast vocabulary (once in Od.).

533 χρυσόθρονος Ἄρτεμις (also ε 123): but Ζ 205 χρυσήνιος Ἄρτεμις;

one or the other—probably the former—is in breach of the formula tradition.

536 Διὸς κούρῃ = Artemis; traditionally Athene.

538 δῖον γένος ἰοχέαιρα: a novel phrase, not in the formula vocabulary.

544 θηρήτορας: a rhapsode's form; the tradition supplied θηρητ-ῆρας.

550 μὲν οὖν: here only in the Iliad; common in classical Attic, foreign to the Epic tradition.

558 'Ιδέω: consonant + εω (for αο) is very rare in the Iliad; Τυδείδεω thrice, Πριαμίδεω Μενοιτιάδεω ἐριβρεμέτεω once each, and the Ionian formula ἀγκυλομήτεω.

561–564 are ridiculous in this place: "they called *the daughter* 'Halcyone' because *the mother, suffering like a halcyon,* wept when Apollo snatched her away"!

565 ἐξ, "because of," is untraditional; only Λ 308 (and Od.).

572 'Ερέβεσφιν (-ευσφιν vulg.): unique and bogus form. "Ερεβος itself is a newcomer to the vocabulary (Π 327, Θ 368, and Od.).

575 θεῶν ἱερῆας ἀρίστους: unique and untraditional phrase.

577 ὅππoθι: a newcomer to the Epic vocabulary (γ 89).

579 οἰνοπέδοιο: unique (Od. twice, but as adjective).

580 ψιλὴν ἄροσιν: words and thing unique in the Iliad (ψιλός Od. twice, ἄροσις once).

586 κεδνότατοι: in a new sense (κ 225 only).

588 πύκ' ἐβάλλετο: the use of πύκα is untraditional (E 70 only).

591 κατέλεξεν: this useful word (46 examples in Od.) is a late intruder upon the Iliad, confined to the purely Ionian compositions IX, X, XIX, XXIV.

598 εἴξας ᾧ θυμῷ: this can only mean "giving rein to his passion"; I suppose it might mean that here too, but the context suggests that the poet intended the opposite.

601 ἐνταῦθα: this very common word has no place whatever in the Epic vocabulary; its kindred ἐνταυθοῖ has crept into Φ 122 and twice into Od.

602 ἐπὶ δώροις: so the main tradition, one of the very rare examples of dative -οις for -οισι in the Iliad (my *Homeric Odyssey* 162 f.); Aristarchus' untranslatable ἐπὶ δώρων was an attempt to get rid of it at all costs.

605 τιμῆς: for τιμήεις, unique phenomenon except Σ 475 τιμῆντα, a contraction equally foreign to the Epic tradition.

It is of course quality, not quantity, which weighs: μὲν οὖν, ἐνταῦθα, τιμῆς are extreme examples of what is clearly a general tendency to compose independently of the traditional Epic formulas. The implication is that the relatively modern poet who introduced Phoenix into the Embassy incorporated into his own work some other poet's narrative, itself of relatively modern composition; and in so doing he followed quite closely the style and vocabulary of his model. The desire to incorporate this wonderful poem—one of the best in all Greek literature—may well have been one of the motives for the new composition. A good example of a phrase taken over and left unadapted to its new surroundings is 528 ἐν δ' ὑμῖν ἐρέω πάντεσσι φίλοισι. The obscurity of 584 καὶ πότνια μήτηρ is caused by transferring without adapting.

The matters discussed in this section are not at all affected by the much-debated question whether the Wrath of Achilles and the Wrath of Meleager are independent of each other or not. Some think that the former was more or less directly inspired by the latter, others reverse the relation. I think that the former of these two parties has the stronger case, but doubt whether either story is in fact dependent on the other. Those who wish to explore this jungle will do well to start by taking a bearing from Noé before plunging into *RE* XV (1931) 446 ff.; *Myth. Lex.* s.v. Meleager; Howald, *Rhein. Mus.* 73 (1924) 402 ff.; Bethe, ibid. 74 (1925) 1 ff.; Sachs, *Philologus* 88 (1933) 16 ff.; Kakridis, ibid. 90 (1935) 1 ff.; and 'Ἀραί (1929); Focke, *Hermes* 82 (1954) 258 ff. As usual I find myself in complete disagreement with Schadewaldt, for whom the brilliantly constructed Wrath of Meleager is a "sehr unorganisches Etwas" (*Iliasstudien* 139).

¹⁰ Schadewaldt (*Iliasstudien* 128) says that Π 61 ff. is an "unambiguous reference back to I 650 ff.; that is acknowledged." It should not be acknowledged, for it is clearly not true. Π 61 ff. may stand entirely by itself, requiring no antecedent of any kind. The correct explanation is given in the Scholia: ἔφην = διενοήθην; not "I said," referring to an antecedent statement, but "I meant," referring to what he assumed or intended. This is normal Epic usage: E 472 f., φῆς που ἄτερ λαῶν πόλιν ἑξέμεν ἠδ' ἐπικούρων, "assumed," not "said,"—as the Scholia say, "Hector would never have *said* anything like that to his allies." X 331 Ἕκτορ, ἀτάρ που ἔφης Πατροκλῆ' ἐξεναρίζων σῶς ἔσσεσθ',—Achilles could not know, and does not care, whether Hector actually *said* it or not (in fact he did not); it is what he *intended* or *expected*. λ 430 ff. ἤτοι ἔφην γε ἀσπάσιος παίδεσσιν ἰδὲ δμώεσσιν ἐμοῖσιν οἴκαδ' ἐλεύσεσθαι,—Agamemnon *thought* to come home welcome etc. δ 171 καί μιν ἔφην ἐλθόντα φιλησέμεν,—Menelaus *meant* to welcome

Odysseus. So Λ 61 f., ἤτοι ἔφην γε = what Achilles *thought*, what he would be likely to say, whether he actually said it or not.

All this used to be well enough known (Ebeling s.v. φημί 422 col. ii).

The only explicit reference to the Embassy in the Iliad (apart from the Nineteenth Book, for which see pp. 311 ff.) is Σ 448–449, part of a long passage athetized by Aristarchus, i.e., known by him to be an intruder upon the standard text. Other alleged references are illusory: (*a*) Λ 59 = Ι 648, but nobody nowadays should suppose that the repetition of a line indicates interdependence of the two passages concerned. (*b*) Focke (l.c. 274 ff.) detects what is not visible to me, a number of "well-considered connexions" with the Embassy, such as Λ 664–668 ("ohne Kenntnis des I 650/5 über die Schiffe Gesagten kaum denkbar"; on the contrary, very easily understandable without any help from I 650–655); Λ 650 f. is said to prove that "irgendwelche Einwirkungen auf Achill schon unternommen waren"; it would never have occurred to me. Other passages quoted are Λ 762 f., Ξ 139–142. All of them are in fact easily and fully intelligible in the light of their own contexts; there is no case whatever for saying that they refer to the Embassy.

11 Schadewaldt, op. cit. 81: "Die Achaier haben den Achill im I nicht 'kniefällig' (d.h. um jeden Preis) gebeten, sondern ihm einen Vergleich angetragen, und die 'Not,' die er nun 'kommen' sieht, ist die gleiche, die er Ende I (650 ff.) als Ziel steckte"; with footnote 1, "Dass das Angebot nur von Agamemnon und seinen Ratgebern ausging, nicht von der Heeresversammlung 'aller' Achaier, betont im besonderen Duckworth, Foreshadowing and Suspense, 87." This is candid enough: he believes that Achilles can now say what he does say, without the least inconsistency, on the grounds (*a*) that the ambassadors were not actually said to "stand round his knees" (i.e., that they did not *implore him with all earnestness* to accept the apology and compensation,—but that is obviously untrue); (*b*) that here it is said to be *the Achaeans* who shall come to him (notice the words "Heeresversammlung 'aller' Achaier," as if πάντας were in the text,—as it would have to be, if Schadewaldt were right; but in fact it is not there). In brief, this interpretation would be too farfetched even if the text would bear it; but the text will not bear it.

12 Focke, l.c. 275: if Achilles says "the Achaeans shall gather round my knees," it is a proof that "eine schlichtere, aber vergebliche Form des Bittens offenbar schon erfolgt (ist), ein I also vorauszusetzen."

13 I mention in passing (it would lead too far afield) that an earlier section of this passage, II 11 ff., shows that Patroclus had not, according to the author of these lines, been sent by Achilles to find out from Nestor what is happening (as he is in Λ, in our Iliad): it would really be ridiculous if Achilles, seeing Patroclus weeping on his return *from that mission*, should begin by saying, "Whatever is the matter now? Have you heard some bad news *from home?*"

14 Schadewaldt, op. cit. 130.

15 It is futile to argue that Achilles does not explicitly *mention* Briseis among the items of compensation which he rejects. Nobody can be left in any doubt that he has rejected *everything:* the omission of an explicit reference to Briseis here is no more significant than in the Nineteenth Book (138 ff.), where Agamemnon happens not to mention Briseis though the sequel shows that she was to be included.

16 On this passage see Cauer, *Grundfragen der Homerkritik* (3rd ed., 1923) 587 ff.

17 Leaf ad loc.; Schadewaldt 129, approved by Noé 87 n. 6.

18 Mazon, *Introduction à l'Iliade* 179 n. 2: "il me semble impossible, étant donné le mouvement, de rapporter les mots εἴ μοι . . . ἤπια εἰδείη à l'attitude générale d'Agamemnon dans le passé. Le présent seul interesse ici Achille"; this is obvious enough,—nobody would ever have thought of taking the words in any other way, if there had not been a special case to plead.

19 Bethe (*Homer* i 73 f.) is eloquent and convincing on the subject of the difference between the Ninth Book on the one hand and the Eleventh and the Sixteenth on the other in their portrayal of the character of Achilles.

20 A further conclusion follows: the Twenty-third Book presupposes the reconciliation of Achilles and Agamemnon. It must therefore have been added to the Iliad later than the Nineteenth; a consequence in harmony with the well-founded belief that the last two Books are among the latest stages in the development of the poem.

21 Not until the reconciliation is over is he even named, and then only in a line which could have been—and which the Alexandrians believed to have been—a later addition to the text (311).

22 See Noé 51 ff., 84 ff. She argues that the allegory in T 91–94 must be *earlier* than that in I 502 ff., on the ground that the former reflects the old Epic conception of *Atê* whereas the latter embodies the post-Homeric conception of mortal responsibility and divine castigation which I have outlined above. It would then follow that the T-passage was composed earlier than the Phoenix-speech, i.e.,

that the reconciliation presupposes the embassy without Phoenix (though Noé believes that after Phoenix was added to the embassy he reacted upon T, hence the mention òf him in 311). I am not convinced by this reasoning: the fact is that no contributor to the Iliad at any date ever departed from the traditional norm in this respect except the Phoenix-poet; the reconciliation-poet is obeying the immemorial law, and that he might well do at any date, whether contemporary with the Phoenix-poet or later. That the one poet had the other's allegory in mind when he composed his own is rendered very probable by the facts that (*a*) allegory is so very rare elsewhere in the Iliad (these are the only two of their kind; Noé 33); (*b*) the two contexts, embassy and reconciliation, are anyway so closely linked. Note also the curious iteration of βλάπτουσ' ἀνθρώπους I 507 = T 94 (though this was athetized).

23 Except the Messenian towns which had been promised in the Ninth Book.

24 Schadewaldt detects the great artist even here. "Im Streit um das Essen kommt das 'Leben wie es ist' zur Sprache, um eben im Gegensatz das höhere Leben des Heros um so tiefer fühlen zu lassen"; we are also to find (but I have failed) "wirklichen Sinn für die Polarität des Lebens und der Dinge."

25 The reconciliation is one of those places where untraditional words and phrases and forms and features of later Greek cluster appreciably more thickly than usual.

a) Phraseology:

130 ὡς εἰπών: traditionally stands at the end of an actual speech; here alone at the end of a *reported* speech.

131 ἔργ' ἀνθρώπων: equivalent to "earth" as opposed to "heaven"; ἔργ' ἀνθρώπων traditionally meant "farmed fields" or the like (Leaf on Π 392).

180 μή τι δίκης ἐπιδευὲς ἔχησθα: the phraseology might pass without comment in an Attic author; it is isolated in the Epic.

186 ἐν μοίρῃ: a novel phrase (χ 54); the use of ἐν with abstracts is only beginning to creep into the Epic (seven other examples in the Iliad, of which four are in the Ninth Book; thrice in Od.).

188 πρὸς δαίμονος: unique in the Epic, apparently "in the sight of the daimon."

220 ἐπιτλήτω κραδίη μύθοισιν: unique and untraditional phrase.

242 ἅμα μῦθος ἔην τετέλεστο δὲ ἔργον: this "no sooner said than done" idea becomes common in archaic and classical Greek; it is not known to the Iliad.

248 κούρητες Ἀχαιῶν: this extraordinary aberration occurs no-

where but in the Reconciliation (cf. 193 above, κούρητας ἀριστῆας Παναχαιῶν). Whoever composed these lines was under the mistaken impression that κούρητες was equivalent to κοῦροι, and was so far from the main road of the tradition that he did not automatically think of the usual formula, ϝελίκωπες 'Αχαιοί. It was presumably the formular verse-end κοῦροι 'Αχαιῶν which led him to create this non-sensical κούρητες 'Αχαιῶν.

259–260 cf. Γ 278 f.; an utterly untraditional notion.

294 ὀλέθριον ἦμαρ, cf. 409 ἦμαρ ὀλέθριον: an untraditional phrase (ὀλέθριος is not in the Epic vocabulary).

298 κουριδίην ἄλοχον: this romantic notion, that Achilles intended to make an honest woman of his concubine, has no place in the Iliad.

309 ἀπεσκέδασεν βασιλῆας: "he *scattered* the kings," a most insensitive use of the language; the traditional vocabulary, true to the life it describes, does not allow its hero to "scatter" kings when he desires them to leave his company.

314 ἀνενείκατο φώνησέν τε: an obscure and untraditional phrase.

359 ff. κόρυθες λαμπρὸν γανόωσαι and θώρηκές τε κραταιγύαλοι are both novel and untraditional phrases, contrary to the formular usages supplied by the older vocabulary (see pp. 285–286).

b) Untraditional words and forms, etc.:

68 ἀσκελέως is not a traditional adverb (nowhere in the Epics; Od. uses ἀσκελές adverbially twice); the traditional way of sayi g what is here expressed thus would presumably be ἀσπερχὲς κεχολῶ θαι ἐνὶ φρεσίν (Π 61). 80 ὑββάλλειν is an untraditional monster. 82 and 166 βλάβομαι is a secondary formation; βλάπτομαι was the traditional form. 83 ἐνδείξομαι is unique in the Epic. 88 ἄτην, for Epic ἄάτηι only Z 356, Ω 28. 94 δ' οὖν is unknown to the Epic. 95 ἄσατο for ἀάσατο (λ 61), a late contraction. 97 and 112 δολοφροσύνη is a novel (indeed unique) abstract. 101 θέαιναι (Θ 5, 20; θ 341) is not an old Epic word. 104 ἐκφανεῖ is a late contraction; Epic ἐκφανέει. 107 ψευστήσεις, 118 ἠλιτόμηνον are neologisms. 120 ἀγγελέουσα is a highly abnormal usage of the future tense. 126 λιπαροπλοκάμοιο, 135 ὀλέκεσκεν, 149 κλοτοπεύειν, 150 ἄρεκτον, 163 (and thrice elsewhere in this Book) ἄκμηνος, are unique. 172 ὅπλεσθαι (Ψ 159) is anomalous. 173 οἰσέτω is a bogus form (Chantraine, *Grammaire homérique* [*GH*] 1.418). 174 ἰανθῆς is a modern contraction (ibid. 1.43). 183 ἀπαρέσσασθαι is unique and untraditional. 186 κατέλεξας is a newcomer (see n. 9 above). 188 ἐπιορκήσω is a newcomer, not elsewhere in the Epic. 189 τέως (in all the MSS) is pure Attic. 194 ἐνεικέμεν is a monstrous form which nobody but an Attic poet was likely to create (Wackernagel,

Sprachl. Untersuch. z. Homer [*SUH*] 111 f.). 201 μεταπαυσωλή was a wretched formation, left severely alone by all men for all time thereafter. 202 ἦσιν, for ἔησιν, is pure Attic. 205 βρωτύν (σ 407) is not the Iliad's word for "food" or "eating." 209 ἰείη is a mere monster, not a part of speech (Chantraine, *GH* 1.284). 210 βρῶσις is unknown to the Iliad (Od. eight times). 218 προβαλοίμην = "excel" is unique. 223 ἄμητος, ὀλίγιστος, 234 f. ὀτρυντύς, are not Epic words. 253 πὰρ ξίφεος is highly abnormal for παρὰ ξίφεος. 255 αὐτόφιν is a bogus form; σιγή is probably a late intruder on the Epic vocabulary (only Γ 8, 134, 420, Δ 431, Η 195 [athet.], and eight times in Od.; the verb only in Ξ 90 and four times in Od.). 259 Γῆ, for Epic γαῖα, is a newcomer (only Γ 104, Ο 24, Φ 63). 261 μή with indicative is untraditional (Κ 329, Ο 41 f.). 262 πρόφασις is unique in the Epic. 263 ἀπροτίμαστος is a novel (and unique) formation. 267 λαῖτμα is an Odyssean word, not in the Iliad. 268 βόσις is yet another novel abstract. 270 διδοῖσθα is another monster (Chantraine, *GH* 1.470), fit company for ἰείη and οἰσέτω. 276 αἰψηρήν is another Odyssean word. 287 Πατρόκλε is a late and almost unique license of prosody in the Iliad (my *Homeric Odyssey* 163). 290 δέχεται: the usage is unique. 292 εἶδον is a flagrant breach of Epic law, elsewhere only Λ 112. 294 κηδείους is not an Epic word. 295 ἔασκες is a monster (for ἐάεσκες; Shipp, *Studies in the Language of Homer* [*SLH*] 38). 302 σφῶν δ' αὐτῶν κῆδε' ἑκάστη was composed very late indeed in the development of the Iliad; for σφέων δ' αὐτάων κήδεα ϝεκάστη. 310 Ἀτρεῖδα: an Attic dual. 321 κακώτερον (Χ 106, Od.) has no place in the traditional vocabulary. 322 τοῦ πατρός, 331 τὸν παῖδα, exceptionally un-Homeric usages of the article. 323 δάκρυον (Π 11, Ω 9) is a newcomer, for Epic δάκρυ. 324 ὅ with first person is a novelty. 325 ῥιγεδανῆς is antitraditional for Epic Ἀργείης; it is not an Epic word. 326 ἠὲ τόν: see Leaf; probably the incoherence is due to want of proper adjustment after interpolation of lines introducing Neoptolemus (of whom the Iliad knows nothing until the late Ω 467).

c) Miscellaneous:

The Reconciliation is relatively rich in metrical anomalies: 35 ἀποειπων is most irregular. 71 ὄιω for ὄίω is always a token of relative lateness of composition. 93 ἄρα ἦ, 194 δῶρα ἐμῆς, and 288 σε ἔλειπον are examples of hiatus of a type absolutely prohibited by the older Epic tradition. The poet is reckless of digamma, as one would expect: 124 ἀνασσέμεν; 302, 332 ἑκαστ-; 75, 102 εἰπ-; 282 ἰκέλη.

The list of anomalies of one kind or another could be appreciably extended (81 ἀκούσαι for ἀκούσειε, Chantraine, *GH* 1.465; 148 μνησώμεθα for μνησόμεθα; abundant ἦν, ἐπήν are symptomatic).

II. The discrepancy between Thucydides and the Iliad was noticed first (so far as I know) by Hermann, *Philol.* 1 (1846) 367 ff. = *Opusc.* 8 (1877) 382 ff. There have been few discussions since, and very few of any value. There is a short and lucid note in M. L. Earle's *Classical Papers* (1912: the author's MS was dated 1905) 142 ff.; cf. also P. Girard, *Mélanges Nicole* (1905) 165 ff. The problem seemed to be solved by D. S. Robertson's brilliant conjecture, published in *CR* 38 (1924) 7; but it was again put in a different perspective both by G. M. Bolling (*The External Evidence for Interpolation in Homer,* 1925, 92 ff.) and by A. W. Gomme (*Historical Commentary on Thucydides* i, 1945, 114 f.).

26 Thucydides I 10.5 ff.: πρὸς τὰς μεγίστας δ᾽ οὖν καὶ ἐλαχίστας ναῦς τὸ μέσον σκοποῦντι οὐ πολλοὶ φαίνονται ἐλθόντες ὡς ἀπὸ πάσης τῆς Ἑλλάδος κοινῇ πεμπόμενοι. αἴτιον δ᾽ ἦν οὐχ ἡ ὀλιγανθρωπία τοσοῦτον ὅσον ἡ ἀχρηματία. τῆς γὰρ τροφῆς ἀπορίᾳ τόν τε στρατὸν ἐλάσσω ἤγαγον καὶ ὅσον ἤλπιζον αὐτόθεν πολεμοῦντα βιοτεύσειν. ἐπειδὴ δὲ ἀφικόμενοι μάχῃ ἐκράτησαν— δῆλον δέ· τὸ γὰρ ἔρυμα τῷ στρατοπέδῳ οὐκ ἂν ἐτειχίσαντο—φαίνονται δ᾽ οὐδ᾽ ἐνταῦθα πάσῃ τῇ δυνάμει χρησάμενοι ἀλλὰ πρὸς γεωργίαν τῆς Χερσονήσου τραπόμενοι καὶ λῃστείαν τῆς τροφῆς ἀπορίᾳ. ᾗ καὶ μᾶλλον οἱ Τρῶες αὐτῶν διεσπαρμένων τὰ δέκα ἔτη ἀντεῖχον βίᾳ τοῖς ἀεὶ ὑπολειπομένοις ἀντίπαλοι ὄντες. περιουσίαν δ᾽ εἰ ἦλθον ἔχοντες τροφῆς καὶ ὄντες ἀθρόοι ἄνευ λῃστείας καὶ γεωργίας ξυνεχῶς τὸν πόλεμον διέφερον, ῥᾳδίως ἂν μάχῃ κρατοῦντες εἷλον· οἵ γε καὶ οὐχ ἀθρόοις ἀλλὰ μέρει τῷ ἀεὶ παρόντι ἀντεῖχον, πολιορκίᾳ δ᾽ ἂν προσκαθεζόμενοι ἐν ἐλάσσονί τε χρόνῳ καὶ ἀπονώτερον τὴν Τροίαν εἷλον.

I begin by making the following points about this passage.

i) μάχῃ ἐκράτησαν means "were victorious in a battle"; the aorist tense can only be used with reference to a stated or otherwise specific occasion. There was, on a particular occasion, a pitched battle, and the Greeks won it. μάχῃ with the aorist of κρατεῖν invariably has this meaning in Thucydides and elsewhere: I 108.3, 109.4, 111.2, 113.2, II 25.3, 26.2, III 91.5, 103.3, VIII 62.2, 107.1. Usually indistinguishable in sense is μάχῃ νικῆσαι (and its passive), eight examples. In Herodotus μάχῃ κρατῆσαι has the same meaning and the same limitation to a stated or otherwise specific occasion: VII 155.1, 157.3, cf. III 39.4. Herodotus uses also νικῆσαι (νικηθῆναι ἐσσωθῆναι) with μάχῃ in the same sense; five examples. (From the above I have of course excluded examples in which the specific reference is explicit, τῇ μάχῃ κρατῆσαι; five examples in Herodotus, one each in Thucydides and Demosthenes.) The phrase μάχῃ κρατῆσαι is apparently uncommon outside Thucydides: only twice in Herodotus, not in Demosthenes or in Drama except Euripides, *Heracles* 612 (where the reference is to a specified occasion).

ii) ἀφικόμενοι goes closely with μάχῃ ἐκράτησαν, as it does in I 109.4 ἀφικόμενος ... μάχῃ ἐκράτησε, cf. 111.2 ἀποβάντες μάχῃ ἐκράτησαν, VIII 23.3 ἀποβάντες ... μάχῃ νικήσαντες. The meaning is "they won a battle on arrival," not "having arrived, they won a battle" (on some other occasion, unconnected with their arrival).

iii) ἐπειδὴ μάχῃ ἐκράτησαν means "after they had won a battle"; that is the normal usage of ἐπειδή with the aorist referring to a definite occasion in past time. As LSJ concisely put it, in this sense "generally the aorist is found, the pluperfect being used only for special emphasis."

iv) οὐδ' ἐνταῦθα means "not even there," that is to say "not even at Troy,"—not even in the field of operations. It has its antecedent a few lines above: "They did not enlist all available forces when they mobilized in Hellas; nor even in the field of operations (where you would specially expect them to do so) did they employ the whole of their army." So also Steup and Classen.

v) φαίνονται δέ cannot be resumptive, as if it were still governed by ἐπειδή, "after they had won a battle, ... and after they seem not to have employed all their forces ..." It must be progressive-apodotic, "after they had won a battle on arrival ... *thereafter* it appears that they did not employ their whole force in the field for ten years." There is no other available apodosis to ἐπειδή, and the sequel ἀλλὰ πρὸς γεωργίαν ... refers to what they did after the initial victory and what they went on doing for ten years; moreover the present tense of φαίνονται would be unintelligible if it were governed, like the aorist ἐκράτησε, by ἐπειδή.

The apodotic δέ has a close parallel in I 18.1 f., where (as here) ἐπειδὴ δέ is followed by a parenthesis, and its progressive apodosis begins immediately after the parenthesis, introduced by δέ. The parenthesis in I 18 is a very long one: but that makes a difference only of degree, not of kind. (See further Denniston, *Greek Particles* 179, though I am not sure that all the examples quoted there are quite of the same kind.)

[27] See esp. Classen ad loc., Bolling l.c. I suppose that it is essentially the same explanation which underlies the Scholia here: it was some other wall, which Homer does not mention. Some editors (and others) have suggested that it might be *any old wall*,—that Thuc. was not thinking of any particular wall: as if τὸ ἔρυμα could mean anything but *"The* Wall," i.e., the well-known one, the one we all remember from the Epic,—but the only wall we remember from

the Epic is the one whose building in the tenth year is described in the Seventh Book.

28 If Herodotus' summary is based on the *Cypria*, and if it is accurate, it is probable that in the *Cypria* the Greeks did fortify their camp at the beginning: II 118 ἐκβᾶσαν ἐς γῆν καὶ ἱδρυθεῖσαν τὴν στρατιήν.

29 See Gomme, *Thuc.* i 114 ff., and cf. Thuc. VI 37.2: Athenagoras assumes that the first Athenian action will be to pitch a camp from their ships; VI 66 f., the Athenians land and at once fortify their camp at the Olympieium; VI 97, again, at Epipolae. "The nearest analogy to the Trojan campaign, as Thuc. sees it, in the Archidamian war, is that against Mytilene (iii 6): the Athenians land troops and win a battle (or rather, the enemy fail to take advantage of a drawn battle), and then, because they have not enough forces to invest the town closely, build two camps which they fortify with a wall; the two sides share the mastery of the land" (Gomme 115).

30 The chief other reason is this: since Thucydides' argument depends on the contrast between (*a*) the difficulties of the Greeks in prosecuting the war during the ten years of the siege, and (*b*) something that happened when they first arrived, it is obvious that that something cannot have been a *defeat* of the Greeks; an initial defeat would not help Thucydides to prove that their subsequent difficulties must have been caused by dispersal of their forces in search of food.

31 Gomme objects further (and it is easy to agree with him) that there is something unnatural in the phraseology in the alleged context ("they would not in the tenth year have built the wall" = "they would have built the wall long before the tenth year"). He discusses also another way of escape: rearrange the words, thus, ἐπειδὴ δὲ ἀφικόμενοι μάχῃ ἐκράτησαν, φαίνονται δ' οὐδ' ἐνταῦθα πάσῃ τῇ δυνάμει χρησάμενοι. δῆλον δέ· τὸ γὰρ ἔρυμα τῷ στρατοπέδῳ οὐκ ἂν ἐτειχίσαντο· ἀλλὰ πρὸς γεωργίαν . . . τραπόμενοι κτλ., "Even after the victory on arrival the Greeks did not use all their forces,—this is obvious, otherwise they would not have had to build the wall, . . ." Gomme himself gives good reason for rejecting this; I add a comment or two: (i) this is a violent alteration of the text; (ii) it presumes that Thucydides would think that the presence of a wall round the camp was evidence that the Greeks were in some difficulty—a presumption contrary to probability; (iii) the passage remains incompatible with the Iliad's tenth-year wall. Gomme says that "in this case, the date at which, according to Homer, the wall was built is left in the background": yes, but not all that far in the background. If the contention is that throughout the ten years the Greeks dispersed

their forces, and that they must therefore build a wall to protect the reduced army in the field, then Homer's belated tenth-year wall will be the worst possible evidence to adduce in favour of that contention; indeed he is the one witness who instantly refutes it, for his Greek army had no wall until the tenth year. Why quote him at all? The statement might have passed unchallenged, but for the proof adduced in its favour.

R. M. Cook has recently suggested (*Proc. Cambr. Philol. Soc.* n.s. 3, 1954–55, p. 3) that οὐκ ἀνετειχίσαντο might be read for οὐκ ἂν ἐτειχίσαντο: the initial victory is proved by the fact that they did not build the wall. Apart from the objection that the absence of a wall could not possibly have been taken by Thucydides to prove success in the initial battle, the conjecture is practically ruled out by the fact that οὐκ ἀνετειχίσαντο should mean "they did not *repair* the wall." This verb and its cognates are very nearly nonexistent. The sense "rebuild" is demonstrable in Xenophon, *Hellenica* IV 8.9 (the noun) and IV 4.18 (the verb); according to LSJ and the Dindorfs' Thesaurus these are the only examples earlier than Josephus.

[32] This second duel was obviously not planned and composed by the author of the first duel: but I do not here discuss further the relation between our passage and its immediate surroundings, except to express general agreement with the observation that the Seventh and Eighth Books were designed to assist the incorporation of the Embassy into an Iliad which had hitherto known nothing of it.

There remains, however, one special problem of some difficulty: I 349–350 (the only later reference to the building of the wall) presupposes the matters described in the Seventh Book; yet the latter (at least this part of it) was not composed earlier than the end of the 5th century, whereas the Embassy was added to the Iliad a long time before that. I 349–350 are not easily detachable from their context (whether alone or together with their immediate surroundings): they appear to be integral, not a later addition. How then can we account for the reference to a tenth-year wall in the Embassy? The likeliest answer is that the Embassy here alludes to a traditional incident of which the Iliad at large took no notice but which the Athenian poet made the starting-point and principal theme of his substantial addition to the Iliad. The question has been much discussed, and various solutions propounded: see e.g. Wilamowitz, *Ilias und Homer* 64 n. 3; Von der Mühll, *Hypomnema* 172; Theiler, *Dichter der Ilias* 165.

[33] I am puzzled by ἀγρόμενοι: its meaning is "gathering ourselves to-

gether," but that seems quite out of place here. What the context requires is an active usage, "collecting (the dead bodies)"; perhaps our poet thought it did mean that.

³⁴ H 334–335 were athetized by Aristarchus. Schol. A has the good note: καθόλου οὖν οἶδε πυρὶ καιομένους τοὺς πάλαι καὶ ἐνταῦθα τιθεμένους ὅπου ἐτελεύτησαν.

³⁵ The Athenian poet has been identified elsewhere in these surroundings, especially (a) in 475, a line athetized by Zenodotus, Aristophanes, and Aristarchus: the extraordinary word ἀνδράποδον (unique in the Epic) is almost certainly an Attic innovation (see Wackernagel, SUH 154; Chantraine, GH 1.233); (b) in 468: Euneos (elsewhere Ψ 747 only) is introduced here for the greater glory of an Athenian family; "he was held to be ancestor of the Attic family Euneidae . . . which played a part in the cult of Dionysus" (Von der Mühll, Hypomnema 143, with references; cf. Wackernagel l.c.; Bethe, Homer i 220 n.).

There are numerous symptoms of relatively late and untraditional composition in this part of the Iliad. Note especially the singular ἵππον, = "cavalry" (342); this is a very late idiom (Aeschylus, Persae 302, 315). 330 ἐσκέδασ' ὀξὺς Ἄρης is untraditional: the Epic vocabulary knows σκέδασε but not ἐσκέδασε; it knows ὀξὺν Ἄρηα as a formular verse-end, but not the nominative ὀξὺς Ἄρης. 332 κυκλέω is found only in Attic drama before Plato (the sense here never recurs. Powell's. Lexicon to Herodotus confuses κυκλέω and κυκλόω: all his examples are of the latter except VIII 16.1 ἐκυκλέοντο d, ἐκυκλεύοντο aP, ἐκυκλεῦντο Reiske; the sense is the same as in 76.1 κυκλούμενοι, "form a circle"; read ἐκυκλοῦντο).

339, 340 αὐτοῖσι, αὐτάων are untraditional uses of the pronoun.

345–432 There is no reason to suppose that 313–482 are not all of a piece. The Athenian poet reveals his hand near the beginning (334–335) and near the end (468, 475). As for 345–432, the amount of unconventional matter is not above the average. If it were known on other grounds that this passage was of very late composition, the following features would need no further explanation:

345 Omission of digamma in the word Ἴλιον, a rarity; the author is indeed unusually negligent of digamma (omitted in 349, 369 εἴπω, 364, 391 οἴκαδε.

353 ἵνα μὴ ῥέξομεν is a miserable piece of prosody (athetized by Aristarchus; cf. Chantraine, GH 2.268).

381 ἠῶθεν: a breach of the Epic convention for representing the sequence of events in time: Idaeus goes to the Greeks "in the early morning"; they hear him; he takes back their message to the

Trojans, who assemble and hear what he has to say,—and the sun has just risen!

384 ἠπύτα κῆρυξ is a novelty.

390 ὡς πρὶν ὤφελλ' ἀπολέσθαι: in the older Epic heralds simply gave the news without personal comment; this aberration has a parallel in Θ 423 f.

394 ἠνώγεον: a novel and odd formation (Chantraine, GH 1.439, Shipp SLH 40); ἤνωγον (conjectured by Bentley) might have been expected.

407 ὑποκρίνονται here only in the Iliad = ἀμείβονται, "answer"; also Od. β 111. But it was not an Attic usage.

409 φειδώ: a new (Odyssean) abstract.

412 τὸ σκῆπτρον: since the "sceptre" has not been explicitly mentioned, this must be simply the definite article; as untraditional a usage of it as you will find anywhere in the Iliad.

414 ἕατο: an untraditional form (Chantraine, GH 1.71). Δαρδανίωνες (Θ 154) is an untraditional name for Δάρδανοι.

416 ἀγγελίην ἀπέειπε: in the older Epic he would have repeated what his message was; we should not thus have been fobbed off with a mere "reported his message."

The short passage 433–441, where the Wall is built, contributes nothing of much interest. ἀμφιλύκη is unique in the Epic but undateable. The scene in Heaven has its share of anomalies: 447 ἐνίψει (this future elsewhere only Od. twice) should be ἐνέψει; 449 τειχίζομαι was not in the Epic vocabulary, nor was ἡρῶι (453, for ἡρῶϊ) Epic prosody; the contraction in ἀθλήσαντε, for ἀεθλ-, recurs five times in Il., twice in Od.; it is of course late. 463 ἀμαλδύνω is a newcomer.

[36] B 192–197, athetized by Aristarchus, were not known to Xenophon: they must have made their way into the vulgate somewhere about the turn from the 5th to the 4th century (see Allen, *Origins and Transmissions* 253; Bolling, *The Athetized Lines of the Iliad* 70 f.). B 853–855 were not in the text recognized by Apollodorus, but 855[ab] were,—these two lines having been added to the Catalogue by Callisthenes about the turn from the 3rd to the 2nd century (see Allen, *Homeric Catalogue of Ships* 156 ff.).

INDEX

Index

343